ORGANIZATIONAL BEHAVIOUR AND THE PHYSICAL ENVIRONMENT

This book looks at how the physical environment of work shapes organizational behaviour, demonstrating that our physical surroundings at work can have a big influence on employee productivity, performance and wellbeing.

Drawing upon the latest research, *Organizational Behaviour and the Physical Environment* provides comprehensive coverage of the different aspects of the physical environment at work – the buildings, furnishings, equipment, lighting, air quality and their configurations. From theories of psychological ownership and work design, to cultural issues and technology in the workplace, its international range of contributors provide voices from Australasia, North America, Europe and the Middle East.

This book will be invaluable supplementary reading for advanced students, researchers and practitioners across the fields of organizational behaviour, HRM, organizational and environmental psychology, and workspace design.

Oluremi B. Ayoko is an Associate Professor of Management at the UQ Business School, University of Queensland, Australia.

Neal M. Ashkanasy is a Professor of Management at the UQ Business School, University of Queensland, Australia.

ORGANIZATIONAL BEHAVIOUR AND THE PHYSICAL ENVIRONMENT

Edited by Oluremi B. Ayoko and
Neal M. Ashkanasy

LONDON AND NEW YORK

First published 2020
by Routledge
2 Park Square, Milton Park, Abingdon, Oxon OX14 4RN

and by Routledge
52 Vanderbilt Avenue, New York, NY 10017

Routledge is an imprint of the Taylor & Francis Group, an informa business

© 2020 selection and editorial matter, Oluremi B. Ayoko and Neal
M. Ashkanasy; individual chapters, the contributors

The right of Oluremi B. Ayoko and Neal M. Ashkanasy to be
identified as the authors of the editorial material, and of the authors
for their individual chapters, has been asserted in accordance with
sections 77 and 78 of the Copyright, Designs and Patents Act 1988.

British Library Cataloguing-in-Publication Data
A catalogue record for this book is available from the British Library

Library of Congress Cataloging-in-Publication Data
A catalog record has been requested for this book

ISBN: 978-1-138-05352-6 (hbk)
ISBN: 978-1-138-05353-3 (pbk)
ISBN: 978-1-315-16723-7 (ebk)

Typeset in Bembo
by Swales & Willis Ltd, Exeter, Devon, UK

MIX
Paper from
responsible sources
FSC
www.fsc.org   FSC™ C013985

Printed in the United Kingdom
by Henry Ling Limited

CONTENTS

FIGURES

TABLES

CONTRIBUTORS

Editors

Oluremi (Remi) B. Ayoko is an Associate Professor of Management at the University of Queensland Business School, Australia. She has had extensive teaching experience across three nations and her research interests include: the physical environment of work, conflict management, teamwork, leadership and diversity. Oluremi has published widely in highly influential journals and serves as an Associate Editor of the *Journal of Management and Organization* (*JMO*) and on the editorial boards of the *International Journal of Conflict Management* (*IJCM*) and *Negotiation and Conflict Management Research* (*NCMR*).

Neal M. Ashkanasy is Professor of Management at the UQ Business School (University of Queensland, Australia). He studies emotion, leadership, culture and ethical behaviour. He has published over 90 peer-reviewed articles and served as Editor-in-Chief of the *Journal of Organizational Behavior* and Associate Editor for the *Academy of Management Review*.

Authors

Rianne Appel-Meulenbroek is Assistant Professor in Corporate Real Estate and Workplace at the Department of Architecture, Building and Planning, Eindhoven University of Technology in the Netherlands. She obtained her PhD in 2014 there as well. She is editor of the *Journal of CRE*, sits on the editorial board of the *Journal of CRE* and acts as reviewer for several other journals. She is chair of the Transdisciplinary Workplace Research (TWR) network and board member of the European Real Estate Society (ERES). In her research, she approaches real estate as a production factor for (knowledge) organizations. She focuses on how corporate real estate (CRE) should be managed and how location, building and workspace design choices add value to driving forces of the users (e.g. productivity of employees, innovativeness of organizations, knowledge-sharing, flexibility).

Peter Bacevice is Director of Research for HLW, a New York-based architecture and design firm. He is also a Research Associate at the University of Michigan's Ross School of Business. He received a PhD in Education from the University of Michigan. Pete's research focuses on the intersection of design and organizational outcomes and the ways in which organizations strategically use design to advance prosocial behaviours.

William J. Bingley is a PhD student in the School of Psychology at the University of Queensland. His research focuses on social identity, communication and emotion.

Christina Bodin Danielsson (PhD) is a practising architect at Brunnberg & Forshed Architects and Associate Professor in Architecture (Human–Environment Interaction), specializing in office design at Chalmers University of Technology, Gothenburg, Sweden. With a Master of Architecture degree from Lund University, Sweden, in 1997, she worked as a practising architect until 2002, when she started her PhD studies at KTH in office design's influence on employees and organizations. Her research, which applies both quantitative and qualitative methods, investigates the office environment's influence on job satisfaction, leadership, workplace conflicts and sick leave rates, among other things. She is the author of many scientific articles, and chapters in various books in her field of expertise, published in English, Swedish and French.

Graham Brown is an Associate Professor and the Tim Price Entrepreneurship Fellow at the Peter Gustavson School of Business, at Canada's University of Victoria. Graham conducts research on territoriality and psychological ownership with a specific focus on how feelings of ownership can simultaneously drive and undermine innovation. His work has been published in the *Academy of Management Review, Organization Science, Journal of Organizational Behavior* and *Organizational Behavior and Human Decision Processes*, and featured in *Harvard Business Review* online. Graham's teaching focuses on the areas of human resource management, leadership and negotiation and he applies these concepts to help others discover and use their passion to lead and create. Dr Brown received his PhD in Organizational Behaviour from the University of British Columbia and has held positions previously at Singapore Management University and the University of British Columbia.

Arran Caza is an Associate Professor in the Asper School of Business at the University of Manitoba, Canada. He earned his PhD in Management and Psychology from the University of Michigan in 2007. His research focuses on age- and culture-related aspects of leadership.

Mylyn Dat is a Master of Organizational Psychology and PhD candidate at the University of Queensland, Australia. Her research focuses on employees' responses to transgressions in the workplace and organizational justice repair.

Matthew C. Davis is an Associate Professor of Organizational Psychology at Leeds University Business School, Leeds, UK. He is an Associate Fellow of the British Psychological Society with expertise in organizational and environmental psychology. Matthew's research includes: socio-technical design, how people interact with their environments and the impact of different office designs. He has researched and consulted with major corporate partners.

Richard de Dear is a Professor of Building Science at the School of Architecture, Design and Planning, the University of Sydney. He has focused his research career on defining what occupants want and need from their built environments, and assessing the performance of buildings in terms of meeting those requirements. He is the editor of academic journals, including *Energy & Buildings* and *Science and Technology for the Built Environment.*

Yvonne A.W. de Kort is a Full Professor Environmental Psychology in the Human–Technology Interaction Group, Eindhoven University of Technology, the Netherlands. She investigates how physical or mediated environments impact restoration from stress and positive emotions, and how physical spaces and communication media influence, shape and enhance social interaction. Current research examines the effects of lighting conditions on mood, performance and social behaviour. Her work has resulted in over 50 peer-reviewed journal articles and numerous chapters, edited volumes and conference papers.

Kimberly D. Elsbach is a Professor of Management and the Stephen G. Newberry Chair in Leadership at the Graduate School of Management, University of California, Davis. She is also an International Research Fellow at the Center for Corporate Reputation, Oxford University, Editor-in-Chief for *Academy of Management Annals*, and co-founder and organizer of the Davis Conference on Qualitative Research. Kim's research focuses on perception – specifically how people perceive each other and their organizations. She has studied these perceptual processes in a variety of contexts ranging from the California cattle industry, and the National Rifle Association, to Hollywood screenwriters. Her most recent work examines how crying at work affects perceptions of professional women at work and how self-perceptions influence one's willingness to adopt ideas in creative collaborations.

Kelly S. Fielding is an Associate Professor in the School of Communication and Arts at the University of Queensland. She received her PhD in Social Psychology from the University of Queensland. Kelly's research focuses on understanding environmental decision-making and developing and testing strategies to promote more uptake of pro-environmental policy and behaviour.

Lyndon Garrett is an Assistant Professor of Management and Organizations at the Boston College Carroll School of Management. He obtained his PhD in Management from the University of Michigan. His research interests include relational and team dynamics at work, and how organizations can cultivate human connection.

Katharine H. Greenaway is a Lecturer at the University of Melbourne School of Psychological Sciences. She obtained her PhD in Social Psychology from the University of Queensland in 2012, after which she was awarded a research fellowship by the Canadian Institute for Advanced Research, and a Discovery Early Career Research Award fellowship by the Australian Research Council. Katharine studies social functioning in three main domains: identity processes, emotion regulation, and human agency.

Gemma L. Irving is a Lecturer in Strategy at the University of Queensland Business School. Her dissertation explored collaboration in open-plan offices, including how employees avoid collaboration when physically proximate and how teams use open-plan offices as scaffolds for learning. Her research interests include organizational space, professional work and learning.

Peter J. Jordan is a Professor of Organizational Behaviour and the Deputy Director of the Work Organization and Wellbeing Research Centre at the Griffith Business School, Griffith University, Australia. Peter's current research interests include emotional intelligence, discrete emotions in organizations, and employee entitlement in organizations.

Jungsoo Kim is a Research Associate at the School of Architecture, Design and Planning, the University of Sydney. He received his PhD in Architectural Science from the University of Sydney. His research interests include human thermal comfort, adaptive behaviour, and indoor environmental quality. He is a member of international research groups such as the International Energy Agency's Energy in Buildings and Communities Programme.

Momo D. Kromah is an Associate Lecturer at the University of Sydney Business School. He completed his PhD in Management at the University of Queensland in 2017 and is also a registered psychologist. His dissertation focused on examining the role, process and consequences of workspace territoriality in the context of organizational change. His research interests include workspace territoriality, psychological ownership, leadership, organizational change and work-integrated learning. He has also worked as a management consultant in a number of public and private organizations.

Pascale Le Blanc is an Associate Professor of Work and Organizational Psychology at the Human Performance Management Group, Department of Industrial Engineering and Innovation Sciences of Eindhoven University of Technology in the Netherlands and Affiliate Researcher at the Department of Psychology of Stockholm University in Sweden. She obtained her PhD in Social Sciences in 1994 from Utrecht University. She has been Associate Editor of the *European Journal of Work and Organizational Psychology* and is currently an editorial board member of the *Scandinavian Journal of Work and Organizational Psychology*. Her research interests focus on the sustainable functioning of organizations and their employees.

Mischel Luong is a Master of Organizational Psychology and PhD candidate at the University of Queensland and an alumna of the University of Melbourne. Her research focuses on the effect of physical spaces on employees in the workplace, with a particular focus on women in male-dominated organizations.

Sharon K. Parker is an Australian Research Council Laureate Fellow, a Professor of Organizational Behavior at the UWA Business School, University of Western Australia, and an Honorary Professor at the University of Sheffield. She is a recipient of the ARC's Kathleen Fitzpatrick Award, and the 2016 Academy of Management OB Division Mentoring Award. Sharon is also a Chief Investigator in the ARC's Centre of Excellence in Population Aging Research (CEPAR), and leads the 'Organizations and the Mature Workforce' research stream. Sharon's research focuses particularly on job and work design, and she is also interested in proactive behaviour, change, wellbeing, development, and job performance. She has published more than 80 internationally peer-reviewed articles, including in top-tier journals such as the *Journal of Applied Psychology*, *Academy of Management Journal*, *Academy of Management Review* and the *Annual Review of Psychology*.

Sharon is a Fellow of the Australian Academy of Social Sciences, and a Fellow of the US Society for Industrial and Organizational Psychology. Sharon is an Associate Editor for the *Academy of Management Annals*, a past Associate Editor of the *Journal of Applied Psychology*, and she has served on numerous editorial boards. She is a past chair of the UWA Academic Promotion Committee. Sharon has attracted competitive research funding worth over $40,000,000, and has worked as a researcher and consultant in a wide range of public and private organizations.

Kim Peters is a Senior Lecturer in Organizational Psychology at the University of Queensland. Her research focuses on social influence processes (including communication and leadership) in social and organizational settings. She has published over 25 peer-reviewed articles in leading journals in social psychology and management science. She has also contributed to 12 edited books and produced 13 industry reports for a range of partners including the European Parliament and Leadership Foundation for Higher Education.

Jon L. Pierce is Professor of Organization and Management in the Department of Management Studies, Labovitz School of Business and Economics, at the University of Minnesota Duluth (USA). He received his PhD in Management and Organizational Behaviour at the University of Wisconsin-Madison. His research interests are focused on the psychology of work and organizations, with a particular focus on psychological ownership and organization-based self-esteem. His teaching focus is in the areas of micro-organizational behaviour and leadership. While working on the theory of psychological ownership he was a visiting scholar in the Department of Psychology at the University of Waikato in New Zealand. He has published nearly a hundred papers appearing in a number of management and organizational behaviour journals (e.g. *Academy of Management Journal and the Review, Journal of Management, Journal of Organizational Behavior*), as well as several books including *Psychological Ownership and the Organizational Context: Theory, Research Evidence, and Application*.

Elizabeth J. Sander is an Assistant Director of Organizational Behaviour at the Bond Business School, Bond University, Australia. Libby's current research interests include the physical work environment in organizations and the role of place and space in entrepreneurial activity and innovation precincts.

Gretchen Spreitzer is the Keith and Valerie Alessi Professor of Business Administration at the Ross School of Business at the University of Michigan, where she is also the Faculty Director of the Center for Positive Organizations. Her research interests include how organizations can enable human thriving at work and the development of people's full potential.

Ileana Stigliani is Assistant Professor of Design and Innovation at the Innovation and Entrepreneurship Department of Imperial Business School, London. She received her PhD in Management from Bocconi University. Her current research focuses on how material artefacts and practices influence cognitive processes – including sensemaking and sensegiving, and perceptions of organizational and professional identities – within organizations.

Ken Tann is Lecturer in Communication Management at the UQ Business School. He completed his PhD in Linguistics and Semiotics at the University of Sydney, and is pioneering the application of social semiotics to research in management and marketing. His work has influenced research across education, social media, restorative justice, and social inclusion in the workplace.

Leonore van den Ende is a Postdoctoral Researcher at the VU University Amsterdam, the Netherlands. She obtained her PhD in Organization Science and has published in journals such as *Long Range Planning* and the *International Journal of Project Management*. Her research interests include organizational change, transition rituals and intercultural collaboration.

Alfons van Marrewijk is Professor of Business Anthropology at the Department of Organization Sciences, VU University Amsterdam, the Netherlands. His research interests includes socio-material world of organizations and complex megaprojects on which he has published books as well as papers in journals such as *Organization Studies* and the *British Journal of Management*. Currently he is project leader of a study on the socio-materiality of infrastructure networks.

Courtney von Hippel is a Senior Lecturer in Social Psychology at the University of Queensland, Brisbane, Australia. She received her PhD in Organizational Behaviour from Ohio State University. Her primary research area focuses on inter-group relations and stereotyping in the workplace.

M.K. Ward completed a PhD in Industrial/Organizational Psychology at North Carolina State University in 2016. Her dissertation focused on the relationships between decision-making styles of entrepreneurs and organizational perfor-mance. M.K.'s prevailing interests include entrepreneurship, performance, work design, organizational neuroscience, and measurement. Other topics of inter-est are judgement and decision-making, mindfulness, affect, and organizations and the natural environment. M.K. has published in peer-reviewed journals such as *Human Resource Management Review* and *Annual Review of Organizational Psychology and Organizational Behavior* (forthcoming). In 2014, she received the Student Research Award from the Association for Psychological Science. She co-edits a column titled 'Organizational Neuroscience' in the journal *Industrial / Organizational Psychologist*. M.K. aims to integrate neuroscience to conduct high-impact research about work design.

Varda Wasserman is a Senior Lecturer at the Department of Management and Economics, The Open University, Israel. She is an organizational sociologist specializing in organizational aesthetics, organizational control and resistance, embodiment and gender identities. Her recent publications are in *Organization Science, Organization Studies, Organization, Gender and Society* and *Culture and Organization*.

Thijs Willems is Postdoctoral Researcher at the Lee Kuan Yew Centre for Innovative Cities at the Singapore University of Technology and Design. He obtained his PhD in Organization Sciences at VU University Amsterdam. His research interests include organization theory, socio-technical systems and infrastructures, and the importance of embodiment in understanding work.

ACKNOWLEDGEMENTS

This project was funded by the Australian Research Council Discovery Grant No. P110102525 to study 'Employee Wellbeing and Productivity: The Role of Territoriality, Conflict and Emotions'.

FOREWORD

I first got to know Neal Ashkanasy at a dinner in 1996 in Cincinnati, Ohio, at our national business conference, the Academy of Management. Even then, Neal was eager to draw attention towards important, but often overlooked, aspects of organizations. Our conversation then was about the critical but oft-ignored topic of emotions in organizations. Today he and his co-author, Oluremi (Remi) Ayoko, are talking about an equally important, and equally overlooked, aspect of organizations and organizing. As you read this foreword, you may not be aware of or appreciate the affordances that the physical medium (e.g. digital or paper) on which you are reading. These affordances make the very act of reading possible. In a similar way, the physical environment makes organizing possible. This is the key argument in this edited book: *Organizational Behaviour and the Physical Environment.*

Such a simple but powerful thesis is not quite as simple as it appears, and needs considerable unpacking in order to be really understood. I was delighted to see that Remi and Neal invited a wide range of contributors to the book, including practising architects as well as management scholars, from all over the world. This helped assure not only a variety of perspectives, but also gives the reader a broader set of studies and theories than what they might get if the contributor pool was shallower. Indeed, although there are a few foundational studies mentioned by several chapters, I was impressed in many ways by how little overlap there is. This gives the reader the impression of how broad and deep and complex this topic really is. Moreover, there is represented here a wide range of perspectives on the physical environment, ranging from more functional views through those that view the physical environment through the lens of socio-materiality and social hermeneutics. The end result is a type of intellectual smorgasbord catering to a variety of tastes, disciplines and interests.

As a whole, the book makes several critical contributions to management scholarship. To begin, it is a comprehensive guide for anyone – academic or practitioner – interested in making organizations better. Authors in this book associate the physical environment with a bevy of critical organizational processes and outcomes including creativity, job performance, job satisfaction, teamwork, psychological ownership, motivation, identity, and even human thriving. At the same time, our physical environment can segregate us (e.g. by gender) and dehumanize us, create stress, erode physical health, and impede change. Fortunately, the authors in this book help disentangle a vast amount of conflicting information, and offer insights into when physical space can be optimized for human wellbeing and performance.

In addition, the book keeps alive questions and controversies that have been inherent in the literature since its inception. To illustrate, is the physical environment best conceived of as something 'outside' the normal realm of human social behaviour (i.e. something that is 'out there')? Indeed, one can conceive of space as existing without us. Buildings continue to stand even if no one is in them. The natural environment continues to surround us whether we are there to appreciate it or not (and perhaps trees really do fall in the woods and make sounds). Thus, we can see the physical world as something that exists apart from us humans, but something we can act upon. Alternatively, is it better to view the material as hopelessly entangled in the social world? If so, we need to view the physical environment not as something that is 'out there', but rather as something that is inseparable from the 'here'. Whether through structuration or similar dynamics, the social and material are inherently connected and mutually influencing. Even more challenging than its relationship to the social are the debates on how agentic the physical environment is. For example, should we conceive of the physical environment as something that is primarily passive and acted upon, or should we view material objects as having a type of material agency that can act upon the world?

Perhaps as importantly as raising these various tensions and issues, as well as outcomes and processes, no one pretends that the role of the physical environment in organizations can be wrapped up in a neat little package. The relationship is inherently complex and the field seems not quite ready to see the 'simplicity on the other side of complexity'. For me, that is a good thing in many ways. Because it helps us as students of organizations realize that as much as we understand, there is still a long way to go. Indeed, the hallmark of a good book is not that it answers all of the questions to be had, but that it opens up new areas of enquiry. This book succeeds in raising new questions and encouraging future research.

In closing, it is perhaps not surprising that Neal asked me to write this foreword. I have been writing about the material world since I started in this profession. In fact, my first 'A' level publication was on the topic of organizational dress way back in 1993 (which may seem like a long time for some of you, but not so long for me). Indeed, I have long played with many of the themes in this book, including the interplay of the physical (e.g. artefacts and environment) and social world (e.g. identity, institutions and organizational behaviour more broadly) – although not using the language of materiality or affordances, nor concepts such as socio-materiality.

Thus, in many ways, reading this book was like coming home to a familiar place that I had not visited for far too long. It is exciting to see how far the field has developed – even in the past ten years. Indeed, some of the chapters use my work with Kim Elsbach in 2008 as depicting a view of the physical environment that is in need of change. And that is exactly how it should be. For a topic as important as this, our thinking needs to evolve, expand and grow. It is wonderful to see how far we have come and to get a glimpse of what lies ahead. Remi and Neal have put together a fine compendium. As you touch the physical pages, or interact with digital images, may you come to enjoy this book as much as I have.

Michael G. Pratt
Chestnut Hill, MA
August 2018

PART I

Introduction

1

INTRODUCTION

Organizational behaviour and the physical environment

Oluremi B. Ayoko and Neal M. Ashkanasy

The chapters in this volume deal with the physical environment of work (PEW), which is critical for employees' effective interactions, productivity and wellbeing. In fact, organizational scholars have known of the important effects of the work environment on the work and productivity of employees since the Hawthorne Studies (Roethlisberger & Dickson, 1939). Building on these classic works, Becker (1988) broadened the debate on the PEW to include connections with workspaces, work patterns, and organizational culture. In this regard, and delving further into the specifics of the physical work environment through the lens of affordances, Fayard and Weeks (2007) showed that the physical and social environments of work are tightly connected. Within this view, the architectural design of workplaces interacts with the way employees construct meaning and ultimately serves to shape employees' formal and informal interactions and behaviours at work.

Similarly, Rafaeli and Pratt (1993) argue that organizational dress such as clothing (e.g. jacket, skirt, trousers) and personal artefacts (e.g. IDs, smocks, jewellery) indicate internal and external organizational processes that also affect individual and organizational outcomes such as compliance, legitimization, organizational image and human resource management. Taking this line of argument further, Pratt and Rafaeli (1997) also show how organizational members employ dress to represent and to negotiate the complex issues inherent to hybrid identities in the workplace. Many decades later, researchers have renewed their effort in exploring the connection between the physical context to work and organizational processes and outcomes for individuals, groups and organizations.

Consistent with this idea, the authors of chapters in this book demonstrate that the physical environment is more than just a physical container for social interactions, but also crucial for the nature, quality, and duration of employee social interactions, behaviours, interaction processes, and outcomes. More specifically, drawing upon theories of psychological ownership, cognitive appraisal, together with existing research on the physical context of work, the authors of the chapters in this volume provide the latest thinking in an engaging approach to the study of how employees' interactions in given physical environments of work shape their behaviours, emotions, wellbeing, and productivity.

Existing work in this area (see Elsbach & Pratt, 2009) suggests that the physical workspaces (e.g. open-plan offices; OPOs) appear to be a double-edged sword. On the one hand, they promote communication and interaction that, in turn, facilitate workplace satisfaction and work effectiveness. They also foster relationships, increase knowledge-sharing, creativity, and idea-generation (Marmot & Eley, 2000); and reduce overhead costs for organizations (Oommen, Knowles & Zhao, 2008). On the other hand, such workspaces are replete with uncontrollable noise and distractions, which often lead to loss of identity and privacy (Bodin Danielsson & Bodin, 2009; Vos & Van der Voordt, 2002), interpersonal conflict (Ayoko & Härtel, 2003), poor motivation (Evans & Johnson, 2000), and lowered satisfaction, productivity and wellbeing (Bodin Danielsson & Bodin, 2009; Hedge, 1982). In this regard, Haapakangas, Helenius, Keekinen, and Hongisto (2008) found that ambient noise in open office settings leads to loss of productivity in comparison with private office settings. Another stream of research suggests that the 'sick building syndrome' (e.g. symptoms of distress, irritation, fatigue, headache and poor concentration; Pejtersen, Allermann, Kristensen & Poulsen, 2006) is linked with OPOs. Altogether, these findings highlight mixed findings and tensions in the research on the physical environment of work that need to be resolved if we are to understand the PEW (Chigot, 2003).

Ayoko and her colleagues (Ayoko & Härtel, 2003; Ayoko, Ashkanasy & Jehn, 2014) propose variously the need for researchers to take a deep look at the relationship between the physical setting of work and how it may impact employee behaviours (e.g. territoriality, see Brown, Lawrence, & Robinson, 2005), emotions, productivity, and wellbeing. This book builds on this previous research and aims partly to resolve physical workplace enigma by developing deeper insights into the role of the PEW, especially in the context of organizational behaviour (OB) research.

In sum, our motivation for this volume is to articulate an evidence-based theoretical background to the PEW, while also providing fresh evidence and understanding as to how the PEW links with work design, task interdependence, and employees' individuality, identity, territoriality, physical activities, emotions, work processes, and wellbeing.

The structure of this volume

Part I: Introduction

Part I comprises three chapters that broadly describe the contradictory and paradoxical nature of the physical environment of work, the mixed findings from previous research in the area, and the rhetoric that surrounds the adoption of differing configurations of workspaces by contemporary organizations. In this part, authors also describe how the physical environment of work shapes employees' innovation and design thinking.

In Chapter 1, Oluremi B. Ayoko and Neal M. Ashkanasy describe the mixed findings of research in the area of the PEW, especially referring to open-plan office design. Additionally, these authors discuss the nature of contemporary configurations and the layout of the physical environment of work from employees' and employers' perspectives.

In Chapter 2, Kimberly D. Elsbach and Ileana Stigliani explore extant research from both organizational scholars and scholars of design and engineering to understand better how features of the PEW might promote creativity by supporting the practice of 'design thinking'. In this respect, the authors conceptualize the physical workspaces as giving rise to design thinking that, in turn, promotes creativity. In particular, and referring to previously published case studies, they examine how common work areas, dedicated project rooms, and private work 'caves' may support the design thinking practices of brainstorming, rapid prototyping, user focus, and experimentation. They also report that features of the physical workspace serve to support different design thinking practices via multiple functions (instrumental, symbolic and aesthetic). Finally and based on their findings, Elsbach and Stigliani suggest possible opportunities for future research on physical work environments and creativity.

Christina Bodin Danielsson, in Chapter 3, addresses holistic office design from an interdisciplinary perspective, including perspectives from the organizational, management, architecture, environmental psychology, and occupational health disciplines. The chapter highlights the impact of office design on the welfare of organizations and its members at different levels. Additionally, in six sections, Bodin Danielsson describes the environmental influences of office design while discussing how office design may shape power, status and hierarchy in the organization, as well as interpersonal and group behaviours. Finally, the author examines the link between office design, job satisfaction, and the psychosocial environment as well as the micro issues of individual employee emotions, well-being and occupational health.

In summary, the authors of Part I set the scene for this volume, providing an overview of research into the PEW as it relates to OB (Chapter 1) and an investigation into how the PEW may stimulate design thinking and creativity (Chapter 2). Finally, adopting theories from multiple disciplines, the author of Chapter 3 gives a holistic view of the role of the PEW in shaping behaviours and attitudes at the individual, group and organizational levels.

Part II: Theoretical background

In Part II, the focus shifts to the theoretical background of the PEW. Our motivation for this volume is to articulate the theoretical background to the PEW, while providing a fresh understanding on how the PEW links to work design, task interdependence, and employees' physical activities, emotions, work processes, and wellbeing. In particular, and drawing on the idea of psychological ownership, an underlying thread of the volume is the importance of employee territoriality and placement identity. The authors in this part examine the foundational issues important for the PEW, such as psychological ownership and employee wellbeing, as well as the quality of workplace environment, individual characteristics, and the socio-technical system thinking inherent in understanding the PEW.

Jon L. Pierce and Graham Brown open Part II with a focus on ownership as a psychological phenomenon (Chapter 4). They review the theory of psychological ownership at both the individual and collective levels, while exploring their associations with the physical work context. They then examine the role of psychological ownership in design as well as other aspects of the physical environment to uncover new areas of impact, especially relating to feelings of ownership relevant to work and organizational contexts.

Next, in Chapter 5, authors Jungsoo Kim and Richard de Dear estimate the relative significance of different environmental qualities on employees' overall evaluations of the workplace. The authors report that the effect of the PEW depends more on employee perceptions than actual environment quality (e.g. thermal comfort, indoor air quality, noise and office layout, its design features and aesthetics). They conclude that this indicates that a certain amount of quality input does not necessarily translate into commensurately desirable output in workplace environment management. Kim and de Dear also address how gender, proximity to windows, and degree of workspace enclosure relate to employee wellbeing and satisfaction.

In Chapter 6, Mischel Luong, Kim Peters, Courtney von Hippel and Mylyn Dat examine how individual characteristics affect the PEW. Using a model of space and identity fit, the authors discuss the motivational implications of self-space identity compatibility at work, in a manner that extends this literature into the domain of workplace space. Indeed, the authors argue that physical workspaces can provide important cues to belonging that affect workers' motivation and organizational commitment. Luong and his colleagues conclude by discussing the implications of their model for diversity management.

Still on how the physical environment can shape, constrain and promote organizational and behavioural outcomes, Matthew C. Davis discusses how the inappropriate approach to workspace design holds the potential to promote undesirable outcomes for employees (Chapter 7). Davis argues that socio-technical systems thinking is a theoretical framework useful in guiding holistic workspace design. This is because this approach encourages a joint consideration of workspace design alongside other organizational systems, such as processes, culture, and organizational structure, which may also help account for the broader context of work. In sum, Davis discusses the value of systemic approaches to workspace design and the associated organizational change using innovative configurations in the PEW such as open-plan and activity-based working.

In summary of Part II, the authors in the opening chapter (Chapter 4) look at the theory of psychological ownership at the individual and collective levels and explore their relationship with the physical work environment. The authors of Chapter 5 explore employee wellbeing and quality of workplace environment and conclude that employee perceptions of their workplace matters probably more than the nature and quality of the physical environment itself. The authors of Chapter 6 extend this idea to include a need for self-space–identity fit. Finally, in Chapter 7 the author addresses the role of socio-technical systems thinking in designing office configurations.

Part III: The physical environment of work and work design

In Part III of this volume, authors address specifically work design issues in relation to the physical environment of work (PEW). The part begins with Chapter 8 by M.K. Ward and Sharon K. Parker, who integrate multiple literatures and propose plausible models of how the workspace potentially shapes the psychological aspects of work. These authors argue that, while there may be other ways that workspace and work design might work together (e.g. they could have interactive effects), one likely scenario is that the role of work design serves to mediate the effects of workspaces on productivity outcomes. Ward and Parker propose possible research directions in this area, especially in entrepreneurial co-working spaces, cognition at work, ageing workforce, and work design profiles.

In the following chapter (Chapter 9), William J. Bingley, Katharine H. Greenaway and Kelly S. Fielding review research on physical greening, and demonstrate that this can positively impact organizational behaviour outcomes such as productivity, stress, and job satisfaction. The authors outline a range of different theoretical explanations for these effects. Finally, Bingley and his associates discuss how the social identity approach can help researchers to understand why greening has positive effects in some contexts but not in others; and how greening may play an important role in encouraging pro-environmental behaviour.

Continuing this line, Varda Wasserman considers in Chapter 10 how the PEW is related to aesthetics. She argues that, while the literature on organizational aesthetics has placed special emphasis on the role of space in constructing social hierarchies and on processes of inclusion and exclusion of various identities, authors to date have paid little attention to gender identities and women's experiences within organizational workspaces. This chapter illuminates the various ways in which the PEW segregates according to gender, and how workspaces are experienced and enacted differently by men and women. Wasserman also highlights a typology of three main theoretical trajectories to examine the ways in which workspaces become gendered. She concludes by offering theoretical arenas for future development of this idea.

In the next chapter, by Leonore van den Ende, Thijs Willems, and Alfons van Marrewijk (Chapter 11), the authors build on extant literature to argue that the relationship between the physical environment and behaviour is complex and characterized by unintended consequences and trade-offs (e.g. Elsbach & Pratt, 2009; Dale & Burrell, 2007). The authors point out that studies nonetheless still treat the PEW and employee behaviour as distinct spheres of organizational life. Van den Ende and her co-authors further challenge this assumption using a socio-material lens and present vignettes of empirical research to demonstrate how the physical environment and behaviour are intrinsically interrelated. They conclude that the physical environment shapes social behaviour and that this behaviour, in turn, shapes how the physical environment is used and perceived.

In the concluding chapter of Part III, Ken Tann and Oluremi B. Ayoko (Chapter 12) continue the discussion of the usefulness of socio-material lens to facilitate a more in-depth understanding of the PEW. Specifically, these authors apply social semiotics to differing office types to explain how the physical environment (e.g. office layout) shapes individual experience. As such, they seek to provide a qualitative understanding of how office design affects aspects such as privacy, interaction, and affinity in a social context. Tann and Ayoko propose a re-examination of these inter-subjectively negotiated meanings as a mediating space between the materiality of the physical environments and the subjective experiences of individuals, groups, and organizations.

Altogether, the authors in Part III collectively bring some additional deeper and differing insights into the relationship between the PEW and work design. The authors of Chapter 8 examine the connection between physical workspace configurations, task characteristics and work design, while, in Chapter 9, the authors lay bare how greening the PEW may impact employee behaviour and space–identity fit, and in Chapter 10, author Wasserman discusses the role of aesthetics. In the last two chapters of Part III (Chapters 11 and 12), the authors adopt a socio-material lens to demonstrate the complex and interconnected relationship between the physical environment and employee behaviour. They also set out the intricate link of the materiality of the physical environments (e.g. office layout) and the subjective experiences of individuals, groups and organizations.

Part IV: Emotions, physical activity, and the physical environment of OB

Opening this part, Gretchen Spreitzer, Peter Bacevice and Lyndon Garrett pick up the topic of thriving (Chapter 13), a critical issue in OB. The authors specifically focus on how the material features that comprise the PEW signal an organization's intent to promote values and to encourage actions that influence the experience of thriving at work. More specifically, Spreitzer and her team examine how workers experience three important aspects of the PEW: (1) open and flexible design office settings; (2) technological approaches for productivity monitoring, communication and collaboration; and (3) the shifting concept of workspace as more people telecommute or work freelance.

In the next chapter (Chapter 14), Rianne Appel-Meulenbroek, Pascale Le Blanc, and Yvonne de Kort picks up the subject of person–environment (PE) fit and the optimization of the physical work environment. The authors review existing evidence from different academic disciplines to identify the effects of the physical workplace on employees, and relate this to the needs–supply fit aspect of person–environment fit theory regarding the three basic human needs at work: competence, autonomy, and relatedness. Through a discussion of individual choice and control, Appel-Meulenbroek and her colleagues seek to emphasize that a one-size-fits-all workplace strategy does not exist, because optimal fit depends on personal characteristics, the task at hand, organizational culture, as well as other aspects.

Elizabeth J. Sander, Arran Caza and Peter J. Jordan next explore the relationship between the PEW and stress (Chapter 15). In this chapter, the authors review research findings concerning the relationship between the physical work environment and stress to summarize the current state of knowledge. Using this summary as a platform, Sander and her co-authors propose evidence-based recommendations as to ways in which the physical environment might be adjusted to reduce stress for employees.

In summary, the authors of the chapters in Part IV deal with the way the PEW may facilitate or constrain employee wellbeing and organizational effectiveness. The authors of the opening chapter of Part IV (Chapter 13) discuss how the material features that comprise the physical environment of work signal an organization's intent to promote values and encourage actions that influence the experience of thriving at work. In Chapter 14, the authors describe the needs–supply fit aspect of person–environment fit theory as a means to understand how the PEW might interact with the three basic human needs at work: competence, autonomy and relatedness. Finally, Sander and colleagues in Chapter 15 address the connection between the PEW and stress, proposing how the PEW might be configured to reduce employee stress.

Part V: The physical environment of OB and the practitioner

Introducing Part V of the book, the authors of Chapter 16 (Momo D. Kromah, Oluremi B. Ayoko, Neal M. Ashkanasy and Gemma L. Irving) draw on place-based theory to explain the nature of employees' emotional attachments to their workspaces, which often results in unintended consequences (i.e. failure of workspace change). Based on a qualitative study involving 19 participants from 9 organizations experiencing various types of organizational change, the authors discuss the role of place attachment and its influence on employees' attitudes and behaviours. Kromah and his associates conclude with theoretical and practical implications of place attachment and its relevance to organizational workspace change.

In the final chapter, Chapter 17, Oluremi B. Ayoko and Neal M. Ashkanasy review the major issues raised by the authors of the chapters in this volume and conclude with some thoughts on how the physical environment of work might be managed effectively.

Conclusion

In the 17 chapters of this edited volume, authors provide an overview of current thoughts and perspectives relating to the PEW and how differing workspace configurations might shape employees' behaviours, attitudes, identity and wellbeing. Indeed, it is especially surprising that it has taken such a long time for the OB field to recognize and to actively investigate the significant impact the physical setting of work may have on employees, groups, and organizations, and how such effects may be managed. It should also be immediately evident from the chapters in the current volume that the topic of the PEW is critical for organizational behaviour research. We offer three reasons why this should be so.

First, contemporary organizations around the world are increasingly spending a significant amount of money on the physical environment of work (redesigning, refurbishing, or building fresh technological-oriented buildings). KPMG Australia has just spent about AUD7 million on what they term 'agile work spaces'. In this regard, the physical environment of work is a persuasive phenomenon and research is needed to examine the impact of these new approaches to workspaces on employee behaviours, attitudes, and productivity. The chapters in the book make this need emphatically clear.

Second, and relatedly, is the impact of the PEW on employees' behaviours (e.g. territoriality). It is clear from the chapters in the book that employees engage in territorial behaviours driven by their psychological need for ownership and identity. The chapters on territoriality and self–space fit phenomena are crucial for helping employers, space and change managers understand why employees clamour for their own workspace where noise and lack of privacy are not distracting.

Third, it is encouraging to see scholars are also aware that the physical environment may directly affect employee wellbeing. Many authors outside the OB field have written about the PEW characteristics of noise and lack of privacy as they affect employees, especially those who work in open-plan offices. Additionally, there is considerable research about the design of work, technology and aesthetics, and how these may affect employee wellbeing. It is clear from the chapters in this volume that managers should address the issues of stress and work design stemming from the PEW to promote employee wellbeing and productivity.

Finally, we note how exciting it is to learn that the PEW is not just a container but a social environment that has capacity to mould individual experience by constraining or enabling various kinds of interactions that may, in turn, impact productivity. What distinguishes the present volume from others on this topic is its primary focus on the PEW and the way it relates this to organizational behaviour (e.g. employees' territoriality) rather than just the general workplace and issues such as lighting, colour, communication, and status. In this regard, we argue that the present volume is unique and represents a new perspective written by experts in the field. We expect the book should make useful reading for both practitioners and academics.

References

Ayoko, O.B., Ashkanasy, N.M., & Jehn, K.A. (2014). Approaches to the study of employees' territoriality, conflict, emotions and well-being. In O.B. Ayoko, N.M. Ashkanasy, & K.A. Jehn (eds.), *Handbook of Conflict Management Research* (pp. 363–381).Cheltenham, UK: Edward Elgar.

Ayoko, O.B., & Härtel, C.E.J. (2003). The role of space as both a conflict trigger and a conflict control mechanism in culturally heterogeneous workgroups. *Applied Psychology: An International Review, 52*, 383–412.

Becker, F.D. (1988). Technological innovation and organizational ecology. In M. Helander (ed.), *Handbook of Human-Computer Interaction* (pp. 1107–1117). New York: North-Holland.

Bodin Danielsson, C., & Bodin, L. (2009). Difference in satisfaction with office environment among employees in different office types. *Journal of Architectural and Planning Research, 26*, 241–257.

Brown, G., Lawrence, T., & Robinson, S.L. (2005). Territoriality in organizations. *Academy of Management Review, 30*, 577–594.

Chigot, P. (2003). Controlled transparency in workplace design: Balancing visual and acoustic interaction in office environments. *Journal of Facilities Management, 2*, 121–130.

Dale, K., & Burrell, G. (2007). *The Spaces of Organisation and the Organisation of Space: Power, identity and materiality at work*. London: Macmillan International Higher Education.

Elsbach, K.D., & Pratt, M.G. (2009). The physical environment in organizations. *Academy of Management Annals, 1*, 181–223.

Evans, G.W., & Johnson, D. (2000). Stress and open-office noise. *Journal of Applied Psychology, 85*, 779–783.

Fayard, A.L., & Weeks, J. (2007). Photocopiers and water-coolers: The affordances of informal interaction. *Organization Studies, 28*, 605–634.

Haapakangas, A., Helenius, R., Keekinen, E., & Hongisto, V. (2008, July). Perceived acoustic environment, work performance and well-being: Survey results from Finnish offices. *Proceedings of the 9th International Congress on Noise as a Public Health Problem* (ICBEN), Foxwoods, CT, USA.

Hedge, A. (1982). The open-plan office: A systematic investigation of employee reactions to their work environment. *Environment and Behavior, 14*, 519–542.

Marmot, A., & Eley, J. (2000). *Office Space Planning: Designing for Tomorrow's Workplace*. New York: McGraw-Hill.

Oommen, V.G., Knowles, M., & Zhao, I. (2008). Should health service managers embrace open plan work environments? A review. *Asia Pacific Journal of Health Management, 3*, 37–43.

Pejtersen, J.H., Allermann, L., Kristensen, T.S., & Poulsen, O.M. (2006). Indoor climate, psychosocial work environment and symptoms in open-plan offices. *Indoor Air, 16*, 392–401.

Pratt, M.G., & Rafaeli, A. (1997). Organizational dress as a symbol of multilayered social identities. *Academy of Management Journal, 40,* 862–898.

Rafaeli, A., & Pratt, M.G. (1993). Tailored meanings: On the meaning and impact of organizational dress. *Academy of Management Review, 18,* 32–55.

Roethlisberger, F.J., & Dickson, W.J. (1939). *Management and the Worker: An Account of a Research Program Conducted by the Western Electric Company, Hawthorne Works, Chicago.* Cambridge, MA: Harvard University Press.

Vos, P., & van der Voordt, T. (2002). Tomorrow's offices through today's eyes: Effects of innovation in the working environment. *Journal of Corporate Real Estate, 4,* 48–65.

2

THE PHYSICAL WORK ENVIRONMENT AND CREATIVITY

How creative workspaces support and encourage design thinking

Kimberly D. Elsbach and Ileana Stigliani

Introduction

Modern organizations are increasingly challenged to generate creative ways of looking at and solving problems. This entails not only rethinking established organizational structures and formal procedures that support creativity, but also crafting physical environments that foster informal processes necessary for creativity. In this vein, previous management research has investigated the role of the physical environment in organizations, and some studies in design and engineering have suggested that the physical environment might promote creativity by supporting 'design thinking' – which may be defined as the use of designerly problem-solving tools (e.g. rapid prototyping, brainstorming) for solving ambiguous and loosely structured problems (Brown, 2008, 2009). Yet, an explicit examination of the role of physical environment in fostering creativity through design thinking is lacking.

In this chapter, we review extant findings from research on creativity and the physical environment, as well as primary evidence from ethnographic case studies of toy designers and product designers, to explore how creative workspaces might promote creativity by encouraging and supporting the practice of design thinking. Our findings suggest that a number of features of the physical work environment (e.g. common work areas, model shops, dedicated project rooms, and private work 'caves') may support and encourage the use of a set of design thinking practices (e.g. brainstorming, rapid prototyping, user focus, and experimentation), which have been shown to enhance creativity in organizations. Further, these features of the physical environment appear to support design thinking through instrumental, symbolic, and aesthetic functions (suggested by extant frameworks of physical environments in organizations) (e.g. Vilnai-Yavetz et al., 2005). Building on these insights, we suggest an agenda for future research that may leverage the role of physical environments in the pursuit of design thinking and creativity.

Extant research on the physical work environment, creativity and design thinking

Physical work environments have been defined as comprising three distinct elements: (1) interior design elements such as furniture, equipment, and décor; (2) interior architectural elements such as size, shape, and arrangement of workspaces, and type/colour of construction materials; and (3) ambient conditions such as lighting, temperature, and sound (Hoff & Öberg, 2015). These dimensions of the physical work environment have been studied by both organizational researchers, as well as researchers from the areas of design and engineering. In the following sections, we provide a brief overview of these two areas of study and their insights regarding how the physical work environment relates to creativity. In doing so, we illuminate some gaps in our understanding of how physical workspaces might promote creativity.

Organizational research on creativity and the physical work environment

Research relating the physical environment to creativity in organizations has gained increasing attention over the past couple of decades (McCoy & Evans, 2002; Dul et al., 2011; Dul & Ceylan, 2014; Hoff & Öberg, 2015), and several conceptual frameworks of this relationship have been published (e.g. Dul & Ceylan, 2011, 2014; Elsbach & Pratt, 2007; Moultrie et al., 2007; Magadley & Birdi, 2009; Oksanen & Ståhle, 2013).

While each of these frameworks is unique, they overlap in their focus on three, primary characteristics of the physical workspace that influence the creativity of employees: (1) *instrumental*, (2) *symbolic*, and (3) *aesthetic characteristics*. These three characteristics have been identified as central to employee responses to the physical work environment (Rafaeli & Vilnai-Yavetz, 2004; Vilnai-Yavetz et al., 2005), and have been shown to have both positive and negative influences on workers (Elsbach & Pratt, 2007). In the following sections, we discuss empirical evidence suggesting that these three dimensions of the physical workspace may influence creativity at work.

Instrumental characteristics of physical workspaces

Extensive research studies in both ergonomics and management suggest that physical workspaces may support and encourage creativity through instrumental means (Dul & Ceylan, 2011; Ceylan et al., 2008). Specifically, research has shown that workspaces that provide opportunities for *both collaboration* and *privacy* may enhance the creativity of workers.

First, the role of collaboration in enhancing creativity has become an increasingly important topic among management practitioners and scholars (Serrat, 2017). Further, researchers have found that collaboration may be encouraged through the design of the physical work environment (Hua et al., 2010). As a result, it is not surprising that researchers have examined how workspaces might be better designed to support and encourage creative collaboration (Becker, 2004; Davenport, 2005).

For example, Hua et al. (2010) examined the importance of individual work-stations as well as three types of collaborative work arrangements (i.e. meeting spaces, shared print/copy spaces, and shared kitchen/coffee areas) for professional workers. Their findings indicate that while individual workstations (e.g. cubicles) were preferred by over 80% of those surveyed for casual conversations, enclosed meeting rooms were strongly preferred (by almost 90% of those surveyed) for the type of collaboration that is necessary for creative work. Further, in support of the general notion that being close together enhances opportunities for creative col-laboration, several studies have shown that physical proximity within a building (Appel-Meulenbroek et al., 2017) and overlap in walking routes to a shared lab (Kabo et al., 2015) increases the chances that workers will collaborate and share knowledge. Finally, the use of information technology has been increasingly the subject of research on creative collaboration. Thus, research on 'blended spaces' (that include both traditional dimensions of group work such as tables and enclosed rooms, and digital facilitators of group work such as computer terminals, screens, and shared digital work surfaces) has shown that these types of technological fea-tures may also be critical to encouraging and supporting creative collaboration (Benyon & Mival, 2015).

At the same time, recent research has also identified the importance of pri-vacy for both creativity and experimentation at work (Elsbach & Pratt, 2007). One issue that has been repeatedly found to detract from creativity at work is distraction from noise or activity nearby (Gifford, 2014). Thus, it is not surprising that privacy at work has been associated with creative and innovative outcomes (Stokols et al., 2002).

In addition, recent research has found that privacy at work can allow workers to engage in unauthorized experimentation that may actually lead to innovative solutions to work problems. In particular, work by Bernstein (e.g. 2012, 2017) has shown that privacy may enhance creativity by allowing such experimentation to take place. Thus, in his study of factory workers in China, Bernstein (2012: 188) found that providing privacy screens had the unintended effect of encouraging workers to experiment with ideas for improving work quality and efficiency (e.g. a 'ton of little tricks' that 'kept production going' or enabled 'faster, easier, and/or safer production'), without fear of being reprimanded for not sticking to assigned tasks and potentially wasting time on experimental solutions that would not work. In this way, allowing workers the opportunity to work in private may also enhance their creativity.

Symbolic characteristics of physical workspaces

A number of studies (e.g. McCoy & Evans, 2002; Ceylan et al., 2008; Magadley & Birdi, 2009) also suggest that symbolic components of the physical environment (i.e. aspects of the physical environment that reflect values and ideals, such as playfulness vs. formality) may influence creativity in organizations. In particular, researchers have found that physical environments that support perceptions and feelings of *freedom* (e.g. ability for self-expression, play, and divergent thinking) may promote creativity (Amabile & Conti, 1999; Amabile et al., 2002).

Perceptions and feelings of freedom at work have been argued to be important to the free flow of ideas and a sense of 'play' at work that is important to divergent thinking and creativity (Amabile et al., 1996). Physical work environments such as 'innovation labs' or other temporary workspaces may create a sense of freedom in employees by distancing them from reminders of the daily work 'grind' (Kristensen, 2004). For example, in a study of an innovation lab used by various groups in the UK, Magadley and Birdi (2009: 320) found that 'getting away' from one's everyday work environment was the aspect of the innovation lab that was most commonly identified by employees as important to 'thinking differently' and, thus, being creative.

In other cases, researchers have found that symbolism that supports feelings and thoughts of freedom may be achieved by workspaces that signal values of self-expression and play. For example, Oksanen and Ståhle (2013: 823) described how the consulting firm, IDEO, encouraged creativity by designing workspaces that symbolically emphasized playfulness and freedom of expression through the types of rooms and non-work areas they included. As they note:

> IDEO embraces values such as creativity, playfulness, open mindedness, and collaboration; similarly their physical workspaces express these values. . . . The IDEO space consists of team project rooms, an open studio for the designers and programmers, a prototyping workshop, a cafe, a community garden, and so forth.

Finally, researchers have shown that the ability to personalize one's workspace (e.g. through mementos, décor, and arrangement) is important to affirming personal distinctiveness and identity, which may be critical to maintaining a sense of personal freedom at work (Elsbach & Pratt, 2007). This is because the ability to personalize one's workspace provides a source of control over the work environment that may help employees gain a sense of freedom at work (Baumeister, 1998). By contrast, Elsbach (2004) found that employees who were denied the opportunity to personalize their workspace – because they had been moved to a non-territorial work environment – found their sense of personal distinctiveness threatened. Such lack of personalization may reduce creativity because it increases stress and negative mood (Scheiberg, 1990; Wells, 2000).

Aesthetic dimensions of physical workspaces

Finally, researchers have shown that aesthetic dimensions of the physical workspace (e.g. aspects of the workspace that influence mood and sensory experience) may influence creativity (Rafaeli & Vilnai-Yavetz, 2004). In particular, this research suggests that aesthetic dimensions of the workspace may influence creativity via their influence on employees' sense of *restoration* (e.g. feelings of physical and emotional rejuvenation and relaxation).

A sense of physical and emotional restoration has been argued to be important to supporting reflection and the 'gestation' of creative thought (Elsbach & Hargadon, 2006; Amabile et al., 2002). In terms of producing such restoration, significant research has shown that a natural or nature-like setting is most effective (Dul & Ceylan, 2011; Ceylan et al., 2008; Hartig et al., 1991, 2003). According to Attention Restoration Theory (Kaplan, 1995), 'nature can support a sense of being away – psychological distance – from worries and other routine mental contents, and from demands on directed attention' (Lymeus et al., 2017). As a result, nature-like settings may allow for the mental restoration needed for creative thought. Such nature-like settings may be achieved in the workspace through access to nature (e.g. through atriums, potted plants, and windows) and the use of natural materials in interior design (e.g. the use of natural wood and natural fibres) (Sundstrom & Sundstrom, 1986).

In addition to nature-like settings, physical work environments that are characterized by cool colours (e.g. blues) and low clutter have been rated as most likely to support creative work by managers (Ceylan et al., 2008). These influences may be related to the effect of colour and clutter on mood and stress (Stone, 2003). That is, both cool colours and low clutter have been shown to lower stress and improve positive mood (Ceylan et al., 2008). Interestingly, visually complex surroundings that are not 'cluttered' may also stimulate creativity (McCoy & Evans, 2002). Thus, these findings suggest that the number and arrangement of objects in a physical environment should be carefully considered when designing for creativity.

Summary

In summary, the above discussion illustrates how organizational researchers have linked the physical work environment to creativity. In general, this research suggests that the physical work environment may influence the creativity of employees through its symbolic and aesthetic (i.e. 'psycho-social') dimensions (e.g. perceptions and feelings of freedom and dynamism (Vithayathawornwong et al., 2003)), or its instrumental dimensions (e.g. spaces large enough and private enough for creative collaboration) (McCoy & Evans, 2002).

Despite this work, we would argue that most of the recent advances in thinking about creativity at work have not come from organizational research. Instead, an explosion of work on creative work has come from researchers studying 'design thinking' as a method of tackling difficult and even ambiguous problems at work (Johansson-Sköldberg et al., 2013; Yoo & Kim, 2015; Bjögvinsson et al., 2012; Mutanen, 2008). We discuss this work next, and suggest that an opportunity exists for linking this recent work on design thinking with insight about the physical work environment to extend our understanding of how workspace is related to creativity.

'Design thinking' research on creativity and the physical work environment

Traditional designers of 'things' (e.g. product designers, building designers) use a systematic approach to problem-solving that employs tools that help them to identify user needs and create solutions that work – although they may not comprise 'optimal' solutions (Liedtka et al., 2009; Liedtka & Ogilvie, 2011). The application of such 'designerly tools' to solve a wide variety of organizational and management problems has over time evolved into a new discipline called 'design thinking' (Brown, 2008; Vogel, 2009).

In general, Seidel and Fixson (2013) suggest that design thinking practices fall into three categories: (1) needfinding practices (i.e. ethnographic observations, in-depth contextual interviews, or customer journeys used to empathize with and understand the needs of end-users); (2) idea-generation practices (i.e. brainstorming and co-creation/co-design used to generate possible solutions to problems); and (3) idea-testing practices (i.e. rapid prototyping used to test ideas on small scale to determine their desirability, technical feasibility and business viability).

The implementation of these practices is inspired by the driving principles of design thinking such as empathy (i.e. the ability to step into other people's shoes), collaboration, iteration and experimentation (Ben Mahmoud-Jouini et al., 2016). In turn, these methods have been successfully used by firms to create new products and services (Sutton & Hoyt, 2016).

While the role of physical work environments in implementing design thinking has not been a focus of scholarly research, there are numerous hints in empirical studies that indicate that the physical work environment may support (or hinder) design thinking practices (Elsbach & Stigliani, 2018). For example, there are a handful of studies that show how the designation of specific 'design labs' or 'design centres' can provide a place for working on creative prototypes or experimenting with new ideas (Rauth et al., 2014; Stigliani & Ravasi, 2012; Terrey, 2009). Thus, in their comparative case study of design thinking implementation across firms, Rauth et al. (2014) found that the creation of dedicated design spaces encouraged and supported the design thinking tools of rapid prototyping and experimentation. As Rauth et al. (2014: 54) reported:

> Interviewees reported the importance of creating dedicated Design Thinking spaces. These spaces had a start-up feel and a flexible interior that allowed for Design Thinking activities and facilitated group work. For example, the space needed to provide material and tools for prototyping and allow participants to display interview results as well as other gathered information. This was usually done through the installation of big whiteboards (or walls painted in a special whiteboard colour) and with furniture that could be flexibly arranged. As such, the physical space was seen as contrasting to established, sometimes cubical, workspaces.

This example suggests that specific design thinking activities (e.g. prototyping) may be best performed in workspaces with specific features (e.g. ready access to materials and tools that may be used to construct prototypes and moveable furniture that can be situated for group work).

In another example, Bailey (2012) described how employees working for a large public sector organization used communal workspaces to post sketches and early prototypes as a way to foster discussions and idea-sharing. As he notes:

> Another effective method of raising awareness was found to be through communicating design processes via communal spaces, posting work on walls of offices, etc., to encourage debate and discussion amongst colleagues. It seems appropriate, therefore, to utilize in-house service design teams to engage relevant staff members in workshops and projects to facilitate the dissemination and practice of design throughout the organization.
>
> *(Bailey, 2012: 5)*

The creation of such communal spaces was purposefully intended to disseminate design thinking capabilities across the organization.

While such examples are few, they suggested to us that our own case studies of designers might help confirm and expand the notion that physical work environments might support and promote design thinking practices. Therefore, we undertook a set of 'second-look' analyses of prior case studies we had performed (Kramer, 2016) to specifically search for evidence linking creative workspaces to design thinking practices. We discuss our findings from these second-look analyses next. We should note that we do not intend to portray our insights as the result of full-blown ethnographic studies, but as illustrative evidence that suggests the need for further study.

Second-look case studies: physical work environments and design thinking

In the following sections, we describe insights gained from taking 'second looks' at two case studies we had performed and published in the last several years. The first case study was led by the first author and involved a study of toy designers originally reported by Elsbach and Flynn (2013). The second case study was led by the second author and involved a study of product designers originally reported by Stigliani and Ravasi (2012). As we discuss below, each of these cases illustrates how certain characteristics of the workspace support the use of specific design thinking tools. In addition, we note how each of these workspace characteristics supports design thinking through instrumental, symbolic, or aesthetic functions of the physical environment (Vilnai-Yavetz et al., 2005). Further, we find that most of the dimensions of the physical environment that support design thinking do so through multiple functions, rather than through a single function. In this way, our reviews link the research on design thinking to extant organizational research on physical environment in organizations.

Case study 1: Toy designers

This case study involved observation and interviews of toy designers working for a large, multinational toy company located in the US. The design centre, where observation took place, housed over 200 toy designers who worked on the development of new toy prototypes. No manufacturing was performed at this site (although construction of prototypes was performed), and while marketing and other administrative staff visited the design centre to confer with toy designers, no administrators (other than clerical staff) were housed on-site.

The physical layout of the 22,000 sq. ft design centre was an open-plan design. Each of five toy groups observed had its own common work area (including large tables for working on prototypes) separated from other groups by moveable partitions. Individual designers had private cubicles adjacent to their group's common workspace. The only enclosed areas housed special machinery (e.g. metal working machines), lab space, and digital video production rooms, plus a few offices for senior staff. Designers could hear their colleagues across the open floor plan, see what others were working on in the public areas, and physically examine prototypes in the design centre.

Observations of these designers revealed how the physical environment promoted the use of design thinking tools in three important ways. We discuss these findings in more detail next and illustrate them with specific observations and commentary regarding a project to develop a new 'track set' for miniature toy cars.

Common workspaces encouraged impromptu brainstorming and rapid prototyping

A first insight from this case study is that common work areas (i.e. large open areas that commonly held a large table upon which toy designs-in-progress were worked) provided an opportunity for impromptu brainstorming and rapid prototyping by designers. Although these common work areas were not formally designated as 'open to all designers', the designers in this setting routinely received informal comments and suggestions from those who were not assigned to work on the projects being developed, but were merely passing by.

This informal collaboration was encouraged by two features of the common work areas that allowed them to promote two design thinking tools. First, the work areas were *large, visible, and centrally located* in the design centre, which made it likely that all designers, including those not working on a project in the common area, would pass by throughout the day. This created opportunities for *impromptu brainstorming* about the projects on display in the work area. These impromptu conversations were a key means for collaboration and for knowledge transfer across divisions. For example, the following conversation occurred when a designer, Tim[1] – who was working on a new project involving micro-cars (very tiny toy cars) – passed by the common area where Alan tinkered with the track set he was developing for a Christmas release:

TIM: Are you trying to get the cars to race upside down on this [pointing] part of the track?

ALAN: Yeah, we wanted the loops to cross here [pointing] and having them upside down there would look pretty cool.

TIM: Well, you might try using some magnets in that part of the track, because that will help the cars stay on track and not fall if they aren't at top speed. I don't know if it would work with these bigger cars, but it works with the micro-cars.

As this example shows, the expertise that Alan had about using magnets in micro-cars may not have been known to Tim, as Alan was working in a different division. The large, visible and centrally located workspace, however, made it easy for Alan to see what was going on and provide a suggestion. In this way, the common workspace allowed for impromptu brainstorming, involving people with different expertise and a distinct point of view.

A second feature of the common work areas that encouraged collaboration and knowledge transfer was that they *contained tools, spare parts*, and *leftover pieces* from past work that was performed in the area in tool carts and containers that were around or underneath the large work table. These artefacts made it easy for passersby to tinker on the edges of the project or even modify the actual project in development. Because the designers knew each other well, and had worked in many divisions over the course of their careers, they were very comfortable letting a designer from outside their project play with it. This allowed experts from other areas tinker with a project in development without ruffling feathers. For example, Marty, another designer who was assigned to the track set project, had the following interaction with Jie, a designer who had begun playing with one of the 'creatures' that popped up when cars raced by:

MARTY: Hey Jie, what are you doing with that monster?

JIE: I'm just seeing how it's designed inside. It's not hollow like I expected, and it weighs a ton. How are you going to get this to pop up at this weight?

MARTY: Well, that's just a prototype we created from a game piece on another project. But, you're right, it should be hollow. We can't really test it correctly without it being hollow.

JIE: Yeah. I might have something in my cube that you could use, or maybe you could just create a hollow monster from some of these spare parts [pointing].

MARTY: Thanks. That's a good idea. Let's see what we have that will work.

In this example, having spare parts and tools readily available allowed the two designers to try something on the spot (i.e. engage in rapid prototyping), without delay.

As the above examples show, the availability of common open workspaces is an important aspect of the physical environment for organizations that want to support design thinking practices among employees. Further, the availability of common workspaces appears to have supported design thinking through both its instrumental functions (i.e. providing a space and materials for tinkering), as well as its symbolic functions (i.e. in signalling the importance of collaboration through its prominence).

Public cubicle walls offered space for prototype/sketch displays, which inspired impromptu brainstorming

A second insight from this case study is that designers used the exterior surfaces of their cubicles to display past project prototypes and drawings, and that these displays inspired fellow designers when they passed by to engage in impromptu brainstorming with the displayer. They also served as a source of general inspiration for fellow designers.

In one such case, a designer, Rick, was walking by the cubicle of Danny, another designer, when he noticed a superhero sketch that was tacked to the outside of Danny's cubicle. Rick and Danny had the following conversation:

RICK: Hey Danny, is that drawing part of the new licensed product line-up we're doing for the new movie?
DANNY: Yeah, I'm trying to work in some of the new gadgets that are featured in the film. I'm not sure I have the size right, or even the way they attach to the costume.
RICK: Well, I'm trying to do the game board design for the same feature, and I didn't even know that they were including 'X' and 'Y' gadgets in the film. Those could be cool as game pieces. Can you show me where you saw those in the movie promotional material?
DANNY: Sure, I need to take a look at them again myself. Maybe we can work on this together to make sure we have the look right. You did the games for the previous movie, didn't you? Maybe we could start with the gadgets you made for that game to check the sizes.

As this example illustrates, prototypes or sketches tacked to the outside of cubicles signalled to others what Danny was working on, and created an opportunity for collaboration and impromptu brainstorming that might not have happened otherwise.

It's also important to note that, although a designer might pass by another designer's cubicle many times, they might only notice a prototype or sketch when it becomes relevant to a current project. Thus, displaying not only current, but also past projects was important for inspiring others and encouraging impromptu brainstorming. In some cases, designers displayed an extensive history of their past projects through prototypes and sketches tacked to their cubicles, which provided a kind of advertisement of expertise, as well as catalogue of ideas for other designers.

These examples emphasize how important the use and the display of visual and physical models were to encouraging the design thinking practice of brainstorming, and hence the sharing of knowledge across employees. They also appeared to serve both instrumental and symbolic functions, as they indicated specific instrumental features of design (e.g. size, material, function) as well as signalled the importance of creative work (by having it prominently displayed).

Cubicle 'caves' promoted experimentation

A final insight from this case study is that some designers created privacy 'caves' by attaching cardboard to the tops and sides of their cubicles. These caves signalled to others to 'leave me alone' and supported private work. This use of private workspaces to enhance creativity contrasts with the other uses of physical environment described, which focus on encouraging collaboration via open workspaces. Interestingly, however, privacy appeared important to experimentation by toy designers.

Similar to the research of Bernstein (2012) described earlier, the first author observed that toy designers who had created privacy 'caves' used them to work on 'unassigned' projects and to experiment with creative ideas in a low-risk way. For example, a designer named Frank told the first author about a new set of graphics he was working on that was based on his personal artwork that he created at home. In this case, Frank was talking to the first author in the hallway about his personal artwork and said:

> What I'm really excited about isn't any current project, but this new set of graphics based on my painting that I do in my free time. I work on it sometimes when I'm stuck on another project, or just want to take a break. I'll show you it in my cube, but you can't tell anyone about it.

Frank said that he could do such 'outside' work because people didn't bother him since he had created his 'cube cave'. He explained that he originally had covered the top of his cube to create a 'dark space' where he could work better with a backlit drawing board, but he found that it also gave him privacy to work on other projects that weren't strictly 'assigned'.

As shown by this example, the possibility to create more private cubicle 'caves' supported employees' use of the design thinking practice of experimentation. In this manner, these privacy caves served the instrumental function of keeping prying eyes out, while also symbolically communicating the importance of individual, creative work (i.e. because management allowed the caves to be built).

Case study 2: Product designers

This case study involved observations of three different product design teams working for global product design and innovation consulting company Continuum Innovation. At the time of the study, the Boston office (where the study was performed) was responsible for formulating guidelines for product design based on consumer analysis, for executing engineering and product design, and for brand-building and communication respectively.

The physical layout of the Boston office (approximately 3,000 sq. ft spread over two floors) was designed as a mix of (a) team project rooms specifically dedicated to individual projects where design teams would meet and work together, (b) an open-plan studio where designers and engineers sat and worked on their desks individually, (c) a model shop where ideas could be translated into functional and 'look and feel' prototypes, (d) a big communal kitchen where employees could have lunch and informal meetings or impromptu brainstorming sessions, (e) some meeting rooms to host meetings with clients, and (f) two libraries – one containing design and architecture books and magazines, and another containing prototypes and physical models from previous projects, as well as various materials such as samples of fabrics, wood, steel, etc.

Similar to the first case study in this chapter, observations provided insights on how certain elements of the Continuum physical environment were conducive to creativity through the promoted use of design thinking practices. In particular, we identified two ways in which the physical work environment led to these outcomes.

Dedicated project rooms encouraged focus on users' needs and brainstorming

An important characteristic of the Continuum studio was the presence of project rooms dedicated to ongoing projects. These rooms were not only used to host project-related meetings such as brainstorming sessions and design critiques, but also as an important repository of tangible evidence collected during the design research (e.g. pictures of people observed or interviewed and of their environments, pictures cut out of magazines and books, competitors' products available on the market, etc.) and of sketches, sticky notes and drawings created by designers – individually or collectively – during the life of the project. The availability of these 'war rooms', as they would call them, promoted three important design thinking practices: focus on users' needs, brainstorming, and co-creation.

As mentioned earlier in this chapter, the identification of users' needs is a crucial aspect of design thinking, and relies on practices such as ethnographic observations, in-depth contextual interviews, and the development of personas and their customer journeys. Designers usually conduct observations and interviews in users' environments (their homes, offices, hospitals, etc.), while they develop personas and their journeys once they are back in the studio. These outputs, together with the evidence collected during the design research, are displayed in the project room, and act as constant reminder of the 'people we are designing for', as designers explained. The three projects observed all had their own dedicated project room, which became small-scale reproduction of users' contexts (i.e. mobile phone stores, hospitals, new parents' houses). This proved very important to focus designers' ideas on issues pertaining to end-users. An excerpt from an ethnographic interview with a designer from Project Holidays clearly illustrates this point:

> In our project room we simulate the users' environment, so we work in our project room constantly channelling these people and surrounded by their artefacts, so for example for the Holidays project, we set up the room as if it was a telecommunication retail store. Because you need to be constantly reminded about the people you are designing for.

Interestingly, observations and interviews with team members also revealed that working in project rooms helped them bounce ideas off each other and combine them together (i.e. engage in impromptu brainstorming). Very often designers compared these rooms as a combination of 'their brains' or as the 'team brain', because the possibility to 'look at other people's thoughts and ideas' allowed designers to more easily and quickly see links and commonalities across ideas. George, a designer from team Holidays, described to the second author the project room as a catalyser of the creative process:

> It's very hard to work at your desk by yourself, because it's like designing in a vacuum. Project rooms are the anti-vacuum. It's a sharing of ideas. It's all these things we're talking about coming together to help you create something. And it's also communicating between the team members, because I could put something up in here that could totally change everybody's attitude towards something.

As an example of such brainstorming, the design of the patient chair developed by the Hospital team was the result of a combination of the best ideas of two young designers. A passage extracted from the field notes taken during a project Hospital 'design critique' illustrates this point:

> David starts explaining that he has developed some sketches based on his latest conversation with Mike about the thickness of the chair seat. In describing the details of the back of the chair, David points out the possibility to have a mechanism to tuck the sheet not in the back, but in the front of the chair, so that it can become an aesthetically appealing element of the chair itself. Observing the sketches, Mike says: 'I like this one . . . even though it does not yet look inviting and soft . . . I wonder what happens if you allow some

thickness at the edge?' He then turns to Geoff's sketches and says: 'I also like this pillow thing; it's very welcoming.' Then referring to David's sketches he adds: 'I like these.' Now, Geoff describes his sketches: 'I used different colours to create a volume inside another volume graphically, as if there was a blanket over the chair.'

Often the brainstorming taking place in the project rooms was supported by the presence of magazines, books and materials taken from the company's libraries. The availability of these artefacts in a project room represented a powerful way to spark the collective development of new ideas. For instance, during brainstorming meetings for a project called 'Holidays', the design team would leaf through design books and magazines as well as materials to seek for concrete examples that could spark their imagination on how to design the new 'Back to School' store windows for their client. One team member explained:

> The materials and the pictures from the magazines act as inspiration because they might drive you to think in a different way, like, 'what would happen if we, instead of, you know, print it on white paper, what would happen if we printed it on this new material?' or 'what would happen if we covered the walls of the store with some really new wallpaper or something?'

The role of the materials selected from the library was also emphasized by the members of the other teams. For example, a designer from team Car explained to the second author that being able to touch tangible samples of fabrics, wood, steel or whatever material available in the material library would lead to group experimentation, as these materials helped spark conversations and ideas about new and original uses of the materials themselves:

> We do use the material library usually in the very first part [of a project], when we try to come up with an idea, and sometimes the material itself will offer some different solutions. . .. The Car project is another big example where we had foams; we were exploring the foam, which is a new material, outside of where they typically are, just to get a sense for different densities, different material qualities, and that does spark new ways of thinking.

As a whole, the above examples suggest that the presence of dedicated project rooms supported the implementation of the design thinking practices of user-focus and brainstorming. Further, they appeared to do this through instrumental functions (e.g. providing a space in which to work, experiment and collaborate), symbolic functions (e.g. signalling the importance of collaboration, experimentation and user experience), and aesthetic functions (e.g. providing opportunities to touch and feel materials and experience what users might experience).

A model shop supported rapid prototyping and experimentation

A second insight from this case study is that the existence of a public model shop (a space with tools and materials where prototypes of product designs could be quickly built) represented an integral part of the creative process, as it was a place where ideas were translated into physical objects, as rough prototypes or more refined 'look and feel' models. This was very important to help designers test their ideas, as the Hospital project leader explained during an informal conversation in the Continuum kitchen:

> You know, the Monday calls and the other formal meetings are good for internal and external communication, whereas most of the creative process takes place here in the model shop, because this is where we can develop ideas, share them among each other, and test them out immediately.

For example, once the design of the patient chair had been defined and a prototype created, a few Hospital team meetings took place in the model shop, where team members and client representatives could sit in the chair prototype and provide further feedback on how to move forward. Thus, during a meeting with some engineers from the client's company, the team realized that the tilting mechanism of the chair needed to be able to accommodate the movements of extreme users, such as very heavy patients. Furthermore, one engineer thought that the back of the chair looked 'too masculine' and so not inviting, as required in the design brief. Mike, the project lead, quickly took some tape from the shelf of the model shop and redefined the contour of the back of the chair in real time.

Interestingly, the presence of a model shop also seemed crucial to overcoming bottlenecks during the process. During an informal conversation in the model shop, Ricky, the model shop manager, revealed to the second author how conversations between designers and model-makers as well as the availability of past products, materials and tools to quickly turn ideas into real things was crucial to overcome barriers or constraints:

> If during a project something that has been designed doesn't work or doesn't look the way they [the designers] thought, and that's where we also get involved. So, they'll be: 'Can you make this work?' And we'll be 'Ok! We have some ideas.' Because, you know, we are generally pretty crafty people that can build just about anything, so they have an idea about how things work or look, so we're good people to talk to about.

As the examples above show, the availability of a model shop, where designers could quickly turn their ideas into tangible models and prototypes, allowed designers to experiment and engage in rapid prototyping. Further, similar to the war rooms, the model shop appeared to do this through functions that were instrumental (providing tools and materials), symbolic (indicating the importance of trying out ideas), and aesthetic (e.g. allowing actual interaction with prototype designs).

Insights and directions for future research

Overall, the insights from extant research and our two, second-look case studies illustrate how workspace features may support the use of several design thinking practices, and, in turn, support organizational creativity. Interestingly, these insights indicate that most of the workspace features that support design thinking do so not only through instrumental functions (such as allowing designers to tinker with prototypes), but also through symbolic and aesthetic functions (such as signalling the importance of creative work or allowing sensorial experience with design prototypes). In this way, these insights suggest how extant organizational work on physical work environments might be integrated with research on design thinking to provide a more complete understanding of the role of workspace features in promoting creativity. We depict in Figure 2.1 the relationships between workspace features, workspace functions, and design thinking practices that enhance

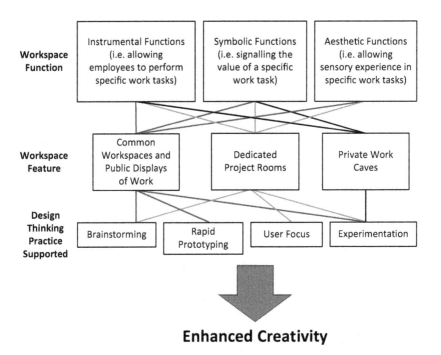

FIGURE 2.1 Relating workspace features, workspace functions and design thinking practices to creativity in organizations

creativity that were suggested by our extant review and case studies. We discuss these relationships in more detail below, and offer some directions for future research suggested by these insights.

Common workspaces and public displays of work support brainstorming and rapid prototyping via instrumental, symbolic, and aesthetic functions

Previous research in design thinking has emphasized that knowledge-sharing during unplanned face-to-face meetings between employees is important for enhancing creativity in organizations (Appel-Meulenbroek et al., 2017). Therefore, if creativity is a high priority, organizations should actively stimulate informal interactions between employees (Heerwagen et al., 2004). As Klijn and Tomic note, creativity appears to be boosted when the workplace 'is borderless, as this facilitates interactions and free chatting among team members' (2010: 335).

Our case studies confirm these notions and emphasize how the use of common spaces and the ability to publicly display prototypes and sketches leads to more spontaneous cross-functional interactions, and hence to more unplanned collaborations and impromptu brainstorming among designers. Moreover, the evidence from our cases suggests that these common spaces may be deliberately placed in central corridors to maximize the chances that designers bump into each other, and thus stimulate knowledge-sharing behaviours. This insight is interesting because it suggests that organizations that wish to pursue creativity need to strategically and *instrumentally* design their workspaces to support collaboration and brainstorming that is critical to design thinking.

Some modern office designers are embracing this type of 'serendipitous communication model' (Peponis et al., 2007) and are creating workplaces for the specific purpose of stimulating these incidental chats, for example, coffee machines, hallways, drop-down seats, etc. Nevertheless, the relationships between casual interactions, and brainstorming and knowledge-sharing need to be empirically tested and studied further in order to better understand how workspaces can be designed and especially where they need to be placed inside a building to stimulate these specific behaviours.

In addition to open spaces, evidence from our case studies suggests that the availability of instrumental tools for tinkering, or even entire model shops, may support the practice of rapid prototyping. Rapid prototyping is a crucial design thinking practice (Brown, 2008; Carlgren et al., 2014) that lets designers test ideas quickly without a huge investment. In turn, these prototypes encourage collaboration by making emerging ideas concrete. Research on how designers work (i.e. Sutton & Hargadon, 1996; Stigliani & Ravasi, 2012) has amply illustrated how this practice is deeply embedded in design teams' behaviour. Moreover, some anecdotal evidence has emerged about the use of rapid prototyping practices in other organizational contexts. For instance, Vetterli et al. (2016) studied the implementation of design thinking at Deutsch Bank, and found that even in non-design contexts, prototypes can be used to spark brainstorming with stakeholders.

In addition to the instrumental functions of common spaces and public displays of prototypes, our case studies suggest that these dimensions of the physical environment served important symbolic and aesthetic functions that also supported the design thinking practices of brainstorming and rapid prototyping. For instance, the visibility and prominence of open workspaces and publicly displayed prototypes signalled, symbolically, that collaborative work and the particular skills of designers were valued in the organizations in which they worked (Elsbach & Flynn, 2013). If these common workspaces had been hidden or the display of past prototypes and sketches discouraged, the opposite signals would have been sent. In addition, the availability of tools and spare parts for tinkering served aesthetic functions of allowing designers to see, feel, and experience designs rather than merely perceiving them in the abstract.

In support of the importance of physical environments in supporting creativity through design thinking, a rising number of organizations have created their own innovation labs, purposefully built and dedicated to enhance and support the creative processes of design thinking (Carstensen & Bason, 2012). These facilities are flexible common spaces where people can work collectively, build and experiment with ideas – thanks to the availability of various tools and materials – or just relax and play. Although this is consistent with previous research on creativity that has linked positive affect with cognitive variation, which then stimulates creativity (Isen et al., 1985; Amabile et al., 2005), empirical research providing evidence of whether and to what extent these spaces effectively support the use of design thinking tools via instrumental, symbolic, and aesthetic functions is scant. Future research studies, thus, need to close this gap.

Dedicated project rooms support user-centredness and brainstorming via instrumental, symbolic, and aesthetic functions

Case study 2 showed how important it is for designers to have dedicated project rooms in order to keep focus on the people they are designing for and to engage in brainstorming of new ideas – a critical dimension of design thinking. In particular, projects rooms help, in an instrumental way, to overcome deficiencies of short-term memory. To solve complex design problems, people need to track lots of moving parts (i.e. evidence from research, user journey, sketches, etc.). As humans, our short-term memory is limited, but our *spatial memory* (memory for physical arrangement and features) is stronger and longer term (Ang & Lee, 2008; Fisk & Sharp, 2003). Plastering a room with notes and other visual materials helps spatial memory, as it allows people to locate information more easily. This, in turn, extends human ability to remember things.

Furthermore, project rooms make it easier to manipulate physical ideas. Re-ordering a prioritized list of sticky notes or redrawing a diagram visually present in front of us is easier than making the same decisions verbally. This is very important for brainstorming, as ideas can be visually created, changed, tweaked and connected more easily (Stigliani & Ravasi, 2012). In so doing, project rooms also help teams work better together. The possibility to visually capture every decision and put it on the wall helps put everyone on the same page, where the project room is the page. The more visual information is put on the walls, the more shared understanding is built.

Dedicated project rooms also serve the instrumental function of helping designers to 'stay focused on their end-users' and 'in the right frame of mind'. This is due to the fact that compared with written text, visual artefacts displayed in a project room enable holistic processing of multiple cues, thus stimulating intuitive cognitive work. Intuition is a unique way of processing information that allows us to non-consciously recognize coherent patterns or other linkages among disparate stimuli (Bowers et al., 1990). Holistic associations, by which individuals (non-consciously) map stimuli onto complex cognitive structures, are therefore considered an essential component of intuition (i.e. Dane & Pratt, 2007). Dane and Pratt (2007) observe how intuitive thinking allows the rapid processing of a large number of cues without conscious effort. Further, it allows addressing unstructured problems, where well-accepted decision rules are absent, more effectively than rational, analytical processes. Intuition has also been linked to the concept of 'flow experience', described as an optimal state of intrinsic motivation where the person is fully immersed in what they are doing, implies 'focused attention' resulting in an increased cognitive performance or 'cognitive rush' (Csikszentmihalyi, 1996; Csikszentmihalyi & Robinson, 1990: 12).

In addition to these instrumental functions, dedicated project rooms have important symbolic functions and aesthetic functions. As noted earlier, the existence of these rooms signals the symbolic importance of the design function in general, and a specific design project in particular. Giving a separate room to a single design project makes salient the importance of that project to a broad audience, including those not familiar with the project. These rooms also provide opportunities to experience, in a sensorial manner, designs as they evolve. Such opportunities are important to supporting rapid prototyping as they allow for a more complete 'user' experience (Brown & Wyatt, 2010).

In support of these multiple functions of dedicated project rooms, more and more organizations, including traditionally non-creative organizations, such as management consulting giant McKinsey, have embraced the practice of dedicating project rooms for cross-functional teams to work. Each sub-group within the team gets its own wall, which functions as a working surface dedicated to customer journeys, technology, business operations, and planning. Each wall is covered with sticky notes capturing tasks, actions, people, and ideas, visible for all to see with the objective to support idea-sharing and faster decision-making (Kilian et al., 2015). Whether this practice is conducive to better innovative performance, though, still remains an empirical question that future studies need to test. In particular, it may be important to determine if and how such rooms support the specific practices of brainstorming and rapid prototyping, and how the physical characteristics of such rooms do this (e.g. through instrumental, symbolic, or aesthetic functions).

Private work 'caves' promote experimentation via instrumental and symbolic functions

The evidence from Case study 1 suggests that designers created private workspaces, which were not strictly 'allowed' by office policies, to allow them to experiment with innovative ideas that were also not strictly part of their work assignments. While the use of private workspaces might sound at odds with the previous discussion of common workspace as conducive to creative work, these findings do fit with recent research findings suggesting that privacy may be important to experimentation in contexts where it is not fully condoned by those in authority (Bernstein, 2012, 2014). Thus, in his study of factory workers in China, Bernstein (2012) found that privacy screens allowed workers to engage in these experiments without fear of being reprimanded for not sticking to assigned tasks and potentially wasting time on experimental solutions that would not work. In contrast, without the privacy screens, Bernstein (2012: 187–188) noted that:

> operators were hiding their most innovative techniques from management so as not to 'bear the cost of explaining better ways of doing things to others' or alternatively 'get in trouble' for doing things differently.

In this manner, the privacy caves created by designers served the instrumental function of hiding their experiments from the view of supervisors.

In addition to these instrumental functions, the presence of the caves also served an important symbolic function: tacitly condoning the activity of private experimentation. Although in design and creativity consulting firms like Continuum this element of the workspace was less salient – due, perhaps, to an organizational culture that highly valued experimentation and tolerated failure – the opportunity to work privately on ideas that are not part of one's formal work assignment may be highly important to creativity in many firms. Criscuolo et al. (2014) call this practice 'bootlegging' and show how engaging in these underground creative activities can improve employees' individual innovative performance. The tacit condoning of these private experiments, thus, provided an important symbolic signal that such experimentation was valued. What we do not know, however, is whether and to what extent private experimentation is ultimately beneficial for the team and the organizational innovative performance. Further, we don't understand how tacit understanding of the value of experimentation is related to specific supervisory behaviours (e.g. is it enough to merely allow private 'caves' to exist, or do supervisors also need to publicly commend the experiments that come out of them?).

Summary: linking workspace features, functions and design thinking

Overall, our exploration of workspace features and their influence on creative work suggests that extant organizational frameworks regarding the functions of physical work environments may be further leveraged by linking them to implementation of design thinking practices. In particular, as noted above, the workspace features that appear to support design thinking practices do so via more than instrumental means. Importantly, these workspace features also provide symbolic signals about the importance and value of creative work, and the tacit approval of unassigned experimentation. Further, in some cases these workspace features provide important aesthetic information to designers that improve their ability to develop prototypes. The role of physical workspace features in providing these symbolic and aesthetic functions is something that has not been discussed by researchers of design thinking, and thus, linking these insights about the functions of workspace features – that originate from organizational research – to the study of design thinking provides important opportunities for future research and for expanding frameworks of physical environments and creativity. We hope this discussion provides a starting point for this future research.

Note

1 All names are pseudonyms, and all projects are disguised from the actual projects being developed.

References

Amabile, T.M., Barsade, S.G., Mueller, J.S., & Staw, B.M. (2005). Affect and creativity at work. *Administrative Science Quarterly*, *50*(3), 367–403.
Amabile, T.M., & Conti, R. (1999). Changes in the work environment for creativity during downsizing. *Academy of Management Journal*, *42*(6), 630–640.
Amabile, T.M., Conti, R., Coon, H., Lazenby, J., & Herron, M. (1996). Assessing the work environment for creativity. *Academy of Management Journal*, *39*(5), 1154–1184.
Amabile, T.M., Hadley, C.N., & Kramer, S.J. (2002). Creativity under the gun. *Harvard Business Review*, *80*, 52–63.
Ang, S.Y., & Lee, K. (2008). Central executive involvement in children's spatial memory. *Memory*, *16*(8), 918–933.
Appel-Meulenbroek, R., de Vries, B., & Weggeman, M. (2017). Knowledge sharing behavior: The role of spatial design in buildings. *Environment and Behavior*, *49*(8), 874–903.
Bailey, S.G. (2012). Embedding service design: The long and the short of it. *ServDes. 2012 Conference Proceedings Co-Creating Services; The 3rd Service Design and Service Innovation Conference; 8–10 February; Espoo, Finland* (pp. 31–41). Linköping, Sweden: Linköping University Electronic Press.
Baumeister, R. (1998). The self. In D.T. Gilbert, S.T. Fiske, & G. Lindzey (eds.), *The Handbook of Social Psychology*, Volume 1 (pp. 680–740). Boston, MA: McGraw-Hill.
Becker, F. (2004). *Office at Work: Uncommon Workspace Strategies That Add Value and Improve Performance*. New York: JohnWiley.
Ben Mahmoud-Jouini, S., Midler, C., & Silberzahn, P. (2016). Contributions of design thinking to project management in an innovation context. *Project Management Journal*, *47*(1), 144–156.
Benyon, D., & Mival, O. (2015). Blended spaces for collaboration. *Computer Supported Cooperative Work (CSCW)*, *24*(2–3), 223–249.

Bernstein, E.S. (2012). The transparency paradox: A role for privacy in organizational learning and operational control. *Administrative Science Quarterly, 5*(2), 181–216.

Bernstein, E.S. (2017). Making transparency transparent: The evolution of observation in management theory. *Academy of Management Annals, 11*(1), 217–266.

Bjögvinsson, E., Ehn, P., & Hillgren, P.A. (2012). Design things and design thinking: Contemporary participatory design challenges. *Design Issues, 28*(3), 101–116.

Bowers, K.S., Regehr, G., Balthazard, C., & Parker, K. (1990). Intuition in the context of discovery. *Cognitive Psychology, 22*(1), 72–110.

Brown, T. (2008). Design thinking. *Harvard Business Review, 86*(1), 84–92.

Brown, T. (2009). *Change by Design: How Design Thinking Transforms Organizations and Inspires Innovation.* New York: Harper Collins.

Brown, T., & Wyatt, J. (2010). Design thinking for social innovation IDEO. *Development Outreach, 12*(1), 29–31.

Carlgren, L., Elmquist, M., & Rauth, I. (2014). Design thinking: Exploring values and effects from an innovation capability perspective. *Design Journal, 17*(3), 403–423.

Carstensen, H.V., & Bason, C. (2012). Powering collaborative policy innovation: Can innovation labs help? *Innovation Journal, 17*(1), 2.

Ceylan, C., Dul, J., & Aytac, S. (2008). Can the office environment stimulate a manager's creativity? *Human Factors and Ergonomics in Manufacturing and Service Industries, 18*(6), 589–602.

Criscuolo, P., Salter, A., & Ter Wal, A.L. (2014). Going underground: Bootlegging and individual innovative performance. *Organization Science, 25*(5), 1287–1305.

Csikszentmihalyi, M. (1996). *Flow and the Psychology of Discovery and Invention.* New York: Harper Collins.

Csikszentmihalyi, M., & Robinson, R.E. (1990). *The Art of Seeing: An Interpretation of the Aesthetic Encounter.* Los Angeles, CA: Getty Publications.

Dane, E., & Pratt, M.G. (2007). Exploring intuition and its role in managerial decision making. *Academy of Management Review, 32*(1), 33–54.

Davenport, T. (2005). *Thinking for a Living: How to Get Better Performances and Results from Knowledge Workers.* Boston, MA: Harvard Business School Press.

Dul, J., & Ceylan, C. (2011). Work environments for employee creativity. *Ergonomics, 54*(1), 12–20.

Dul, J., Ceylan, C., & Jaspers, F. (2011). Knowledge workers' creativity and the role of the physical work environment. *Human Resource Management, 50*(6), 715–734.

Dul, J., & Ceylan, C. (2014). The impact of a creativity-supporting work environment on a firm's product innovation performance. *Journal of Product Innovation Management, 31*(6), 1254–1267.

Elsbach, K.D. (2004). Interpreting workplace identities: The role of office décor. *Journal of Organizational Behavior, 25*(1), 99–128.

Elsbach, K.D., & Flynn, F.J. (2013). Creative collaboration and the self-concept: A study of toy designers. *Journal of Management Studies, 50*(4), 515–544.

Elsbach, K.D., & Hargadon, A.B. (2006). Enhancing creativity through 'mindless' work: A framework of workday design. *Organization Science, 17*(4), 470–483.

Elsbach, K.D., & Pratt, M.G. (2007). 4 the physical environment in organizations. *Academy of Management Annals, 1*(1), 181–224.

Elsbach, K.D., & Stigliani, I. (2018). Design thinking and organizational culture: A review and framework for future research. *Journal of Management, 44*(6), 2274–2306.

Fisk, J.E., & Sharp, C.A. (2003). The role of the executive system in visuo-spatial memory functioning. *Brain and Cognition, 52*(3), 364–381.

Gifford, R. (2014). Environmental psychology matters. *Annual Review of Psychology, 65.*

Gruber, M., De Leon, N., George, G., & Thompson, P. (2015). Managing by design. *Academy of Management Journal, 58*(1), 1–7.

Haner, U.E. (2005). Spaces for creativity and innovation in two established organizations. *Creativity and Innovation Management, 14*(3), 288–298.

Hartig, T., Mang, M., & Evans, G.W. (1991). Restorative effects of natural environment experiences. *Environment and Behavior, 23*(1), 3–26.

Hartig, T., Evans, G.W., Jamner, L.D., Davis, D.S., & Gärling, T. (2003). Tracking restoration in natural and urban field settings. *Journal of Environmental Psychology, 23*(2), 109–123.

Heerwagen, J.H., Kampschroer, K., Powell, K.M., & Loftness, V. (2004). Collaborative knowledge work environments. *Building Research and Information, 32*(6), 510–528.

Hoff, E.V., & Öberg, N.K. (2015). The role of the physical work environment for creative employees: A case study of digital artists. *International Journal of Human Resource Management, 26*(14), 1889–1906.

Hua, Y., Loftness, V., Kraut, R., & Powell, K.M. (2010). Workplace collaborative space layout typology and occupant perception of collaboration environment. *Environment and Planning B: Planning and Design, 37*(3), 429–448.

Isen, A.M., Johnson, M.M., Mertz, E., & Robinson, G.F. (1985). The influence of positive affect on the unusualness of word associations. *Journal of Personality and Social Psychology, 48*(6), 1413.

Johansson-Sköldberg, U., Woodilla, J., & Çetinkaya, M. (2013). Design thinking: Past, present and possible futures. *Creativity and Innovation Management, 22*(2), 121–146.

Kabo, F., Hwang, Y., Levenstein, M., & Owen-Smith, J. (2015). Shared paths to the lab: A sociospatial network analysis of collaboration. *Environment and Behavior, 47*(1), 57–84.

Kaplan, S. (1995). The restorative benefits of nature: Toward an integrative framework. *Journal of Environmental Psychology, 15*(3), 169–182.

Kilian, J., Sarrazin, H., & Yeon, H. (2015). Building a design-driven culture. London: McKinsey Digital.

Klijn, M., & Tomic, W. (2010). A review of creativity within organizations from a psychological perspective. *Journal of Management Development, 29*(4), 322–343.

Kramer, R.M. (2016). Worth a second look? Exploring the power of post-mortems on postmortems. In K.D. Elsbach & R.M. Kramer (eds.), *Handbook of Qualitative Organizational Research: Innovative Pathways and Methods* (pp. 411–420). New York: Routledge.

Kristensen, T. (2004). The physical context of creativity. *Creativity and Innovation Management, 13*(2), 89–96.

Liedtka, J., & Ogilvie, T. (2011). *Designing for Growth: A Design Thinking Tool Kit for Managers.* New York: Columbia Business School Publishing.

Liedtka, J., Rosen, R., & Wiltbank, R. (2009). *The Catalyst: How You Can Become an Extraordinary Growth Leader.* New York: Crown Business.

Lymeus, F., Lundgren, T., & Hartig, T. (2017). Attentional effort of beginning mindfulness training is offset with practice directed toward images of natural scenery. *Environment and Behavior, 49*(5), 536–559.

Magadley, W., & Birdi, K. (2009). Innovation labs: An examination into the use of physical spaces to enhance organizational creativity. *Creativity and Innovation Management, 18*(4), 315–325.

McCoy, J.M., & Evans, G.W. (2002). The potential role of the physical environment in fostering creativity. *Creativity Research Journal, 14*(3–4), 409–426.

Moultrie, J., Nilsson, M., Dissel, M., Haner, U.E., Janssen, S., & Van der Lugt, R. (2007). Innovation spaces: Towards a framework for understanding the role of the physical environment in innovation. *Creativity and Innovation Management, 16*(1), 53–65.

Mutanen, U.M. (2008). Developing organisational design capability in a Finland-based engineering corporation: The case of Metso. *Design Studies, 29*(5), 500–520.

Oksanen, K., & Ståhle, P. (2013). Physical environment as a source for innovation: Investigating the attributes of innovative space. *Journal of Knowledge Management, 17*(6), 815–827.

Peponis, J., Bafna, S., Bajaj, R., Bromberg, J., Congdon, C., Rashid, M., Warmels, S., Zhang, Y., & Zimring, C. (2007). Designing space to support knowledge work. *Environment and Behavior, 39*(6), 815–840.

Rafaeli, A., & Vilnai-Yavetz, I. (2004). Emotion as a connection of physical artifacts and organizations. *Organization Science, 15*(6), 671–686.

Rauth, I., Carlgren, L., & Elmquist, M. (2014). Making it happen: Legitimizing design thinking in large organizations. *Design Management Journal, 9*(1), 47–60.

Scheiberg, S.L. (1990). Emotions on display. *American Behavioral Scientist, 33*(2), 330–338.

Seidel, V.P., & Fixson, S.K. (2013). Adopting design thinking in novice multidisciplinary teams: The application and limits of design methods and reflexive practices. *Journal of Product Innovation Management, 30*(S1), 19–33.

Serrat, O. (2017). Harnessing creativity and innovation in the workplace. In *Knowledge Solutions* (pp. 903–910). Singapore: Springer Singapore.

Stigliani, I., & Ravasi, D. (2012). Organizing thoughts and connecting brains: Material practices and the transition from individual to group-level prospective sensemaking. *Academy of Management Journal, 55*(5), 1232–1259.

Stokols, D., Clitheroe, C., & Zmuidzinas, M. (2002). Qualities of work environments that promote perceived support for creativity. *Creativity Research Journal, 14*(2), 137–147.

Stone, N.J. (2003). Environmental view and color for a simulated telemarketing task. *Journal of Environmental Psychology, 23*, 63–78.

Sundstrom, E., & Sundstrom, M.G. (1986). *Workplaces: The Psychology of the Physical Environment in Offices and Factories.* Cambridge: Cambridge University Press Archive.

Sutton, R.I., & Hargadon, A. (1996). Brainstorming groups in context: Effectiveness in a product design firm. *Administrative Science Quarterly*, 685–718.

Sutton, R.I., & Hoyt, D. (2016). Better service, faster: A design thinking case study. *Harvard Business Review, 94*, 2–6.

Terrey, N. (2009). Distributed design management in a large public-sector organization: Methods, routines, and processes. *Design Management Journal, 4*(1), 48–60.

Vetterli, C., Uebernickel, F., Brenner, W., Petrie, C., & Stermann, D. (2016). How Deutsche Bank's IT division used design thinking to achieve customer proximity. *MIS Quarterly Executive, 15*(1), 37–53.

Vilnai-Yavetz, I., Rafaeli, A., & Yaacov, C.S. (2005). Instrumentality, aesthetics, and symbolism of office design. *Environment and Behavior, 37*(4), 533–551.

Vithayathawornwong, S., Danko, S., & Tolbert, P. (2003). The role of the physical environment in supporting organizational creativity. *Journal of Interior Design, 29*(1–2), 1–16.

Vogel, C.M. (2009). Notes on the evolution of design thinking: A work in progress. *Design Management Review, 20*(2), 16–27.

Wells, M.M. (2000). Office clutter or meaningful personal displays: The role of office personalization in employee and organizational well-being. *Journal of Environmental Psychology, 20*(3), 239–255.

Yoo, Y., & Kim, K. (2015). How Samsung became a design powerhouse. *Harvard Business Review, 93*(9), 73–78.

3

HOLISTIC OFFICE DESIGN

From an organizational and management perspective

Christina Bodin Danielsson

Introduction

This chapter investigates the subject of office design's impact on the welfare of organizations and their employees from an organizational and management perspective. In doing so, it reviews the subject from a holistic approach, hereby meaning an approach that connects an organizational and management perspective on the subject with the perspectives of other disciplines that deal with the influence of the office environment on employees and organizations. In addition to the field of organizational behaviour, it includes perspectives from fields such as architecture, environmental psychology and occupational health. Along with this, a holistic approach means, from my point of view, an approach that investigates the environmental influence of the office on employees and organizations at various levels, i.e. individual, group, and organizational.

Because of the described holistic approach to the subject, the chapter introduces the reader to both different disciplines within an interdisciplinary research field, but also to factors of great variety important to organizational success and welfare, such as employee branding, leadership, social support, and workplace conflicts with an emphasis on empirical-based research. Since I, as the author, am a practising architect and researcher specializing in office design, the chapter also introduces the reader to some of my own research of relevance in the context.

In the chapter, the different issues reviewed in relation to the subject of office design's impact on the welfare of organizations and their members are highly interlinked with one another as a consequence of their nature and the approach applied in this review. As result of this, the same issue will sometimes appear in various sections of the text. The advantage of this structure is that it makes it very apparent how interlinked the influence of various factors are to one another and that together dictate office design's impact on the welfare of individuals and organizations. However, by showing the interlinked connection between the factors in the structure of the text, the risk increases of difficulties to follow the movements between different sections and themes in the chapter. Despite this, there are, in my opinion, more advantages than disadvantages of such an interlinked structure to the subject in the text, as this makes clear the interdisciplinary nature of office design's impact on the welfare of organizations and their members.

The chapter is structured into six sections that describe different aspects of office design's impact on the welfare and success of organizations and their members. All but two sections include a subsection that describes specific design features in the office design linked to the subject of the section. The first section is a brief introduction to the office's environmental impact on employees and organizations. The following section, 'Office design from an organizational and management perspective', describes how office architecture relates to the concepts of power, status and hierarchy. The section also introduces the reader to the two most well-established models used to analyse the office environment from a management perspective, which many latter models in this field are based on. Finally, this section finishes by describing office design as a strategic management tool based on the knowledge of the two previous sections.

The next section, 'Office design in relation to interpersonal relationships', describes how office architecture relates to interaction and collaboration. A subsection describes architectural features linked to collaboration and teamwork in the office. 'Office design in relation to creativity, innovation and performance' describes how organizational success today not only includes traditional parameters such as efficiency and performance, but also creativity and innovation – clearly reflected in the view on office design today. This section includes a longer subsection on architectural features in office design that relate to these issues at an individual and group level.

'Office design in relation to job satisfaction and the psychosocial work environment' focuses on office design's relation to employees' job satisfaction and to psychosocial factors important to job satisfaction. A subsection looks at the features of office design that relate to job satisfaction and to the psychosocial work environment.

The final section, 'Components of a holistic office design from an organization and management perspective', is a discussion and conclusion of the chapter as a whole, taking a holistic approach to the content of the chapter.

Environmental influences of office design

The office environment's influence operates by various factors, where the most dominant is the office layout determined by choice of office type and design of plan layout. The choice of office type stands between the different office types defined in contemporary office design, for example between cell offices (individual office rooms) or traditional open-plan offices. (For detailed discussion of defined office types, see e.g. research by Bodin Danielsson et al., 2015, and Bodin

Danielsson, 2008). The design of plan layout deals with the arrangements and sizes of rooms in the office, for example placements of cell offices and workspaces with open-plan layout, etc. The design of the plan layout also deals with connections between spaces, which includes placement and size of openings between different spaces as well as placement and size of windows, etc. The office layout, by its combination of office type and plan layout, holds a central position for the office impact on employees and organizations for several reasons. First, it influences equality, openness and collectivity in an organization's culture (Kallio, Kallio, & Blomberg, 2015). Second, it sets the framework for the environmental condition, for example ability for privacy, and the influence of environmental factors such as lighting and noise on office occupants (e.g. Heerwagen, 1990; Jahncke & Halin, 2012; Kupritz, 1998). Also the architectural design and architectural elements used have been found to exert environmental influence on office employees' work attitudes and behaviours (Bodin Danielsson, 2015; Danielsson, 2005). This environmental influence can either be a stimulus, i.e. generate positive influences, or a stressor, with negative consequences at both individual and organizational levels. The latter include psychological and behavioural reactions, such as difficulty to focus and confusion, but also withdrawal or aggressiveness and hostility, feelings of indifference and fatigue (e.g. Cohen, Evans, Stokols, & Krantz, 1991; Sauter & Murphy, 1995). Additionally, there is a symbolic dimension to the environmental influence of office environment related to status and hierarchy, with implications for previous aspects as well as others, for example employee branding. Hence, the office environment's influence on organizations and their employees extends over a large area, expressed in various ways in workplaces. This chapter gives only a brief overview of this.

Office design from an organizational and management perspective

Architecture holds strong symbolic value because of its association with power, status, and hierarchy. It has been used religiously and politically through history as a method to signal this. We see this use of architecture as a 'leadership and management tool' in religious buildings, such as pyramids, temples, and cathedrals, as well as in buildings of authority/power, such as castles and fortresses, but also in courthouses and town halls.

Power, status, and hierarchy

In organizational theory, space is analysed in relation to culture, power, and politics in general, and in an office context even more so. Schein (2010) classified the physical environment as a cultural artefact, sending messages by the space in which people work. This approach is taken a step further by Pfeffer (1981), who relates space to power and politics within organizations, claiming people who strive for power and status in organizations modify the impact of cultural artefacts such as language and ceremonials. Position within space often conveys status (Homans, 1992), even when placed in an organizational framework, since the hierarchical dimension is always present – either consciously or unconsciously. Hence, the change of office environment can send various messages – a symbol that concretely represents abstract values (Trice & Beyer, 1993). Thus, the change from cell office, i.e. an individual room, to an open-plan office where colleagues share workspaces may in an organizational context signal a change in cultural norms or in status (for more on defined office type in contemporary office design, see e.g. Bodin Danielsson, 2008; Bodin Danielsson et al., 2015). The game of status can lead to odd and irrational behaviour, as exemplified by a study of dysfunctional project work between two departments at a university (Barclay & York, 2001).

Because of lack of common, neutral space in the building, project space was allocated in one of the departments to which it belonged. This resulted in tension between project members, and not much got done as the energy was focused on organizational games between the departments instead of on the project.

Models to analyse office design in an organizational context

There is a lack of empirical-based research on architecture's influence in an organizational context despite its recognized association with power, status, and hierarchy (e.g. Ashkanasy, Ayoko, & Jehn, 2014; Pratt & Rafaeli, 2001; Vilnai-Yavetz, Rafaeli, & Schneider Yaacov, 2005). Most studies in this area are theoretical and often focus on models of how to analyse and understand architecture from a management and corporate perspective. This may be due to the sensitive and abstract nature of the subject, as well as the empirical difficulty in assessing experiences of this among office employees.

An early model was developed by Steele (1973) to analyse the office environment from a management perspective based on six identified main functions: (1) shelter and security, (2) social contact, (3) symbolic identification, (4) task instrumentality, (5) pleasure, and (6) growth. Another well-established model was developed by Davis (1984), in which the office environment's influence on employees and organizations is instead analysed based on three elements: (1) physical structure, (2) physical stimuli, and (3) symbolic artefact, chosen because of their likely pervasive effect on managerial behaviour, in his opinion. The physical structure (1) includes the architectural design of the office and physical placement of furniture within this. While the physical stimuli (2) includes aspects of the physical setting that intrude on managers' and employees' awareness and behaviour. The final element, the symbolic artefact (3), individually and collectively guides the interpretation of the social setting at the office, thus is of special interest from a branding perspective. This includes, for example, the architectural design of the office determined by material, colour, type, and style of furniture and choice of artefacts such as artwork, photographs, etc. Symbolic artefacts, whether we are aware of it or not, communicate information about the organization and its members with multiple interpretations, resulting in intended and unintended consequences. According to

Davis (1984), symbolic artefacts convey four main types of messages about a workplace: (a) professional image cues, (b) status cues, (c) task effectiveness cues, and (d) aesthetic cues. Typical status cues through architecture are: accessibility, size of workspace, furniture design, and location in building (Sundstrom, 1986).

Office design as a strategic management tool

With the emergence of the 'new economy', i.e. the transition from a manufacturing economy to a service-based economy during the so-called dot-com era in the late 1990s, a conscious and outspoken use of office design as a strategic tool was introduced (e.g. Van Meel & Vos, 2001). The most well-known example of this approach is perhaps Google's. It uses office design as an important part of the corporate branding of the company, linked to recruitment, innovation, competitiveness, leadership, etc. (e.g. Bodin Danielsson, Wulff, & Westerlund, 2013). Branding by office design can thus include both external branding, i.e. towards the market, clients, and competitors, and employee branding, i.e. internal branding towards employees as a means to increase job satisfaction, commitment, innovation, etc. However, successful corporate branding, where office design today is often a central component, is difficult. It requires organization-wide support, which involves the whole organization from top to bottom and across functional units in realizing the corporate brand, according to Hatch and Schultz (2003). In their view, the brand is, along with the audience, formed by the interplay between strategic vision, organizational culture, and the corporate images held by stakeholders (e.g. users, clients, and competitors). It must be 'real', i.e. part of the DNA of the organization and not something developed by external PR strategists. Fundamental to this approach to office design is the belief that it influences attitudes and behaviour of organizational members. The fact is, however, that today, more than 30 years after Davis (1984) presented his hypothesis that the office environment affects the behaviour and attitudes of organizational members, there is a lack of empirical research that backs up the hypothesis. Instead, most of the research in this area is theoretical (e.g.Vilnai-Yavetz et al., 2005).

Despite a lack of empirical research regarding office design's impact from a branding perspective, some exists. For example, one recent study on architecture's influence on employees' attitudes in relation to work in various office types found this to influence both their perception of the workplace and the organization as a whole (Bodin Danielsson, 2015). This study found that mainly the aesthetic dimension of the office architecture and not the functional had a positive influence on this. Results also showed that employees working in offices with shared workspaces and facilities had a greater focus on the aesthetics of the office than those in individual or smaller shared offices. They also had more focus on the social dimension of the office architecture than those working in individual or smaller shared offices, who had their focus on the individual workspace. In the article it is hypothesized to be a consequence of what in sociology is called social responsiveness (Asplund, 1988), which means it is a natural reaction for humans to be social when the physical environment enables this. This theory may also explain why research has found that offices with open-plan layout can enhance the social climate of the workplace (Hedge, 1982) and why physical proximity between colleagues in the office is positive for friendship and interaction between colleagues (Conrath, 1973). Another study on the office architecture's importance from a branding and experience perspective investigated employees' office experiences and what role different components of the architecture play for positive versus negative experiences (Danielsson, 2005). Employees' positive experiences were to a greater extent found to depend on the architectural quality of the office than on its size or category of office type. Although this indicates that the architectural design is of greater importance from an employee branding perspective, it does not automatically mean the other two dimensions are irrelevant. In fact, office type per se appears to play a significant role for office employees' environmental satisfaction and this differs significantly between employees in different office types (Bodin Danielsson & Bodin, 2009). The study found that cell-office employees reported significantly higher environmental satisfaction than others did – especially in terms of noise and privacy issues and workspace design. Only satisfaction with office design's support for interaction in the workplace was significantly less in cell offices than in other office types.

Together, the two studies described here indicate, in line with Davis's theory (1984), that office architecture can play the 'role of a value carrier' for the psychosocial work environment and organizational culture. Although the architecture played the role of an invisible background in employees' daily work activities and as such was taken for granted and not much thought of, results indicated that the office architecture influenced employees' feelings and attitudes towards the workplace and organization. Those with positive experiences of the office's architecture were more positive towards their workplaces, but also more positive towards management and the organization as a whole. An additional important finding of these studies was the dominant role of aesthetics for employees' experiences of work. It indicates that aesthetics in the office environment is not unnecessary, nor a luxury, since it influences office employees' whole workplace experience and is thereby important for an organizational perspective.

There is an association between office design and organizational culture – either the organization recognizes this or not. This is something that is further emphasized in an organizational change process. A failure in this can sometimes be traced back to a lack of consideration of the physical environment for the change process (Barclay & York, 2001). Support for this theory is found in a recent Dutch study that compares successful and non-successful office transitions from cell offices to activity-based flex offices in a large nationwide organization (Brunia, De Been, & Van der Voordt, 2016). This study found that the success of the transition depended on both the architectural design of the office and on managerial factors. Regarding architecture, the plan layout was central for employees' satisfaction with transition, because of its impact on key factors for this, such as level of openness and subdivision of space, number and diversity, but also accessibility of work environments for different work activities. Furthermore, employees' satisfaction correlated positively with access to workspaces that consisted of enclosed rooms, enabling regulation of distraction and privacy when needed. While instead satisfaction with office transition correlated negatively with large open workspaces with low ability for seclusion or privacy in the new office. The researchers' conclusion was that architectural features central for a successful office transition were features that influence both communication and concentration opportunity in the office (Brunia et al., 2016). Managerial factors important for employees' satisfaction with their new flex offices related to the implementation process of this, where management's commitment and ways of communication were central, but also if and how employees could influence the implementation process.

Office design in relation to interpersonal relationships and group behaviour

From an organizational perspective, group behaviour is of specific interest, as an organization consists of groups of individuals, thus its performance not only depends on employees' individual performance, but also on how they collaborate and perform together. Many of the most impressive and innovative solutions for many decades have also been the product of teamwork (Mesmer-Magnus et al., 2017). We find examples of this in businesses such as software and game development, as well as the movie industry with companies like Pixar Animation Studios, etc. (Catmull, 2008). Individuals relate and operate in relation to each other in a context set and regulated by the organization, where the physical environment is one of the parameters often used for this purpose. The reason for this is that the physical environment influences different aspects important to the welfare and success of organizations that involves interpersonal relations and group behaviour.

Interaction and collaboration

These two outcomes of interpersonal relationships and group behaviours have become increasingly important to organizations since diversity of information, experience, and values today are key factors to organizational success (Jackson, 1992).

In the knowledge-based society of today, work has become increasingly complex, resulting in one of its major characteristics being the high degree of multidisciplinary collaboration (Davenport, 1998). Thus the dependency on teams to collaborate effectively is why collective information processing is more critical to organizational success (Hinsz, Tindale, & Vollrath, 1997). Building collaborative organizations is today both a key factor for organizational success and for survival on the global, competitive market, almost independently of labour market sector or line of business (Beyerlein, Freedman, McGee, & Moran, 2003). Furthermore, patterns of interactions in an organizational context are not only important because much of the work today is collaborative, but also because they define the culture of the organization and/or its subgroups (Barclay & York, 2001).

Teamwork

In addition to being flatter and more decentralized, collaborative organizations are based on the group/team. In order to succeed, this basic building block for its structure depends on team diversity – diversity of information, experience, and values (Jackson, 1992). Software development companies are examples of organizations that rely on project teams, and, like all collaborative organizations, it is crucial to them be able to utilize the expertise and knowledge of participants without overwhelming individual members. For this to succeed, team cognition is a key factor to retrieve and access team members' knowledge, as this, per se, can explain significant differences between team performances (DeChurch & Mesmer-Magnus, 2010). It is defined as the emergent state that involves the distribution, organization, and representation of knowledge in a group and that enables collective action (Hollingshead & Brandon, 2003).

Architectural features of the office: collaboration and teamwork

Recognizing interaction and collaboration as well as teamwork as important to organizations today, the question is what influence the office design has for these outcomes.

The social dimension of architecture and space is well established in various studies – for example, that opportunities for interactions can be built into work environments (Haner, 2005, p. 293), in turn influencing the creativity and innovation at the workplace. We know that both the spatial layout and physical distances in the office influence co-workers' interaction (Conrath, 1973; Estabrook & Sommer, 1972; Lang, Burnette, Moleski, & Vachon, 1974).

It has for example been found that the frequent daily interaction happens often not further than 18 metres (59 feet) from the office employee's workstation (Sailer & Penn, 2009). This could explain why physical proximity between employees correlates with friendship (Szilagyi & Holland, 1980), and hereby support in social networks decreases with distances (Mok & Wellman, 2007). Additionally, proximity to co-workers in many cases fosters collaboration at the workplace (e.g. Allen, 1997; Becker & Sims, 2001; Hua, Loftness, Heerwagen, & Powell, 2011). However, proximity to co-workers is not all positive, as the sense of having co-workers too close can be detrimental for collaboration (Hua et al., 2011). Hence, simple openness, i.e. a vast open floor plan with high visibility, is not automatically a support for collaboration. The explanation for this is probably partly because proximity relates to spatial density, which in turn is associated with the sense of crowding, which is an environmental stressor. Crowding may cause physiological arousal (Aiello, Epstein, & Karlin, 1975; Evans, 1979), whose stress symptoms are both behavioural (e.g. reduced ability to be social and creative, increased intention of job turnover) and physiological (e.g. high blood pressure) (Oldham, 1988). Besides described dimensions, crowding can also be a result of more social stimulation and interaction, but also more interference with activities than desired (Stokols, 1972).

Research tells us that distances and openness in the workspace have positive influences for collaboration and teamwork, but also that proximity can, if the office is not carefully designed, be negative. Architectural design features supportive for collaboration are, for example, easy access to shared spaces such as meeting rooms and kitchen/coffee area and high percentage of spaces for shared service and amenities in the office (Hua et al., 2011). From a teamwork perspective, other architectural features are also supportive such as ability to easily exhibit and post work-related artefacts in the workspace (Bodin Danielsson, 2013). These facilitate the sharing of thoughts and ideas between team members, thus are often used in offices for architects and designers that work in project teams (Stigliani & Ravasi, 2012). The lean office design concept that intends to enhance efficiency and improvements of the work process builds on this idea of visualization and sharing of ideas, but also on good overview of the work process (Bodin Danielsson, 2013).

Office design in relation to creativity, innovation and performance

Organizational success is today more than ever related to outcomes such as employees' capacity for creativity and innovation, although traditional outcomes such as efficiency and performance are still important. The role office design has for these outcomes is debated. Some researchers claim that the work environment, where the physical dimension is important, is the dominant factor for corporate creativity (Robinson & Stern, 1997, p. 39). While others are more sceptical, such as Csikszentmihalyi, an authority on creativity, who has doubts that it can scientifically be proved that pleasant environments enhance creativity (Csikszentmihalyi, 1996, p. 135). Office design's impact on efficiency and performance is less controversial. This debate concerns instead mainly how to accurately assess performance and efficiency of knowledge work. Nevertheless, our scientific knowledge about the influence of office design in this field is sparse because of the lack of empirical research. Despite this, I attempt in the latter part of this section to present some empirical research on the subject.

Efficiency and performance

For organizations, there is always a focus on efficiency and performance. Today we see, however, a shift in their focus with regard to this, with more emphasis on team processes, which is also apparent with regard to office design. This shifted focus is a result of 'innovative' business teamwork being proved to be more efficient than solo work, dispersed in individual rooms (Becker, Sims, & Schoss, 2003). Despite this shift in focus, the individual performance is always of interest, as reflected in the office research, for example in studies on noise disturbance influence on creativity and performance in writing (e.g. Keus van de Poll & Sörqvist, 2016).

Creativity and innovation

These two outcomes occupy many organizations today. Traditionally the focus has been on individuals' creativity, but we see now also a shift towards creative processes of teamwork because of several factors. This includes an exponential growth of knowledge and specialization in recent decades, which poses great challenges on the individual's learning capacity and ability to be creative (see review in Haner, 2005). Because of the increased focus on innovation and creativity, the interest for innovative workplaces has also grown. Cornell University, for example, has a research programme called the International Workplace Studies Program (IWSP) that focuses on innovative workplace strategies. However, most of this research is theoretical, concerned with developing models of how to study the work environment and creativity relationship (e.g. Amabile, Conti, Coon, Lazenby, & Herron, 1996; Dul & Ceylan, 2010).

Architectural features of the office: creativity, innovation and performance

The most dominant architectural feature of the office, the office layout – determined by plan layout and choice of office type (e.g. cell office, traditional plan offices, etc.) combined – influences employees' performance and behaviour in the office (e.g. Haynes, 2008b; Lee, 2010). In addition to office layout, other architectural features of the office influence employees' creativity and innovation, as well as efficiency and performance. Before describing these influences of office design, it should be noted that the influence of office design on creativity and innovation is complex. This is partly because activities during creative and innovative processes can be convergent or divergent in nature and can be individual or team efforts (Haner, 2005).

Proximity

Proximity and distances relate directly to the office layout. From efficiency and performance perspectives, these two design factors are important to teamwork since proximity facilitates communication between team members, but also planning and coordination. For scientific and technological organizations, which rely heavily on creativity and innovation, proximity between team members and shared workspace is especially central (e.g. Allen, 1977; Becker et al., 2003; Teasley, Covi, Krishnan, & Olsson, 2000). The number of colleagues with which a project member consults contributes to best performance, which is maintained with high levels of communication between colleagues outside their organization (Allen, Tushman, & Lee, 1979). This distance is crucial; the same study found that face-to-face interactions between team members may decline greatly after 30 metres (98.5 feet) and, despite strong organizational connections, frequent interactions may already decline at 50 metres (164 feet). Also, vertical distribution matters. One study found, for example, that if co-workers are distributed on different floor plans, the communication between them may reduce by 50% (Estabrook & Sommer, 1972). Consequently, scientists on the same floor plan collaborate more often than those on different floors or in other buildings (Becker et al., 2003).

Windows and lighting

Office layout and the placement of windows controls both the amount and quality of daylight. Together with artificial lighting, these sources of light are central for the work environment situation for several reasons. Light illuminates the space and hereby enables work assignments, orientation, and movement in space, but it also affects the architectural experience of the space (Veitch, Stokkermans, & Newsham, 2013). Additionally, light regulates human biology and physiology critical to performance (Aries, 2005). For example, it has been found that cognitive performance varies in accordance with circadian patterns (Blatter & Cajochen, 2007). Lighting induced positive affect on workplace satisfaction (Veitch, Charles, Farley, & Newsham, 2007), but also work engagement, which is why good lighting conditions have been suggested to be used to enhance goodwill and promote desirable work behaviours (Veitch et al., 2013). However, when discussing light we have to bear in mind that too much light is not good in the office context, and is not an unusual problem in modern office buildings with glass facades. It is important to limit the exposure when it causes glare and unpleasant solar heat gain to avoid discomfort and difficulty working on computer screens as well as problems with heating and cooling in the office (Veitch, 2005)

Noise

This is the major stressor in open-plan offices, and as such influences not only employees' satisfaction and annoyance, but also their performance (e.g. Brocolini, Parizet, & Chevret, 2016; Sundstrom, Town, Rice, Osborn, & Brill, 1994). Disturbance is highly determined by the architectural design of the office (Frontczak et al., 2012), with plan layout and choice of office type influencing both the exposure and spread of noise, i.e. co-workers' conversations and one-minute requests, sounds from telephones and office equipment (Ayr, Cirillo, Fato, & Martellotta, 2003; Roelofsen, 2002). Thus, more problems are reported in office types with open-plan layouts than in cell offices (e.g. Bodin Danielsson & Bodin, 2009). Additionally, the acoustic and visual privacy is affected by architectural elements and internal furniture arrangements, but also by choice of material and volume of space (Payne, 2013).

Noise disturbance has been found to have several negative effects at an individual level. This includes negative effects such as fatigue, but also decreased motivation (Jahncke & Halin, 2012) and work performance (Banbury & Berry, 2005). In the latter study by Banbury and Berry (2005), it was for example found that 99% of the participants reported impairment of their concentration due to office noise. That both lack of acoustic and visual privacy is problematic for the individual performance has been found. Lack of privacy in both regards has been found to lead to a decline in performance, especially for tasks such as word processing and numbers' calculation (see review in Al Horr et al., 2016, p. 9). The negative effect of low perceived acoustic and visual privacy on employees with highly complex tasks shows not only in their performance and satisfaction at an individual level, but it may have effects at a group level as it has been found to have negative effects on employees' attitudes and reactions to the workspace (Maher & von Hippel, 2005).

Architectural support of the work process

Regarding the impact of office design on work processes and performance, this influences the individual employee. However, this aspect of office design operates and shows at a group level. The office environment and the work process should match – meaning that the office layout, to improve productivity, must complement the work process of organization, for example by an office layout that facilitates the workflow (see reviews in Al Horr et al., 2016; Haynes, 2008). In fact, there is even an office design – lean office design – that is designed with this purpose only (Bodin Danielsson, 2013).

The office layout affects behaviour in the workplace in different ways. Thus, an office layout focused on the process of the organization can support this in various ways. At a group level, for example, by focusing on teamwork and interaction, visual contact and meetings between different groups and departments can be enabled. At an individual level, the balance between distraction and stimulation in the design of the plan layout is the focus, as this is crucial for the individual's productivity in terms of, for example, writing and calculating (e.g. Keus van de Poll & Sörqvist, 2016; Maher & von Hippel, 2005). This is important as distraction has the most negative impact on employees' perceived productivity, while at the same time in many cases interaction is the most positive (Haynes, 2008), and both are largely determined by the plan layout of the office. Work assignments and needs related to these vary depending on the job and occupational position; people also have different personalities and needs related to these. Nevertheless, research has found that in most cases, to work efficiently, office employees need an office that enables distraction-free work, but also informal interaction with colleagues (Heerwagen, Kampschroer, Powell, & Loftness, 2004). In line with this, a case study of two 'innovative' offices, designed to enhance creativity, found that spaces for communication and interaction, but also for privacy, are crucial (Haner, 2005).

Architectural elements and design features

There are some indications architectural design regarding aesthetics and colour schemes in indoor environments could affect performance and productivity

(Mahnke, 1996; Özturk, Yilmazer, & Ural, 2012). Foremost, physical features such as spatial diversity within the office have positive influences on this (Ehler et al., in Haner, 2005). This includes for example a division into different zones in terms of activities and needs related to these, for example a division into an action zone, an interaction zone and a retreat zone (see Bauer, Haner & Rieck, 2001, in Haner, 2005). Of interest here is that accessibility of a mixture of office types within the office appears to correlate with employees' rating of 'motivation', 'attractiveness of the work environment', 'wellbeing' and rating of 'office performance' (Ehler et al., in Haner, 2005). With regard to creativity, we know that a supportive social–organization work environment and positive mood motivate creative behaviour and facilitate the generation of more ideas (Amabile et al., 1996; Davis, 2009; Isen, Daubman, & Nowicki, 1987). It has been hypothesized that the physical environment can enhance creativity (Amabile et al., 1996, p. 249), and there have also been some attempts to identify design features that enhance this. In a study by Dul and Ceylan (2010), office employees were rated on elements in their social–organizational and physical work environment, and whether this correlated with employees' self-rated creative performance. They found that high rates of creative work environment correlated with high rates of creative performance.

Office design in relation to job satisfaction and the psychosocial work environment

Additional factors important to organizational success include employees' job satisfaction, highly related to motivation (Herzberg, Mausner, & Bloch Snyderman, 2003). The reason for the interest in job satisfaction is that organizational success goes beyond employee contributions to organizational effectiveness by immediate task performance (e.g. Weiss & Merlo, 2015). Job satisfaction is a contextual attitude with desirable responses at both individual and organizational level (Bradley, Petrescu, & Simmons, 2007). From an organizational perspective it is important because of its association with employees' organizational commitment, counterproductive work behaviour, intent to quit, and turnover (e.g. Brief & Weiss, 2002; Bruursema, Stacey, Kessler, & Spector, 2011; Carsten & Spector, 1987; George & Jones, 1996; Leiter & Maslach, 1988; Tett & Meyer, 1993). Additionally, job satisfaction is associated with ill-health, for example stress disorders, mental ill-health and job-related burnout (Lee & Ashforth, 1996; Maslach, 1982). All of the described outcomes associated to job satisfaction are problematic at an individual level, but also very costly at an organizational and societal level (Bäck, Andersson, & Hedin, 2015; European Commission, 2002). Furthermore, job satisfaction is associated positively with factors important to organizational success, such as organizational citizenship behaviour (OCB), i.e. when colleagues voluntarily help others on the job (Organ & Ryan, 1995), to group creativity (Valentine, Godkin, Fleischman, &

Kidwell, 2011), but also innovation and performance (Shipton, West, Parkes, Dawson, & Patterson, 2006).

Job satisfaction and psychosocial dimensions of work

Job satisfaction is linked with several psychosocial factors ranging from leadership, relationships with colleagues to job design and characteristics (Spector, 1997). The psychosocial work environment is central for employees' health and wellbeing (Karasek & Theorell, 1990; Robbins, Peterson, Tedrick, & Carpenter, 2003). Leadership per se is of specific interest to organizational success for several reasons. It has a direct impact on workplace performance (Rosete & Ciarrochi, 2005), on subordinates' job satisfaction and motivation (e.g. Locke & Henne, 1986; Lok & Crawford, 2004), but also on employees' health and wellbeing (Kivimäki et al., 2003; Nyberg, Westerlund, Magnusson Hanson, & Theorell, 2008).

Architectural features of the office: job satisfaction and psychosocial work environment

Although job satisfaction and different aspects of this is well researched, there is a lack of research about job satisfaction and other psychosocial factors in relation to office design. The sparse research in this field applies mainly two perspectives to the subject – one emphasizes the positive aspects of open, shared workspaces (Britner, 1992), and another, more critical perspective, sees negative consequences on employee health as well as behaviours (Fischer, 1997). One area – leadership and its impact on employees' attitudes and behaviour in relation to office design and the change of this – has, however, gained some attention (e.g. Lines, 2004; McElroy & Morrow, 2010). These studies tend to see office design as a strategic tool to implement change without organizational resistance. Yet another argument is that employee participation will lead to better decisions (Kim & Mauborgne, 1998), but it must then be done carefully and with respect (Vischer, 2005). One study found leadership, for example, to be important for the success of the implementation of the activity-based office type, the flex office, a somewhat extreme office type with flexible and non-personal work environment for employees (Brunia et al., 2016). In addition to leadership style and managers' attitudes to this special office type, the study also found that architectural design features played an important role in employee satisfaction with the shift to this office type, for example degree of openness in workspaces, access, and design of supportive back-up work environment. Nevertheless, the fact is that our knowledge is sparse about office design's impact on job satisfaction and the psychosocial environment – a consequence of lack of empirical research.

The area of office design's impact on employees' health and wellbeing is a special interest to me as both a practising architect and researcher. Hence, I have in various studies investigated what impact choice of office design has on job satisfaction and other psychosocial factors. My colleagues and I have found significant difference in job satisfaction between employees in various office types (Bodin Danielsson & Bodin, 2008). The best results were found in shared-room offices (two to three people per workspace) and the activity-based flex office (good access to supportive work environments and non-personal workstations), followed by the cell office (individual office room). For details on office type definitions, see, for example, the study by Bodin Danielsson et al. (2015) and Bodin Danielsson (2008).

In the study above on job satisfaction, my colleagues and I hypothesize that identified differences in job satisfaction may be due to the different architectural and functional features of the studied office types that support different factors important to job satisfaction (Bodin Danielsson & Bodin, 2008). For example, in shared-room offices, employees reported high on cooperation, which could be a result of the small group (two to three people) sharing a workspace possibly fostering strong group identity and cohesion (Svedberg, 1992). The higher satisfaction with realistic goals at work in the flex office may be a result of flex office employees reporting well on the item goals at work, but on the other hand may be a result of independent work assignments, a functional feature of this office type.

The headquarter office of Prevent in Stockholm, Sweden.

An office with activity-based flex office design (built in 2016)

Prevent is an expert organization on work environment in Sweden. The organization is owned by both the association of enterprises and of unions, where its work is to inform and educate organizations in the public and private sector about the subject.

The organization worked formerly in an office with open-plan and combi-offices when the management decided to go for an activity-based flex office design. This is an office design focused on work activity instead of ownership, where employees have non-personal workstations, but instead are offered good access to supplementary workspaces, i.e. back-up rooms, of various kinds within the office. When Prevent decided to implement the flex office, with non-personal workstations, a prerequisite for introducing this was that the office design guaranteed a good working environment for all members of the workforce, including its disabled employees. That this implementation of scientific knowledge on good office environment was successful in the Prevent office was also revealed in a longitudinal study that followed the move to flex offices of four different organizations (Rolfö, 2018), which found that the Prevent office stood out because of a very high work environment satisfaction among the employees.

FIGURE 3.1 Touch down workstations and supportive workspaces of various types in the background; this includes back-up rooms for concentrated work and workstations in open workspace

FIGURE 3.2 A work area for teamwork in the middle of the picture; on the left side of this, we see a back-up room with two workstations for collaborative work, and on the right side, an area with regular workstations in an open workspace

FIGURE 3.3 A meeting room for four people, and behind this an individual back-up room for concentrated work

FIGURE 3.4 A breakout and lounge area with both high tables and low seating behind this on the left side

FIGURE 3.5 Lounge area with low seating, and behind this is an education room, which is booked in advance; the board next to the door shows if the room is booked and by whom

FIGURE 3.6 Library area – a seating area for reading and calm talks

Architects: Brunnberg & Forshed Architects Ltd. (Copyright owner of the photos)

Photographer: Krister Bengtsson

(Photos of a flex office for organization Prevent. Prevent, an organization owned by both the association of enterprises and of unions, works with information and education in the field of work environments, contacted my firm to design a flex office for them).

In another recent study, a colleague and myself studied office employees' satisfaction with the contributions that office design makes to job satisfaction and related outcomes (Bodin Danielsson & Theorell, 2018). We found employees' satisfaction to vary highly between employees in different office designs and that in office designs where employees reported poor access to supportive facilities, such as back-up rooms and other supplementary work environments, they also reported more dissatisfaction with the contribution that workspace makes. My research interests expand into the area of office design's relationship to different psychosocial factors important for health and wellbeing as well as the general work environment at the office. Accordingly, in one study I and some colleagues investigated office design's influence on employees' perception of managerial leadership between employees in different office types in a large, nationwide survey (Bodin Danielsson et al., 2013). The study design did not enable control for all possible factors that influence employees' perception of leadership; the choice fell on treating the following four major background factors as confounders: age, sex, job rank, and labour market sector (private/public). There are certainly more factors that influence employees' relationship to managers, but we control for some of the major. For example, the latter confounder was controlled for because of the high rates of complaints on leadership in the public sector compared with the private. Our analysis showed, after control for these background factors, significant differences in employee–manager relationships between office types. For example, we found that the best perception of managerial leadership was reported among employees in medium-sized open-plan offices, where employees and managers often share workspace. In the study, we suggested that employees and closest managers sharing workspace may be good from an employee–manager relationship perspective since physical proximity between colleagues appears to be beneficial for communication and development of friendship (Festinger, Schacter, & Back, 1950; Szilagyi & Holland, 1980). Our hypothesis is further supported by research that has found that a visibly and audibly present manager is positive for the perception of supervisor friendliness.

Because of the negative effects that conflicts have for both individuals and organizations (e.g. Fuller et al., 2003; Grandey, Kern, & Frone, 2007; Jehn, 1997), some colleagues and I have also studied office type's association to workplace conflicts. In terms of workplace conflicts, we found in a study that there is less risk for conflicts in offices with open-plan layouts (Bodin Danielsson et al., 2015). In the four studies presented here, we suggest that identified differences in terms of studied outcomes are related to the defining features of the different office designs/office types, since these determine degree of disturbance and environmental stress, but also the stimulation and social interaction the employees are exposed to at their workplaces.

Components of a holistic office design from an organizational and management perspective

This chapter tells us that the impact of office design operates at both an individual and organizational level: at an individual level, influencing employees' wellbeing, satisfaction, emotions, and attitudes, but also creativity and innovations; at team and organizational levels it affects performance and efficiency crucial to the success and competitiveness of organizations.

Depending on focus, different approaches are applied when analysing office design. Within organizational and management the environmental influence of the office is considered to operate via the needs and symbolic value associated with its design (e.g. Davis, 1984; Steele, 1973). Recently, the emotional aspect of office design has gained interest, since employee attitudes in relation to this are a consequence of its influence on, for example, social cohesion and conflicts, highly influenced by emotions (Ashkanasy et al., 2014). Environmental psychology and occupational health research focus more on employees' health and wellbeing, or performance (Bodin Danielsson & Bodin, 2008; Bodin Danielsson, Chungkham, Wulff, & Westerlund, 2014; Evans & Johnson, 2000; Jahncke, Hygge, Halin, Green, & Dimberg, 2011).

Independently of focus, research tells us that office design's influence on employees and organizations is complex. For the individual, the workplace concerns psychological factors such as control and non-verbal self-expression, but also functional factors such as work opportunities and sharing of space and facilities with colleagues (Bodin Danielsson, 2008). Important here is the in-built symbolic value of architecture associated with power, status, and hierarchy. The strategic management use of office design utilizes this, since, because of factors described in this chapter, it is part of an organization's culture, and as such, it may play a role in both defining and changing this. Thus, it can be used for both employee and corporate branding, towards the outside market. In order to succeed in branding, however, this has to represent the ethos of the organization (Dean, Ottensmeyer, & Ramirez, 1997).

To conclude, this chapter introduces the reader to a holistic approach towards office design from an organizational and management perspective by presenting research from a variety of disciplines on the subject of office design's influence on employees and organizations. More specifically, a holistic approach means an analysis of office design's influence at various levels, i.e. micro and macro level, but foremost an analysis that includes other perspectives than the purely organizational perspective. It includes the environmental and architectural perspective to issues studied, but also an occupational health perspective because of the impact environmental influence has in this regard. Architecture can contribute with its contextual approach to environmental influences that depend on the aesthetic and functional aspects of the built environment and the architectural design of this. Environmental psychology, which looks at behaviour and psychological aspects on the office environment at the individual level, can contribute with these perspectives on the matter. Finally, occupational health, by nature an interdisciplinary field – which spans from epidemiology, stress medicine to behaviour science – can contribute with insight on the health and wellbeing aspects of the office environment's influence on employees and organizations. By linking the different fields to each other, theories and methods used in the different fields will not only be introduced to the subject of office design's influences, but established models within each field will also be able to develop.

In summary, a holistic approach to office design from an organizational and management perspective means an inclusion of many dimensions of office design's influence on employees and organizations that encompasses the welfare of both.

References

Aiello, J. R., Epstein, Y. M., & Karlin, R. A. (1975). Effects of crowding on electrodermal activity. *Sociological Symposium, 14*, 42–57.

Al Horr, Y., Arif, M., Kaushik, A., Mazroei, A., Kaytafygiotou, M., & Elsarrag, E. (2016). Occupant productivity and office indoor environment quality: A review of the literature. *Building and Environment, 105*, 1–21. doi: https://dx.doi.org/10.1016/j.buildenv.2016.06.001.

Allen, T. J. (1977). *Managing the Flow of Technology*. Cambridge, MA: MIT Press.

Allen, T. J. (1997). *Architecture and Communication Among Product Development Engineers, WP #165–97, Soan WP#3983*. Cambridge, MA: International Center for Research on the Management of Technology, Massachusetts Institute of Technology (MIT).

Allen, T. J., Tushman, M. L., & Lee, D. M. (1979). Modes of technology transfer as a function of position in the R&D spectrum. *Academy of Management Journal, 22*(4), 694–708.

Amabile, T. M., Conti, R., Coon, H., Lazenby, J., & Herron, M. (1996). Assessing the work environment for creativity. *Academy of Management, 39*(5), 1154–1184.

Aries, M. B. C. (2005). *Human Lighting Demands: Healthy Lighting in an Office Environment*. Eindhoven: Technische Universiteit Eindhoven.

Ashkanasy, N., Ayoko, O., & Jehn, K. A. (2014). Understanding the physical environment of work and employee behavior: An affective events perspective. *Journal of Organizational Behavior, 35*(8), 1169.

Asplund, J. (1988). *Det sociala livets elementära former (The Elementary Structure of Social Life)*. Gothenburg, Sweden: Korpen.

Ayr, U., Cirillo, E., Fato, I., & Martellotta, F. (2003). A new approach to assessing the performance of noise indices in buildings. *Applied Acooustics, 64*, 129–145. doi:10.1016/S0003-682X(02)00075-0.

Bäck, C., Andersson, K. B., & Hedin, J. (2015). *Företagens erfarenheter av sjukförsäkringen och sjukfrånvarons utveckling (Business Experience of Health Insurance and Development of Sickness Absence)*. Stockholm, Sweden: Confederation of Swedish Enterprise.

Banbury, S., & Berry, D. (2005). Office noise and employee concentration: Identifying caues of disruption and potential improvements. *Ergonomics, 48*(1), 25–37.

Barclay, L., & York, K. (2001). Space at work: Excercises in the art of understanding physical indicators of culture. *Journal of Management Education, 25*(1), 54–69.

Becker, F., & Sims, W. (2001). *Offices That Work: Balancing Communication, Flexibility and Cost*. Ithaca, NY: Cornell University (International Workplace Studies Program).

Becker, F., Sims, W., & Schoss, J. (2003). *Interaction, Identity and Collocation: What Value Is a Corporate Campus?* Ithaca, NY: Cornell University (International Workplace Studies Program).

Beyerlein, M., Freedman, S., McGee, G., & Moran, L. (2003). *Beyond Teams: Building the Collaborative Organization*. San Francisco, CA: Jossey-Bass/Pfeiffer.

Blatter, K., & Cajochen, C. (2007). Circadian rhythms in cognitive performance: Methodological constraints, protocols, theoretical underpinnings. *Physiology and Behavior, 90*, 196–208.

Bodin Danielsson, C. (2008). Office experiences. In H. Schifferstein & P. Hekkert (eds), *Product Experience* (pp. 605–628). San Diego, CA: Elsevier Scientific Publications.

Bodin Danielsson, C. (2013). An explorative review of the lean office concept. *Journal of Corporate Real Estate, 15*(3/4), 167–180. doi:10.1108/JCRE-02-2013-0007.

Bodin Danielsson, C. (2015). Aesthetics versus function in office architecture: Employees' perception of the workplace. *Nordic Journal of Architectural Research, 2*, 11–40.

Bodin Danielsson, C., & Bodin, L. (2008). Office type in relation to health, wellbeing and job satisfaction among employees. *Environment and Behavior, 40*(5), 636–668. doi:10.1177/0013916507307459.

Bodin Danielsson, C., & Bodin, L. (2009). Differences in satisfaction with office environment among employees in different office types. *Journal of Architectural and Planning Research, 26*(3), 2241–2257. doi:http://www.jstor.org/stable/43030872.

Bodin Danielsson, C., Bodin, L., Wulff, C., & Theorell, T. (2015). The relation between office type and workplace conflict: A gender and noise perspective. *Journal of Environmental Psychology, 42*, 161–171. doi:doi.org/10.1016/j.jenvp.2015.04.004.

Bodin Danielsson, C., Chungkham, H. S., Wulff, C., & Westerlund, H. (2014). Office design's impact on sick leave rates. *Ergonomics, 57*(2), 139–147. doi:10.1080/00140139.2013.871064.

Bodin Danielsson, C., & Theorell, T. (2018). Office employees' perception of workspace contribution: A gender and office design perspective. *Environment and Behavior.* doi:10.1177/0013916518759146.

Bodin Danielsson, C., Wulff, C., & Westerlund, H. (2013). Is perception of leadership influenced by office environment? *Journal of Corporate Real Estate, 15*(3/4), 194–212. doi:10.1108/JCRE-03-2013-0008.

Bradley, S., Petrescu, A., & Simmons, R. (2007). The impacts of human resource management practices and pay inequality on workers' job satisfaction. *British Journal of Industrial Relations, 43*(2).

Brief, A. P., & Weiss, H. M. (2002). Organizational behavior: Affect in the workplace. *Annual Review of Psychology, 53*, 279–307.

Britner, J. M. (1992). The impact of physical surroundings on customers and employees. *Journal of Marketing, 56*(2), 57–71.

Brocolini, L., Parizet, E., & Chevret, P. (2016). Effect of masking noise on cognitive performance and annoyance in open plan offices. *Applied Acoustics, 114*, 44–55. doi:10.1016/j.apacoust.2016.07.012.

Brunia, S., De Been, I., & Van der Voordt, T. J. M. (2016). Accommodating new ways of working: Lessons from best practices and worst cases. *Journal of Corporate Real Estate, 18*(1), 30–47. doi:http://dx.doi.org/10.1108/JCRE-10-2015-0028.

Bruursema, K., Stacey R. Kessler, S. R., & Spector, P. E. (2011). Bored employees misbehaving: The relationship between boredom and counterproductive work behaviour. *Work and Stress, 25*(2), 93–107. doi:10.1080/02678373.2011.596670.

Carsten, J. M., & Spector, P. E. (1987). Unemployment, job satisfaction, and employee turnover: A meta-analytic test of the Muchinsky model. *Journal of Applied Psychology, 72*(3), 374–381.

Catmull, E. (2008). *How Pixar Fosters Collective Creativity.* Boston, MA: Harvard.

Cohen, S., Evans, G., Stokols, D., & Krantz, D. (1991). *Behavior, Health, and Environmental Stress.* New York: Plenum Press.

Conrath, C. W. (1973). Communication patterns, organizational structure, and man: Some relationships. *Human Factors, 15*(5), 459–470. doi:10.1177/001872087301500503.

Csikszentmihalyi, M. (1996). *Creativity: Flow and the Psychology of Discovery and Invention.* New York: Harper Collins.

Danielsson, C. (2005). Applying Lynch's theory on office environments. *Nordic Journal of Architectural Research*, (4), 69–78.

Davenport, T. H. (1998). Successful knowledge management projects. *Sloan Management Review*, *39*(2), 43–57.

Davis, M. A. (2009). Understanding the relationship between mood and creativity: A meta-analysis. *Organisational Behavior and Human Decision Processes*, *108*, 25–38.

Davis, T. (1984). The influence o physical environment in offices. *Academy of Management Review*, *9*(2), 271–283.

Dean, J. W., Ottensmeyer, E., & Ramirez, R. (1997). An aesthetic perspective on organizations. In C. L. Cooper & S. Jackson (eds), *Creating Tomorrow's Organizations: Handbook for Future Research in Organizational Behavior* (pp. 419–437). Chichester: John Wiley and Sons.

DeChurch, L. A., & Mesmer-Magnus, J. R. (2010). The cognitive underpinning of effective teamwork: A meta-analysis. *Journal of Applied Psychology*, *95*(1), 32–53.

Dul, J., & Ceylan, C. (2010). Work environments for employee creativity. *Ergonomics*, *54*(1), 12–20.

Estabrook, M., & Sommer, R. (1972). Social rank and acquaintanceship in two academic buildings. In W. Graham & K. H. Roberts (eds), *Comparative Studies in Organizational Behavior* (pp. 122–128). New York: Holt, Rinehart & Winston.

European Commission. (2002). *Guidance of Work-related Stress: Spice of Life or a Kiss of Death?* Luxemburg: Official Publications of the European Communities.

Evans, G. (1979). Behavioral and physiological consequences of crowding in humans. *Journal of Applied Social Psychology*, *9*, 27–46.

Evans, G., & Johnson, D. (2000). Stress and open-office noise. *Journal of Applied Psychology*, *85*(5), 779–783. doi:10.1037/0021-9010.85.5.779.

Festinger, L., Schacter, S., & Back, K. (1950). *Social Pressures in Informal Groups: A Study of Human Factors in Housing*. Stanford, CA: Stanford University Press.

Fischer, G. N. (1997). *Individuals and Environment: A Psychological Approach to Workspace*. New York: Walter de Gruyte.

Frontczak, M., Schiavon, S., Goins, J., Arens, E., Zhang, H., & Wargocki, P. (2012). Quantiative relationships between occupant satisfaction and satisfaction aspects of indoor environmental quality and building design. *Indoor Air*, (22), 119–131. doi:10.1111./j.1600-0668.2011.00745.x.

Fuller, J. A., Stanton, J. M., Fisher, G. G., Spitzmüller, C., Russel, S. S., & Smith, P. (2003). A lengthy look at the daily grind: Time series analysis of events, mood, stress, and satisfaction. *Journal of Applied Psychology*, *88*(6), 1019–1033

George, J. M., & Jones, G. R. (1996). The experience of work and turnover intentions: Interactive effects of value attainment, job satisfaction, and positive mood. *Journal of Applied Psychology*, *81*, 318–325.

Grandey, A., Kern, J., & Frone, M. R. (2007). Verbal abuse from outsiders versus insiders: Comparing frequency, impact on emotional exhaustion, and the role of emotional labor. *Journal of Occupational Health Psychology*, *12*(1), 63–79. doi:10.1037/1076-8998.12.1.63.

Haner, U.-E. (2005). Spaces for creativity and innovation in two established organisations. *Creativity and Innovation Management*, *15*, 288–298.

Hatch, M. J., & Schultz, M. (2003). Bringing the corporation into the corporate branding. *European Journal of Marketing*, *37*(7/8), 1041–1064. doi:10.1108/0309560310477654.

Haynes, B. P. (2008). Impact of workplace connectivity on office productivity. *Journal of Corporate Real Estate*, *10*(4), 286–302.

Haynes, B. P. (2008b). The impact of office layout on productivity. *Journal of Facilities Management, 6*(3), 189–201.

Hedge, A. (1982). The open plan office: A systematic investigation of employee reactions to their work environment. *Environment and Behavior, 14*(5), 519–542. doi: 10.1177/0013916582145002.

Heerwagen, J. (1990). Affective functioning, light hunger and room brightness preferences. *Environment and Behavior, 22*(5), 608–635.

Heerwagen, J. H., Kampschroer, K., Powell, K. M., & Loftness, V. (2004). Collaborative knowledge work environments. *Building Research and Information, 32*(6), 510–528. doi: 10.1080/09613210412331313025.

Herzberg, F., Mausner, B., & Bloch Snyderman, B. (2003). *The Motivation to Work* (6th ed.). New Brunswick, NJ: Transaction Publishers.

Hinsz, V. B., Tindale, R. S., & Vollrath, D. A. (1997). The emerging conceptualization of groups as information processes. *Psychological Bulletin, 121*, 43–64.

Hollingshead, A., & Brandon, D. P. (2003). Potential benefits of communication in transative memory systems. *Human Communication Research, 29*(4), 607–615.

Homans, G. C. (1992). *The Human Group.* New Brunswick, Canada: Transaction Publishers.

Hua, Y., Loftness, J. H., Heerwagen, J., & Powell, K. M. (2011). Relationship between workplace spatial settings and occupant-perceived support for collaboration. *Environment and Behavior, 43*(6), 807–826.

Isen, A. M., Daubman, K. A., & Nowicki, G. P. (1987). Positive affect facilitates creative problem solving. *Journal of Personality and Social Psychology, 52*, 1122–1131.

Jackson, S. (1992). Team composition in organizations. In S. Wochel, W. Wood, & J. Simpson (eds), *Group Process and Productivity* (pp. 1–12). London: Sage.

Jahncke, H., & Halin, N. (2012). Performance, fatigue and stress in open-plan offices: The effects of noise and restoration on hearing impaired and normal hearing individuals. *Noise and Health, 14*(60), 260–272.

Jahncke, H., Hygge, S., Halin, N., Green, A. M., & Dimberg, K. (2011). Open-plan office noise: Cognitive performance and restoration. *Journal of Environmental Psychology, 31*, 373–382. doi:10.1016/j.jenvp.2011.07.002.

Jehn, K. A. (1997). A qualitative analysis of conflict types and dimensions in organizatioanl groups. *Administrative Science Quarterly, 42*, 530–557.

Kallio, T. J., Kallio, K.-M., & Blomberg, A. J. (2015). Physical space, culture and organisational creativity: A longitudinal study. *Facilities, 33* (5/6), 389–411. doi: 10.1108/F-09-2013-0074.

Karasek, R., & Theorell, T. (1990). *Healthy Work: Stress, Productivity, and the Reconstruction of Working Life.* New York: Basic Books.

Keus van de Poll, M., & Sörqvist, P. (2016). Effects of task interruption and background speech on word processed writing. *Applied Cognitive Psychology.* doi:10.1002/acp.3221.

Kim, W. C., & Mauborgne, R. (1998). Procedural justice, strategic decision making and the knowledge economy. *Strategic Management Journal, 19*(4), 323–338.

Kivimäki, M., Head, J., Ferrie, J. E., Shipley, M. J., Vahtera, J., & Marmot, M. G. (2003). Sickness absence as a global measure of health: Evidence from mortality in the Whitehall II prospective cohort study. *British Journal of Management, 327*(7411), 364. doi:10.1136/bmj.327.7411.364.

Kupritz, V. W. (1998). Privacy in the work place: The impact of building design. *Journal of Environmental Psychology, 18*, 341–356. doi:10.1006/jevp.1998.0081.

Lang, J., Burnette, C., Moleski, W., & Vachon, D. (1974). *Designing for Human Behavior: Architecture and the Behavioral Sciences.* Stroudsburg, PA: Dowden, Hutchinson, and Ross.

Lee, R. T., & Ashforth, B. E. (1996). A meta-analytic examination of the correlates of the three dimensions of job burnout. *Journal of Applied Psychology, 81*(2), 123–133.

Lee, Y. S. (2010). Office layout effecting privacy, interaction, and acoustic quality in LEED-certified buildings. *Building and Environment, 45*, 1594–1600.

Leiter, P., & Maslach, C. (1988). The impact of interpersonal environment on burnout and organizational commitment. *Journal of Organizational Behavior, 9*, 297–308.

Lines, R. (2004). Influence of participation in strategic change: Resistance, organizational commitment and change goal achievement. *Journal of Change Management, 4*(3), 193–215. doi:10.1080/1469701042000221696.

Locke, E. A., & Henne, D. (1986). Work motivation theories. In C. L. Cooper & R. I. T. (eds), *International Review of Industrial and Organizational Psychology* (pp. 1–35). Chichester: John Wiley.

Lok, P., & Crawford, J. (2004). The effect of organisational culture and leadership style on job satisfaction and organisational commitment: A cross-national comparison. *Journal of Management Development, 23*(4), 321–338.

Maher, A., & von Hippel, C. (2005). Individual differences in employee reactions to open-plan offices. *Journal of Environmental Psychology, 25*(2), 219–229. doi:10.1016/j.jenvp.2005.05.002.

Mahnke, F. H. (1996). *Color, Environment, and Human Response: An Interdisciplinary Understanding of Color and Its Use as a Beneficial Element in the Design of the Architectural Environment.* New York: Van Nostrand Reinhold.

Maslach, C. (1982). *Burnout: The Cost of Caring.* Englewood Cliffs, NJ: Prentice Hall.

McElroy, J. C., & Morrow, P. C. (2010). Employee reactions to office redesign: A naturally occurring quasi-field experiment in a multi-generational setting. *Human Relations, May*(63), 609–636.

Mesmer-Magnus, J., Ashley, A., Niler, J. A., Plummer, G., Larson, L. E., & DeChurch, L. A. (2017). The cognitive underpinnings of effective teamwork: A continuation. *Career Development International, 22* (5), 507–519. doi:10.1108/CDI-08-2017-0140.

Mok, D., & Wellman, B. (2007). Did distance matter before the Internet? Interpersonal contact and support in the 1970s. *Social Networks, 29*(3), 430–461. doi:10.1016/j.socnet.2007.01.009.

Nyberg, A., Westerlund, H., Magnusson Hanson, L., & Theorell, T. (2008). Managerial leadership is associated with self-reported sickness absence and sickness presenteeism among Swedish men and women. *Scandinavian Journal of Public Health, 36*, 803–811. doi:10.1177/1403494808093329.

Oldham, G. R. (1988). Effects of changes in workspace partitions and spatial density on employees reactions: A quasi-experiment. *Journal of Applied Psychology, 73*(2), 253–258.

Organ, D. W., & Ryan, K. (1995). A meta-analytic review of attitudinal and dispositional predictors of organizational citizenship behavior. *Personnel Psychology, 48*, 775–802.

Özturk, E., Yilmazer, S., & Ural, S. E. (2012). The effects of achromatic and chromatic color schemes on participants' task performance in appraisals of an office environment. *Color Res. Appl., 37*, 359–366.

Payne, S. R. (2013). The production of a perceived restorativeness soundscape scale. *Applied Acoustics, 74*, 255–263.

Pfeffer, J. (1981). *Power in Organizations.* Marshfield, MA: Pitman.

Pratt, M. G., & Rafaeli, A. (2001). Symbols as language of organizational relationships. In B. Staw & R. Sutton (eds), *Research in Organizational Behavior: An Annual Series of Analytical Essays and Critical Reviews* (Vol. 23, pp. 93–132). Amsterdam: JAI.

Robbins, M. J., Peterson, M., Tedrick, T., & Carpenter, J. R. (2003). Job satisfaction on NCAA Division III athletic directions: Impact on job design and time on task. *International Sport Journal, 7*(2).

Robinson, A. G., & Stern, S. (1997). *Corporate Creativity: How Innovation and Improvement Actually Happen*. San Francisco, CA: Berrett-Koehler Publishers.

Roelofsen, P. (2002). The impact of office environments on employee performance: The design of the workplace as a strategy for productivity enhancement. *Journal of Facilities Management, 1* (3), 247–264. doi:https://doi.org/10.1108/14725960310807944.

Rolfö, L. (2018). *Planning and Designing Flexible Office Work Environments: Processes and Outcomes* (doctoral degree), School of Technology and Health, The Royal Institute of Technology (KTH), Stockholm.

Rosete, D., & Ciarrochi, J. (2005). Emotional intelligence and its relationship to workplace performance outcomes of leadership effectiveness. *Leadership and Organization Development Journal, 26*(5), 388–399.

Sailer, K., & Penn, A. (2009). *Spatiality and Transpatiality in Workplace Environments*. Paper presented at the 7th International Space Syntax Symposium, Stockholm, Sweden.

Sauter, S. L., & Murphy, L. R. (eds). (1995). *Organizational Risk Factors for Job Stress*. Washington, DC: American Psychological Association.

Schein, E. H. (2010). *Organizational Culture and Leadership*. 4th ed. San Francisco: Jossey-Bass.

Shipton, H. J., West, M. A., Parkes, C. L., Dawson, J. F., & Patterson, M. G. (2006). When promoting positive feelings pays: Aggregate job satisfaction, work design features, and innovation in manufacturing organizations. *European Journal of Work and Organizational Psychology, 15*(4), 404–430. doi:10.1080/13594320600908153.

Spector, P. E. (1997). *Job Satisfaction: Application, Assessment, Causes, and Consequences*. London: SAGE.

Steele, F. (1973). *Physical Settings and Organisational Development*. Reading, MA: Addison-Wesley.

Stigliani, I., & Ravasi, D. (2012). Organizing thoughts and connecting brains: Material practices and the transition from individual to group-level prospective sensemaking. *Academy of Management, 55*(5), 1232–1259.

Stokols, D. (1972). On the distinction between density and crowding. *Psychological Review, 79*(3), 275–277.

Sundstrom, E. (1986). *Work Places: The Psychology of the Physical Environment in Offices and Factories*. New York: Cambridge University Press.

Sundstrom, E., Town, J. P., Rice, R. W., Osborn, D., & Brill, M. (1994). Office noise, satisfaction, and performance. *Environment and Behavior, 26*(2), 195–222.

Svedberg, L. (1992). *Gruppsykologi – Om den inre och yttre scenen – teori och tillämpning (Group Psychology – About the Internal and External Scene)*. Lund: Studentlitteratur.

Szilagyi, A., & Holland, W. (1980). Changes in social density: Relationships with functional interaction and perceptions of job characteristics, role stress, and work satisfaction. *Journal of Applied Psychology, 65*(1), 28–33. doi:10.1037/0021-9010.65.1.28.

Teasley, S., Covi, L., Krishnan, M. S., & Olsson, J. S. (2000). *How Does Radical Collocation Help a Team Succeed?* Paper presented at the ACM Conference on Computer Supported Cooperative Work, New York.

Tett, R. P., & Meyer, J. P. (1993). Job satisfaction, organizational commitment, turnover intention, and turnover: Path analyses based on meta-analytic findings. *Personnel Psychology, 46*, 259–293.

Trice, H. M., & Beyer, J. M. (1993). *The Culture of Work Organizations*. Englewood Cliffs, NJ: Prentice-Hall.

Valentine, S., Godkin, L., Fleischman, G. M., & Kidwell, R. (2011). Corporate ethical values, group creativity, job satisfaction and turnover intention: The impact of work context on work response. *Journal of Business Ethics, 98,* 353–372. doi:10.1007/s10551-010-0554-6.

Van Meel, J., & Vos, P. (2001). Funky offices: Relections on office design in the 'new economy'. *Journal of Corporate Real Estate, 3*(4), 322–334.

Veitch, J., Charles, K., Farley, K., & Newsham, G. (2007). A model of satisfaction with open-plan office conditions: COPE field findings. *Journal of Environmental Psychology, 27,* 177–189.

Veitch, J. A. (2005). Light, lighting, and health: Issues for consideration. *LEUKOS: The Journal of the Illuminating Engineering Society of North America, 2*(2), 85–96. doi:10.1582/LEUKOS.2005.02.02.001.

Veitch, J. A., Stokkermans, M., & Newsham, G. (2013). Linking lighting appraisals to work behaviors. *Environment and Behavior, 45*(2), 198–214. doi:10.1177/0013916511420560.

Vilnai-Yavetz, I., Rafaeli, A., & Schneider Yaacov, C. (2005). Instrumentality, aesthetics, and symbolism of office design. *Environment and Behavior,* 533–551.

Vischer, J. (2005). *Space Meets Status: Designing Workplace.* London: Routledge, Taylor & Francis.

Weiss, H. M., & Merlo, K. L. (2015). Job satisfaction. In *International Encyclopedia of the Social and Behavior Sciences* (2 ed., pp. 832–838). https://doi-org.focus.lib.kth.se/10.1016/B978-0-08-097086-8.22029-1: Elsevier.

PART II

The theoretical background to the physical environment of organizational behaviour

4

PSYCHOLOGICAL OWNERSHIP AND THE PHYSICAL ENVIRONMENT IN ORGANIZATIONS

Jon L. Pierce and Graham Brown

The office is an integral part of the work experience for employees and the second largest operating expense for most companies. Indeed, organizations such as Aldar in the United Arab Emirates spend millions of dollars (US$272 million) on design to make architectural statements about the company, both for its employees and other stakeholders. Companies also spend money on the interior with a variety of goals, including increased collaboration: witness, for example, Facebook's campus (US$269 million)[1] in Menlo Park, California.

Not surprisingly, research into how people experience environmental conditions at work is a growing and necessary area of study. As noted by Vischer (2008), 'until the 1980s, there was insufficient research on "workspaces"' (p. 97), since then there has been increasing attention on the impact that the workplace has on the employees' work experience. While there is considerable research on the physical and functional[2] aspects of design, the psychological impact is still not well understood. This chapter is intended to contribute to this gap by exploring the impact that psychological ownership (PO) has in the workplace. In doing so, we consider the impact of PO across the spectrum of the physical work environment from the building itself (i.e. architecture), to physical objects (i.e. workspaces) within the building; and from design choices that affect the interactions between employees (i.e. desk-sharing), including the individual worker's physical proximity to the main office (i.e. telecommuting). Through a lens of PO we explore the impact that design has on the development of feelings of ownership, the objects for which people develop these feelings, and the consequences and implications of ownership at work. We acknowledge up front that we are unable to cover all aspects of the physical environment and instead address a sample of topics as illustrations of the connections between psychological ownership and the physical environment. We start with a review of the theory of psychological ownership as both an individual-level phenomenon and as a collective cognition. In the second part of the chapter our focus is on the emergence and manifestation of the sense of ownership within the physical work and organizational context. More specifically, we discuss targets (i.e. workspaces) to which the sense of ownership attaches, design and physical context predictors of the emergence of these ownership feelings, and finally the individual and organizational effects that are created by PO. In the third section of this chapter we consider practical and research implications for designing workspaces and managing employees through designs that our review of the psychological ownership literature suggests.

Psychological ownership in organizations

Across cultures and time the concept of ownership has taken on a number of different conceptualizations. In Marxistic/Leninistic communist societies (e.g. China under Chairman Mao), as well as kibbutz arrangements, personal ownership of objects was discouraged and virtually non-existent. Mao, for example, introduced collective ownership of objects, thereby limiting personal ownership.[3] There have also been cultures, such as certain clans of the Sami, the nomadic people of the Arctic North, who believed that one cannot own many earthly objects (e.g. land, huts), as ownership is informed by those things that one can take with them into the next life (e.g. one's soul).[4] Rousseau (1762) noted that civil society most likely began when a person fenced off a plot of land and took it into his head to claim it as mine and others respected his assertion, suggesting to us that ownership may be seen as a social relationship (cf. Heider, 1958; Rudmin, 1994). Somewhat similarly, it has been observed that children by the age of three frequently employ first possession to ascribe ownership (Friedman, 2008; Friedman & Neary, 2008; Shaw, Li & Olson, 2012). Throughout much of the world, ownership has been approached as the legal right of possession, where the rights and responsibilities that accompany this state are defined and protected by the host country's legal system. Ownership, as the legal right of possession, (Monks & Minow, 2001), can be defined in terms of a 'bundle of rights' (e.g. the right to exercise control over and use of the target of ownership; the right to be fully informed about the status of the target of ownership; as well as a physical and/or financial stake in the owned object).

Stemming from the recent work of Etzioni (1991), Pierce, Rubenfeld, and Morgan (1991), and Wilpert (1991), the idea of ownership as a psychological state got traction. Pierce et al. (1991), in their study of employee ownership as an organizational arrangement, noted that they typically pass along a financial stake in the organization (cf. employee stock ownership plans – ESOPs) to its employees, thereby making them employee owners. Such arrangements, however, typically fall short in meeting expectations as to the true meaning of ownership and what it means to be an owner. Missing in design and application is the full bundle of rights to which many have grown accustomed. Typically missing from many employee ownership schemes, with an exception being the worker-owned and -controlled cooperative, is the right to information about and control over the owned object. This mental model as to the meaning of ownership carries with it the notion that ownership is, in part, a psychological state which they referred to as psychological ownership. Etzioni (1991) expressed it well when he noted that ownership is a 'dual creation, part attitude, part object, part in the "mind" and part real' (p. 466). Much earlier, James (1890, p. 291–293) wrote that:

> a man's Self is the sum total of all that he can call his, not only his body and his psychic powers, but his cloths and his house, his wife and children . . . his reputation and works, . . . if they wax and prosper, he feels triumphant; if they dwindle and die he feels cast down . . . not necessarily the same degree for each . . ., but in much the same way for all.

Building off of this idea, Pierce, Kostova, and Dirks (2001, 2003, p. 299) defined *psychological ownership* (PO) as that state where an individual feels as though the target of ownership (or a piece of that target) is theirs (i.e. it is MINE!). The core of this psychological state is feeling of possessiveness, being psychologically tied to an object, and experiencing the object as part of the extended self (Belk, 1988; Dittmar, 1992; Furby, 1978; James, 1890). As noted by James (1890), 'there is a fine line between that which is "me" and that which is considered "mine"', and as such psychological ownership essentially responds to the question: what do I feel is mine and a part of me?

There are two competing perspectives that have been taken with regard to the genesis of this psychological state. There are those who believe that the human condition carries with it the innate possessive tendency (e.g. Ardrey, 1966; Burk, 1900; Darling, 1937; Porteous, 1976). Quite naturally people mark and defend territory, collect and hoard various objects claiming them as their own. Such possessive and property-related behaviour is commonly observed in children, even before their use of possessive (ownership) related words (Ellis, 1985). McDougall (1908/1923, p.75) wrote, 'The impulse to collect and hoard various objects is displayed in one way or another by almost all human beings, and seems to be due to a true instinct.' Many scholars (e.g. Beaglehole, 1932; Lewis & Brook, 1974; Litwinski 1942; Seligman, 1975), however, contend that attitudinal, motivational, and behavioural expressions of ownership are an outgrowth of socialization practices carried out in society. As children begin to explore their environment, others begin to draw the lines that demark *meum* and *tuum* (mine and yours) through such expressions as 'not yours, don't touch,' 'here is your bucket and ball'. Bridging this divide is a socio-biological perspective. Litwinski (1942) and somewhat later Dittmar (1992) took a socio-biological perspective, noting that possessive actions and assertions that appear in children very early in life are most likely an outgrowth of an innate tendency, which gets reinforced, very quickly, by the socialization practices to which they were exposed.

Psychological ownership theory as an individual psychological state

The original theorizing on psychological ownership can be found in the works of Pierce, Kostova, and Dirks (2001, 2003), with a more targeted focus dealing with organizational change found in the work of Dirks, Cummings, and Pierce (1996), and Brown, Lawrence, and Robinson's (2005) focus on territoriality. Psychological ownership theory addresses the roots (i.e. motivational states) that underpin the emergence of a sense of ownership, the routes (i.e. experiences) travelled to the emergence of ownership feelings, attributes of targets to which psychological ownership attaches itself, and several personal and organization-related effects some of which are positive (e.g. job satisfaction, in-role performance, stewardship) and others negative (e.g. stress, burden of responsibility, refusal to share) in nature. The construct psychological ownership appears to have originated at the individual level of analysis, which was followed by similar theorizing focused on the sense of ownership as a collective cognition referred to as collective psychological ownership (CPO) (Pierce & Jussila, 2010).

Uniqueness of the sense of ownership

There are several constructs in the organizational sciences that depict the psychological relationship that connects the individual with work and organizational context, thereby raising questions as to the uniqueness of the construct PO and/or its relationship with these constructs. Psychological ownership has been conceptually differentiated from job satisfaction, affective commitment, identification, internalization, psychological empowerment, and experienced meaningfulness in terms of the constructs' conceptual core, question answered, motivational base, development, type of state, and selected consequences (e.g. Brown, Pierce, & Crossley, 2014b; Pierce et al., 2001, 2003). In addition, there is empirical evidence suggesting discrimination from organizational commitment, satisfaction, organization-based self-esteem, job involvement, insider status, organizational justice, organizational optimism, future orientation, territoriality, accountability, organization identity, collective psychological ownership, organizational identification and internalization (cf. Avey, Avolio, Crossley, & Luthans, 2009; Brown et al., 2014b; Chi & Han, 2008; Knapp, Smith, & Sprinkle, 2014; O'Driscoll, Pierce, & Coghlan, 2006; Pierce, Jussila, & Li, 2017a; Qian, Lin, Han, Tian, Chen, & Wang, 2015; Van Dyne & Pierce, 2004).

The roots of psychological ownership

The theory of PO identifies four motives (i.e. the effectance motive, and the needs for self-identity, home, and stimulation) that illuminate reasons for the emergence of PO. These motives are not seen as the cause of the sense of ownership, yet they facilitate our understanding of why the sense of ownership is commonplace.

White (1959) noted that a natural part of the human condition is the motivation to explore and to interact effectively with one's environment. Building off of his work, Furby (1978) noted that the motivation for possessive behaviour is embedded in what White (1959) refers to as the effectance or competence motive. This motivation manifests itself in attempts to master one's environment through understanding and control, which serves to bring controlled objects into the citadel of the self, making them a part of the extended self (Belk, 1988; Dittmar, 1992; Furby, 1978; James, 1890). This led Pierce et al. (2001, 2003) to suggest that the motivation for and the experienced state of ownership is, in part, grounded in the effectance and competence motive such that the strength and duration of experienced control over an object results in feelings of ownership for that object. Thus, object control serves to satisfy the effectance/competence motive, coupled with the resultant feeling of efficacy, which is pleasure-producing *per se.*

The need for self-identity is seen as a second motive that underpins the emergence and is satisfied by a sense of ownership. Objects are frequently employed as symbolic expressions of the self, serving to help one come to know thyself, to express thyself to others (Dittmar, 1992), and aid in maintaining the continuity of one's self-identity across time (cf. Csikszentmihalyi & Rochberg-Halton, 1981; Dittmar, 1992; Kamptner, 1989, 1991; Mead, 1934; Porteous, 1976). Note, for example, the decoration of homes and offices commonly reflects the interests and personality of their occupants. Thus, possession and the sense of ownership serve to satisfy the need for self-identity.

Home or having a place in which to dwell is seen as the third motive which serves as the reason for the existence of a sense of ownership. According to Heidegger (1927) and Polanyi (1962), being at home is realized when that in which we inhabit ceases to be an object, as it has become a part of us. Thus, the individual has infused themselves into time and space, having found within it meaning, comfort, and security. Being at home is psychological in nature, whether in reference to experiencing a physical place (e.g. within four walls on a plot of land), or something more abstract as being at home in one's language, within familiar sights, sounds, smells, and foods.

Finally, theorizing on PO has proposed the need for stimulation as a fourth reason for the sense of ownership. Possessions are sought after and brought into one's personal space as a way of fulfilling the human need for arousal/activation (Darling, 1937; Duncan, 1981; Kamptner, 1989; Scott, 1966). Possessions serve as objects of attention, manipulation, enhancement, and protection, thereby serving and satisfying a basic human need for stimulation

In sum, when one or more of these motives is activated it can be seen as the glue that serves to attach an individual to certain objects. As to be discussed next, critical to the emergence of PO is the intersection between a target possessing the right characteristics (e.g. visible and attractive), an aroused need, and a particular experience (e.g. experienced control over an object) or set of experiences with the potential target of ownership. Later in the chapter we apply this specifically to the physical environment and consider how different objects like one's workspace or even one's office building (place of work) can satisfy the motives and are thus potential targets for the development of PO.

The routes to PO's emergence

In the discussion that follows, we comment on the role played by three proximal experiences that have been theorized as leading to the emergence of PO. In the previous section, we noted that there are four latent needs (i.e. effectance motive, need for self-identity, need for home [having a place in which to dwell], and the need for stimulation) that serve as the roots for (i.e. the reason for) PO. While not seen as the cause of PO, these 'roots' make the individual ready to engage in a relationship, whereby certain objects become a part of the extended self. To be discussed later are the properties of the objects that are seen as playing an important role in the emergence of this psychological state.

The three direct routes to PO are experienced control over, intimate knowing of, and investment of the self into the target of ownership. Current theorizing also suggests that an individual only needs to travel down one of these paths for the sense of ownership to materialize.

Early in the developmental process children have already begun to develop a sense and understanding of ownership (cf. Friedman, 2008; Friedman & Neary, 2008). When their motor skills first develop, objects that can be controlled are experienced as part of the self and they are commonly referred to as 'me' and 'mine' (cf. Isaacs, 1933; Kline & France, 1899; Seligman, 1975), while those objects that cannot be similarly controlled are experienced as 'not-self', not me nor mine. Thus, Furby (1978) among others (e.g. Prelinger, 1959; Tuan, 1984) have reasoned that the more one controls an object, and the longer that that object is controlled, it increasingly becomes experienced as one's possession, referred to as mine, and experienced as a part of the extended self (Belk, 1988; Furby, 1978). Object control is seen as satisfying the effectance (competence) motive.

James (1890) suggested that through a living relationship a sense of ownership for an object emerges and it becomes a part of that which one considers him/ herself. Similarly, Beaglehole (1932) reasoned that as we increasingly come to an intimate knowing of an object, person, or place, it becomes a part of the self. Much like the gardener who, after ploughing and tilling the soil, planting the seed, caring for and nourishing the plantings, becomes rooted within the garden. Accompanying this intimate knowing of the garden it becomes 'theirs', and a part of the self (Weil, 1952). The emergence of this intimate relationship is seen as serving the need for both home and stimulation.

Finally, investment of the self into the target of ownership is seen as a third path down which travels give rise to feelings of target ownership. Flowing from the self appears to reflect Locke's (1690) thinking when he noted that we own ourselves, we own our labour, and therefore we are most likely to feel that we own that which we create, shape, attend to, nurture, and protect. Investment of the self into an object is likely to serve to satisfy the effectance motive, the need for stimulation, an expression of one's self-identity while providing domicile (home) within which to dwell.

Current theorizing on PO has identified several sources of work environment structure that potentially put one onto one or more of the three routes (e.g. experienced target control, intimate knowing) to PO. In general, situational strength (Mischel, 1973) plays a major role, with PO most likely emerging in weak as opposed to strong situations, as it is under these conditions that the person (e.g. one's personality, motives, attitudes) as opposed to the situation plays a major role shaping one's behaviour. Among the structural forces giving rise to weak situational strength are complex job/work design, organically designed social systems, non-routine technology, participatory management processes (e.g. planning, organizing, decision-making), and leadership styles.

As will be discussed later in the chapter, workspaces provide opportunities to experience all of these routes. However, there are other design considerations and work arrangement choices that organizations make that can hinder or facilitate any of these routes and thus the development of PO.

The emergence of psychological ownership

Across time, the individual with their latent needs interacts with many objects (material and non-material in nature). Most likely the vast majority of person–object interactions do not result in the emergence of the sense of ownership, as people do not come to a sense of ownership for each and every object with which they come into contact.

Target attributes that are seen as having the capacity to satisfy one or more of the motives that underpin this psychological state play a critical role in the object becoming experienced as an extended part of the self. Among those target attributes are *visibility* and *attractiveness* as the target needs to get and hold the attention of the psychological owner for the unfolding process associated with the emergence of PO to take place. *Accessibility* (openness, receptivity) is seen as important, enabling the individual to embed themselves within the object, both within time and space, thereby giving rise to a sense of security and comfort. Thus, accessibility is seen as a critical target attribute as it facilitates satisfaction of the need for a place in which to dwell. Targets that are attractive, *socially esteemed* and *self-revealing* allow for the assimilation of the target as a personal anchor in time and space, thereby enabling the individual to employ attributes of the target as an expression of one's identity, aiding satisfaction of the need for self-identity. Finally, target *malleability* is seen as contributing to the satisfaction of the need for stimulation, as well as the effectance motive while promoting feelings of efficacy.

In sum, the emergence of PO appears to be at the confluence of a set of latent needs and target attributes that serve to satisfy one or more of these needs. Also, as a part of this emergent process is the individual's experienced control over the target of ownership, coming to intimately know that target, and/or the investment of their self into the target. Thereby the individual becomes psychologically tied to the target as it becomes a part of the extended self and feelings of ownership manifest themselves. Later in the chapter we discuss the many objects at work that have the capacity to satisfy one or more of the motives, and how different organizations vary in the autonomy employees have over their workspace and the way they do their work.

Theorized effects of psychological ownership

Current theorizing on PO suggests both a positive as well as a dark side. In addition to possessions being pleasure-producing *per se* (Furby, 1978), many of its effects stem from the fact that possessions come to be a part of the extended self (Belk, 1988; Furby, 1978; James, 1890). Driven by the self-regulatory motivational mechanisms, the needs for self-protection, self-verification (consistency), and self-enhancement (Dipboye, 1977; Korman, 2001; Swann, 1984), people strive to protect, verify, and enhance that to which the self is attached. As a consequence, feelings of ownership have been hypothesized to be positively related to, for example, the assumption of responsibility, stewardship, satisfaction, affective commitment, empowerment, territorial behaviours, protection and discretionary performance-related behaviour, experienced meaningfulness, a sense of attachment (e.g. belongingness, as in being a member of community), and the promotion of organizational change that is evolutionary, additive, and/or self-initiated in nature (e.g. Dirks et al., 1996; Pierce et al., 2001, 2003). On the negative side, the sense of ownership has been linked conceptually with resistance to imposed, revolutionary, and subtractive change, refusal to share (e.g. information-/knowledge-hoarding), stress, and a burden of responsibility (e.g. Baer & Brown, 2012; Dirks et al., 1996; Pierce et al., 2003). Current theorizing does not take us much beyond this point informing our thinking about when the sense of ownership turns from positive to negative, or when the dark side simply emerges. Both the positive and negative effects of a sense of ownership can be exacerbated or avoided through the physical work environment and, more specifically, the design choices organizations make to support or hinder a sense of ownership – a point we will discuss later.

Theory of psychological ownership as a collective cognition

Before examining the relationship between the physical environment and PO, it is important to acknowledge that feelings of ownership can also be a collective phenomenon, which itself is also impacted by the organization's physical design choices. Psychological ownership at the individual level appears to manifest itself in terms of personal feelings of exclusive ownership (e.g. that is my fly rod), and in terms of a personal recognition that others may experience a sense of ownership for the same object (i.e. this is our commons). In the later instance the pronoun 'our' is a dual possessive pronoun, thereby inclusive of the notion that the commons is mine, as well as an acknowledgment that others may also refer to the same commons with the words mine and/or ours. In studies of work teams, one may ask each member of the team to express either the strength of their own feelings of ownership (mine or ours) for a particular target (e.g. this is my [our] workspace), or to ask the respondent to indicate the extent to which they believe that members of their work team feel a sense of ownership for the same workspace. Then the aggregation of those responses across each member of the team reveals team-level experienced ownership (team ownership) for the workspace in question.

The construct collective psychological ownership (CPO) as discussed in this section is phenomologically a different construct than that which has been just been described. In the discussion that follows we focus on the theory of CPO (Pierce & Jussila, 2010), where the construct is seen as a 'collective cognition', a single and shared mindset that is an outgrowth of shared experiences, and a collective negotiation of the meaning of those experiences resulting in a team coming to the sense of their joint possessive reality. The construct is seen as somewhat similar to what Bandura (1997) refers to as collective efficacy, which is seen as an emergent group-level phenomenon and not simply the sum of individual efficacy beliefs.

Collective psychological ownership: the construct

Scholars (e.g. Cooke, 2015; Gibson, 2001; Gibson & Earley, 2007; Weick & Roberts, 1993) have acknowledged that under certain conditions a group can develop a 'mind of its own'.

More specifically, Furby (1980) noted the existence of a collective psychology of possession; similarly Druskat and Pescosolido (2002) observed that collective notions of ownership are commonplace, noting that 'shared mental models among the members of a work team has a positive effect on team processes and effectiveness' (p. 284; cf. Klimoski & Mohammed, 1994; Levine & Moreland, 1991; Mathieu et al., 2000). Building off of these observations, informed by the psychology of possession and property, and current theorizing on PO at the individual level, Pierce and Jussila (2010) provided a theory of collective psychological ownership. They conceptually defined *collective psychological ownership* as 'the collectively held sense (feeling) that this target of ownership (or a piece of that target) is collectively "ours"' (p. 812).

Cooke (2015, p.416), in her discussion of team cognition, describes the emergence of this shared mental model as taking place through team members' interactions where they 'coordinate cognitively with one another, integrating ideas and creating new knowledge' (cf. Grand, Braun, Kuljanin, Kozlowski, & Chao, 2016). Unlike PO at the individual level, which resides in the mind of the psychological owner, CPO resides at the intersection of experiences, shared in both time and space among members of a collective around a particular target of ownership (e.g. tasks performed). Thus, CPO by its very nature is inextricably tied to context where group members (e.g. a work team), sharing their collective experiences, cognitively congeal with one another in their coming to a collective sense of possession (cf. Cooke, 2015). Similar to communications and marriage, two relational phenomena, CPO cannot be meaningfully understood at the individual level as the collective is the unit of analysis (Cooke, 2015).

Further insight into the emergence of CPO can be gained by borrowing from the work of Kozlowski and Klein (2000) and their discussion of variables with shared unit properties. Building off of their work, Pierce and Jussila (2010, pp. 812–813) envisioned CPO's emergent process as occurring in three stages. First, as objects become grounded psychologically, they become for the individual 'mine' as the individual finds themselves present in them (Kline & France, 1899), and they become a part of the 'extended self' (Belk, 1988; Dittmar, 1992). Second, the individual recognizes that not only are they psychologically tied to the object, but so are others. Thus, there is a shift in their personal reference from the self (i.e. a personal feeling that the target is MINE) to the group and the inclusion of others (i.e. the personal sense that the target is OURS). Third, 'interactive dynamics' (i.e. verbal and non-verbal language) 'create an emergent property that is more than the sum of the individual attributes' (Bandura, 1997, pp. 477–478); whereby agreement among team members emerges, and the construct is transformed from the individual to the group level and that collective cognitive/affective state that the target of ownership is 'ours' emerges. It is through this process that there is a transition from a state characterized as 'not us' to a state of 'us'; and the target of ownership becomes a part of the collective's 'extended sense of "us"', much as owned objects become a part of the 'extended self' at the individual level (Belk, 1988; Dittmar, 1992). Thus, it is through collective action and interactive dynamics (i.e. explicit communications; 'group processes involving the acquisition, storage, transmission, manipulation, and use of information'; Gibson, 2001, p. 122; cf. Chan, 1998; Gibson & Earley, 2007; Morgeson & Hofmann, 1999) around a shared object–experience relationship that the collective sense of ownership for a particular target (e.g. workspace) amongst team members emerges.

The distinction between PO at the individual level and CPO as a collective phenomenon, and recognition of the existence of both, is important as each manifests itself in the shared work environment. Organizational decisions around the type of work environment and policies related to resources can impact the formation of CPO. In turn, collective ownership has implications for the experience of the physical work environment by individual employees.

The roots of CPO

To be party to a collective sense of ownership the individual needs to experience themselves as a psychological owner, just not exclusively so. It has also been argued that the conditions that give rise to personal feelings of ownership are a necessary though not a sufficient condition for the emergence of CPO. Thus, one or more of the motives that underpin PO at the individual level (i.e. the motives for effectance, self-identity, home, and/or stimulation) needs to be manifest. In addition, it has been reasoned (Pierce & Jussila, 2010) that the social-identity motive plays a key role in the emergence of the collective sense of ownership.

According to Tajfel (1981) the social-identity motive is that part of the self-concept that propels the individual to experience themselves as being a part of a group, and to be recognized by others as a part of a particular group of people. Thus, for an individual to be party to claiming a particular target as 'ours', they must want to be part of those doing the claiming, and to be comfortable with others seeing and associating them with that group. Like the role played by other motives (e.g. effectance, home) underpinning the emergence of the collective sense of ownership, fulfilment of the social-identity motive is satisfying. Design plays an important role in the promotion of the social-identity motive and thus the development of CPO.

The routes to collective psychological ownership's emergence

Current theorizing identifies three routes (experiences, paths travelled) to this psychological state, placing each experience as a direct determinant to the emergence of CPO. These three experiences closely parallel the routes to the emergence of PO at the individual level, though the path is jointly, as opposed to solo, travelled. Thus, as members of a social system (e.g. work team) collectively recognize and experience that, they: (1) share and jointly experience control over a target of ownership (e.g. tasks to be performed), (2) have come to intimately know and collectively negotiate the meaning of that target, and/or (3) they have mutually invested their related selves into that target CPO manifests itself (Pierce & Jussila, 2010). Within virtually any context (e.g. work team, worker-owned cooperatives), each of these three proximal experiences is influenced by more distal forces. For example, within work organizations, self-governing work teams, enriched job design, non-routine technology, transformational leadership, and an organically designed organization are likely to play a major role. In addition, as we will discuss later in the chapter, there are a number of forces in the physical environment that support and hinder the development of CPO. There are also interesting dynamics between PO and CPO that we will discuss below. For example, office designs that foster CPO may reduce individual territorial behaviour, as members broaden those whom have access and rights to the object.

Emergent thinking about the relationship between psychological ownership and the physical environment

Building on our review of the extant PO literature, in this section we provide some thinking about new and as of yet unexplored roles and relationships played by PO within the work and organizational context. Specifically we address the connection between PO and design (noting that design includes architectural building design, interior design, and psychological and social conceptualizations of the physical environment). Adapting a view that people and the environment should not be viewed as separate entities, but rather as aspects of a single transactional whole (Altman, 1975), we present arguments positioning PO as both an independent and dependent variable in the physical environment–psychological ownership relationship. We also recognize that in many instances ownership feelings will also act as both a carrier and changer of the relationship between other variables within the work and organizational environment.

This section will be divided into three parts. First, we identify the primary targets of ownership that have been the focus of research at both the individual and collective levels of analysis. Specifically, we discuss how workspaces and buildings manifest as targets of ownership. Second, and by drawing upon two major reviews of the PO literature (i.e. Dawkins, Tian, Newman, & Martin, 2017; Pierce & Jussila, 2011), we comment on design criteria and issues that influence predictors of the sense of ownership that primarily stem from the physical work and organizational context. Finally, drawing upon these two literature reviews, we summarize the individual and organizational effects stemming from individual- and collective-level psychological ownership.

Work and organizational targets of ownership

The theoretical and empirical PO literature at the individual level of analysis has almost exclusively focused on two organizational targets of ownership, namely organization- and job-based psychological ownership (Bernard & O'Driscoll, 2011; O'Driscoll et al., 2006; Peng & Pierce, 2015; Ramos, Man, Mustafa, & Ng, 2014), with some exceptions, such as the exploration of ownership feelings for 'any object' (e.g. idea, tools, key relationships, work project; Brown et al., 2014a), change proposals (Baer & Brown, 2012), workspaces (Brown & Zhu, 2016), franchise brand (Hou, Hsu, & Wu, 2009), business ventures (Hsu, 2013), and ownership beliefs and ownership behaviours (Wagner, Parker, & Christiansen, 2003). There has also been some exploration of PO outside of the organizational sciences, with a focus on such topics as environmentalism, healthcare, information technology, lectures, franchises, entrepreneurship, and consumer behaviour. In the most comprehensive study of the relationship between the routes and PO to date, Brown and his colleagues (2014b) observed a positive relationship between all three routes (control, intimate knowing, and investment of the self into the job) with PO. They also provided evidence suggesting that each of these three route variables mediate the positive relationship between job design complexity and psychological ownership.

Workspaces are prime targets for ownership as they have the capacity to satisfy one or more of the motives that underpin this psychological state. As noted above, objects that have attributes of *visibility* and *attractiveness* are more likely to be targets of ownership because they get and hold the attention of the owner. In addition, objects that are *accessible* (i.e. openness, receptivity) facilitate the need for a place in which to dwell. Similarly, objects that allow the owner to express themselves and affirm their identity (i.e. attribute of *social esteem*), satisfy the need for self-identity. Finally, objects that are *malleable* contribute to the satisfaction of the need for stimulation, as well as the effectance motive and feelings of efficacy. Workspaces also vary in their desirability and attractiveness to employees and allow both the expression of one's identity and the ability to exert influence. Experienced control over the workspace, coming to intimately know that workspace, and/or the investment of the self into the workspace provide the paths down which the individual travels in becoming psychologically tied to that workspace. Through one or more of the conditions the workspace becomes a part of the extended self and feelings of personal ownership emerge. Recognizing the role of psychological ownership and how it is formed helps predict the types of connections that employees will form with different workspace arrangements. There is a range of typical workspaces in organizations and we describe the relationship between these types and PO in Table 4.1. The implications of these different choices will be discussed later in this chapter.

As discussed above, the emergence of CPO closely parallels the routes to the emergence of PO at the individual level, though the path is jointly travelled, as opposed to one travelled alone. Work on CPO has been largely centred on the job (i.e. the work that a team is called upon to perform; e.g. Pierce et al., 2017a; Pierce, Li, Jussila, & Wang, 2017b). We, however, believe that the building in which people work is another potential target of CPO. Architecture, as a symbol, carries a message about the owner and inhabitants and is used to inspire and influence. For example, the Supreme Court building in Jerusalem is revered by many as a symbol of justice. The contours of the building seem to shut out corruption and people gain a sense of pride and assurance from its presence. Similarly, corporate architecture is a way of infusing the corporation, its activities, and products with meaning and is important for shaping corporate culture. For example, the original design of the Volvo plant in Kalmar, Sweden, was rejected because it was too old fashioned. The new building was redesigned to reflect the values (e.g. democracy, creativity, and technical innovation) that the president wanted people to think about when they thought Volvo (Berg & Kreiner, 1990).

Architecture may facilitate identification with the organization as employees note that this is where I work, my place of work, and this is where we work and our building. As discussed above, for an individual to be party to claiming a particular target as 'ours', they must want to be part of those doing the claiming, and to be comfortable with others seeing and associating them with that group. While the architecture may not be malleable, members can come to know the building intimately and the building can be a source of pride that members want to be associated with, thus satisfying the social identity need of the organizational member, as well as their need for home (a place in which to dwell).

TABLE 4.1 Workspace type as a target of PO

Office type	PO space	Control	Investment of self	Intimate knowing
Private office	High	High	High	High
Cubicle	Moderate	Moderate	Moderate	Moderate
Open plan	Low	Low	Low	Low
Benching	None	None	None	None
Hoteling	Low	Moderate*	Low	Low

*Temporary

Physical context predictors of the sense of ownership

Observed predictors of individual-level psychological ownership

Reviews of the extant empirical PO literature reveal that several organizational factors have been found to influence ownership feelings. At the individual level there have been observations of a positive relationship with several sources of work environment structure: technology routinization (e.g. Pierce, O'Driscoll, & Coghlan, 2004), job complexity (e.g. Brown et al., 2014b; Liu, Wang, Lee, & Hui, 2009), management practices (e.g. self-management and participative decision-making; Liu et al., 2009; Asatyan & Oh, 2008; Han, Chiang, & Chang, 2008), employee stock ownership plans (e.g. Chi & Han 2008; Chiu & Lai, 2007), leadership (e.g. transformational, passive, ethical, benevolent; Avey et al., 2009; Avey, Wernsing, & Palanski, 2012; Bernard & O'Driscoll, 2011; Zhu, Chen, Li, & Ahou, 2013), autonomy (e.g. Hassen, Voordeckers, Lambrecht, & Koiranen, 2014; Mayhew, Ashkanasy, Bramble, & Gardner, 2007), and control (e.g. Peng & Pierce, 2015).

To understand how workspaces and office design affect the formation of PO, it is necessary to characterize key features of the building environment. Kupritz (1998) provided an analysis of the properties of buildings and separated these into field characteristics and barriers. Field characteristics are things such as corridors, breakout spaces, and neighbouring desks that may affect the ability to control one's environment and create a sense of home and are thereby likely to hinder the development of individual PO. In contrast, partitions and doors support the development of these paths and ultimately increase opportunities for developing individual PO. Both field characteristics and barriers directly affect the development of psychological ownership through the routes but also indirectly through changes in crowding and privacy.

As previously discussed, workspaces are targets for ownership. One of the paths through which these feelings develop is the personalization of one's workspace. The act of marking both allows one to express aspects of their identity to others while also exerting control over the object (Edney & Buda, 1976; Halpern, 1995; Wineman, 1986). As shown in Table 4.1, the ability to express oneself is limited in certain workspace arrangements, with private offices affording the greatest opportunity to express one's identity and arrangements such as hot-desking or benching (i.e. when employees are not assigned to a particular/dedicated workstation [e.g. desk], but work from any station that happens to be available at the time) providing (at best) temporary opportunities to express one's identity. Research has shown that personalization has been linked to increases in organizational identification (Knight & Haslam, 2010); however, it remains to be tested whether the act of personalizing one's individual space (thereby increasing PO) may decrease CPO as it signals distinctiveness (i.e. co-workers' differences), which may undermine social identity.

Changes in the design of office layouts are also likely to influence the formation of individual PO. Increasingly organizations are switching from individual offices to shared offices or cubicles in open floor plan designs. This spatial downsizing has several potential advantages for the organization, including reduced operating costs, increased work efficiency, and increased communication (Duffy, 2007; Pile, 1976). Fewer walls provide more floor space, allowing a higher spatial density of workers to the office. However, increasing spatial density is not without costs. Research on crowding shows that increasing spatial density decreases privacy (Becker, 1981; Oldham & Rotchford, 1983), which is the need to exercise control over one's accessibility to others (Altman, 1975) and reflects concerns about status and control (Vischer, 2008). With decreased privacy, workers experience decreased work satisfaction, involvement, and motivation (Dean, 1977; Marans & Spreckelmeyer, 1981). Moreover, people who share offices are less able to regulate access to themselves and their space, and more likely to perceive territorial invasions (Wollman, Kelly, & Bordens, 1994), which decreases job satisfaction (Rafaeli & Sutton, 1987). In addition to physical intrusions by other people, noises and smells (among other things) can be very stressful. The inability to express oneself and lack of control undermine the employee's ability to develop feelings of ownership.

Similarly, the move to alternative work arrangements such as hot-desking and telecommuting, which have created a more mobile workforce, may also influence the formation of individual PO. New office designs are now more likely to include breakout space, collaborative space, and contemplative space in contrast to the traditional workspace settings consisting of assigned desks and formal meeting rooms. This results in a more mobile workforce where people are not tied to a desk or even a building. Telecommuting, for example, purports a number of benefits to the organization, with six out of ten employers identifying cost savings as a significant benefit to telecommuting (Oseland & Webber, 2012). IBM, for example, claims that telecommuting has globally slashed real estate costs by US$50 million (Oseland & Webber, 2012) and 46% of companies that allow telecommuting say it has reduced attrition (Oseland & Webber, 2012).

This has implications for the organization and the worker as mobile workers will have fewer opportunities to develop PO to their workspace. As shown by Brown and Zhu (2016), ownership of a workspace is related to feelings of ownership for the organization. Both of these changes have significant impact on the ability of people to form relationships and may increase the territorial conflict from multiple claims. On the positive side, the agile or mobile worker may not be as affected by the design or lack of privacy because they have the ability to find and control the information or others' access to them. Thus, the design of the physical environment that creates agile and mobile workers may actually support PO towards one's job, as suggested by Brown et al. (2014b) in their study of the relationship between job design and PO.

Observed predictors of CPO

Two empirical investigations were found that looked at predictors of the emergence of CPO. In their construct validation work with CPO, Pierce et al. (2017a) reported observing a positive relationship between job complexity and CPO from both their Chinese and Finnish samples. In addition, Pierce et al. (2017b) observed a significant and positive relationship between CPO and team work complexity and team self-management. In addition, they observed that the three route variables (i.e. experienced control exercised over the job, intimate knowing of the job, and investment of the collective selves into the job) were significantly related to CPO. Finally, they reported observing that two of the three route variables (i.e. collective intimate knowing, and investment of the collective's selves) mediated the relationship between team work complexity and team self-management, and CPO. They speculated that the role played by power distance in the Chinese culture may have contributed to the failure to find support for the mediation effect of experienced control. In high power distant cultures, control is supposed to be exercised by those higher in the social structure.

Earlier we discussed the three routes to CPO as members of a social system (e.g. work team) collectively recognize and experience that they, for example, share and jointly experienced control over a target of ownership (e.g. tasks to be performed), and they have mutually invested their related selves into that target, CPO manifests itself (Pierce & Jussila, 2010). The design and layout of space can play a major role in the development and demise of these feelings. As above, we suggested that shared workspaces or communal type spaces may undermine individual PO, the move to shared workspaces and workspace arrangements such as benching may help facilitate collective ownership over a work area rather than a specific workspace. This is illustrated by a team of workers who worked in 'The Cage', as described in Richard and Dobyns' (1957) classic article in *Human Organization*. Employees often play a role in shaping the space in which they work, which may facilitate a sense of collective ownership. The workers in 'The Cage' moved furniture and office objects around to create a specific space that was for the members of their team. This would seem to create a sense of collective ownership to the space, but also reinforce the identity of the team – this conjecture is supported by the results observed when the team lost their defining space. When the company decided to relocate two divisions together on one floor, 'The Cage' was changed, and while the members of 'The Cage' were still a unit, they no longer had their own space – and the results were disastrous, as employee morale declined rapidly and work efficiency dropped. This example illustrates several important aspects of the design–psychological ownership relationship that we will discuss later in the chapter. The physical environment has the ability to influence the paths to PO, but in turn it is also impacted by employees' feelings of ownership to their workspaces and organizations. At the one end, architecture may seem far removed from the daily experience of an employee, but the symbolism of the building plays an important role in the relationship of the employee(s) and the organization. At the other end, crowding and privacy represent the consequences of design decisions that similarly influence the development of PO.

As with individual PO, flexible or alternative work arrangements also have an impact on the formation of CPO. Hoteling (e.g. the reserving of a desk or office space for some period of time) treats offices as public spaces, similar to a library carousel. The offices are on a first come, first served basis and are relatively void of identity, especially given that there are multiple users of any one office. Hotelers share an office with other workers, some who they know and others who are complete strangers, sometimes even working for a different organization. Hoteling may decrease satisfaction because people have fewer ownership opportunities or spaces to which they can become attached and express their identity. Similarly, telecommuting may actually weaken the ties that bind organizations and their members (Wiesenfeld, Raghuram, & Garud, 1998) and may undermine CPO because there is less social identity, limited shared understanding or common experiences (limited intimate knowing), and few if any opportunities to control and express oneself.

Observed effects of individual and collective levels of psychological ownership

While research on the role of the physical environment in organizations is limited, we draw from related research to suggest that creating opportunities through design that foster a sense of ownership is likely to positively impact a variety of outcomes, including satisfaction, organizational commitment, and performance.

Psychological ownership has been related to several work-related attitudes and behaviours. In the following, we explore specific outcomes that are related to the physical work environment and design choices that organizations make in creating working environments for employees. Design is critical in providing opportunities for ownership. When employees feel ownership, their needs at work are met and this results in a variety of positive outcomes. Having a workspace of one's own, for example, can help the employee regulate access to themselves, provide a mechanism for self-expression and increase their sense of control at work. These design choices, such as office layouts, flexible work arrangements, and workspace types, provided by companies affect the development of both individual and collective psychological ownership, prevent or allow the continuation of ownership, and in doing so thwart or satisfy various important needs, including effectance, expression of identity, and sense of home.

Design choices that provide opportunities for ownership will affect control and privacy (Bluyssen, Aries, & van Dommelen, 2011; Veitch, Charles, Farley, & Newsham, 2007), as well as the ownership of the workspace itself (Brown & Zhu, 2016). When employees lack targets for ownership, their needs are less likely to be met. For example, a study by Keeling, Clements-Croome, and Roesch (2015) found that mobile workers find it difficult to adapt to the office when they are there. Thus, having one's own space provides the feeling that one can control interactions and may negatively affect satisfaction. For hotelers and telecommuters, the strong desire towards marking spaces to create a sense of home and express oneself is evident. Employees may even try to get the same space repeatedly (Katz-Stone, 1999) and may mark the space with personalizations to express their identity while they are in occupancy. Marking may actually be good for one's wellbeing and sense of connection to the organization (e.g. Wells, 2000). For example, when residents of a psychiatric ward were allowed to personalize their territories, the social atmosphere in the ward improved (Gifford, 1997). Similarly, positive health effects were observed by Cram and Paton (1993) in their study of elderly women who were given the opportunity to decorate their nursing home living quarters with their prized possessions, which appeared to arrest some of the debilitating effects commonly associated with institutionalization. In the context of ownership these behaviours make sense, as the person tries to foster a connection and attachment to the space, as well as maintaining memories of a different time and space. If employees have specific spaces, this may reduce anxiety and conflict among employees. At a group level, this may also help facilitate positive interactions among employees (Elsbach, 2004). For example, neighbourhoods where owners personalized their front yards were more cohesive (Brown & Werner, 1985) and satisfied with their neighbourhood (Brown, Brown, & Perkins, 2004).

In contrast, by sharing an office or not having a permanent space of one's own, people are less able to regulate access to their space. This in turn may have detrimental effects for the individual and organization: 'if employees feel they cannot exert control through voice or other constructive means, they might try to demonstrate control in ways that are more destructive for the organization' (Ashforth & Lee, 1990; Folkman & Lazarus, 1980; Greenberger & Strasser, 1986). People need control over their immediate environment and decisions that directly affect them (Greenberger & Strasser, 1986; Wortman & Brehm, 1975). Indeed, a felt lack of control has many detrimental effects, including reduced motivation, stress-related ailments, and even sabotage or other forms of deviance (see Greenberger & Strasser, 1986, for a review).

Leaman and Bordass (1999) estimated that design, management and the use of space can account for up to 15% of an organization's turnover. For example, when a resident of a neighbourhood is not satisfied with their space or the larger neighbourhood, they make efforts to move (Speare, 1974; Stokols & Shumaker, 1982) or withdraw from the social functioning and contribution of the neighbourhood (Brown, Brown, & Perkins, 2004). Similarly, when an organizational member is not happy with their physical environment, and this likely extends beyond their own office (cubicle), they may enact efforts to find a better environment. Workplaces that encourage individual routes of ownership, such as expression of self, benefit from decreased turnover and absenteeism (Steele, 1986; Wells, 2000).

Psychological ownership may also buffer against the negative effects of crowding. In an effort to save money, organizations that downsize offices and other workspaces risk that the increase in density may also lead to crowding. Crowding creates a situation of overstimulation and may lead to a variety of negative outcomes, including reduced citizenship behaviour (Bell, Fisher, Baum, & Green, 1990) and increased conflict (Paulus, McCain, & Cox, 1981). On complex tasks, performance decreases when crowding increases (Paulus, Annis, Seta, Schkade, & Matthews, 1976), likely due to increased distractions and arousal (Sanders, 1983). Crowding also decreases motivation and persistence on complex tasks (Evans, 1979).

The choice to create opportunities (targets) to which individuals can exert control and express themselves may provide important buffers to increasing office density. Moreover, the creation of 'home' through a possession creates a psychological sanctuary against the lack of privacy and overcrowding that might exist at work. Organizational choices around the physical environment and design play a major role in shaping this relationship.

Design that affords ownership opportunities is also likely to lead to positive affect at work. We are particularly interested in the affective evaluation of an object (i.e. workspace) because we believe that the attitude someone has towards their owned objects at work can be a significant factor in their experience at work. As outlined by affective events theory (Weiss & Cropanzano, 1996), moods and emotions at work are considered mediating mechanisms through which features of the work environment impact subsequent attitudes and behaviours (Fisher & Ashkanasy, 2000). Similarly, we believe that objects in the work environment can engender feelings and that PO will be related to these feelings. These feelings towards objects in the organization may be an important part on an individual's evaluative experience at work.

These ownership feelings may also extend to help someone feel more confident and perform their job more effectively. Psychological ownership towards a workspace may confer benefits for negotiation (Brown & Baer, 2011) and decision-making (Taylor &, Lanni, 1981). Salacuse and Rubin (1990) were among the first to explicitly discuss the importance of location in negotiation and suggested that meeting in '(My) Place' provides a sense of familiarity, allows control over layout, and allows greater access to information.

On the downside, if employees have developed PO, changes to office design may be more disruptive to the worker and lead to more territorial behaviour. For example, workspace personalization and space appropriation behaviours increase when organizations move to denser and more open office configurations (Wells & Thelen, 2002). The powerful desire for one's 'own' space in the organization may lead people to claim space, which can result in conflict and territorial infringement. People with fixed offices are less likely to be infringed, but people who share offices are more likely to perceive territorial invasions (Wollman et al., 1994). As a result, people with PO may engage in territorial defending behaviours, including hoarding (Brown & Robinson, 2007; Webster et al., 2008), resulting in reduced creativity (Baer & Brown, 2012) and increased conflict (Brown & Robinson, 2011).

Collective psychological ownership experienced effects

Two empirical investigations were found that looked at effects associated with the emergence of CPO. As a part of their efforts to develop and validate a measure of CPO, Pierce et al. (2017a) observed several individual- and group-level relationships. At the individual level CPO was related to job satisfaction, affective commitment, organizational citizenship behaviours, experienced responsibility, personal initiative, and individual-level PO. At the group level they reported observing a positive relationship with group potency and supervisor ratings of performance effectiveness, and a negative relation with social loafing. In addition, a positive relationship between CPO and supervisor ratings of employee performance effectiveness has been observed (Pierce et al., 2017b).

Collective psychological ownership of space (e.g. workstations, commons) may facilitate protection, enhancement, and the decoration of that space with markers that express the group's identity. On the negative side, CPO may result in the polarization of the collective's behaviour towards increased risk-taking. Finally, we speculate that CPO may also lead to other negative outcomes when the sense of ownership gets disrupted, as evidenced in the previously described case of 'The Cage'.

Integration and application

Design has a major impact on work outcomes. A study by Oldham and Fried (1987) showed that that the independent and joint effects of the workspace characteristics accounted for 24% of the variance in employee turnover, 31% of the variance in work satisfaction, and 34% of the variance in discretionary withdrawal. Although these results are often discussed as direct outcomes from design, we believe that much of this can be understood through a lens of PO.

While the role and importance of PO has not been explicitly acknowledged in design, our chapter suggests that there is good reason to start designing to facilitate feelings of ownership. Historically a major motivation for design has been cost-efficiency and, more recently, to increase collaboration; however, our research and discussion presented in this chapter suggests a more complex relationship. Employees come to work with a variety of important needs. Given the amount of time people spend at work and, for many, the importance of work to a person's identity, the workplace is a critical aspect of a person's life. Design choices that increase density or have employees share desks to save money may reduce opportunities for ownership. Similarly, strategies to increase collaboration that force employees to rotate between spaces may undermine employees' ability to express themselves. As presented above, the formation of PO fulfils important human needs and allows employees to focus on their work and to feel a greater commitment to the organization. In contrast, when employees' needs are not met, they look elsewhere for employment. The choices that organizations make regarding work arrangements may undermine the formation of PO and thus indirectly and unintentionally undermine the employee's commitment to the organization.

The physical environment provides a dynamic palette for exploring organizational behaviour. The paths to ownership development are parts of this design and provide managers with insights into creating ownership and understanding employee frustration as a result of frustrated needs. We acknowledge that we have not exhausted the list of objects within this context to which the sense of individual or collective ownership could attach, while focusing on a few broad categories including the building architecture, interior office layout, and the employee's workspace(s). Our exploration applies to more than just the objects we have discussed in this chapter and, for that matter, beyond the physical environment itself.

Also, in large part, missing from our discussion are other forces or factors in the work and organizational context that spawn the emergence of PO. In simple terms, it has been argued that feelings of ownership are more likely to emerge under conditions of weak situational strength (Mischel, 1973), as it is under such conditions that the individual and work group have a greater opportunity to express themselves through the exercise of control and to invest themselves into different parts of the work and organizational context.

With this acknowledgement, we turn our attention to discuss additional directions for application and research. For managers and organizations, acknowledging the feelings that employees have towards objects in the physical work environment and how these feelings satisfy important needs is an area that calls for more research attention.

As organizations adopt approaches that increase the interchangeableness of workspaces, employees lose the ability to personalize and mark the boundaries of their surroundings. This has not been fully considered and our discussion of PO helps elucidate the importance of personal space, as it is one of the more malleable targets for ownership. Organizations need to be sensitive to the fact that they are expected to satisfy the needs of the employees, and those workplaces that succeed in doing so are likely to 'win the war for talent'. Managers that continue to discourage personalizations that would otherwise help root an employee have to be aware that this behaviour may undermine the employee's commitment to the organization. Conversely, the manager that understands the importance of PO will find ways to help mobile workers and those without permanent desks find alternative targets to develop PO towards. This is evident in looking at Table 4.1, where certain types of workspaces appear to be limited in the ability to foster feelings of ownership. We provided the typical setup, but with this information and understanding how PO is developed through the routes, organizations can develop strategies for employees to generate feelings of control by allowing them to book the same space, even in open seating offices. Similarly, creative organizations may find ways that allow individuals to invest themselves in their workspaces despite not having a private office.

From a research angle, we have to first acknowledge that, although rooted in theory and related research, many of the arguments we have presented need testing to verify. Extending from this, there are several other interesting research ideas that would also advance our understanding of the PO. Among these is to further explore the relationship between PO and CPO. Our review of the literature suggests that work arrangements that promote mobility, such as hot-desking, are likely to decrease an individual sense of exclusive PO, in the accompaniment of the emergence of CPO because everyone shares and uses spaces collectively. On the other hand, flexible work arrangements, including telecommuting or agile work, may decrease CPO because workers do not share a common workspace.

Research on PO and territoriality would also provide insights into how to promote feelings of ownership, but avoid some of the potential negative aspects of territoriality. Research in this area has already shown that while PO has benefits for how the individual feels, it can be negatively interpreted by co-workers (Brown & Zhu, 2016). Research by Brown, Crossley, and Robinson (2014a) identified a potential boundary condition of trust amongst co-workers as influencing when this relationship is likely to be more or less damaging. However, more research is needed to understand additional moderators as well as the relationship between CPO and collective territoriality. The physical environment is a great context for testing these relationships and exploring ways to solve these potential dilemmas.

In closing, we note that feelings of ownership can possibly attach to many different facets, material and non-material in nature, that make up the work and organizational context that have not been highlighted in this chapter. Among them are intra-organization social systems (e.g. work teams), and objective materials (e.g. instruments of work such as computers). Also worthy of consideration are relationships (e.g. my leader), personal responsibilities (e.g. job duties), mental processes (e.g. work attitudes and ideas), personal attributes (e.g. skills and knowledge), actions (e.g. work processes) and work outcomes (e.g. services rendered). There is a need for scholarship addressing many different aspects of the workplace that have been noted in this chapter.

Notes

1 www.washingtonpost.com/news/the-switch/wp/2015/11/30/what-these-photos-of-facebooks-new-headquarters-say-about-the-future-of-work/?utm_term=.fbdfa413a2b0. http://greenbuildingelements.com/2016/05/12/facebook-spends-269-million-headquarters/
2 As reviewed by Vischer (2008), in the context of the physical work environment physical comfort refers to basic human needs such as safety, hygiene, and accessibility (usually achieved through applying existing building codes and standards). Functional comfort refers to the degree to which the environment supports the users' tasks. Our focus is on a psychological comfort, which includes feelings of belonging, ownership, and control over the workspace.
3 Personal conversations with Chinese scholars Dr Dahui Li (University of Minnesota Duluth) and Dr Jianyou Wang (Nankai University, China, and the Confucian Centre, Glasgow, Scotland).
4 Personal conversations with the late Rudolph Johnson, University of Minnesota Duluth, librarian. Mr Johnson was born in Kirkenes in northern Norway of parents with Norwegian and Sami ancestry, and for a period of time he lived in Lapland. His grandfather was of the reindeer herder Porsanger clan of Karasjohka and he also had relations to the reindeer people of Guovdageaidnu.

References

Altman, I. (1975). *The Environment and Social Behavior: Privacy, Personal Space, Territory, and Crowding.* Monterey, CA: Brooks/Cole Publishing.
Ardrey, R. (1966). *The Territorial Imperative.* New York: Atheneum.
Asatyan, V. S., & Oh, H. (2008). Psychological ownership theory: An exploratory application in the restaurant industry. *Journal of Hospitality and Tourism Research, 32,* 363–386.

Ashforth, B. E., & Lee, R. T. (1990). Defensive behavior in organizations: A preliminary model. *Human Relations, 43*(7), 621–648.

Avey, J. B., Avolio, B. J., Crossley, C, D., & Luthans, F. (2009). Psychological ownership: Theoretical extensions, measurement and relation to work outcomes. *Journal of Organizational Behavior, 30*, 173–191.

Avey, J. B., Wernsing, T., & Palanski, M. (2012). Exploring the process of ethical leadership: The mediating role of employee voice and psychological ownership. *Journal of Business Ethics, 107*, 21–34.

Baer, M., & Brown, G. (2012). Blind in one eye: How psychological ownership of ideas affects the types of suggestions people adopt. *Organizational Behavior and Human Decision Processes, 118*, 60–71.

Bandura, A. (1997). *Self-efficacy: The Exercise of Control.* New York: W. H. Freeman.

Beaglehole, E. (1932). *Property: A Study in Social Psychology.* New York: Macmillan.

Becker, F. D. (1981). *Workspace: Creating Environments in Organizations.* New York: Praeger.

Belk, R. W. (1988). Possessions and the extended self. *Journal of Consumer Research, 15*, 139–168.

Bell, P. A., Fisher, J. D., Baum, A., & Green, T. C. (1990). *Environmental Psychology.* 3rd edition. New York: Holt, Rinehart, and Winston.

Berg, P. O., & Kreiner, K. (1990). Corporate architecture: Turning physical settings into symbolic resources. *Symbols and Artifacts: View of the Corporate Landscape*, 41–67.

Bernard, F., & O'Driscoll, M. (2011). Psychological ownership in small family-owned businesses: Leadership style and nonfamily-employees' work attitudes and behaviours. *Group and Organization Management, 36*, 345–384.

Bluyssen, P. M., Aries, M., & Van Dommelen, P. (2011). Comfort of workers in office buildings: The European HOPE project. *Building Environment, 46*, 190–200.

Brown, B. B., & Werner, C. M. (1985). Social cohesiveness, territoriality, and holiday decorations: The influence of cul-de-sacs. *Environment and Behavior, 17*, 539–565.

Brown, G., & Baer, M. (2011). Location in negotiation: Is there a home field advantage? *Organizational Behavior and Human Decision Processes, 114*(2), 190–200.

Brown, G., Brown, B. B., & Perkins, D. D. (2004). New housing as neighborhood revitalization: Place attachment and confidence among residents. *Environment and Behavior, 36*(6), 749–775.

Brown, G., Crossley, C., & Robinson, S. L. (2014a). Psychological ownership, territorial behaviour and contributions to collective performance: The critical role of an environment of trust. *Personnel Psychology, 67*, 577–485.

Brown, G., Lawrence, T. B., & Robinson, S. L. (2005). Territoriality in organizations. *Academy of Management Review, 30*, 577–594.

Brown, G., Pierce, J. L., & Crossley, C. (2014b) Job design, psychological ownership, and work effects: A test of a mediated model. *Journal of Organizational Behavior, 35*, 463–485.

Brown, G., & Robinson, S. L. (2007). The dysfunction of territoriality in organizations: Research companion to the dysfunctional workplace. *Management Challenges and Symptoms, 252.*

Brown, G., & Robinson, S. L. (2011). Reactions to territorial infringement. *Organization Science, 22*, 210–224.

Brown, G., & Zhu, H. (2016). 'My workspace, not yours': The impact of psychological ownership and territoriality in organizations. *Journal of Environmental Psychology, 48*, 54–64.

Burk, C. (1900). The collecting instinct. Pedagogical Seminary, 7, 179–207.

Chan, D. (1998). Functional relations among constructs in the same content domain at different levels of analysis: A typology of composition models. *Journal of Applied Psychology, 83*, 234–246.

Chi, N-W., & Han, T-S. (2008). Exploring the linkages between formal ownership and psychological ownership for the organization: The mediating effects of organizational justice. *Journal of Occupational and Organizational Psychology, 81,* 691–711.

Chiu, W. C. K., & Lai, G. W. F. (2007). Psychological ownership and organizational optimism amid China's corporate transformation: Effects of an employee ownership scheme and a management-dominated board. *International Journal of Human Resource Management, 18,* 303–320.

Cooke, N. J. (2015). Team cognition as interaction. *Current Directions in Psychological Science, 24,* 415–419.

Cram, F., & Paton, H. (1993). Personal possessions and self-identity: The experiences of elderly women in three residential settings. *Australian Journal of Aging, 12,* 19–24.

Csikszentmihalyi, M., & Rochberg-Halton, E. (1981). *The Meaning of Things: Domestic Symbols and the Self.* Cambridge: Cambridge University Press.

Darling, F. F. (1937). *A Herd of Red Deer.* London: Oxford University Press.

Dawkins, S., Tian, A. W., Newman, A., & Martin, A. (2017). Psychological ownership: A review and research agenda. *Journal of Organizational Behavior, 38,* 163–183.

Dean, R. G. (1977). *Equilibrium Beach Profiles: US Atlantic and Gulf Coasts.* Department of Civil Engineering and College of Marine Studies, University of Delaware.

Dipboye, R. L. (1977). A critical review of Korman's self-consistency theory of work motivation and occupational choice. *Organizational Behavior and Human Performance, 18,* 108–126.

Dirks, K. T., Cummings, L. L., & Pierce, J. L. (1996). Psychological ownership in organizations: Conditions under which individuals promote and resist change. In R. W. Woodman & W. A. Pasmore (eds), *Research in Organizational Change and Development, 9,* 1–23.

Dittmar, H. (1992). *The Social Psychology of Material Possessions: To Have Is to Be.* New York: St. Martin's Press.

Druskat V. U., & Pescosolido, A. T. (2002). The content of effective teamwork mental models in self-managing teams: Ownership, learning and heedful interrelating. *Human Relations, 55,* 283–314.

Duffy, F. (2007). Justifying place in a virtual world. In: *Connected Real Estate: Essays from Innovators in Real Estate, Design, and Construction.* Nottinghamshire, UK: Torworth Publishing.

Duncan, N. G. (1981). Home ownership and social theory. In S. Duncan (ed.), *Housing and Identity: Cross-cultural Perspectives,* (pp. 98–134). New York: Holmes and Meier.

Edney, J. J., & Buda, M. A. (1976). Distinguishing territoriality and privacy: Two studies. *Human Ecology, 4*(4), 283–296.

Ellis, L. (1985). On the rudiments of possessions and property. *Social Science Information, 24,* 113–143.

Elsbach, K. D. (2004). Interpreting workplace identities: The role of office décor. *Journal of Organizational Behavior, 25,* 99–128.

Etzioni, A. (1991). The socio-economics of property. *Journal of Social Behavior and Personality, 6,* 465–468.

Evans, G. W. (1979). Behavioral and physiological consequences of crowding in humans. *Journal of Applied Social Psychology, 9*(1), 27–46.

Fisher, C. D., & Ashkanasy, N. M. (2000). The emerging role of emotions in work life: An introduction. *Journal of Organizational Behavior,* 123–129.

Folkman, S., & Lazarus, R. S. (1980). An analysis of coping in a middle-aged community sample. *Journal of Health and Social Behavior,* 219–239.

Friedman, O. (2008). First possession: An assumption guiding inferences about who owns what. *Psychonomic Bulletin and Review, 15,* 290–295.

Friedman, O., & Neary K. R. (2008). Determining who owns what: Do children infer ownership from first possession? *Cognition, 107,* 829–849.

Furby, L. (1978). Possessions: Toward a theory of their meaning and function throughout the life cycle. In P. B. Baltes (ed.), *Life Span Development and Behavior* (pp. 297–336). New York: Academic Press.

Furby, L. (1980). The origins and early development of possessive behaviour. *Political Psychology, 2*(1), 30–42.

Gibson, B. G. (2001). From knowledge accumulation to accommodation: Cycles of collective cognition in work groups. *Journal of Organizational Behavior, 22,* 121–134.

Gibson, B. G., & Earley, P. C. 92007). Collective cognition in action: Accumulation, interaction, examination, and accommodation in the development and operation of group efficacy beliefs in the workplace. *Academy of Management Review, 32,* 438–458.

Gifford, R. (1997). *Environmental Psychology: Principles and Practice.* Boston: Alyn & Bacon.

Grand, J. A., Braun, M. T., Kuljanin, G., Kozlowski, S..W. J., & Chao, G. T. (2016). The dynamics of team cognition: A process-oriented theory of knowledge emergence in teams. *Journal of Applied Psychology, 101,* 1353–1386.

Greenberger, D. B., & Strasser, S. (1986). Development and application of a model of personal control in organizations. *Academy of Management Review, 11,* 164–177.

Halpern, A. (1995). *On the Placement and Morphology of Clitics.* Center for the Study of Language (CSLI).

Han, T-S., Chiang, H-H., & & Chang, A. (2008). *Employee Participation, Psychological Ownership, and Knowledge Sharing: Mediating Role of Organizational Commitment.* Paper presented at the Annual Meeting of the Academy of Management, Los Angeles, CA.

Hassen, B., Voordeckers, W., Lambrecht, F., & Koiranen, M. (2014). The CEO autonomy–stewardship relationship in family firms: The mediating role of psychological ownership. *Journal of Family Business Strategy, 5,* 312–322.

Heidegger, M. (1927/1967). *Being and Time.* Trans. by J. Macquarrie & E. Robinson. Oxford: Basil Blackwell.

Heider, F. (1958). *The Psychology of Interpersonal Relations.* New York: Wiley.

Hou, S. T., Hsu, M. Y., & Wu, S. H. (2009). Psychological ownership and franchise growth: An empirical study of a Taiwanese taxi franchise. *International Journal of Entrepreneurial Behaviour and Research, 25,* 415–435.

Hsu, D. (2013). This is my venture: The effect of psychological ownership on intention to re-enter entrepreneurship. *Journal of Small Business and Entrepreneurship, 26,* 387–402.

Isaacs, S. (1933). *Social Development in Young Children.* London: Routledge.

James, W. (1890). *The Principles of Psychology.* New York: Holt.

Kamptner, N. L. (1989). Personal possessions and their meaning in old age. In S. Spacapan & S. Oskamp (eds), *The Social Psychology of Aging* (pp. 165–196). London: SAGE.

Kamptner, N. L. (1991). Personal possessions and their meaning: A life-span perspective. In F. W. Rudmin (ed.), To have possessions: a handbook on ownership and property. [Special Issue] *Journal of Social Behavior and Personality, 6*(6), 209–228.

Katz-Stone, A. 1999. Office as hotel. *Washington Business Journal,* Jan 29 – Feb 4.

Keeling, T., Clements-Croome, D., & Roesch, E. (2015). The effect of agile workspace and remote working on experiences of privacy, crowding and satisfaction. *Buildings, 5,* 880–898.

Klimoski, R., & Mohammed, S. (1994). Team mental model: Construct or metaphor. *Journal of Management, 20,* 403–437.

Kline, L., & France, C. J. (1899). The psychology of mine. *Pedagogical Seminary and Genetic Psychology*, *6*, 421–470.

Knapp, J., Smith, B., & Sprinkle, T. (2014). Clarifying the relational ties of organizational belonging: Understanding the roles of perceived insider status: Psychological ownership, and organizational identification. *Journal of Leadership and Organizational Studies*, *21*, 273–285.

Knight, C., & Haslam, S. A. (2010). The relative merits of lean, enriched, and empowered offices: An experimental examination of the impact of workspace management strategies on wellbeing and productivity. *Journal of Experimental Psychology: Applied*, *16*(2), 158.

Korman, A. H. (2001). Self-enhancement and self-protection: Toward a theory of work Motivation. In M. Erez, U. Kleinbeck, & H. Thierry (eds), *Work Motivation in the Context of a Globalizing Economy* (pp. 121–130). Mahwah, NJ: Lawrence Erlbaum Associates.

Kozlowski, S. W. J., & Klein, K. J. (2000). A multilevel approach to theory and research in organizations: Contextual, temporal, and emergent processes. In K. J. Klein & S. W. J. Kozlowski (eds), *Multilevel Theory, Research, and Methods in Organizations: Foundations, Extensions, and New Directions* (pp. 3–90). San Francisco, CA: Jossey-Bass.

Kupritz, V. W. (1998). Privacy in the workplace: The impact of building design. *Journal of Environmental Psychology*, *18*, 341–356.

Leaman, A., & Bordass, B. (1999). Productivity in buildings: The 'killer' variables. *Building Research and Information*, *27*(1), 4–19.

Levine, M., & Moreland, R. L. (1991). Culture and socialization in work groups. In L. B., Resnicek, J. M. Levine, & S. D. Teasley (eds), *Perspectives on Socially Shared Cognition* (pp. 157–279). Washington, DC: American Psychological Association.

Lewis, M., & Brook, J. (1974). Self, other, and fear: Infants' reactions to people. In M. Lewis & L. S. Rossenblum (eds), *The Origins of Fear* (pp. 165–194). New York: Wiley.

Litwinski, L. (1942). Is there an instinct of possession? *British Journal of Psychology*, *22*, 240–251.

Liu, J., Wang, H., Lee, C., & Hui, C. (2009). *Psychological Ownership: The Importance of Perceived Control.* A Renmin University of China, Beijing China Working Paper.

Locke, J. (1690). *Two Treatises of Government.* London: Awnsham Churchill

Marans, R. W., & Spreckelmeyer, K. F. (1981). *Evaluating Built Environments: A Behavioral Approach.* Survey Research Center, Institute for Social Research, University of Michigan.

Mathieu, J. E., Heffner, T. S., Goodwin, G. F., Salas, E., & Cannon-Bowers, J. A. (2000). The influence of shared mental models on team processes and performance. *Journal of Applied Psychology*, *85*, 273–283.

Mayhew, M. G., Ashkanasy, N. M. Bramble, T., & Gardner, J. (2007). A study of the antecedents and consequences of psychological ownership in organizational settings. *Journal of Social Psychology*, *147*, 477–500.

McDougall, W. (1908/1923). *An Introduction to Social Psychology.* London: Methuen.

Mead, G. H. (1934). *Mind, Self and Society.* Chicago, IL: University of Chicago Press.

Mischel, W. (1973). Toward a cognitive social learning reconceptualization of personality. *Psychological Review*, *80*, 252–283.

Monks, R. A. G., & Minow, N. (2001). *Corporate Governance.* Oxford: Blackwell.

Morgeson, F. P., & Hofmann, D. A. (1999). The structure and function of collective constructs: Implications for multilevel research and theory development. *Academy of Management Review*, *24*, 249–265

O'Driscoll, M. P., Pierce, J. L., & Coghlan, A. M. (2006). The psychology of ownership: Work environment structure, organizational commitment, and citizenship behaviour. *Group and Organization Management*, *31*, 388–416.

Oldham, G. R., & Fried, Y. (1987). Employee reactions to workspace characteristics. *Journal of Applied Psychology*, 72(1), 75.

Oldham, G.R. & Rotchford, N.L. (1983). Relationships between office characteristics and employee reactions: A study of the physical environment. *Administrative Science Quarterly*, 28, 542–556.

Oseland, N., & Webber, C. (2012). Flexible working benefits collated evidence and case studies. *Occasional Paper*, 3, 12.

Paulus, P. B., Annis, A. B., Seta, J. J., Schkade, J. K., & Matthews, R. W. (1976). Density does affect task performance. *Journal of Personality and Social Psychology*, 34(2), 248.

Paulus, P., McCain, G., & Cox, V. (1981). Prison standards: Some pertinent data on crowding. *Federal Probation*, 45, 48.

Peng, H., & Pierce, J. L. (2015) Job- and organization-based psychological ownership: Relationship and outcomes. *Journal of Managerial Psychology*, 30, 151–168.

Pierce, J. L., Kostova, T., & Dirks, K. T. (2001). Towards a theory of psychological ownership in organizations. *Academy of Management Review*, 26, 298–310.

Pierce, J. L., Kostova, T., & Dirks, K. T. (2003). The state of psychological ownership: Integrating and extending a century of research. *Review of General Psychology*, 7, 84–107.

Pierce, J. L., & Jussila, I. (2010). Collective psychological ownership within the work and organizational context: Construct introduction and elaboration. *Journal of Organizational Behavior*, 31, 810–834.

Pierce, J. L., & Jussila, I. (2011). *Psychological Ownership and the Organizational Context: Theory, Research, and Application*. Northhampton, MA: Edward Elgar.

Pierce, J. L., Jussila, I., & Li, D. (2017a). Development and validation of an instrument for assessing collective psychological ownership in organizational field settings. *Journal of Management and Organization*, 24(6), 776–792.

Pierce, J. L., Li, D., Jussila, I., & Wang, J. (2017b). *An Empirical Observation of the Emergence of Collective Psychological Ownership in Work Team Context*. Labovitz School of Business & Economics, University of Minnesota, Working Paper.

Pierce, J. L., O'Driscoll, M. P., & Coghlan, A. M. (2004). Work environment structure and psychological ownership: The mediating effects of control. *Journal of Social Psychology*, 144, 507–534.

Pierce, J. L., Rubenfeld. S., & Morgan, S. (1991). Employee ownership: A conceptual model of process and effects. *Academy of Management Review*, 16, 121–144.

Pile, J. F. (1976). *Interiors: 3rd Book of Offices*. New York: Watson-Guptill Publications.

Polanyi, M. (1962). *Personal Knowledge*. London: Routledge and Kegan Paul.

Porteous, J. D. (1976). Home: The territorial core. *Geographical Review*, 66, 383–390.

Prelinger, E. (1959). Extension and structure of the self. *Journal of Psychology*, 47, 13–23.

Qian, J., Lin, X., Han, Z. R., Tian, B., Chen, G. Z., & Wang, H. (2015). The impact of future time orientation on employees' feedback-seeking behaviour from supervisors and co-workers: The mediating role of psychological ownership. *Journal of Management and Organizations*, 221, 336–349.

Rafaeli, A., & Sutton, R. I. (1987). Expression of emotion as part of the work role. *Academy of Management Review*, 12(1), 23–37.

Ramos, H., Man, T., Mustafa, M., & Ng, Z. (2014). Psychological ownership in small family firms: Family and non-family employees' work attitudes and behaviours. *Journal of Family Business Strategy*, 5, 300–311.

Richard, C., & Dobyns, H. (1957). Topography and culture: The case of the changing cage. *Human Organization*, 16(1), 16–20.

Rousseau, J. J. (1762/1950). *The Social Contract*. New York: E. P. Dutton.

Rudmin, F. W. (1994). Property. In W. Lonner & R. Malpass (eds), *Psychology and Culture* (pp. 55–58). Provo, UT: Association for Consumer Research.

Salacuse, J. W., & Rubin, J. Z. (1990). Your place or mine? Site location and negotiation. *Negotiation Journal, 6*(1), 5–10.

Sanders, A. (1983). Towards a model of stress and human performance. *Acta Psychologica, 53*(1), 61–97

Scott, W. E. (1966). Activation theory and task design. In W. E. Scott & L. L. Cummings (eds), *Readings in Organizational Behavior and Human Performance* (pp. 188–202). Homewood, IL: R. D. Irwin.

Seligman, M. E. P. (1975). *Helplessness*. San Francisco, CA: Freeman.

Shaw, A., Li, V., & Olson, K. R. (2012). Children apply principles of physical ownership to ideas. *Cognitive Science, 36*, 1383–1403.

Speare, A. (1974). Residential satisfaction as an intervening variable in residential mobility. *Demography, 11*(2), 173–188.

Steele, F. (1986). *Making and Managing High Quality Workplaces: An Organizational Ecology*. New York: Teachers' College Press.

Stokols, D., & Shumaker, S. A. (1982). The psychological context of residential mobility and well-being. *Journal of Social Issues, 38*(3), 149–171.

Swann, W. (1984). Self-verification: Bringing social reality into harmony with the 'self'. In J. Suls & A. Greenwald (eds), *Psychological Perspectives on the Self, 2* (pp. 33–66). Hillsdale, NJ: Erlbaum.

Tajfel, H. (1981). *Human Groups and Social Categories*. Cambridge: Cambridge University Press.

Taylor, R. B., & Lanni, J. C. (1981). Territorial dominance: The influence of the resident advantage in triadic decision making. *Journal of Personality and Social Psychology, 41*, 909–915.

Tuan, Y. F. (1984). *Dominance and Affection: The Making of Pets*. New Haven, CT: Yale University Press.

Van Dyne, L., & Pierce, J. L. (2004). Psychological ownership and feelings of possession: Three field studies predicting employee attitudes and organization citizenship behaviour. *Journal of Organizational Behavior, 25*, 439–459.

Veitch, J. A., Charles, K. E., Farley, K. M. J. & Newsham, G. R. (2007). A model of satisfaction with open-plan office conditions: COPE field findings. *Journal of Environmental Psychology, 27*, 177–189.

Vischer, J.C. (2008). Towards an environmental psychology of workspace: How people are affected by environments for work. *Architectural Science Review Volume, 51*(2), 97–108.

Wagner, S. H., Parker, C. P., & Christiansen, N. D. (2003). Employees that think and act like owners: Effects of ownership beliefs and behaviours on organizational effectiveness. *Personnel Psychology, 56*, 847–871.

Webster, J., Brown, G., Zweig, D., Connelly, C. E., Brodt, S., & Sitkin, S. (2008). Beyond knowledge sharing: Withholding knowledge at work. In *Research in Personnel and Human Resources Management* (pp. 1–37). Emerald Group Publishing Limited.

Weick, K. E., & Roberts, K. H. (1993). Collective mind in organizations: Heedful inter-relating on flight decks. *Administrative Science Quarterly, 38*, 357–381.

Weil, S. (1952). *The Need for Roots: Prelude to a Declaration of Duties Towards Mankind*. London: Routledge and Kegan Paul.

Weiss, H. M., & Cropanzano, R. (1996). Affective events theory: A theoretical discussion of the structure, causes and consequences of affective experiences at work. In B. M. Saw & L. L. Cumming (eds), *Research in Organizational Behaviour* (pp. 1–75). Greenwich, CT: JAI Press.

Wells, M. M. (2000). Office clutter or meaningful personal displays: The role of office personalization in employee and organizational wellbeing. *Journal of Environmental Psychology, 20*, 239–255.

Wells, M. M., & Thelen, L. (2002). What does your workspace say about you? The influence of personality, status, and workspace on personalization. *Environment and Behavior, 34*, 300–321.

White, R. W. (1959). Motivation reconsidered: The concept of competence. *Psychological Review, 66*, 297–330.

Wiesenfeld, B. M., Raghuram, S., & Garud, R. (1998). Communication patterns as determinants of organizational identification in a virtual organization. *Journal of Computer-Mediated Communication, 3*(4).

Wilpert, B. (1991). Property, ownership, and participation: On the growing contradictions between legal and psychological concepts. *International Handbook of Participation in Organizations: For the Study of Organizational Democracy, Co-operation, and Self-management, 2*, 149–164.

Wineman, J. D. (1986). *Behavioral Issues in Office Design*. Van Nostrand Reinhold Company.

Wollman, N., Kelly, B. M., & Bordens, K. S. (1994). Environmental and intrapersonal predictors of reactions to potential territorial intrusions in the workplace. *Environment and Behavior, 26*, 179–194.

Wortman, C. B., & Brehm, J. W. (1975). Responses to uncontrollable outcomes: An integration of reactance theory and the learned helplessness model. *Advances in Experimental Social Psychology, 8*, 277–336.

Zhu, H., Chen, C., Li, X., & Ahou, Y. (2013). From personal relationships to psychological ownership: The importance of manager–owner relationship closeness in family businesses. *Management and Organization Review, 9*, 295–318.

The authors contributed equally to this chapter, and the ordering of their names was determined by a coin toss.

We appreciate the contributions of our many colleagues who aided our understanding of psychological ownership and its presence in the work and organizational context.

5

EMPLOYEE SATISFACTION AND THE QUALITY OF WORKPLACE ENVIRONMENT

Jungsoo Kim and Richard de Dear

Introduction

Occupant wellbeing is deemed a key performance indicator of commercial buildings. Especially in so-called 'premium-grade' office buildings in Australia (PCA, 2012), making occupants feel comfortable in their workplace is widely regarded as an important performance target for the building's facilities management team. The underlying logic is that the environmental quality of the workplace has a significant impact on the employees' wellbeing, workplace satisfaction, and productivity. In effect, the largest proportion of building energy use is attributed to the provision of comfort indoors during the operation of building service systems (e.g. heating, ventilation, air-conditioning and lighting).[1] Creating comfortable indoor environments has compelling economic implications as human resources account for the largest proportion of total costs in the lifecycle of a building (Brill, Margulis, Konar, & BOSTI, 1985; Kats, Alevantis, Berman, Mills, & Perlman, 2003). A study reports that the potential savings and productivity gains from improved workplace environments (e.g. reduced absenteeism and health-care costs) amount to US\$20–160 billion per annum for the United States alone (Fisk, 2000). The observation of health symptoms such as headaches, dizziness, eye and nose irritation, fatigue and respiratory problems in workplaces has led to the term sick building syndrome (SBS) (WHO, 1983). The linkage between such health symptoms reported by employees and physical indoor parameters such as office noise, lighting, thermal condition, and air quality has served to heighten the awareness of workplace environmental quality (Haapakangas, Hongisto, Hyönä, Kokko, & Keränen, 2014; Robertson, McInnes, Glass, Dalton, & Burge, 1989; Seppänen, 1999; Wargocki, Wyon, Baik, Clausen, & Fanger, 1999; Witterseh, Wyon, & Clausen, 2004). Over recent decades, the topic of indoor environmental quality (IEQ) has generated increased research activity in response to organizations' awareness of the significance of workplace environments to well-being of their office workforces.

The way that people respond to the overall quality of a workplace environment is largely influenced by their perception of the various environmental aspects, such as thermal comfort, indoor air quality, noise, lighting, and office spatial characteristics (e.g. office layout, design features and aesthetics). However, the relationship between workers' overall satisfaction with their workspace, and the condition of individual environmental aspects within those spaces, seems to be very complex. How different environmental factors influence office workers' overall perception of their workplace is a long way from being fully understood. The IEQ literature is dominated by studies that concentrate on isolated effects of single environmental factors on office occupants' comfort, satisfaction, and wellbeing. These studies underpin definitions of comfortable or acceptable thresholds for each environmental parameter in the relevant standards or guidelines. On the other hand, there are studies indicating that, in real-life settings, occupants' perceived comfort is not explained deterministically by one single IEQ component (Bluyssen, 2010). Discrepancies observed in field settings between the perceived and the actual building performance on specific environmental factors supports this argument; for example, sometimes meeting the requirements of the relevant standards doesn't guarantee a reasonable level of occupant satisfaction (Arens, Humphreys, de Dear, & Zhang, 2010; Haghighat & Donnini, 1999). Leaman and Bordass (2007), based on their office occupant surveys, argue that occupants perceive the environment holistically, trading off good features against the not-so-good. This implies that a priority of different workplace environmental features needs to be established in order to figure out which has the most significant impact on individuals and organizations.

Indeed it is very difficult to anticipate or predict office occupants' attitudes about, and affective responses to, their surrounding environment. Sometimes poor condition of certain environmental factors doesn't necessarily translate into overall workplace dissatisfaction. This is perhaps because the factor was deemed unimportant by the occupants, or there was another very good feature in the workplace that was compensating for the poor environmental component. On the other hand, sometimes an entire workplace is roundly criticized because of the poor condition of just one particular environmental factor. Exploring the mechanisms behind office employees' environmental satisfaction leads to a series of enquiries: does every environmental component of the workplace contribute *equally* to an employee's satisfaction with the total work environment? Does an environmental aspect affect employee workplace satisfaction in *both* positive and negative ways, or only in *one direction*, either positively (satisfier) or negatively (dissatisfier), or in both directions but *with different gravities*?

Basic factors and bonus factors

The literature suggests that employee reaction towards the workplace environment is not always observed as anticipated because improvements to individual environmental conditions do not correspond uniformly to increases one's overall workplace satisfaction. That is, overall satisfaction is not just an average of satisfaction with each environmental dimension (Bluyssen, 2010), signalling nonlinear relationships: small inputs but much larger consequences, or vice versa (Leaman & Bordass, 2001). Subjective averaging (i.e. comparing good and bad features of indoor environment and performing trade-offs between them) could occur, making it even more difficult to understand the cause-and-effect mechanisms behind overall evaluation of the workplace environment (Humphreys, 2005).

In the discipline of marketing research, the general consensus is that quality attributes fall into three categories (Anderson & Mittal, 2000; Brandt, 1988; Kano, 1984). This three-factor structure of customer satisfaction, typically known as Kano's model, categorizes product qualities according to the direction of their effect on satisfaction. Adapting this three-factor satisfaction model to the office building context, workplace environmental attributes can be classified into three categories (Kim & de Dear, 2012): (1) *basic factors* ('must-have' and 'expected' factors are used synonymously in the marketing literature) are those that are expected or presumed, thus regarded as minimum requirements. Excellence on these factors doesn't necessarily improve satisfaction, but they can cause dissatisfaction if they are deficient in some way. Thus the magnitude of the impact resulting from under-performance is greater than the impact resulting from positive performance (negative asymmetry). (2) *Bonus factors* (synonyms include 'excitement' and 'attractive' factors) are not normally expected, so they can have a strong positive impact when these are fulfilled. Thus the impact on satisfaction resulting from positive performance is greater than that from under-performance (positive asymmetry). (3) *Proportional factors* (synonyms include 'performance' and 'one-dimensional' factors) impact satisfaction or dissatisfaction proportionally. When they perform well, end-users will be satisfied, and when they perform poorly, end-users will be dissatisfied.

In order to define the functional dependence of overall workplace satisfaction upon a variety of individual environmental qualities, the empirical test was performed on an office occupant survey (BOSSA[2]) dataset. BOSSA is an officially accredited occupant survey tool within Australia's building sustainability rating schemes, including the National Australian Built Environment Rating System (NABERS) and Green Star Performance. BOSSA's online questionnaire was administered to office building occupants, assessing their satisfaction with various workplace environmental quality topics such as workspace design and fit-out, thermal comfort, indoor air quality, visual comfort, and office acoustics. The survey respondents rated their satisfaction level with each questionnaire item on a seven-point bipolar scale (e.g. dissatisfied–satisfied), which was coded with numerical values ranging from −3, through 0, to +3 for the statistical analysis (Table 5.1). The analysis is based on a total of 756 survey responses (55.4% response rate) collected from 13 contemporary office buildings (13 organizations) located in capital cities in Australia. The participating organizations were engaged in various businesses, such as construction, financial services, professional services, public administration, and real estate.

TABLE 5.1 List of office employee survey questionnaire items used in the analysis

Environmental factor	Survey questions	Rating scale (7-point)
1. External view	Please rate your satisfaction level with the *external view* from you normal work area.	Dissatisfied – Satisfied
2. Access to daylight	Please rate your satisfaction level with the *access to daylight* from your normal work area.	Dissatisfied – Satisfied
3. Temperature in winter	Please rate your satisfaction level with the *temperature* conditions of your normal work area in *winter*.	Dissatisfied – Satisfied
4. Temperature in summer	Please rate your satisfaction level with the *temperature* conditions of your normal work area in *summer*.	Dissatisfied – Satisfied
5. Air freshness	Please rate your satisfaction level with the overall *air freshness* in your normal work area.	Dissatisfied – Satisfied
6. Noise	Please rate you satisfaction level with the overall *noise* in your normal work area.	Dissatisfied – Satisfied
7. Lighting comfort	Please rate your satisfaction level with the *lighting comfort* of your normal work area (e.g. amount of light, glare, reflections, contrast).	Dissatisfied – Satisfied
8. Amount of space	Please rate your satisfaction level with the *amount of space* available to you at your normal work area.	Dissatisfied – Satisfied
9. Interaction with colleagues	How do you rate your normal work area's layout in terms of allowing you to *interact with your colleagues*?	Dissatisfied – Satisfied
10. Visual aesthetics of workspace	Please rate your satisfaction level with the *visual aesthetics of your normal work area*.	Dissatisfied – Satisfied
11. Comfort of furnishing	Please rate how comfortable your work area's *furnishings* are (including chairs, desk, equipment, etc.).	Uncomfortable – Comfortable
12. Adjustability of workspace	My normal work area can be *adjusted (or personalized) to meet my preferences*.	Disagree – Agree
13. Visual privacy	My normal work area provides adequate *visual privacy* (not being seen by others).	Disagree – Agree
14. Perceived control	Please rate your satisfaction level with the *degree of freedom to adapt* your normal work area (air-conditioning, opening the window, lighting, etc.) to meet your own preferences.	Dissatisfied – Satisfied
15. Visual aesthetics of building	Please rate the overall *visual aesthetics of this building*.	Dissatisfied – Satisfied
16. Workspace overall	All things considered, how satisfied are you with the *overall comfort of your normal work area*?	Dissatisfied – Satisfied

In order to estimate the positive and negative impacts of individual workspace attributes listed in Table 5.1 on the employee's overall assessment of workspace, a multiple regression analysis was conducted by dividing the survey samples into three groups: (1) those who are highly satisfied with the IEQ factor (respondents who rated their satisfaction at the top two levels, i.e. +3 or +2 votes), (2) those who are highly dissatisfied with the IEQ factor (respondents who rated their satisfaction at the lowest two levels, i.e. −3 or −2), and (3) those who are indifferent to the IEQ factor (respondents who rated their satisfaction level in the middle of the scale, i.e. +1, 0, or −1). Then the statistical model enables the prediction of change in outcome (i.e. overall workspace satisfaction) due to a unit change in the predictor from the baseline category (i.e. from indifferent to either satisfied or dissatisfied). Thus the increase or decrease in overall satisfaction, depending on whether an occupant is satisfied or dissatisfied with a particular workspace environmental factor, can be estimated. This analytical approach has been frequently used in marketing research in order to identify nonlinear relationships between attribute performance and overall satisfaction (e.g. Anderson & Mittal, 2000; Matzler, Fuchs, & Schubert, 2004)

Regression coefficients representing positive impact (b_1) and negative impact (b_2) on overall workspace satisfaction, followed by the resulting category (i.e. *basic, bonus,* or *proportional*) of each questionnaire item are listed in Table 5.2. Environmental factors reporting insignificant regression coefficients for both b_1 and b_2 remained undefined for its category. Three questionnaire items had their impact on overall workspace satisfaction oriented towards the positive direction. These are 'external view', 'interaction with colleagues', and 'visual privacy', being only associated with increments in overall workspace satisfaction rating (i.e. classified as *bonus factors*). For example, an attractive view through a window can be beneficial to occupant overall comfort, but a poor quality or absence of view doesn't necessarily result in a decline in overall workspace satisfaction. In other words, window view only matters when it is deemed satisfactory. In contrast, six environmental factors (access to daylight, temperature in winter, temperature in summer, noise, amount of space, and visual aesthetics of workspace) exerted exclusively negative impacts on overall workspace satisfaction; their positive impacts were statistically insignificant. Therefore, these factors were categorized as *basic factors*. In other words, these qualities are minimum requirements for office building occupants. Therefore if a building fails to meet employee expectations on these factors, their workplace satisfaction will be significantly eroded. The remaining IEQ factors (air freshness, comfort of furnishing, perceived control, and visual aesthetics of building) had their impacts in both positive and negative directions with approximately equal magnitudes (determined by comparing 95% confidence intervals of b_1 and b_2), placing them in the *proportional factor* category.

Window proximity

In the previous section, access to outdoor view through a window appeared be a 'luxury' element of the workplace environment (i.e. classified as a *bonus factor*).

TABLE 5.2 Positive and negative impacts of different environmental factors on employees' overall workspace evaluation, and the resulting categorization into *basic, bonus,* and *proportional* group

Environmental factor	Regression coefficients		Category
	Positive impact (b_1)	Negative impact (b_2)	
1. External view	0.26** [0.09, 0.43]	N.S.	**Bonus**
2. Access to daylight	N.S.	−0.34** [−0.60, −0.08]	*Basic*
3. Temperature in winter	N.S.	−0.25* [−0.46, −0.03]	*Basic*
4. Temperature in summer	N.S.	−0.30** [−0.52, −0.09]	*Basic*
5. Air freshness	0.42** [0.24, 0.60]	−0.27** [−0.45, −0.08]	Prop.
6. Noise	N.S.	−0.21* [−0.38, −0.03]	*Basic*
7. Lighting comfort	N.S.	N.S.	–
8. Amount of space	N.S.	−0.50** [−0.80, −0.20]	*Basic*
9. Interaction with colleagues	0.22** [0.06, 0.39]	N.S.	**Bonus**
10. Visual aesthetics of workspace	N.S.	−0.29* [−0.53, −0.04]	*Basic*
11. Comfort of furnishing	0.17* [0.00, 0.33]	−0.29* [−0.56, −0.02]	Prop.
12. Adjustability of workspace	N.S.	N.S.	–
13. Visual privacy	0.28* [0.05, 0.51]	N.S.	**Bonus**
14. Perceived control	0.33** [0.10, 0.57]	−0.43** [−0.60, −0.26]	Prop.
15. Visual aesthetics of building	0.21** [0.05, 0.37]	−0.30* [−0.55, −0.05]	Prop.

(1) R^2=0.62 of regression model, Constant (b_0) = 0.47
(2) Significance level of regression coefficients: **$p<0.01$, *$p<0.05$, N.S.>0.05
(3) Lower and upper bound of Confidence Intervals (95%) are in brackets
(4) *Basic* (Basic factor), **Bonus** (Bonus factor), Prop. (Proportional factor)

In fact, the positive effects of view and sunlight through windows upon occupants' mood, satisfaction, and wellbeing have already been widely addressed in the research literature (e.g. Aries, Veitch, & Newsham, 2010; Boubekri, Hull, & Boyer, 1991; Markus, 1967). Indeed, empirical studies have implied that being close to a window can buffer other negative aspects experienced in buildings (Leather, Pyrgas, Beale, & Lawrence, 1998; Yildirim, Akalin-Baskaya, & Celebi, 2007). To explore further this question of how employees' perception of workplace environments changes depending on whether or not an external window is present close to their workspace, a subsequent analysis was carried out on the BOSSA survey dataset.

The questionnaire collected information about the distance to external windows ('3m or less' or 'over 3m') from each respondent's regular work area. Table 5.3 summarizes the mean rating scores for different environmental attributes, depending on the respondent's workspace location with respect to window proximity. The BOSSA questionnaire has overall questions on how employees perceive their productivity and health as being influenced negatively or positively by the quality of their workspace environments. In addition to the 16 survey questions presented in Table 5.1, these two overall questions (perceived productivity and health) are also included in the analysis. The occupant group with close window proximity expressed higher satisfaction levels for most of the parameters assessed. The biggest gap was observed for 'external view' and 'access to daylight' with approximately 1.5 unit differences in the seven-point rating scale, followed by 'perceived control', 'workspace aesthetics', 'overall comfort', and 'perceived health'.

Since windows are commonly regarded as the source of outdoor view and sunlight, higher satisfaction levels with 'external view' and 'access to daylight' from respondents sitting near a window has been confirmed. However, the results suggest that proximity to windows can positively affect occupant perceptions of many other, non-window-related environmental aspects as well. According to Table 5.3, it seems that workspaces close to a window are perceived by their occupants to be more spacious, aesthetically more pleasing, more comfortable, productive, healthy, and adaptive. This result is in line with that reported by Kaplan (1993) – the availability of a view influenced other aspects of satisfaction with workspace environment including job satisfaction, overall health, and sense of having control over

TABLE 5.3 Difference of group mean satisfaction rating (ranging from −3 = 'very dissatisfied' to +3 = 'very satisfied') for various workplace indoor environmental aspects, depending on window proximity

Workplace environmental aspects	Window proximity		t-test	
	3m or less	Over 3m	Mean difference	Sig. (p-value)
Workspace overall satisfaction	0.92	0.49	0.43	$p<0.001$
Perceived productivity	0.64	0.31	0.33	$p<0.01$
Perceived health	0.39	−0.02	0.41	$p<0.001$
External view	1.12	−0.27	1.39	$p<0.001$
Access to daylight	1.74	0.17	1.57	$p<0.001$
Temperature in winter	0.49	0.46	0.03	N.S.
Temperature in summer	0.54	0.53	0.01	N.S.
Air freshness	0.25	0.03	0.22	N.S.
Noise	−0.21	−0.19	−0.02	N.S.
Lighting comfort	0.86	0.59	0.27	$p<0.05$
Amount of space	1.55	1.30	0.25	$p<0.05$
Interaction with colleagues	1.12	1.03	0.09	N.S.
Visual aesthetics of workspace	0.72	0.26	0.46	$p<0.001$
Comfort of furnishing	1.04	0.76	0.28	$p<0.05$
Adjustability of workspace	0.29	0.17	0.12	N.S.
Visual privacy	−0.89	−1.23	0.34	$p<0.01$
Perceived control	−0.35	−0.89	0.54	$p<0.001$
Visual aesthetics of building	0.91	0.74	0.17	N.S.

the work area. Kaplan (1993) emphasizes on '*micro-restorative experience*' as the main reason for the view through a window having a positive impact with respect to workplace wellbeing. That is, even a moment's glance to outdoors can provide a respite from tasks and demands at work.

Gender difference

Providing an optimal workplace environment that can secure the wellbeing of a majority of office employees has been the primary goal of many organizations' facilities management practice, in particular in the context of large commercial office buildings in which individual occupants' ability to control their surrounding environments (e.g. operating windows, air-conditioners, or blinds) is usually very limited. What's often observed is that workplace indoor environments deemed satisfactory by a certain group of people may not be satisfactory to another. People often react in very much different ways under the same indoor environmental condition, leading to a presumption that various personal or psychosocial factors play a role in shaping employee perception of the quality of workspace environment (e.g. Haghighat & Donnini, 1999; Kostiainen et al., 2008; Lahtinen, Huuhtanen, Kähkönen, & Reijula, 2002). In effect, gender is a factor that has been widely investigated in the literature. Debates on the gender difference can be found in the research field of thermal comfort, indoor air quality, and sick building syndrome (SBS) (e.g. Cena & de Dear, 1999; Stenberg & Wall, 1995; Zweers, Preller, Brunekreef, & Boleij, 1992).

Kim et al. (2013) conducted a comprehensive literature survey on this topic. A total of 35 published research articles were included in their review, a majority of which were field studies utilizing questionnaire surveys with or without accompanying physical measurements of indoor environments. The study samples reflected office workforces in different continents (including North and South America, Asia, Middle East, Europe and Oceania), with sample sizes varying from 20 up to over 7,000 people. The results of their literature survey indicated that female office workers had higher prevalence of health symptoms in the workplace. Women were more likely to suffer from SBS symptoms such as fatigue, headache, and irritated eyes in their workplace environments than men. Furthermore, the results also suggested that the female office occupants expressed dissatisfaction with thermal environments of their workplaces more frequently than the male occupants.

A large-scale building occupant survey dataset was analysed to further explore gender differences in employees' perception of various workplace environmental issues (Kim et al., 2013). The survey database from CBE (Center for the Built Environment) at the University of California, Berkeley, was used for the statistical analysis. The database contained over 38,000 satisfaction ratings for various indoor environmental aspects, collected from hundreds of buildings in different countries including Australia, Canada, Finland, and the USA (Zagreus, Huizenga, Arens, & Lehrer, 2004). Kim et al. (2013) reported that the female group's satisfaction level was consistently lower than that of the male group across all IEQ aspects investigated in the CBE survey (Table 5.4).

TABLE 5.4 Difference of group mean satisfaction rating (ranging from −3 = 'very dissatisfied' to +3 = 'very satisfied') for various workplace indoor environmental aspects, between female and male respondents

Workplace environment aspects	Female	Male	Mean difference	Sig.
Overall satisfaction	0.83	0.86	−0.03	N.S.
Temperature	−0.37	0.18	−0.55	$p<0.001$
Air quality	0.10	0.53	−0.43	$p<0.001$
Amount of light	1.28	1.43	−0.15	$p<0.001$
Visual comfort	0.86	1.06	−0.20	$p<0.001$
Noise level	0.14	0.29	−0.15	$p<0.001$
Sound privacy	−0.89	−0.53	−0.36	$p<0.001$
Amount of space	0.93	1.04	−0.10	$p<0.001$
Visual privacy	0.50	0.68	−0.18	$p<0.001$
Ease of interaction	1.30	1.43	−0.13	$p<0.001$
Comfort of furnishing	1.02	1.13	−0.11	$p<0.001$
Adjustability of furniture	0.76	0.91	−0.15	$p<0.001$
Colours and textures	0.73	0.86	−0.13	$p<0.001$
Building cleanliness	0.97	1.17	−0.20	$p<0.001$
Workspace cleanliness	0.76	1.09	−0.32	$p<0.001$
Building maintenance	0.93	1.03	−0.11	$p<0.001$

The differences in the office employees' responses to various aspects of indoor environment, as shown in Table 5.4, suggest there is a discrepancy between the two sexes. However, before generalizing further, potential other factors that may have confounded the gender differences should be considered. That is, the frequently reported females' health symptoms or complaints at workplaces could be affected by other personal or occupational characteristics such as lack of control of work, job-related stress, and low job satisfaction resulting from low position within the organizational hierarchy. For example, it is known that work-related symptoms were the highest in clerical or secretarial workers, followed by technical or professional workers, and lowest among managers (Burge, Hedge, Wilson, Bass, & Robertson, 1987). Therefore, to take into account the effects of seniority and work characteristics, the potential confounding factors (age and type of work) collected during the background survey were included in the analysis. In the current logistic analysis (Table 5.5), the values of odds ratios (OR) represent the likelihood of expressing dissatisfaction with different workplace environment issues resulting from gender difference, adjusted for seniority (age) and work characteristics (an OR greater than 1 indicates that the event in question is more likely to occur in the experimental group compared with the reference group). Male gender was set as the reference (OR=1) in the analyses. Therefore, ORs reported in Table 5.5 indicate the probability that female employees express dissatisfaction with individual IEQ factors relative to their male counterparts. For instance, OR=1.84 for temperature can be interpreted as females being 1.84 times more likely to be dissatisfied with temperature of their workspace than males. The results shown in Table 5.4 indicated that female gender was associated with higher levels of dissatisfaction than males on all the workspace IEQ issues addressed in the survey, particularly indoor thermal (OR=1.84), air quality (OR=1.7) and cleanliness (OR=1.79–2.14) related issues.

Degree of enclosure: open-plan or cellular offices

In recent decades, the office work environment has transformed from cellular offices to open-plan configurations. By removing internal walls, open-plan offices promised tangible economic benefits, such as increased net usable area, higher occupant density, and ease of reconfiguration (e.g. Duffy, 1992; Hedge, 1982). The open-plan office has become the norm across the commercial property sector because of its occupational space efficiency – more people can be accommodated within a smaller space compared with traditional cellular offices. Without internal walls and doors to demarcate personal territories, large numbers of employees share a common environment – conducting conversations, making phone calls, sharing feedback, holding impromptu meetings, or concentrating on an individual task.

As the open-plan layout has become almost universal, its impact on organizations and their employees' workplace satisfaction and work performance has been studied. Numerous research articles have pointed out negative impacts of

TABLE 5.5 Results of logistic regression model for workspace dissatisfaction associated with gender (adjusted for age and work characteristics)

Workspace environment aspects	Odds ratios
Temperature	1.84*** [1.65; 2.05]
Air quality	1.70*** [1.48; 1.96]
Amount of light	1.56*** [1.28; 1.90]
Visual comfort	1.28** [1.09; 1.51]
Noise level	NS
Sound privacy	1.35*** [1.23; 1.49]
Amount of space	NS
Visual privacy	NS
Ease of interaction	1.35** [1.10; 1.66]
Comfort of furnishing	1.37** [1.12; 1.67]
Adjustability of furniture	1.53*** [1.29; 1.82]
Colours and textures	1.48*** [1.25; 1.73]
Building cleanliness	1.79*** [1.51; 2.11]
Workspace cleanliness	2.14*** [1.82; 2.51]
Building maintenance	1.30** [1.10; 1.52]

***$p<0.001$, **$p<0.01$, NS=Not Significant ($p>0.05$)

Note: Odds ratios (ORs) represent the likelihood of female employee expressing dissatisfaction with an environmental aspect (OR=1 for males as the reference). 95% Confidence Intervals (CI) for OR shown in brackets.

the open-plan workplace, including a significant decrease in occupant satisfaction (Sundstrom, Herbert, & Brown, 1982), increased distraction and loss of privacy (Kaarlela-Tuomaala, Helenius, Keskinen, & Hongisto, 2009), and perceived performance decrements (Brennan, Chugh, & Kline, 2002). Other studies have attributed sick building syndrome (SBS) to the open-plan office layout, with symptoms such as fatigue, headache, and concentration difficulties (Klitzman & Stellman, 1989; Pejtersen, Allermann, Kristensen, & Poulsen, 2006). Many studies report that internally generated noise, in particular irrelevant but intelligible speech from co-workers, negatively impacts performance on tasks requiring cognitive processing (Banbury & Berry, 2005; Hongisto, 2005). Furthermore, it is argued that exposure to uncontrollable noise can be linked with a fall in task motivation (Evans & Johnson, 2000). Employees in open-plan work environments tend to experience excessive uncontrolled social contact and interruptions, known as over-stimulation (Maher & von Hippel, 2005; Oldham, 1988), which can exacerbate negative reactions toward the workplace environment.

The open-plan layout was originally intended to facilitate communication and collaboration between co-workers, streamlining information flows within an organization, but there are also negative consequences. Acoustical problems such as distraction by unwanted noise (e.g. phones ringing, audible conversation, typing or other office-equipment noise) and lack of sound privacy have featured prominently in the research literature. A study by Kim and de Dear (2013), based on the CBE dataset containing 42,000 survey responses from office workers in more than 300 different buildings, reported that acoustics, privacy, and the proxemics issues (e.g. background noise, unintentional listening to nearby speech, and being seen by others) were the most problematic aspects of working in open-plan offices. In their study, people in open-plan offices showed considerably higher workplace dissatisfaction rates (survey responses falling into the lowest two categories on the seven-point satisfaction scale, i.e. 'very dissatisfied' and 'dissatisfied') than those in enclosed private offices. In particular, about two-thirds of the people in open-plan workplaces expressed dissatisfaction with the condition of sound privacy in their offices, while the dissatisfaction rate for people in enclosed offices fell below 10% on most of the survey items investigated (see Table 5.4 for the entire questionnaire items).

In an attempt to empirically quantify pros (facilitated interaction between co-workers) and cons (noise and privacy problems) of the open-plan working environment, Kim and de Dear (2013) evaluated the trade-off between the positive impact of 'ease of interaction' and the negative impact of noise and loss of privacy on the employee overall perception of the workplace. Their multiple regression analysis produced two regression coefficients (b_1 and b_2): b_1 increasing overall workspace satisfaction when the individual environmental aspect was perceived to be satisfactory, and b_2 decreasing overall satisfaction when the individual environmental aspect was perceived to be unsatisfactory (Table 5.6). The absolute value of the regression coefficients can be interpreted as the strength of each predictor's impact on employee overall workplace

TABLE 5.6 Positive and negative impacts of the environmental aspects on open-plan office occupants' overall workspace satisfaction

Predictor	Positive impact (Regression coefficients b_1)	Negative impact (Regression coefficients b_2)
Ease of interaction	**0.21****	−0.19**
Noise level	0.23**	**−0.41****
Sound privacy	0.08**	**−0.20****
Visual privacy	0.21**	**−0.46****

Dependent variable: Overall satisfaction with workspace, ** $p<0.01$

satisfaction. The analysis estimated the positive impact (b_1) of ease of interaction on overall workspace satisfaction was 0.21, whereas the negative impacts (b_2) of noise, poor sound, and visual privacy was 0.41, 0.20 and 0.46 respectively. According to this predictive model, when employees in an open-plan office perceive that their workplace environment improves their interaction with colleagues, but degrades quality of acoustics, sound and visual privacy, the disadvantages outweigh the benefits (their overall workspace satisfaction level shows a net decrease of 0.86 units, i.e. $0.21 - 0.41 - 0.20 - 0.46 = -0.86$). In the open-plan working environment, predicted decrements in overall workspace satisfaction due to unsatisfactory privacy and acoustic issues were bigger than the predicted increment accruing from ease of communication. This means that even when employees are satisfied with interactions in open-plan office environments, their overall workspace will eventually fall due to uncontrollable acoustical and privacy issues.

Conclusions

This chapter rests on the hypothesis that the significance of a workplace environmental factor differs depending on how it is perceived by employees. The empirical analysis identified nonlinear links (assumed causal pathways) between various environmental aspects and employee overall workspace satisfaction, which indicated that a certain amount of input doesn't necessarily translate into commensurately desirable output. Therefore, predicting overall workplace satisfaction level without taking into account nonlinearity of effects can lead to systemic over- or under-estimation of the significance of environmental aspects on overall workspace satisfaction.

Some environmental aspects demonstrated this differential impact on employee overall evaluation of the workplace. Those factors, namely thermal comfort, access to daylight, background noise, amount of individual workspace, and workspace aesthetics, showed negative asymmetry, becoming more critical when employees' evaluations of these factors was negative or below expectation (labelled *basic factors*). What this implies is that even the most vigorous effort to improve performance on a *basic factor* can't guarantee a corresponding improvement in employees' workplace satisfaction outcomes. For *basic factors*, the consequences of their negative impact outweighed their positive effects. Apparently employees refrain from praising the workplace for its excellent *basic* environmental factors, but they would be much more forthcoming in criticizing the workplace environment if it failed to meet their expectations on these *basic* dimensions. It seems that these factors are deemed as 'must-have' elements to fulfil employees' needs in the workplace. *Basic factors* do not figure as sources of 'excitement' or 'delight', adding richness to occupants' experience of the workplace. This implies that focusing on negative aspects can be more efficient for maintaining employee satisfaction in the workplace's environmental management practices. In contrast to *basic factors*, some other factors showing positive bias in their effects on overall workplace satisfaction were also revealed. 'External view' was identified as a *bonus factor*. External view through a window can be deemed to give office workers a pleasurable experience in the workplace, suggesting that a quality external view may mitigate or compensate for the negative aspects of a workplace environment. Satisfaction with external view from one's workstation significantly contributed to enhanced overall workplace satisfaction. Being near a window with a view outdoors also had positive effects on the occupants' perception of diverse environmental qualities unrelated to windows. Furthermore, those who had close proximity to a window perceived themselves as being more productive and healthy, compared with their counterparts without immediate access to an external window. These empirical findings suggest that close proximity to window is a strong contributor of employee well-being and satisfaction in the workplace. It appears that a window is a source of favourable workplace environmental experience, affording adaptive and restorative opportunities in an office building scenario and, in turn, maximizing satisfaction.

This chapter also explored the effects of employees' demographic characteristics (i.e. gender) and degree of workspace enclosure (i.e. cellular or open-plan) on employee perception of the various workplace environmental qualities. The comprehensive literature survey indicated the general consensus of previous studies that gender differences exist, particularly in sick building syndrome prevalence and indoor thermal discomfort. Statistical analyses based on the CBE occupant survey database strongly corroborated the previous research findings highlighting females' consistently lower satisfaction across all indoor environmental factors included in the analysis. The statistical model predicted that females are more likely to express dissatisfaction with IEQ than males, and that this tendency was most prominent for indoor air quality and thermal comfort, regardless of respondents' age and work characteristics. These findings signal that female employees can be more sensitive or critical to indoor environmental factors, particularly those issues that are related to a building's environmental service (heating, ventilation, and air-conditioning) systems.

This chapter also showed that the degree of enclosure in office layout plays a role in the employee perception of workplace environments. Enclosed private offices clearly outperformed open-plan layouts in most aspects, particularly in acoustics, privacy, and the proxemics issues. The statistical analysis based on the CBE occupant survey database confirmed the negative effects of open-plan layout typically reported by earlier studies, i.e. privacy loss, noise distraction, feeling of crowding, and unwanted social interactions and interruptions. The pros and cons of open-plan offices, quantified through a statistical model, suggest that the benefits of enhanced interaction between co-workers were outweighed by the penalties of increased noise levels and decreased privacy that come with the open-plan office configuration. Therefore these negative aspects resulting from an open-plan layout shouldn't be overlooked in strategic management of the workplace environment.

A series of empirical analyses introduced throughout this chapter indicated dynamic relationships between individual workplace environmental qualities and employee satisfaction. That is, they can differ between market segments (group differences), and they can change over time. Sometimes, a workplace quality deemed important to one group of employees is not very important to others. Sometimes, a quality deemed satisfactory to one group can be unsatisfactory to another. And sometimes a basic or minimum requirement for one group is an attractive bonus for another. Similarly, the expectations of the same person could change as time goes by. That is, an attribute once regarded as a bonus factor could transform into a basic factor as people become accustomed to it and take it for granted.

It appears that minimizing the gap between employee expectations and its perceived condition is the key to strategic workplace environment management. The three-way classification of environmental factors can help better understand those relationships. Focus on negatives for the *basic factors* is essential to *maintaining* overall workplace satisfaction levels, but striving for the positive *bonus factors* is the best strategy for *enhancing* satisfaction.

Notes

1 Heating, ventilation, and air-conditioning (HVAC) and lighting account for approximately 70% of energy end use in office buildings (DCCEE, 2012).
2 BOSSA is a post-occupancy evaluation tool developed by the Indoor Environmental Quality Laboratory at the University of Sydney (Cândido, Kim, de Dear, & Thomas, 2016).

References

Anderson, E. W., & Mittal, V. (2000). Strengthening the satisfaction-profit chain. *Journal of Service Research, 3*(2), 107–120.
Arens, E., Humphreys, M. A., de Dear, R., & Zhang, H. (2010). Are 'class A' temperature requirements realistic or desirable? *Building and Environment, 45*(1), 4–10.
Aries, M. B. C., Veitch, J. A., & Newsham, G. R. (2010). Windows, view, and office characteristics predict physical and psychological discomfort. *Journal of Environmental Psychology, 30*(4), 533–541.
Banbury, S. P., & Berry, D. C. (2005). Office noise and employee concentration: Identifying causes of disruption and potential improvements. *Ergonomics, 48*(1), 25–37.

Bluyssen, P. M. (2010). Towards new methods and ways to create healthy and comfortable buildings. *Building and Environment, 45*(4), 808–818.

Boubekri, M., Hull, R. B., & Boyer, L. L. (1991). Impact of window size and sunlight penetration on office workers' mood and satisfaction: A novel way of assessing sunlight. *Environment and Behavior, 23*(4), 474–493.

Brandt, R. D. (1988). How service marketers can identify value-enhancing service elements. *Journal of Service Marketing, 2*(3), 35–41.

Brennan, A., Chugh, J. S., & Kline, T. (2002). Traditional versus open office design: A longitudinal field study. *Environment and Behavior, 34*(3), 279–299.

Brill, M., Margulis, S. T., Konar, E., & BOSTI. (1985). *Using Office Design to Increase Productivity.* Buffalo, NY: Workplace Design and Productivity, Inc.

Burge, S., Hedge, A., Wilson, S., Bass, J. H., & Robertson, A. (1987). Sick building syndrome: A study of 4373 office workers. *Annals of Occupational Hygiene, 31*(4 A), 493–504.

Cândido, C., Kim, J., de Dear, R., & Thomas, L. (2016). BOSSA: A multidimensional post-occupancy evaluation tool. *Building Research and Information, 44*(2), 214–228.

Cena, K., & de Dear, R. (1999). Field study of occupant comfort and office thermal environments in a hot, arid climate. *ASHRAE Transactions, 105,* 204–217.

DCCEE. (2012). *Baseline Energy Consumption and Greenhouse Gas Emissions in Commercial Buildings In Australia.* Department of Climate Change and Energy Efficiency, Commonwealth of Australia.

Duffy, F. (1992). *The Changing Workplace.* (P. Hannay, ed.). London: Phaidon.

Evans, G. W., & Johnson, D. (2000). Stress and open-office noise. *Journal of Applied Psychology, 85*(5), 779–783.

Fisk, W. J. (2000). Health and productivity gains from better indoor environment and their relationship with building energy efficiency. *Annual Review of Energy and the Environment, 25,* 537–566.

Haapakangas, A., Hongisto, V., Hyönä, J., Kokko, J., & Keränen, J. (2014). Effects of unattended speech on performance and subjective distraction: The role of acoustic design in open-plan offices. *Applied Acoustics, 86,* 1–16.

Haghighat, F., & Donnini, G. (1999). Impact of psycho-social factors on perception of the indoor air environment studies in 12 office buildings. *Building and Environment, 34*(4), 479–503.

Hedge, A. (1982). The open-plan office: A systematic investigation of employee reactions to their work environment. *Environment and Behavior, 14*(5), 519–542.

Hongisto, V. (2005). A model predicting the effect of speech of varying intelligibility on work performance. *Indoor Air, 15*(6), 458–468.

Humphreys, M. A. (2005). Quantifying occupant comfort: Are combined indices of the indoor environment practicable? *Building Research and Information, 33*(4), 317–325.

Kaarlela-Tuomaala, A., Helenius, R., Keskinen, E., & Hongisto, V. (2009). Effects of acoustic environment on work in private office rooms and open-plan offices: Longitudinal study during relocation. *Ergonomics, 52*(11), 1423–1444.

Kano, N. (1984). Attractive quality and must be quality. *Journal of the Japanese Society for Quality Control, 14*(2), 147–156.

Kaplan, R. (1993). The role of nature in the context of the workplace. *Landscape and Urban Planning, 26*(1–4), 193–201.

Kats, G., Alevantis, L., Berman, A., Mills, E., & Perlman, J. (2003). *The Costs and Financial Benefits of Green Buildings: A Report to California's Sustainable Building Task Force.* Sacramento, CA: California Department of Resources – Recycling and Recovery.

Kim, J., & de Dear, R. (2012). Nonlinear relationships between individual IEQ factors and overall workspace satisfaction. *Building and Environment, 49*(1), 33–40.

Kim, J., & de Dear, R. (2013). Workspace satisfaction: The privacy–communication trade-off in open-plan offices. *Journal of Environmental Psychology, 36*(0), 18–26.

Kim, J., de Dear, R., Cândido, C., Zhang, H., & Arens, E. (2013). Gender differences in office occupant perception of indoor environmental quality (IEQ). *Building and Environment, 70*(0), 245–256.

Klitzman, S., & Stellman, J. M. (1989). The impact of the physical environment on the psychological wellbeing of office workers. *Social Science and Medicine, 29*(6), 733–742.

Kostiainen, T., Welling, I., Lahtinen, M., Salmi, K., Kähkönen, E., & Lampinen, J. (2008). Modeling of subjective responses to indoor air quality and thermal conditions in office buildings. *HVAC and R Research, 14*(6), 905–923.

Lahtinen, M., Huuhtanen, P., Kähkönen, E., & Reijula, K. (2002). Psychosocial dimensions of solving an indoor air problem. *Indoor Air, 12*(1), 33–46.

Leaman, A., & Bordass, B. (2001). Assessing building performance in use 4: The Probe occupant surveys and their implications. *Building Research and Information, 29*(2), 129–143.

Leaman, A., & Bordass, B. (2007). Are users more tolerant of 'green' buildings? *Building Research and Information, 35*(6), 662–673.

Leather, P., Pyrgas, M., Beale, D., & Lawrence, C. (1998). Windows in the workplace: Sunlight, view, and occupational stress. *Environment and Behavior, 30*(6), 739–762.

Maher, A., & von Hippel, C. (2005). Individual differences in employee reactions to open-plan offices. *Journal of Environmental Psychology, 25*(2), 219–229.

Markus, T. A. (1967). The function of windows: A reappraisal. *Building Science, 2*(2), 97–121.

Matzler, K., Fuchs, M., & Schubert, A. K. (2004). Employee satisfaction: Does Kano's model apply? *Total Quality Management and Business Excellence, 15*(9–10), 1179–1198.

Oldham, G. R. (1988). Effects of changes in workspace partitions and spatial density on employee reactions: A quasi-experiment. *Journal of Applied Psychology, 73*(2), 253–258.

PCA. (2012). *A Guide to Office Building Quality.* Sydney: Property Council of Australia.

Pejtersen, J., Allermann, L., Kristensen, T. S., & Poulsen, O. M. (2006). Indoor climate, psychosocial work environment and symptoms in open-plan offices. *Indoor Air, 16*(5), 392–401.

Robertson, A. S., McInnes, M., Glass, D., Dalton, G., & Burge, P. S. (1989). Building sickness: Are symptoms related to the office lighting? *Annals of Occupational Hygiene, 33*(1), 47–59.

Seppänen, O. A. (1999). Association of ventilation rates and CO2 concentrations with health and other responses in commercial and institutional buildings. *Indoor Air, 9*(4), 226–252.

Stenberg, B., & Wall, S. (1995). Why do women report 'sick building symptoms' more often than men? *Social Science and Medicine, 40*(4), 491–502.

Sundstrom, E., Herbert, R. K., & Brown, D. W. (1982). Privacy and communication in an open-plan office: A case study. *Environment and Behavior, 14*(3), 379–392.

Wargocki, P., Wyon, D. P., Baik, Y. K., Clausen, G., & Fanger, P. O. (1999). Perceived air quality, sick building syndrome (SBS) symptoms and productivity in an office with two different pollution loads. *Indoor Air, 9*(3), 165–179.

WHO. (1983). *Indoor Air Pollutants: Exposure and Health* (Vol. EURO Report). Copenhagen: WHO Regional Office for Europe.

Witterseh, T., Wyon, D. P., & Clausen, G. (2004). The effects of moderate heat stress and open-plan office noise distraction on SBS symptoms and on the performance of office work. *Indoor Air, Supplement, 14*(8), 30–40.

Yildirim, K., Akalin-Baskaya, A., & Celebi, M. (2007). The effects of window proximity, partition height, and gender on perceptions of open-plan offices. *Journal of Environmental Psychology, 27*(2), 154–165.

Zagreus, L., Huizenga, C., Arens, E., & Lehrer, D. (2004). Listening to the occupants: A web-based indoor environmental quality survey. *Indoor Air, Supplement, 14*(8), 65–74.

Zweers, T., Preller, L., Brunekreef, B., & Boleij, J. S. M. (1992). Health and indoor climate complaints of 7043 office workers in 61 buildings in the Netherlands. *Indoor Air, 2*(3), 127–136.

6

FITTING INTO THE WORKPLACE

The motivational implications of self-space identity compatibility at work

Mischel Luong, Kim Peters, Courtney von Hippel, and Mylyn Dat

The French writer and poet, Noel Arnaud (cited in Bachelard, 1964, p. 137), famously stated: '*I am the space where I am.*' In doing so, he implied that the spaces that we occupy are intrinsically interlinked with our identities – our sense of who we are. There is a growing body of evidence that supports this possibility. We know, for instance, that people decorate their personal spaces with objects to convey what matters to them (e.g. Graham, Gosling, & Travis, 2015). For example, a person who places a high value on family may fill their home with photographs of family members, while a person who places a high value on adventure may instead display mementos from their travels. We also know that people are reasonably good at reading identities from these decorative cues. For instance, observers are able to form accurate judgements of a target's openness, extraversion, and conscientiousness merely by looking at their bedrooms (Gosling, Ko, Mannarelli, & Morris, 2002; Perez-Lopez, Aragonés, & Amérigo, 2017). This suggests that people express their identities onto their spaces in ways that are informative and meaningful to those around them.

These space-crafting efforts are not limited to people's personal spaces (e.g. homes and bedrooms), as they have been shown to occur in a range of public spaces, including workplaces. In the office, employees have been observed to decorate their desks in ways that convey aspects of their identity much as they do at home (e.g. Byron & Laurence, 2015; Elsbach, 2003; Gosling et al., 2002; Wells & Thelen, 2002). For instance, while some employees decorate their offices with family photos, others decorate them with awards and diplomas. However, a desire to make efficient and flexible use of space or to create an aesthetic that reflects the organization's actual or aspirational identity, leads many workplaces to limit the extent to which people are able to craft their spaces – if they don't prevent such behaviours entirely (Goodrich, 1986; Worthington, 2006).

While the organizational implications of employees' personalization of their workspaces appears to be mixed (e.g. facilitating work motivation versus the creation of territorial boundaries that exclude colleagues), there is evidence that policies that prohibit or discourage the decoration of offices can have negative consequences, with workers reporting elevated levels of identity threat (Elsbach, 2003, 2004; Wasserman & Frenkel, 2011).

To the extent that workplaces limit people's ability to craft and choose their spaces, they may be a major locus for people's daily experiences of self-space identity incompatibility – of *not* fitting with the spaces where they are. Our aim in this chapter is to explore the underpinnings and implications of self-space identity compatibility for workers and their organizations. We outline a *Workplace Self-Space Identity Model* that argues that people are sensitive to the compatibility between their own identities and those that are symbolized by workplace spaces, and that the resultant perceptions of compatibility are likely to affect organizational identification and motivation. We also discuss one contextual factor that may moderate the consequences of self-space compatibility: the stability of the organizational context. Finally, we consider the implications of our model for an organization's capacity to attract and motivate a diverse workforce.

Workplace Self-Space Identity Model

The Workplace Self-Space Identity Model is summarized in Figure 6.1. This model argues that workplace spaces can activate mental representations that relate to a person's own identity as well as the identities of other individuals and groups who belong to the organization. Importantly, when these self-space identities are activated simultaneously, they are likely to be accompanied by an evaluation of their compatibility. Drawing on the extensive literature on organizational fit (Kristof, 1996; Kristof-Brown, Zimmerman, & Johnson, 2005), this model argues that perceptions of self-space identity compatibility should generally boost workers' sense of belonging and work motivation, while perceptions of incompatibility should erode them. While this suggests that organizations that can foster compatibility between the identities of their workers and those that are represented by their spaces may well reap benefits, this is mostly likely to occur in stable organizational contexts. In a changing context, self-space identity compatibility may foster identity inertia (a reluctance to engage in any actions that may erode the current state of compatibility) and thereby reduce the willingness of workers to engage with, or adapt to, the change. An implication of this reasoning is that the consequences of self-space *incompatibility* for organizations need not always be negative. In particular, when self-space identity incompatibility fosters identity reactivity (efforts to change the self or the space in ways that increase congruence), organizations may benefit from workers' efforts to adopt an identity valued by the organization or to bring about necessary organizational change.

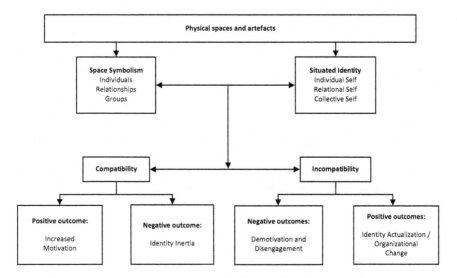

FIGURE 6.1 The Workplace Self-Space Identity Model

As an illustration, consider an example of a junior employee who has been employed as part of a large corporation's graduate programme. When she arrived, she was shown to her workstation, which is situated among a sea of cubicles occupied by her junior peers. When she has cause to visit the top floor of the organization, she is struck by the large offices of the C-suite executives, which are decorated with an austere dark palate, filled with plush furnishings of leather and heavy wood, and completely bare of any decorations of a personal or frivolous nature. To her, this space speaks to the power and status of these executives (as well as the myriad benefits of career progression). It simultaneously makes her very aware of her own lowly status. In other words, this space both verifies the importance and achievements of the executives who occupy it and tells this junior employee that she is very much out of place: *who she is* sits in stark contrast to *who the space is for*. In this situation, many workers may find this feeling of incompatibility discouraging, highlighting as it does the hierarchical nature of the organization and (perhaps) the absence of common cause between the executives and those they seek to lead. However, this particular employee aspires towards such elevated organizational heights herself and feels confident in her ability to reach them. Consequently, this event actually fuels her drive to make the sacrifices to her non-work life that will help her to get ahead and acquire this aspirational, high-powered identity for herself.

In articulating these dynamics, our Workplace Self-Space Identity Model contributes to the growing body of work on the psychological implications of workplace space in at least three ways. First, we integrate work in the social identity tradition (e.g. social identity theory; Tajfel & Turner, 2004; self-categorization theory; Turner, Hogg, Oakes, Reicher, & Wetherell, 1987) with research on workplace identity symbols (e.g. Elsbach, 2004; Ornstein, 1986) to understand how workplace spaces can activate identity constructs that relate to the self and the organization, and thereby inform perceptions of self-space identity compatibility. Second, while existing work has focused on the implications of space for workers' job satisfaction, we draw on work on organizational fit and belonging to extend our theorizing to worker motivation (e.g. Cheryan, Plaut, Davies, & Steele, 2009). Third, we consider the implications of our model for organizational change and diversity management. Here we argue that self-space compatibility may foster worker resistance to organizational change, including efforts to increase the inclusion of under-represented and lower-status groups within the organization. In the sections that follow, we summarize the empirical work that supports our claims in greater detail.

Workplace spaces activate identities

The central premise of the *Workplace Self-Space Identity Model* is that spaces are sources of meaning for those who occupy them. This is not surprising when one considers that the spaces that we inhabit, whether built or natural, personal or public, surround and scaffold the important experiences, activities, and relationships that make up the tapestry of our lives. Processes of associative learning mean that when people enter spaces (especially ones that are, or are similar to, familiar spaces), they are unlikely to experience them as a set of neutral dimensions and arrangements. Instead, they are likely to respond to their spaces in ways that are consistent with the nature of the experiences, activities, and relationships that they have previously experienced in them (or expect to experience in the future). In line with this claim, there is a rich history of scholarship that has examined the symbolic and cultural meanings that reside in various physical spaces, and the artefacts within them (e.g. Appleyard, 1979; Elsbach & Pratt, 2007; Gosling et al., 2002; Proshansky, Fabian, & Kaminoff, 1983).

Although this perspective has been relatively under-represented in organizational science (Warren, 2002; see also Kemp, Angell, & McLoughlin, 2015; cf. Vilnai-Yavetz & Rafaeli, 2006), there is a growing body of work that is exploring the symbolism of workplace spaces (by which we mean the organization's building, furnishings, décor, ambient conditions, and arrangement of objects and artefacts within it). Among other things, this work has shown that workplace spaces are perceived as meaningful by those who occupy or encounter them. For instance, previous work has shown that organizations whose lobbies contain artwork and magazines are perceived as warm and comfortable, while those whose lobbies contain authority symbols, such as emblems, flags, and restrictive signs, are perceived as exerting high levels of control and restricting worker autonomy (Ornstein, 1986, 1992; see also Ridoutt, Ball & Killerby, 2002). This corresponds with Earle's (2003, pp. 250–251) claim that 'the space an organization occupies is its physical manifestation . . . parallels can be drawn between the quality and character of an organization's office space and such things as the company's concern for detail and a propensity to cut corners'.

Organizational leaders are not oblivious to these symbolic possibilities, and in some cases try to design their workplace space in ways that they believe will express important aspects of the organization's actual or aspirational identity (Cappetta & Gioia, 2006). For instance, a recent article in *The Economist* (2017) describes how the ride-hailing firm, Uber, is attempting to counter its reputation for secretive and dodgy dealings by building an entirely transparent head office. Further, in what promises to be the most expensive corporate headquarters ever built, the donut-shaped Apple Park is described by its architect as a 'true utopian vision', and by Apple's CEO, Tim Cook, as an embodiment of the perfection and eye to detail that workers are expected to aspire to in their own work (Moore, 2017).

Importantly, there is evidence that organizational spaces not only convey meaning about an organization's culture, values, and aspirations, but also about the identities of the individuals and collectives who work in it. At the individual level, there is evidence that employees infer the attributes, values, and interests of their colleagues on the basis of their desk and office decorations (Elsbach, 2004; Gosling et al., 2002; Wells & Thelen, 2002). At the collective level, organizational spaces also communicate information about its social groups (especially those who dominate and are highly valued within it). For instance, Dale and Burrell (2007; see also Wasserman, 2012) have argued that many organizational spaces communicate a masculine (rather than feminine) identity, which signals that these workplaces are the primary domain of men (and those with stereotypically masculine attributes and interests). This corresponds with the arguments of feminist researchers (e.g. Rose, 1993) who have claimed that in their corporate work, architects (who are predominantly male) preference design elements that are directly or indirectly associated with Western masculinity rather than femininity (e.g. through the use of phallic symbols, straight lines, and angular shapes versus soft, round shapes). There is evidence that organizational spaces can signal other collective identities, too, including those related to nationality (e.g. European versus Western identities; Wasserman & Frenkel, 2011) and age (e.g. Gen X identity represented by the 'fun' and communal workplaces of Google and Facebook; Lamm & Meeks, 2009).

At the same time as informing an understanding of who the (valued) *members* of an organization are, workplace spaces can also shape people's understandings of who they themselves are. In other words, people's identities are *situated*, reflecting aspects of their immediate social and physical context (Alexander & Wiley, 1981). This claim is consistent with self-categorization theory (Turner et al., 1987; Turner, Oakes, Haslam, & McGarty, 1994), which argues that people can construe their identities at multiple levels of abstraction and that how people categorize themselves (and the meaning of these categories) is contextually determined. That is, a person's sense of self can be informed by a sense of who they are as a unique individual (i.e. a personal identity) as well as who they are as a member of a collective, such as a social group, role, or relationship (i.e. a social identity). Further, the specific identity that is most salient at a given point in time (informing how people understand and respond to a situation) is determined by the person's readiness to use the category as well as its relevance to the immediate social context (Ashforth & Johnson, 2001; Turner et al., 1994). For instance, while an individual could think of themselves as a witty individual, a loyal spouse, or a migrant when they are at home, they may instead think of themselves as an expert, a manager, or a team member when they are at work (e.g. Ashforth & Johnson, 2001; Ellemers, 2001).

While self-categorization theory and the related empirical literature has focused primarily on the role of the immediate *social* context in identity salience, there is some work that shows that physical workplace spaces can also shape people's identities. Specifically, Millward, Haslam and Postmes (2007) found that employees who worked in a hot-desking environment identified more strongly with the organizational identity than employees who had fixed desks that were co-located with the other members of their team. These latter workers in turn identified more strongly with their team. In another study of the impact of hot-desking, Elsbach (2003) found that the reduced opportunities for personalization of these spaces meant that some employees experienced identity threat associated with their inability to craft a space that captured the positive unique aspects of their personal identity.

In sum, this work shows that workplace spaces are meaningful. Among other things, these spaces inform workers' understandings of who other members of the organization are as well as a situated sense of who they themselves are. In the next section, we will explain how the capacity for workplace spaces to simultaneously activate self and organizational identities may affect a worker's sense of organizational belonging and, as a result, their work motivation.

The motivational consequences of self-space identity compatibility

We propose that workers will be highly sensitive to the congruence between the self-space identities that are activated by a particular workplace space. This expectation is based on the extensive body of work that has shown that people are sensitive to the degree of fit between their personal qualities and their work environment. People who perceive that their personal qualities (their attributes, values, and abilities) are congruent with relevant aspects of the organizational environment experience a range of positive workplace consequences (Kristof, 1996; Kristof-Brown & Guay, 2011; Edwards, Caplan, & Van Harrison, 1998). For instance, people who perceive their values as compatible with those of the organization are especially attracted to the organization and likely to remain within it (e.g. Devendorf & Highhouse, 2008; Lane & Gibbons, 2007; Moss & Frieze, 1993; Schneider, 1987). In a similar way, workers who perceive that their interests and abilities are congruent with the requirements of their job express greater levels of job satisfaction and motivation (e.g. Kristof-Brown et al., 2005).

Building on this work, we suggest that workers will attend to the congruence between their situated identity and the identities symbolized by the workplace space and that judgements of high levels of congruence will inform feelings of comfort and belonging – *of fitting into the space*. A sense of incongruence will instead inform a sense of discomfort and insecurity – *of being out of place*. Evidence for this possibility is provided by Wasserman and Frenkel (2011), who described how the relocation of the Israeli Ministry of Foreign Affairs from a Kibbutz-like building to a modern European one was perceived by some employees as a rejection of core aspects of their Israeli identity, reducing their sense of comfort and belonging at work. Similar patterns have been noted in the context of religious spaces. Here, there is evidence that Christians have higher self-esteem when they are placed in cathedrals rather than mosques, and that Catholic students experience less negative affect when they are in rooms that include prominent depictions of the crucifix (Bilewicz & Klebaniuk, 2013; Ysseldyk, Haslam, & Morton, 2016).

If self-space identity congruence does affect belongingness in these ways, theories in the self-determination and self-categorization traditions suggest that these congruence perceptions are likely to have important motivational consequences. Specifically, according to self-determination theory, the need to belong is a fundamental human motivation (Baumeister & Leary, 1995; Deci & Ryan, 2002; Maslow, 1943). According to self-categorization theory, perceptions of belonging increase the likelihood that people will identify with a given social group, and subsequently internalize its goals and norms (e.g. Tajfel & Turner, 1979; see also Ellemers, De Gilder, & Haslam, 2004; Jetten, Spears, & Manstead, 1996; Noel, Wann, & Branscombe, 1995). In line with this, there is evidence that junior surgeons and marine commando recruits who have greater feelings of belonging are more motivated in their careers, and less likely to consider opting out from them (Peters, Ryan, Haslam, & Fernandes, 2012; Peters, Ryan, & Haslam, 2015). Importantly, there is some evidence that interventions that increased feelings of belonging among students (for instance, by normalizing the hard work that is required to succeed) and policewomen (by informing them that their leadership style was similar to leading police officers) boosted self-reported career motivation and performance (Peters, Haslam, Ryan, & Fonseca, 2013; Smith, Lewis, Hawthorne, & Hodges, 2013; Walton & Cohen, 2011). These dynamics can also account for findings that casual staff, who are less likely to feel that they belong in their organization, are less motivated than full-time staff (De Gilder, 2003; Veenstra, Haslam, & Reynolds, 2004), pointing to some deleterious consequences of a lack of belonging.

In sum, this theoretical and empirical work leads us to expect that workers who perceive high compatibility between their own identity and those symbolized by the workplace space will experience a sense of belonging that will motivate them to achieve the organization's goals. Although there is to our knowledge no direct evidence for these claims, there is some indirect evidence that is consistent with the possibility that self-space identity compatibility may fuel motivation. For example, there is a well-established home advantage for sporting teams, who are more likely to win when they play at their home ground than when they play away (Loughead, Carron, Bray, & Kim, 2003). A recent laboratory study also found some support for the possibility that working in spaces that maximize self-space identity congruence may boost task productivity (Greenaway, Thai, Haslam, & Murphy, 2016). Finally, a large-scale survey by the American Society of Interior Designers (Earle, 2003) found that the company's physical workplace impacted applicants' decisions to accept a job offer, and employees' decisions to remain within the organization. Further, this survey found that workers who were more satisfied with their organization's workplace space were also more satisfied with their job. Although this study is not able to speak to the specific role of self-space identity compatibility, it does show that workers' evaluations of their workplace space matter for important organizational behaviours.

While our argument thus far suggests that self-space identity compatibility will have positive motivational (and thus performance) consequences, there is reason to expect that many workplaces actively undermine this compatibility. This can be understood by considering two aspects of organizational life: the layout of modern office space and the strong tradition of managerial control over the design and decoration of workplaces (for reviews see Knight & Haslam, 2010a, 2010b). Contemporary workplaces can be divided into two major office environments: the conventional office and 'lean' open-plan office configurations (Danielsson & Bodin, 2009; Haslam & Knight, 2010). Where conventional offices comprise individual offices or, at a minimum, separate cubicles that are separated with partitions, open-plan offices have few, if any, interior boundaries or partitions between employees. While conventional offices provide opportunities for identity expression, open-plan offices are usually 'lean' spaces devoid of extraneous non-work-related artefacts, such as photographs or other personal decorative items (Danielsson & Bodin, 2009; Haslam & Knight, 2010). The cost-efficiency of open-plan offices means that they are the office configuration of choice, despite consistent findings that employees in such spaces express a lack of privacy, reduced satisfaction with their physical work environment, and lower levels of satisfaction with and productivity in their job (e.g. Danielsson & Bodin, 2009; Davis, 1984; Haslam & Knight, 2010; De Croon, Sluiter, Kuijer, & Frings-Dresen, 2005).

In addition, as discussed above, organizations often seek to design their workplace spaces in order to convey their culture, values, and identity (or at least the culture that they would like to encourage). In these cases, managers may want to exert control over the space to ensure that employees keep to 'message'. Thus, by designing workplace spaces in a top–down fashion with little concern to the identities of those who occupy them, and limiting opportunities for workers to express their identities, organizations may be eroding workers' perceptions of self-space compatibility and feelings of belonging. To the extent that this also erodes workers' identification with the organization and motivation to achieve its goals, this may have negative performance implications. In the next section, we consider the possibility that the beneficial impacts of self-space compatibility may be most apparent in stable organizational contexts, and that in times of change, there may be some benefits to self-space incompatibility.

Self-space identity incongruity in times of change

Contemporary organizations are faced with unprecedented pressures to adapt to volatile, increasingly connected economies. Organizations who are able to change in ways that maintain or increase their alignment with their environment are more likely to secure long-term performance and survival (e.g. Audia, Locke, & Smith, 2000; Dixon, Meyer & Day, 2010). However, attempts to change often fail, and one of the major factors is an organization's failure to successfully engage their workers in the change (e.g. Armenakis & Harris, 2009; Rafferty & Restubog, 2010). While a number of factors are implicated in workers' resistance to change, including uncertainty and concerns around job security, there is evidence that identity threat can play a major role. In particular, workers who perceive that the change will negatively affect a valued aspect of their identity are particularly likely to resist the change (e.g. Amiot, Terry, Jimmieson, & Callan, 2006; Armstrong-Stassen, 2005). This work suggests that employees may be resistant to organizational change if it threatens the identities that underpin their perceptions of self-space identity compatibility (and informs their sense of belonging in the organizational space). In this way, we suggest that a consequence of self-space congruence may be *identity inertia*. In an illustration of such a process, Wasserman and Frenkel (2011) described how employees of the Israeli Ministry of Foreign Affairs ignored rules around the decoration of their new building in order to introduce artefacts (e.g. a Persian carpet, strong colours) that reinforced the non-Ashkenazi Jewish identity that the organization, through its new space, was attempting to weaken. This case study suggests that organizations that seek to change compatible spaces are likely to encounter a degree of resistance on the part of workers, which may promote organizational disidentification and departure.

A corollary of the above is that self-space incongruity may be advantageous in a changing environment. This is because incongruity may promote *identity reactivity* where workers seek to resolve the incongruity (and sense of a lack of belonging) by changing who they are in the workplace space, or which identities are represented by the space. For instance, where self-space identity incongruence reflects a gap between the self and aspirational organizational identities (i.e. identities that the worker perceives as desirable), workers may seek to change their own identity in ways that allow them to actualize these desired identities (Markus & Nurius, 1986; see also Ashforth & Schinoff, 2016). In the organizational literature there is evidence that workers who have such desired identities in the workplace are more motivated to grow in their role and may attain high levels of achievement (Strauss, Griffin, & Parker, 2012; Strauss & Parker, 2015). However, whether workers are able to sustain their efforts to realize a desired identity is likely to depend on their self-efficacy and the social validation that they receive in the process (Ashforth & Schinoff, 2016). For individuals who do not receive social validation, particularly after sustained efforts, we would expect the more typical self-space incompatibility demotivation dynamics.

Another response to self-space identity incompatibility is workplace crafting. For instance, employees who feel low self-space identity congruence may seek to buffer against this threat by projecting their identity outwards onto their work-place space, thus achieving local identity compatibility (e.g. Droseltis & Vignoles, 2010). One common way of doing this is by personalizing the workspace with artefacts that reflect the worker's identity, whether this is related to the workplace (e.g. in the form of certificates, awards) or non-work identities (e.g. related to hobbies, sports club membership, family). Indeed, there is evidence that the major-ity of workers exert significant effort in personalizing their workplaces (Byron & Laurence, 2015; Sundstrom & Sundstrom, 1986; Wells & Thelen, 2002), even in hot-desking situations (Brunia & Hartjes-Gosselink, 2009). There is also evi-dence that such personalization may increase workers' sense of control at work, and even help them to cope with work-related stress (Wells, Thelen, & Ruark, 2007). Although the empirical literature described here is mostly concerned with the local implications of desk decorations, it is possible that such space-crafting could have broader implications for cultural change within the organization. For instance, if workers in a particular area changed their space in ways that captured desirable organizational identity (e.g. one that values diversity and inclusion) this could impact on the organization and future space-crafting in a bottom–up way.

The change dynamics that we have described above are quite general, and we suggest that they can be relevant to workplace diversity too. In particular, organi-zations not only have to cope with rapid changes in the competitive landscape and technology; they also need to cope with transformations in the composition of their workforce. In Western contexts, organizations have become increasingly diverse, with white males no longer a majority in most US workplaces (Toossi, 2012). If organizations are going to capitalize on the benefits of diversity, they need to consider whether their physical spaces foster a sense of belonging among *all* employees. For example, posting conference social event posters that depict women in a sexualized fashion (Biernat & Hawley, 2017), and 'creative spaces' focusing on foosball and ping-pong, are examples of how workspaces may (unin-tentionally) make some employees feel marginalized (see also Cheryan, Meltzoff, & Kim, 2011; Cheryan et al., 2009). Such physical aspects of the workspace likely explain why majority employees tend to view their workplace as more inclu-sive and supportive than they are perceived by minority employees (Mor Barak, Cherin, & Berkman, 1998). If workspaces are designed with majority employees in mind, their experience of the workplace will inevitably be more positive. It is also the case that as minority groups become more prevalent in organizations and attempt to craft the workplace space so that it better reflects who they are, majority group members and organizational leaders may exhibit identity inertia and actively resist such attempts. It behoves diversity practitioners to consider the important role that workplace spaces can play in the identity responses of majority and minor-ity members, and consequently their feelings of belonging.

Conclusion

Physical spaces are imbued with symbolic meaning, which impact our everyday psychological processes, functioning, and identity experiences; workplaces are no exception. To our knowledge, there is no general framework of how these processes (and their implications for worker and organizational identities) impact an employees' belonging in the workplace. To bridge this gap, we have presented the *Workplace Self-Space Identity Model*, which describes the process of evaluating identity fit in a given environment. We suggest that high self-space compatibility is important for employee motivation, while low self-space compatibility can prompt employees to craft their local environment or actualize a desired identity. Within the context of the changing world, we argue that compatibility can come at the cost of identity inertia – unwillingness to engage with change and realizing other desired identities. We suggest the dynamic between self and space has important implications for diversity management in the workplace. Taken together, the role of physical spaces in the workplace, though often overlooked, can provide a novel and practical perspective to addressing a range of important personnel and organizational issues.

References

Alexander, C. N., & Wiley, M. G. (1981). Situated activity and identity formation. *Social Psychology: Sociological Perspectives*, 269–289.

Amiot, C. E., Terry, D. J., Jimmieson, N. L., & Callan, V. J. (2006). A longitudinal investigation of coping processes during a merger: Implications for job satisfaction and organizational identification. *Journal of Management*, 32(4), 552–574.

Appleyard, D. (1979). The environment as a social symbol: Within a theory of environmental action and perception. *Journal of the American Planning Association*, 45(2), 143–153. https://doi.org/10.1080/01944367908976952.

Armenakis, A. A., & Harris, S. G. (2009). Reflections: Our journey in organizational change research and practice. *Journal of Change Management*, 9(2), 127–142.

Armstrong-Stassen, M. (2005). Coping with downsizing: A comparison of executive-level and middle managers. *International Journal of Stress Management*, 12(2), 117.

Ashforth, B. E., & Johnson, S. A. (2001). Which hat to wear? The relative salience of multiple identities in organizational contexts. In M. A. Hogg & D. J. Terry (eds), *Social Identity Processes in Organizational Contexts* (pp. 31–48). Philadelphia, PA: Psychology Press.

Ashforth, B. E., & Schinoff, B. S. (2016). Identity under construction: How individuals come to define themselves in organizations. *Annual Review of Organizational Psychology and Organizational Behavior*, 3(1), 111–137. https://doi.org/10.1146/annurev-orgpsych-041015-062322.

Audia, P. G., Locke, E. A., & Smith, K. G. (2000). The paradox of success: An archival and a laboratory study of strategic persistence following radical environmental change. *Academy of Management Journal*, 43(5), 837–853.

Bachelard, G. (1964). *The Poetics of Space*. Boston, MA: Beacon Press.

Baumeister, R. F., & Leary, M. R. (1995). The need to belong: Desire for interpersonal attachments as a fundamental human motivation. *Psychological Bulletin*, 117(3), 497.

Biernat, M., & Hawley, P. H. (2017). Sexualized images in professional contexts: Effects on anticipated experiences and perceived climate for women and men. *Journal of Applied Social Psychology*. https://doi.org/10.1111/jasp.12461.

Bilewicz, M., & Klebaniuk, J. (2013). Psychological consequences of religious symbols in public space: Crucifix display at a public university. *Journal of Environmental Psychology, 35,* 10–17. https://doi.org/10.1016/j.jenvp.2013.03.001.

Brunia, S., & Hartjes-Gosselink, A. (2009). Personalization in non-territorial offices: A study of a human need. *Journal of Corporate Real Estate, 11*(3), 169–182. https://doi.org/10.1108/14630010910985922.

Byron, K., & Laurence, G. A. (2015). Diplomas, photos, and tchotchkes as symbolic self-representations: Understanding employees' individual use of symbols. *Academy of Management Journal, 58*(1), 298–323. https://doi.org/10.5465/amj.2012.0932.

Cappetta, R., & Gioia, D. A. (2006). Fine fashion: Using symbolic artifacts, sensemaking, and sensegiving to construct identity and image. In A. Rafaeli & M. G. Pratt (eds), *Artifacts and Organizations: Beyond Mere Symbolism* (pp. 199–219). Mahwah, NJ: Lawrence Erlbaum Associates.

Cheryan, S., Meltzoff, A. N., & Kim, S. (2011). Classrooms matter: The design of virtual classrooms influences gender disparities in computer science classes. *Computers and Education, 57*(2), 1825–1835. https://doi.org/10.1016/j.compedu.2011.02.004

Cheryan, S., Plaut, V. C., Davies, P. G., & Steele, C. M. (2009). Ambient belonging: How stereotypical cues impact gender participation in computer science. *Journal of Personality and Social Psychology, 97*(6), 1045–1060. https://doi.org/10.1037/a0016239.

Dale, K., & Burrell, G. (2007). *The Spaces of Organisation and the Organisation of Space: Power, Identity and Materiality at Work.* Basingstoke: Palgrave Macmillan.

Danielsson, C. B., & Bodin, L. (2009). Differences in satisfaction with office environment among employees in different office types. *Journal of Architectural and Planning Research, 26*(3), 241–257.

Davis, T. R. V. (1984). The influence of the physical environment in offices. *Academy of Management Review, 9*(2), 271–283. https://doi.org/10.5465/AMR.1984.4277654.

De Croon, E., Sluiter, J., Kuijer, P. P., & Frings-Dresen, M. (2005). The effect of office concepts on worker health and performance: a systematic review of the literature. *Ergonomics, 48*(2), 119–134. https://doi.org/10.1080/00140130512331319409.

De Gilder, D. (2003). Commitment, trust and work behaviour: The case of contingent workers. *Personnel Review, 32*(5), 588–604.

Deci, E. L., & Ryan, R. M. (2002). Overview of self-determination theory: An organismic-dialectical perspective. In E. L. Deci & R. M. Ryan (eds), *Handbook of Self-determination Research* (pp. 3–33). Rochester, NY: University Rochester Press.

Devendorf, S. A., & Highhouse, S. (2008). Applicant–employee similarity and attraction to an employer. *Journal of Occupational and Organizational Psychology, 81*(4), 607–617.

Dixon, S. E., Meyer, K. E., & Day, M. (2010). Stages of organizational transformation in transition economies: A dynamic capabilities approach. *Journal of Management Studies, 47*(3), 416–436.

Droseltis, O., & Vignoles, V. L. (2010). Towards an integrative model of place identification: Dimensionality and predictors of intrapersonal-level place preferences. *Journal of Environmental Psychology, 30*(1), 23–34. https://doi.org/10.1016/j.jenvp.2009.05.006.

Earle, H. A. (2003). Building a workplace of choice: Using the work environment to attract and retain top talent. *Journal of Facilities Management, 2*(3), 244–257.

Edwards, J. R., Caplan, R. D., & Van Harrison, R. (1998). Person–environment fit theory. *Theories of Organizational Stress, 28,* 67.

Ellemers, N. (2001). Social identity, commitment and work behavior. In M. A. Hogg & D. J. Terry (eds), *Social Identity Processes in Organizational Contexts* (pp. 101–114). Philadelphia, PA: Psychology Press.

Ellemers, N., De Gilder, D., & Haslam, S. A. (2004). Motivating individuals and groups at work: A social identity perspective on leadership and group performance. *Academy of Management Review, 29*(3), 459–478.

Elsbach, K. D. (2003). Relating physical environment to self-categorizations: Identity threat and affirmation in a non-territorial office space. *Administrative Science Quarterly, 48*(4), 622. https://doi.org/10.2307/3556639.

Elsbach, K. D. (2004). Interpreting workplace identities: The role of office décor. *Journal of Organizational Behavior, 25*(1), 99–128. https://doi.org/10.1002/job.233.

Elsbach, K. D., & Pratt, M. G. (2007). The physical environment in organisations. *The Academy of Management Annals, 1*(1), 181–224.

Goodrich, R.J. (1986), Corporate culture and office design. In J. T. Black, K. S. Roark, & L. S. Schwartz (eds), *The Changing Office Workplace* (pp. 65–79). Washington, DC: The Urban Land Institute.

Gosling, S. D., Ko, S. J., Mannarelli, T., & Morris, M. E. (2002). A room with a cue: Personality judgments based on offices and bedrooms. *Journal of Personality and Social Psychology, 82*(3), 379–398. https://doi.org/10.1037//0022-3514.82.3.379.

Graham, L. T., Gosling, S. D., & Travis, C. K. (2015). The psychology of home environments: A call for research on residential space. *Perspectives on Psychological Science, 10*(3), 346–356. https://doi.org/10.1177/1745691615576761.

Greenaway, K. H., Thai, H. A., Haslam, S. A., & Murphy, S. C. (2016). Spaces that signal identity improve workplace productivity. *Journal of Personnel Psychology, 15*(1), 35–43.

Haslam, S. A., & Knight, C. (2010). Cubicle, sweet cubicle. *Scientific American Mind, 21*(4), 30–35.

Jetten, J., Spears, R., & Manstead, A. S. (1996). Intergroup norms and intergroup discrimination: Distinctive self-categorization and social identity effects. *Journal of Personality and Social Psychology, 71*(6), 1222.

Kemp, L. J., Angell, L., & McLoughlin, L. (2015). The symbolic meaning of artifacts for the workplace identity of women in academia. *Gender in Management: An International Journal, 30*(5), 379–396. https://doi.org/10.1108/GM-07-2013-0080.

Knight, C., & Haslam, S. A. (2010a). The relative merits of lean, enriched, and empowered offices: An experimental examination of the impact of workspace management strategies on well-being and productivity. *Journal of Experimental Psychology: Applied, 16*(2), 158–172. https://doi.org/10.1037/a0019292.

Knight, C., & Haslam, S. A. (2010b). Your place or mine? Organizational identification and comfort as mediators of relationships between the managerial control of workspace and employees' satisfaction and well-being: Space and organizational identification. *British Journal of Management, 21*(3), 717–735. https://doi.org/10.1111/j.1467-8551.2009.00683.x.

Kristof, A. L. (1996). Person-organization fit: An integrative review of its conceptualizations, measurement, and implications. *Personnel Psychology, 49*(1), 1–49.

Kristof-Brown, A. L., Zimmerman, R. D., & Johnson, E. C. (2005). Consequences of individuals' fit at work: A meta-analysis of person–job, person–organization, person–group, and person–supervisor fit. *Personnel Psychology, 58*(2), 281–342. https://doi.org/10.1111/j.1744-6570.2005.00672.x.

Kristof-Brown, A., & Guay, R. P. (2011). Person–environment fit. In S. Zedeck (ed.), *APA Handbook of Industrial and Organizational Psychology, Vol 3: Maintaining, Expanding, and Contracting the Organization* (pp. 3–50). Washington, DC: American Psychological Association. https://doi.org/10.1037/12171-001.

Lamm, E., & Meeks, M.D. (2009). Workplace fun: The moderating effects of generational differences. *Employee Relations, 31*(6), 613–631.

Lane, D. J., & Gibbons, F. X. (2007). Am I the typical student? Perceived similarity to student prototypes predicts success. *Personality and Social Psychology Bulletin, 33*(10), 1380–1391.

Loughead, T. M., Carron, A. V., Bray, S. R., & Kim, A. J. (2003). Facility familiarity and the home advantage in professional sports. *International Journal of Sport and Exercise Psychology, 1*(3), 264–274.

Markus, H., & Nurius, P. (1986). Possible selves. *American Psychologist, 41*(9), 954.

Maslow, A. H. (1943). A theory of human motivation. *Psychological Review, 50*(4), 370.

Millward, L. J., Haslam, S. A., & Postmes, T. (2007). Putting employees in their place: The impact of hot desking on organizational and team identification. *Organization Science, 18*(4), 547–559.

Moore, R. (23 Jul, 2017). The billion-dollar palaces of Apple, Facebook and Google. *Guardian.* Retrieved from www.theguardian.com/artanddesign/2017/jul/23/inside-billion-dollar-palaces-of-tech-giants-facebook-apple-google-london-california-wealth-power

Mor Barak, M. E., Cherin, D. A., & Berkman, S. (1998). Organizational and personal dimensions in diversity climate: Ethnic and gender differences in employee perceptions. *Journal of Applied Behavioral Science, 34*(1), 82–104.

Moss, M. K., & Frieze, I. H. (1993). Job preferences in the anticipatory socialization phase: A comparison of two matching models. *Journal of Vocational Behavior, 42*(3), 282–297.

Noel, J. G., Wann, D. L., & Branscombe, N. R. (1995). Peripheral ingroup membership status and public negativity toward outgroups. *Journal of Personality and Social Psychology, 68*, 127–127.

Ornstein, S. (1986). Organizational symbols: A study of their meanings and influences on perceived psychological climate. *Organizational Behavior and Human Decision Processes, 38*(2), 207–229. https://doi.org/10.1016/0749-5978(86)90017-8.

Ornstein, S. (1992). First impressions of the symbolic meanings connoted by reception area design. *Environment and Behavior, 24*(1), 85–110. https://doi.org/10.1177/0013916592241004.

Perez-Lopez, R., Aragonés, J. I., & Amérigo, M. (2017). Primary spaces and their cues as facilitators of personal and social inferences. *Journal of Environmental Psychology, 53*, 157–167. https://doi.org/10.1016/j.jenvp.2017.07.008.

Peters, K., Haslam, S. A., Ryan, M. K., & Fonseca, M. (2013). Working with subgroup identities to build organizational identification and support for organizational strategy: A test of the ASPIRe model. *Group and Organization Management, 38*(1), 128–144.

Peters, K., Ryan, M. K., & Haslam, S. A. (2015). Marines, medics, and machismo: Lack of fit with masculine occupational stereotypes discourages men's participation. *British Journal of Psychology, 106*(4), 635–655.

Peters, K., Ryan, M., Haslam, S. A., & Fernandes, H. (2012). To belong or not to belong. *Journal of Personnel Psychology, 11*(3), 148–158. https://doi.org/10.1027/1866-5888/a000067.

Proshansky, H. M., Fabian, A. K., & Kaminoff, R. (1983). Place-identity: Physical world socialization of the self. *Journal of Environmental Psychology, 3*(1), 57–83. https://doi.org/10.1016/S0272-4944(83)80021-8.

Rafferty, A. E., & Restubog, S. L. D. (2010). The impact of change process and context on change reactions and turnover during a merger. *Journal of Management, 36*(5), 1309–1338.

Ridoutt, B. G., Ball, R. D., & Killerby, S. K. (2002). First impressions of organizations and the qualities connoted by wood in interior design. *Forest Products Journal: Madison, 52*(10), 30–36.

Rose, G. (1993). *Feminism and Geography: The Limits of Geographical Knowledge.* Minneapolis, MN: University of Minnesota Press.

Schneider, B. (1987). The people make the place. *Personnel Psychology, 40*(3), 437–453.

Smith, J. L., Lewis, K. L., Hawthorne, L., & Hodges, S. D. (2013). When trying hard isn't natural: Women's belonging with and motivation for male-dominated STEM fields as a function of effort expenditure concerns. *Personality and Social Psychology Bulletin, 39*(2), 131–143. https://doi.org/10.1177/0146167212468332.

Strauss, K., & Parker, S. K. (2015). Intervening to enhance proactivity in organizations: Improving the present or changing the future. *Journal of Management.* https://doi.org/10.1177/0149206315602531.

Strauss, K., Griffin, M. A., & Parker, S. K. (2012). Future work selves: How salient hoped-for identities motivate proactive career behaviors. *Journal of Applied Psychology, 97*(3), 580.

Sundstrom, E., & Sundstrom, M. G. (1986). *Work Places: The Psychology of the Physical Environment in Offices and Factories.* Cambridge: Cambridge University Press Archive.

Tajfel, H., & Turner, J. C. (1979). An integrative theory of intergroup conflict. *Social Psychology of Intergroup Relations, 33*(47), 74.

Tajfel, H., & Turner, J. C. (2004). The social identity theory of intergroup behavior. In J. T. Jost & J. Sidanius (eds), *Key Readings in Social Psychology: Political Psychology: Key Readings* (pp. 276–293). New York: Psychology Press.

The Economist (Apr 29, 2017). Sofas and surveillance. Retrieved from www.economist.com/business/2017/04/29/technology-firms-and-the-office-of-the-future

Toossi, M. (2012). Projections of the labor force to 2050: A visual essay. *Monthly Labor Review, 135,* 3.

Turner, J. C., Hogg, M. A., Oakes, P. J., Reicher, S. D., & Wetherell, M. S. (1987). *Rediscovering the Social Group: A Self-categorization Theory.* Oxford: Basil Blackwell.

Turner, J. C., Oakes, P. J., Haslam, A. S., & McGarty, C. (1994). Self and collective: Cognition and social context. *Personality and Social Psychology Bulletin, 20*(5), 454–463. https://doi.org/10.1177/0146167294205002.

Veenstra, K., Haslam, S. A., & Reynolds, K. J. (2004). The psychology of casualization: Evidence for the mediating roles of security, status and social identification. *British Journal of Social Psychology, 43*(4), 499–514.

Vilnai-Yavetz, I., & Rafaeli, A. (2006). Managing artifacts to avoid artifact myopia: Artifacts and organizations. *Beyond Mere Symbolism,* 9–21.

Walton, G. M., & Cohen, G. L. (2011). Sharing motivation. *Social Motivation,* 79–101.

Warren, S. (2002). 'Show me how it feels to work here': Using photography to research organisational ethics. *Ephemera: Theory and Politics in Organization, 2*(3), 224–245.

Wasserman, V. (2012). Open spaces, closed boundaries: Transparent workspaces as clerical female ghettos. *International Journal of Work Organisation and Emotion, 5*(1), 6–25.

Wasserman, V., & Frenkel, M. (2011). Organizational aesthetics: Caught between identity regulation and culture jamming. *Organization Science, 22*(2), 503–521.

Wells, M., & Thelen, L. (2002). What does your workspace say about you? The influence of personality, status, and workspace on personalization. *Environment and Behavior, 34*(3), 300–321. https://doi.org/10.1177/0013916502034003002.

Wells, M., Thelen, L., & Ruark, J. (2007). Workspace personalization and organizational culture: Does your workspace reflect you or your company? *Environment and Behavior, 39*(5), 616–634. https://doi.org/10.1177/0013916506295602.

Worthington, J. (2006). *Reinventing the Workplace.* 2nd ed. Oxford: Architectural Press.

Ysseldyk, R., Haslam, S. A., & Morton, T. A. (2016). Stairway to heaven? (Ir)religious identity moderates the effects of immersion in religious spaces on self-esteem and self-perceived physical health. *Journal of Environmental Psychology, 47,* 14–21. https://doi.org/10.1016/j.jenvp.2016.04.016.

7

SOCIO-TECHNICAL SYSTEMS THINKING AND THE DESIGN OF CONTEMPORARY WORKSPACE

Matthew C. Davis

Introduction

The physical environments in which people work have long been acknowledged as playing a key role in helping to shape, constrain, and promote a range of behavioural and organizational outcomes – from creativity to wellbeing, performance to communication, job satisfaction to sick leave (Bodin Danielsson, Chungkham, Wulff, & Westerlund, 2014; Davis, Leach, & Clegg, 2011). Public, corporate, and academic interest in the effects that office environments in particular may have upon their occupants has grown since the widespread emergence of 'open-plan' offices in the 1960s (Brookes & Kaplan, 1972) and the subsequent complaints from workers regarding these environments (e.g. *Business Week*, 1978). While some firms are still on the transition from traditional enclosed (often individual private offices) to open-plan (offices largely without interior walls or visual obstructions, housing three to many hundreds of workers), many more are embarking on what seems set to become the next big shift in office design. They are adopting activity-based working (ABW) or multi-modal offices, embodying a less static view of what employees require from their workspace (Brunia, De Been, & van der Voordt, 2016). With more choice regarding office design it raises the questions as to how organizations decide what is the most effective office configuration for their needs, and how to approach the process of design itself.

In this chapter I consider physical work environments, specifically office space, from a socio-technical systems thinking (STST) perspective (e.g. Cherns, 1976). I begin by outlining a key problem within office design regarding the prioritization of efficiency over user needs and narrow thinking regarding successful design. Next, I introduce STST as an approach to place the physical workspace in a broader organizational context. Then, I present the core STST principles most applicable to the challenge of undertaking workspace design and management of the requisite change. Finally, I conclude with a reflection on the challenges posed by applying STST to this domain.

The problem of top–down design and the prioritization of efficiencies

Traditionally many office environments have been designed based upon generic assumptions regarding the needs of workers (Kaarlela-Tuomaala, Helenius, Keskinen, & Hongisto, 2009) or as a result of decision-making primarily aimed around 'efficient' use of space (Duffy, 2000; Vischer, 2005). This is reflected in the rise and now ubiquitous nature of open-plan office formats – introduced with the aim of reducing barriers to communication and increasing information flows (De Croon, Sluiter, Kuijer, & Frings-Dresen, 2005), popularized through the significant financial savings they delivered (Davis et al., 2011; Laing, 2006). Some potential downsides for open-plan occupants have been recognized, particularly with regards to increased density and openness, for example, elevated distraction and interruption, lower satisfaction, organizational commitment and wellbeing (Bodin Danielsson et al., 2014; De Croon et al., 2005; Elsbach & Pratt, 2007; Oldham, Cummings, & Zhou, 1995). Nonetheless, this seems to have little changed the calculus regarding optimal workspace design, with financial and narrow operational concerns prioritized (Davis et al., 2011; Duffy, 2000).

As physical workspace constitutes the second largest financial overhead for most firms, after staff costs (McCoy, 2005), the desire to continue to reduce costs by creating further efficiencies in the design and use of space is unlikely to abate. This trend may be witnessed in the embrace of ABW across an increasing number of organizations (Vos & van der Voordt, 2001; Wohlers & Hertel, 2017) as well as through other innovations such as use of co-working spaces and greater client-side or home working (Cascio, 2000; Göçer, Göçer, Ergöz Karahan, & İlhan Oygür, 2017). ABW typically produces a reduction in requisite office space through a combination of hot-desking (non-reservable desks that are available to employees as and when required) and reduced individual workstations, coupled with increased task spaces, e.g. discussion areas, team rooms, quiet spaces. The rationale being that a mix of such spaces reduces the proportion of time that areas of the office are left unoccupied and increases the efficiency of the office space, e.g. fewer assigned desks are left empty for long periods while their occupants attend meetings in traditional conference rooms.

I argue that the desire to reduce overhead and to manage workspace efficiently has driven myopic thinking as to what constitutes successful design and that this is problematic. User and broader organizational implications of differing workspace designs are often reduced to secondary concerns or 'user acceptance' issues, to be managed once occupants arrive in their new offices (Davis et al., 2011; Vischer, 2005). This view runs contrary to calls that have been made across disciplines to view workspace as an integral part of the overall organizational system and to recognize that workspace affects how individuals go about their work, the technologies they need, and affect their day-to-day experience (e.g. Allen & Henn, 2007; Becker & Steele, 1995; Blyth & Worthington, 2001; Haynes, 2007; Turner & Myerson, 1998). I present STST as an established framework and set of principles with which to engage in holistic design, countering top–down and efficiency-driven prevailing mindsets. As I will explain through this chapter, STST explicitly promotes the consideration of contingencies and interactions between workspace and other aspects of the organizational system, in addition to balancing competing stakeholder interests (Davis et al., 2011; Ridgway et al., 2008). I will demonstrate the applicability of this approach to workspace design through examples relating to ABW and open-plan offices. We first consider the origins of STST and its core philosophy.

Origins of socio-technical systems thinking and its core philosophy

STST developed from seminal work conducted at the Tavistock Institute in the 1940s and 1950s, initially examining the impact of introducing advanced machinery within the coal mining industry (e.g. Emery, 1959; Trist & Bamforth, 1951). These and other studies, in the beginning focusing on heavy industries (e.g. Emery, 1959), then later on the introduction of advanced manufacturing technologies, information systems, and information technologies (e.g. Mumford, 1983), demonstrated the inter-related nature of human and technical aspects of work systems and contributed to the development of STST theory and principles (Davis, Challenger, Jayewardene, & Clegg, 2014; Eason, 2014).

The consistent underlying STST philosophy that has emerged argues that any organization can be considered a complex system consisting of many interdependent components, both social and technical, e.g. people, culture, goals, processes, technology, and infrastructure, with a change in any one aspect of the system causing change or adaptation elsewhere (Clegg et al., 2017). The interrelated nature of organizational systems is illustrated in Figure 7.1, with the lines between the nodes in the hexagon demonstrating the relationships and contingencies present in any system (see Davis et al., 2014, for further discussion of these inter-relationships). Furthermore, STST suggests that systems will work at their best when both the social and technical aspects are 'jointly optimized' (Cherns, 1976), i.e. designed or redesigned with consideration as to the inter-relationships and contingencies between different parts of the system. This way of thinking highlights the need to avoid considering any one part of a system in isolation and to recognize that other parts of the system are connected and may support, inhibit, or constrain desired outcomes. For example, the effective utilization of machinery was contingent on the prevailing culture and organization of work processes in Trist and Bamforth's original coal mining studies.

FIGURE 7.1 Hexagonal socio-technical systems framework, illustrating inter-related nature of organizational systems

Source: Reproduced from Clegg et al. (2017) under a CC-BY 4.0 license (http://creativecommons.org/licenses/by/4.0/).

As discussed previously, financial and other technical factors have been prioritized in organizations' approach to workspace design. Francis Duffy, a prominent architect, captures this prevailing mindset, reflecting that 'the design of the working environment has been considered by the vast majority of clients as a marginal and technical matter, best left to experts to sort out' (Duffy, 2000, p. 371). The design of workspace in relative isolation mirrors that which has been observed by STST researchers over many years in the design and introduction of new technologies and information systems (Eason, 2008). This siloed thinking reflects an expert-led 'techno-centric' mindset and the primacy of technology, or in this case the physical infrastructure, over the other aspects of the system within which it resides and interacts. This is a particular problem when one considers that the success of increasingly popular concepts such as ABW are reliant upon wider system factors, requiring, for example: that individuals work in roles that encompass varied tasks requiring different types of space; individuals have the autonomy to decide where and when to work; individuals are willing to embrace change; technologies that enable workers to get up and take their work with them are available; a culture of trust exists to allow individuals to work out-of-sight or from home (Brunia et al., 2016; Laing, 2006).

Thanks to the long pedigree of STST, there already exists a large body of knowledge, developed across various problem domains, regarding effective socio-technical design (see Hughes, Clegg, Bolton, & Machon, 2017; Mumford, 2006), which could be used to approach the problem of workspace design. In the next section, key principles to approach such design are discussed in detail.

Key socio-technical systems principles applied to workspace design

Various sets of 'principles' to guide the design of socio-technical systems or to evaluate and explain their performance (success, maladaptation, or failure), have been proposed, based upon observation and analysis of system design and redesign in various contexts (e.g. Cherns, 1976, 1987; Clegg, 2000; Mumford, 1983). These principles provide a well-established framework to approach the process of workspace design, promoting holistic design and stakeholder engagement. They also provide insights regarding the form of the design itself and how to manage the attendant change. The eight principles that are particularly pertinent to the design of workspace are discussed in turn below using Cherns (1987) and Clegg (2000) as organizing lexicons. These principles are summarized in Table 7.1.

1. Open systems perspective

STST suggests that system components should be designed in relation to one another and with reference to current and future environmental demands (Cherns, 1976). This principle also encapsulates the overarching idea that a change to one part of the system may have implications elsewhere (Davis et al., 2014), e.g. that a change to the physical layout of an office may result in changes

TABLE 7.1 Socio-technical systems principles applied to workspace design

STST principle	Description	Applied to workspace
1. Open systems perspective	A change to one part of the system may have implications elsewhere. These changes may be unanticipated.	Workspace cannot be viewed in isolation. Workspace design may influence how employees feel and behave, how tasks and processes are ordered, etc. Successful workspace design may require attendant changes to other parts of the system (e.g. technology, culture, processes).

2. Organizational choice	Designers should specify as little as possible, allowing users to decide how to solve their design problem.	Designers should not impose a design solution or close off potential designs at the outset. Employees should be empowered to decide what space is appropriate for their work and how, when, and where they work.
3. Controlling problems at source	Systems are most effective when they make problems visible and easy to resolve as they arise.	Workspace may be designed to facilitate fast decision-making and knowledge-sharing to resolve problems as they are identified. Workspace can be designed to be flexible, enabling employees to respond to change.
4. Boundary location and information flows	Physical, social, and technological boundaries can affect information flows.	The interaction between technologies and workspace design may support the easy flow of information. Co-location and reductions in physical barriers may ease communication and understanding between groups.
5. Congruence and support	Any change to part of the system needs to be congruent with, and supportive of, related components.	Workspace should reflect organizational goals, culture, and ways of working. The workspace may support or inhibit individual work practices. Evaluation of individual needs and tasks should be used to tailor workspace to support these. Diverse employee and organizational needs may require multi-modal workspace.
6. Quality of life and experience at work	Design of any system component can change the nature of work and the experience for employees.	Evaluation of the impact of workspace design on employees needs to be built into initial design phases. Technically optimal solutions may produce lagging employee impacts (e.g. stress). Behavioural impacts should be balanced against financial and technical outcomes.
7. User participation and ownership	Successful design requires users to actively participate in the design process and to take ownership of the practical implementation.	Occupants should be involved in the design process (contributing functional, social, and technical needs) and participate in decision-making (e.g. about space, furniture, and aesthetics). Occupants should be responsible for how space will be used and the handover from designers.
8. Design is open-ended	Design is never finished and is an open-ended process that needs to adapt to a changing world.	Organizations' and individuals' needs will change over time. Workspace should be designed to be adaptable, never viewed as 'complete', and occupants equipped to re-evaluate their space requirements over time.

to the organization of teams and processes. This implies that physical workspace should be designed in a way that is both adaptable and responsive (links to principles 3 and 7 below), to enable the organizational system to respond to changes in the external environment (c.f., Mumford, 2006). If client needs or internal functions change, the workspace should be easily adaptable and reconfigurable. Similar flexibility is required with regards to IT and technical infrastructure, acknowledging that technologies and software as yet unknown may be deployed at scale within organizations, or ones that are currently ubiquitous may disappear. For example, as witnessed with the loss of typing pools, large server rooms and, increasingly, the demise of static PC workstations (Laing, 2006). Indeed, the recognition that work organization may change rapidly was one of the drivers of the adoption of open-plan layouts (Davis et al., 2011; De Croon et al., 2005), with the rise in popularity of ABW reflecting in part that technologies are now highly mobile (Gillen, 2006; Wohlers & Hertel, 2017).

2. Organizational choice

This principle relates to the ideas of 'minimal critical specificity' (Cherns, 1976, 1987), that designers should limit formal specification of form, function, or process to only that which needs to be decreed, e.g. expected outcomes or safety processes, with the detail of how to accomplish tasks or to organize work left to individuals and groups as far as possible. In other words, 'workers should be told what to do but not how to do it' (Mumford, 2006, p. 322). The rationale being that designers can never foresee all eventualities or contingencies that may arise in the real world. Clegg (2000) extends this reasoning to conclude that there are always multiple design solutions to any given problem and that design should reflect the needs of the business, employees, and users rather than designers' preferences or convenience.

While these ideas may appear obvious, the overwhelming prevalence of open-plan offices (Bodin Danielsson et al., 2014; Davis et al., 2011) suggests that this design has become the unquestioned norm, rather than a considered choice for many organizations. The specification of open-plan designs a priori reflects design and operational bias on the part of designers and managers. This constrains the configuration of the space, organization of individuals, and ways of working. STST would argue that beyond the unavoidable constraints, occupants should be permitted to decide what space is appropriate for their work requirements and to decide where, when, and how they accomplish their work. These sentiments are becoming increasingly popular through ABW and flexible work–home arrangements (Daniels, Lamond, & Standen, 2001; Göçer et al., 2017; Knight & Haslam, 2010). This does not necessarily mean that such arrangements will necessarily be appropriate, rather that they should be on the table as options at the start of the design process.

3. Controlling problems at source

The idea of controlling problems or 'variance' at source (Cherns, 1976, 1987) has become one of the most well known of the socio-technical principles (e.g. Waterson, 2005) and refers to systems operating most effectively where they are designed to make problems visible and to enable them to be resolved where and when they occur. This idea has been applied extensively in manufacturing and technology implementations (Clegg & Davis, 2016; Eason, 2008). The idea extends to broader notions of building opportunities for control and empowerment within systems to improve performance outcomes (enabling systems to respond to unexpected events, uncertainty, and complex problems with variable solutions) and provide psychological benefit to workers (Clegg, 2000; Mumford, 1995).

The workspace literature has identified that the configuration of workspace holds the potential to both enable and constrain individual choice, control, and the opportunity to take action to manage problems quickly and directly (Elsbach & Pratt, 2007). Physical design can therefore be used to actively help promote the broader aim of control of variance of source and, by extension, system resilience and innovation. For example, open-plan offices have been lauded for enabling fast decision-making and discussion of problems (e.g. Brennan, Chugh, & Kline, 2002; Brookes & Kaplan, 1972), with breakout and informal discussion spaces increasingly being incorporated into a range of office types to aid this objective (Bodin Danielsson et al., 2014; Morrow, McElroy, & Scheibe, 2012), enabling problems to be resolved as and when they arise. Provision of task or activity spaces provides examples as to design options that enable workers to be reactive, able to respond to changes in task requirements, work demands or to resolve unexpected problems without, for example, having to book meeting rooms or project space in advance (cf., Allen, Bell, Graham, Hardy, & Swaffer, 2004; Duffy, 1997; Göçer et al., 2017; Laing, 2006).

4. Boundary location and information flows

The design of physical, social, and technological boundaries, structures, and processes can act as barriers to communication and inhibit information flowing to those who require it and effective knowledge exchange (Cherns, 1976, 1987). These concerns are readily observable with regards the design of workspace, with, for example, walls and barriers, as well as sheer physical distance, able to impede access and interaction with colleagues (Allen & Henn, 2007). STST suggests that the design of workspace should aim to make physical and organizational barriers as indistinguishable as possible. Where boundaries exist within the work process, e.g. tasks passing between different groups, this presents an opportunity for learning and knowledge-sharing (Mumford, 2006) and may be aided by co-location, whereby colleagues can observe other aspects of the work process (Oldham &

Brass, 1979). Exemplifying this principle, Hall and Ford (1998) report the redesign of a manufacturing space that resulted in the removal of physical barriers separating white- and blue-collar teams. Following the change, empathy, cross-team understanding, communication, and problem resolution increased.

While open-plan designs very visibly seek to remove physical barriers to communication, they also present a trade-off with individual needs of workers for privacy and control (Davis et al., 2011). Office configurations such as ABW or open-plan designs that provide areas to retreat to for quiet working may present an opportunity for workers to better manage this tension between the need for privacy and the benefits of interaction (Laing, 2006; Wohlers & Hertel, 2017). Nonetheless, boundary reduction needs to be more nuanced than simply considering physical walls or furniture and be applied to the related aspects of the work organization (see related principles 1 and 5). In essence, holistic design is required. Consideration should be given as to the placement of teams, the organizational structure, working practices, and information systems or technologies needed to support easy free flow of information and ideas within these spaces.

5. Congruence and support

This principle refers to the need for any design and the implicated change to working arrangements to be congruent with and supported by related system components and practices, e.g. culture, goals, and technologies (Clegg, 2000). This idea is fundamental in anticipating how and why similar office designs may perform differently in varying contexts (e.g. the inconsistencies and paradoxes that are observed in the outcomes for white-collar workers in open-plan offices, e.g. Davis et al., 2011; De Croon et al., 2005; Elsbach & Pratt, 2007; Wohlers & Hertel, 2017). This poses the question: is the workspace congruent with what workers are being asked to do, how work processes are structured, current organizational hierarchies, required information flows, reward systems, and goals? The assertion being that system performance and outcomes will be enhanced where the different aspects of the system are aligned, as opposed to where they undermine or oppose one another (Clegg & Walsh, 2004; Mumford, 2006). Successful design will flow from recognition of the relationship between the workspace and related aspects of the organizational system.

The necessity of congruence between workspace design and broader organization factors is illustrated by observations from the workspace literature. Previous evaluations of occupant reactions to open-plan offices have highlighted differential effects across workers dependent upon job role or seniority (Charles & Veitch, 2002), with negative outcomes when the spaces fail to provide adequate provision for the range of tasks and interactions that are performed, e.g. Kaarlela-Tuomaala et al. (2009). This suggests that workspaces may need to be multi-modal to reflect user needs, in other words incorporate a variety of office concepts within a single building. For example, a department may require different sets of spaces (e.g. individual offices, ABW, traditional open-plan) to accommodate the type of workers and individual preferences within their teams. This way of thinking underscores the importance of considering relevant aspects of job design and considering techniques such as job analysis and process mapping to develop an understanding of the existing structures and ways of working with which the physical workspace may support, impede, or interact (see Ridgway et al., 2008). The nature of the work will also influence the use and success of space, e.g. work involving confidential projects or client-centred interactions requiring different types of spaces from those where individuals work with non-sensitive material (cf. Davis et al., 2011; Sundstrom, Town, Rice, & Osborn, 1994). Workspace design should not occur without reference to these factors.

The importance of this principle can be further emphasized when one considers the interaction that may occur between the physical environment with organizational goals and culture. Encouraging collaborative work practices where individuals are measured and rewarded on the basis of individual performance is difficult (Clegg, 2000). Similarly, environments designed to encourage team work and cross-team information-sharing are unlikely to fulfil their objectives when individuals are incentivized to focus on their own work tasks or individual performance outcomes. Other system components, such as processes and technologies, may also be considered as contingencies here. The provision of mobile devices (e.g. laptops and mobile telephony) and software (e.g. video-conferencing, instant or professional messaging services), together with supporting technical infrastructure (e.g. high-quality wifi, mobile network access, cloud hosting) and requisite training or information, may be crucial to determining whether workers are able to utilize different task spaces to their full, to easily hot-desk or to work from home or client or remote locations (Allen et al., 2004; Brunia et al., 2016; Laing, 2006). Furthermore, the role of management expectations or culture has been highlighted as a success factor within post-occupancy studies (e.g. Hongisto, Haapakangas, Varjo, Helenius, & Koskela, 2016; Laing, Duffy, Jaunzens, & Willis, 1998; Ridgway et al., 2008; Vischer, 2005). For example, presenteeism or close supervision and allocation of work may place constraints on individuals' opportunities to decide where and when to work (e.g. in the case of more flexible office designs) or to use breakout or coffee spaces within more traditional open-plan offices. These observations support the argument that design is holistic and congruence between workspace design and the wider organization cannot be ignored.

6. Quality of life and experience at work

Mumford (1983, 1995) demonstrated how the design of technologies, information systems, work processes, and environments can tangibly alter the nature of the work that individuals engage in, for example, by increasing levels of surveillance, reducing individual autonomy, de-skilling, or fragmenting tasks. These observations are recognizable too in research specifically examining the relationship between the design of workspace and occupant responses and behaviours. For example, the configuration and design of workspace has been related to behavioural outcomes such as the levels of feedback individuals receive (Oldham & Brass, 1979), opportunities for friendships or the quality of co-worker relations (Brookes & Kaplan, 1972; Zalesny & Farace, 1987), job satisfaction (Sundstrom, Burt, & Kamp, 1980; Veitch, Charles, Farley, & Newsham, 2007; Zalesny & Farace, 1987) and work motivation (Oldham & Brass, 1979).

Mumford (e.g. 1983) emphasizes the consideration of values within socio-technical systems design and the responsibility that designers and managers have to design work and organizational systems that enhance employees' quality of life. This aim has often been criticized as being idealistic or too humanistic (Pasmore, 1994). However, when it comes to the design of workspace I would argue that there are good reasons to question whether the most technically efficient design (e.g. in terms of the highest occupancy rate or density of workers within the floor space) is necessarily the optimal overall system state. The technical, procedural, or financial gains from differing designs need to be balanced against the impact on occupants and their resultant behaviour or organizational outcomes. For example, design decisions that optimize occupancy, e.g. implementing hot-desking, reducing the distance between desks, or increasing the openness, may produce negative short-term psychological changes. These impacts may include reducing psychological privacy (e.g. Sundstrom, Herbert, & Brown, 1982), perceived control (e.g. Lee & Brand, 2010) or increasing cognitive load (e.g. Kaarlela-Tuomaala et al., 2009), with implications then for task performance and other organizational outcomes (Block & Stokes, 1989; Brennan et al., 2002; Kim & de Dear, 2013). Furthermore, it is clear from research in this domain that the influence of workspace design on occupants may include long-lasting and potentially lagging effects (Bodin Danielsson et al., 2014; De Croon et al., 2005; Oldham et al., 1995), e.g. general wellbeing or physical health (Danielsson & Bodin, 2008), withdrawal from the office itself (Oldham & Fried, 1987) and ultimately the desire to seek a new job (Carlopio, 1996). Consequently, short-term gains in terms of reduced build or lease costs may be offset by longer-term costs relating to reduced resilience, performance, or skills retention, e.g. stemming from increased staff turnover, absence, or fatigue. Actively seeking to enhance employees' quality of life may be perceived as idealistic. However, it seems entirely rational to try to evaluate the likely employee impact of different workspace options as an explicit design stage (cf. Clegg et al., 2017; Davis et al., 2011) if we wish to avoid or mitigate undesirable organizational outcomes. This view balances the efficiency mindset and recognizes that design that reduces financial costs in one part of the system may result in financial or non-financial costs elsewhere.

7. User participation and ownership

This principle draws across the ideas of both user participation in (Cherns, 1976, 1987), and more active 'ownership' during, design and implementation of the resulting change (Clegg, 2000; Mumford, 1983). STST case studies and evaluations have consistently demonstrated that successful design requires users to be both involved in the process of design, e.g. inputting to requirements and decisions, but also to feel that they own the design and take responsibility for how it will work in practice (Clegg & Walsh, 2004; Mumford, 2006; Nadin, Waterson, & Parker, 2001). STST scenario planning techniques (e.g. Clegg et al., 1996; Hughes et al., 2017) have been used to develop the initial design brief for architects and designers, engaging users in the process of actively considering their various needs, associated system contingencies and to take the lead in evaluating the impact of different design scenarios (e.g. Ridgway et al., 2008).

The emphasis within STST on broad stakeholder engagement and multi-disciplinary design teams is a major contribution towards avoiding top–down or techno-centric design. The value and applicability of user participation and ownership to workspace design are evident in the wider literature relating to workspace design, e.g. in terms of identifying users' functional needs or technology requirements, re-evaluating working practices, building acceptance of concomitant change, improving understanding regarding timings, and the process of the design itself (Allen et al., 2004; Foland, Rowlen, & Watson, 1995; Vischer, 2005). This participation is a key step in design and acts as an important counterbalance to the experts or other members of the design team and can serve to challenge their preconceptions (see principle 2). Participation also provides valuable on-the-ground information from front-line workers with intimate knowledge of the reality of carrying out work tasks and how a change in physical layout or associated ways of working may impact themselves or their teams (Clegg & Walsh, 2004; Davis et al., 2011). The active involvement of workers within the design process can itself provide an opportunity for autonomy and empowerment (see principle 3) and provide beneficial satisfaction and interpersonal outcomes (e.g. Foland et al., 1995).

Adopting user participation is likely to be more labour- and time-intensive than more 'top–down' approaches; however, studies have demonstrated that outcomes are better where employees have been involved in the design of their office, rather than having a design imposed upon them (Foland et al., 1995). The infamous case of Chiat/Day, where employees rebelled against a radical office redesign (akin to ABW) and forced changes to its design and use (Vischer, 2005), reinforces the value of both user engagement and subsequent evaluation (see principle 8). This supports the argument that whether employees are formally provided with the opportunity to design or redesign their space, if it fails to meet their needs, they will attempt to change it (or undermine it) through other means (Chapman, Sheehy, Heywood, Dooley, & Collins, 1995; Davis et al., 2011).

8. Design is open-ended

Finally, STST incorporates the idea that design is never finished and that it is an open-ended iterative process (e.g. Cherns, 1987). This reflects the need for systems to continually adapt, to the changing nature of the external environment and the demands that they encounter – to meet this challenge it is necessary that 'design never stops' (Mumford, 2006, p. 323). Clegg (2000) stresses the need for evaluation to be inherent in the design process itself and for this to be embraced as an opportunity to learn and (by extension) to improve. Cherns (1987) views such evaluation as a core task for those individuals within the system itself, an opportunity for them to apply their skills and knowledge (see also principles 3 and 7) and not a task to be left to external experts (e.g. architectural consultants).

These ideas run contrary to standard practice and suggest that workspace design should not be viewed as a discrete activity that is complete once a space has been designed, refurbished, or reconfigured. Rather, workspace design should be considered as an activity to be repeated and decisions reviewed regularly. The further implication (tied to principles 3 and 7) is that this is a process that has to be connected to the occupants' own experiences and structures set in place to enable them to surface complaints and ideas for improvements. For example, Davis and Offut (2015) report an employee involvement process and staggered launch of a new ABW office, to enable employees to shape the initial design and for early movers to 'live' in the part-completed office, feedback on the reality of the space and help iterate the design prior to final completion.

The evaluation of current and prospective workspace by employees can be supported by the use of existing socio-technical tools and the results used to refine and iterate designs. Many of these tools have been applied extensively in human factors and macro ergonomics to analyse existing systems and identify relevant interrelationships and dependencies, e.g. HFACS, Accimap, STAMP, STS Hexagon (see Davis et al., 2014)

Open-ended design and the notion of open systems reflect the awareness that an organization's and individual's relationship with space will change and evolve over time. The need to be responsive and adaptable can be seen in the trend towards ABW in modern organizations, with the spaces enabling individual employees to evaluate and essentially craft their own workspace day-by-day (shifting between task spaces as appropriate). However, at a more macro level, the extent to which most workers are able to influence the design of their office remains limited, with the industry still predominantly organized around design–build or similar processes that see architectural, engineering, or furniture companies contracted to deliver a design concept, but rarely contracted to support iteration over time.

Limitations and challenges in applying STST

The discussion thus far has focused on making the case for workspace to be considered from an STST perspective and the potential for these ideas to be applied to help manage the design and implementation of office environments. It is important to acknowledge both limitations of STST in general and the challenges that relate to the application of STST to workspace design.

A great strength of STST is its long history and depth of supporting case studies. However, the application and development of STST has predominantly concerned the design and implementation of IT systems or industrial machinery (Davis et al, 2014; Mumford, 2006). This relative narrowness of application is a limitation and means that some of the claims regarding application of principles to physical workspace and buildings design have received only limited direct exploration (Ridgway et al, 2008). Additional research and validation of the principles in this context are required. The technology change literature has also illustrated that where STST has been applied, the tendency is often still for the technology to take precedence, with the social and work structures designed around this (Clegg, 2000; Eason, 2008). There is a danger that the same may occur within workspace design, whereby engineering, architectural, and cost constraints may be imposed early in the design process, resulting in STST being used to fit the organization around the already planned space.

The STST approach raises two key sets of challenges in terms of application specifically to the design of workspace.

First, the highly multi-disciplinary nature of the literature relating to office evaluation and office (re)design (Davis et al., 2011) reflects the complexity of the problem domain, the range of influences on success (both technical, psychological, and organizational) as well as the skill-set required to approach this problem. STST argues that any design is systemic and that no one discipline has all of the answers (Clegg, 2000); this rings particularly true when considering the design of office environments. As I have discussed in this chapter, it is difficult to disentangle the influence of component parts of this puzzle and there can be unintended consequences from failing to take account of the relationship that workspace has with other parts of the system. This challenges organizational behaviour scholars and practitioners to work closely with colleagues from architectural, engineering, information systems, management, and other relevant disciplines to recognize the value in alternative approaches and to overcome barriers of terminology or methodology. I suggest that to understand differences in outcomes and to theorize appropriately, we need to think of extra-person system factors not simply as noise or potential confounding variance to be controlled and ignored, but as part of what we are seeking to explain and offering explanatory value in understanding the organizational behaviour that is observed. Wohlers and Hertel (2017) offer a good example of a theoretical framework incorporating workspace, psychological, organizational, and technological factors that may inform such work. A collaborative approach seems imperative both for the development of a more complete understanding regarding the interaction between individuals or groups and their physical surroundings, but also to the active application of our knowledge regarding human behaviour and perceptions – an endeavour that is likely to contribute to better design (for both employees and organizations) in practice.

Second, applying a socio-technical approach either to workspace design or its evaluation requires both time and commitment (Davis et al., 2014). In practical terms, the ongoing data collection required to enable STST principles to be tested, or for iterative design and redesigns to be evaluated, is time-intensive. It requires us to develop deep and trusting relationships with organizations to enable data to be gathered on multiple occasions, to reassure them that access will be honoured and that results will be of practical value. This style of partnership is also important if we as researchers want to influence the design of new workspaces, to develop and refine tools or techniques to improve the design process itself, or simply to be present at the opportune time to collect data from participants prior to an office change. It is my own frequent frustration that even where one has good relationships with managers and executives within a firm, events can sometimes move faster than one expects and the window for data collection can rapidly disappear. The need for speedy data collection suggests that we need to invest in the development of more innovative, less obtrusive and quicker to deploy research methods. For example, making use of performance data already held by an organization, using movement data collected through bluetooth or wifi, or the establishment of well-verified short psychometric measures. Furthermore, the research concerning the physical workspace has often resulted in contradictory findings (e.g. relating to levels of communication within apparently similar office types). As indicated previously, there are many contextual and broader systems-related factors that might lie behind this; superficial knowledge of the organization is unlikely to aid the identification of these.

In conclusion, the ongoing organizational need to reduce costs and manage facilities efficiently suggests that the problem of establishing what constitutes the optimum office design is unlikely to abate. Practice to date has often prioritized cost and space efficiencies over broader system considerations and led to top–down design. STST offers a well-established and robust set of principles to guide the design of workspace and offers insights into how to balance the competing needs of individuals, organizations, and designers. While applying STST poses challenges, it also presents an opportunity to promote holistic design that maintains the interests of workers and supports organizational effectiveness in its broadest sense.

References

Allen, T., Bell, A., Graham, R., Hardy, B., & Swaffer, F. (2004). *Working without Walls: An Insight into the Transforming Government Workplace.* London: DEGW.

Allen, T. J., & Henn, G. W. (2007). *The Organization and Architecture of Innovation: Managing the Flow of Technology.* Oxford: Elsevier.

Becker, F. D., & Steele, F. (1995). *Workplace by Design: Mapping the High-performance Workscape.* San Francisco, CA: Jossey-Bass Inc.

Block, L. K., & Stokes, G. S. (1989). Performance and satisfaction in private versus nonprivate work settings. *Environment and Behavior, 21*, 277–292.

Blyth, A., & Worthington, J. (2001). *Managing the Brief for Better Design.* London: Taylor & Francis Group.

Bodin Danielsson, C., Chungkham, H. S., Wulff, C., & Westerlund, H. (2014). Office design's impact on sick leave rates. *Ergonomics, 57*(2), 139–147. doi:10.1080/00140139.2013.871064.

Brennan, A., Chugh, J. S., & Kline, T. (2002). Traditional versus open office design: A longitudinal study. *Environment and Behavior, 34*(3), 279–299. doi:10.1177/0013916502034003001.

Brookes, M. J., & Kaplan, A. (1972). The office environment: Space planning and affective behavior. *Human Factors and Ergonomics in Manufacturing, 14*(5), 373–391.

Brunia, S., De Been, I., & van der Voordt, T. J. M. (2016). Accommodating new ways of working: Lessons from best practices and worst cases. *Journal of Corporate Real Estate*, *18*(1), 30–47. doi:10.1108/JCRE-10-2015-0028.

Business Week (1978). The trouble with open offices. *Business Week* (7 August), *88*, 84–5.

Carlopio, J. R. (1996). Construct validity of a physical work environment satisfaction questionnaire. *Journal of Occupational Health Psychology*, *1*(3), 330–344.

Cascio, W. F. (2000). Managing a virtual workplace. *Academy of Management Executive*, *14*(3), 81–90. doi:10.5465/AME.2000.4468068.

Chapman, A. J., Sheehy, N. P., Heywood, S., Dooley, B., & Collins, S. C. (1995). The organizational implications of teleworking. In C. L. Cooper & I. T. Robertson (eds), *International Review of Industrial and Organizational Psychology* (Vol. *10*, pp. 229–248). Chichester: John Wiley & Sons Ltd.

Charles, K.E.,& Veitch, J.(2002). *Environmental Satisfaction in Open-Plan Environments: 2. Effects of Workstation Size, Partition Height and Windows.* Institute for Research in Construction, National Research Council Canada.

Cherns, A. (1976). The principles of sociotechnical design. *Human Relations*, *29*(8), 783–792.

Cherns, A. (1987). Principles of sociotechnical design revisited. *Human Relations*, *40*(3), 153–161. doi:10.1177/001872678704000303.

Clegg, C. W. (2000). Sociotechnical principles for system design. *Applied Ergonomics*, *31*(5), 463–477. doi:10.1016/S0003-6870(00)00009-0.

Clegg, C. W., Cooch, P., Hornby, P., Maclaren, R., Robson, J. I., Symon, G. J., & Carey, N. (1996). Tools to incorporate some psychological and organisational issues during the development of computer-based systems. *Ergonomics*, *39*(3), 482–511.

Clegg, C. W., & Davis, M. C. (2016). Automation/advanced manufacturing technology/ computer-based integrated technology. In S. G. Rogelberg (ed.), *The Sage Encyclopedia of Industrial and Organizational Psychology* (2nd ed.). Thousand Oaks, CA: SAGE.

Clegg, C. W., Robinson, M. A., Davis, M. C., Bolton, L., Pieniazek, R., & McKay, A. (2017). Applying organizational psychology as a design science: A method for predicting malfunctions in socio-technical systems (premists). *Design Science*, *3*, 1–31. doi:10.1017/ dsj.2017.4.

Clegg, C. W., & Walsh, S. (2004). Change management: Time for a change! *European Journal of Work and Organizational Psychology*, *13*(2), 217–239. doi:10.1080/13594320444000074.

Daniels, K., Lamond, D., & Standen, P. (2001). Teleworking: Frameworks for organizational research. *Journal of Management Studies*, *38*(8), 1151–1185.

Danielsson, C. B., & Bodin, L. (2008). Office type in relation to health, well-being, and job satisfaction among employees. *Environment and Behavior*, *40*(5), 636–668. doi:10.1177/0013916507307459.

Davis, M. C., Challenger, R., Jayewardene, D. N. W., & Clegg, C. W. (2014). Advancing socio-technical systems thinking: A call for bravery. *Applied Ergonomics*, *45*(2, Part A), 171–180. doi:http://dx.doi.org/10.1016/j.apergo.2013.02.009.

Davis, M. C., Leach, D. J., & Clegg, C. W. (2011). The physical environment of the office: Contemporary and emerging issues. In G. P. Hodgkinson & J. K. Ford (eds), *International Review of Industrial and Organizational Psychology* (Vol. *26*, pp. 193–235). Chichester: Wiley.

Davis, M. C., & Offutt, R. (2015). *Activity Based Working: A Classic Case of Change Management?* Paper presented at the 2015 Academy of Management Annual Meeting, Vancouver, Canada.

De Croon, E., Sluiter, J., Kuijer, P. P., & Frings-Dresen, M. (2005). The effect of office concepts on worker health and performance: A systematic review of the literature. *Ergonomics*, *48*(2), 119–134. doi:10.1080/00140130512331319409.

Duffy, F. (1997). *The New Office*. London: Conran Octopus.

Duffy, F. (2000). Design and facilities management in a time of change. *Facilities, 18*(10/11/12), 371–375. doi:10.1108/02632770010349592.

Eason, K. (2008). Sociotechnical systems theory in the 21st century: Another half-filled glass? In D. Graves (ed.), *Sense in Social Science: A Collection of Essays in Honour of Dr. Lisl Klein* (pp. 123–134).

Eason, K. (2014). Afterword: The past, present and future of sociotechnical systems theory. *Applied Ergonomics, 45*(2, Part A), 213–220. doi:https://doi.org/10.1016/j.apergo.2013.09.017.

Elsbach, K. D., & Pratt, M. G. (2007). Chapter 4: The physical environment in organizations. *Academy of Management Annals, 1*(1), 181–224. doi:10.1080/078559809.

Emery, F. E. (1959). *Characteristics of Socio-Technical Systems*. Tavistock Institute Document Number 527. London: Tavistock Institute.

Foland, S. S., Rowlen, S., & Watson, S. (1995). *Team Space and Empowerment: A Formula for Success*. Paper presented at the World Workplace '95, IFMA Annual Conference, Miami.

Gillen, N. M. (2006). The future workplace, opportunities, realities and myths: A practical approach to creating meaningful environments. In J. Worthington (ed.), *Reinventing the Workplace* (2nd ed., pp. 61–78). Oxford: Architectural Press.

Göçer, Ö., Göçer, K., Ergöz Karahan, E., & İlhan Oygür, I. (2017). Exploring mobility and workplace choice in a flexible office through post-occupancy evaluation. *Ergonomics*, 1–17. doi:10.1080/00140139.2017.1349937.

Hall, D. J., & Ford, T. Q. (1998). A quality approach to factory design. *Industrial Management and Data Systems, 6*, 241–245.

Haynes, B. P. (2007). Office productivity: A theoretical framework. *Journal of Corporate Real Estate, 9*(2), 97–110.

Hongisto, V., Haapakangas, A., Varjo, J., Helenius, R., & Koskela, H. (2016). Refurbishment of an open-plan office: Environmental and job satisfaction. *Journal of Environmental Psychology, 45*, 176–191. doi:http://dx.doi.org/10.1016/j.jenvp.2015.12.004.

Hughes, H. P. N., Clegg, C. W., Bolton, L. E., & Machon, L. C. (2017). Systems scenarios: A tool for facilitating the socio-technical design of work systems. *Ergonomics, 60*(10), 1319–1335. doi:10.1080/00140139.2017.1288272.

Kaarlela-Tuomaala, A., Helenius, R., Keskinen, E., & Hongisto, V. (2009). Effects of acoustic environment on work in private office rooms and open-plan offices: Longitudinal study during relocation. *Ergonomics, 52*(11), 1423–1444.

Kim, J., & de Dear, R. (2013). Workspace satisfaction: The privacy–communication trade-off in open-plan offices. *Journal of Environmental Psychology, 36*, 18–26. doi:http://dx.doi.org/10.1016/j.jenvp.2013.06.007.

Knight, C., & Haslam, S. A. (2010). Your place or mine? Organizational identification and comfort as mediators of relationships between the managerial control of workspace and employees' satisfaction and well-being. *British Journal of Management, 21*(3), 717–735. doi:10.1111/j.1467-8551.2009.00683.x.

Laing, A. (2006). New patterns of work: The design of the office. In J. Worthington (ed.), *Reinventing the Workplace* (2nd ed., pp. 29–49). Oxford: Architectural Press.

Laing, A., Duffy, F., Jaunzens, D., & Willis, S. (1998). *New Environments for Working: The Redesign of Offices and Environmental Systems for New Ways of Working*. London: Construction Research Communications Ltd.

Lee, S. Y., & Brand, J. L. (2010). Can personal control over the physical environment ease distractions in office workplaces? *Ergonomics, 53*(3), 324–335. doi:10.1080/00140130903389019.

McCoy, J. M. (2005). Linking the physical work environment to creative context. *Journal of Creative Behavior, 39*(3), 169–191.

Morrow, P. C., McElroy, J. C., & Scheibe, K. P. (2012). Influencing organizational commitment through office redesign. *Journal of Vocational Behavior, 81*(1), 99–111. doi:http://dx.doi.org/10.1016/j.jvb.2012.05.004.

Mumford, E. (1983). *Designing Secretaries: The Participative Design of a Word Processing System.* Manchester: Manchester Business School.

Mumford, E. (1995). *Effective Systems Design and Requirements Analysis: The Ethics Approach.* Basingstoke: Macmillan.

Mumford, E. (2006). The story of socio-technical design: Reflections on its successes, failures and potential. *Information Systems Journal, 16*(4), 317–342. doi:10.1111/j.1365-2575.2006.00221.x.

Nadin, S. J., Waterson, P. E., & Parker, S. K. (2001). Participation in job redesign: An evaluation of the use of a sociotechnical tool and its impact. *Human Factors and Ergonomics in Manufacturing, 11*(1), 53–69.

Oldham, G. R., & Brass, D. J. (1979). Employee reactions to an open-plan office: A naturally occurring quasi-experiment. *Administrative Science Quarterly, 24*(2), 267–284. doi:10.2307/2392497.

Oldham, G. R., Cummings, A., & Zhou, J. (1995). The spatial configuration of organizations. In G. Ferris (ed.), *Research in Personnel and Human Resources Management* (Vol. *13*, pp. 1–37). Greenwich, CT: JAI Press.

Oldham, G. R., & Fried, Y. (1987). Employee reactions to workspace characteristics. *Journal of Applied Psychology, 72*(1), 75–80. doi:10.1037/0021-9010.72.1.75.

Pasmore, W. A. (1994). *Creating Strategic Change: Designing the Flexible, High Performing Organization.* New York: Wiley.

Ridgway, K., Cerulli, C., Davis, M., Challenger, R., Wiseall, S., Hill, P., & Clegg, C. (2008). *Designing the Factory of the Future.* Paper presented at the International Conference on Applied Human Factors and Ergonomics (AHFEI), Las Vegas, USA.

Sundstrom, E., Burt, R. E., & Kamp, D. (1980). Privacy at work: Architectural correlates of job satisfaction and job performance. *Academy of Management Journal, 23*(1), 101–117. doi:10.2307/255498.

Sundstrom, E., Herbert, R. K., & Brown, D. W. (1982). Privacy and communication in an open-plan office: A case study. *Environment and Behavior, 14*(3), 379–392. doi:10.1177/0013916582143007.

Sundstrom, E., Town, J. P., Rice, R. W., & Osborn, D. P. (1994). Office noise, satisfaction, and performance. *Environment and Behavior, 26*(2), 195–222.

Trist, E. L., & Bamforth, K. W. (1951). Some social and psychological consequences of the longwall method of coal-getting: An examination of the psychological situation and defences of a work group in relation to the social structure and technological content of the work system. *Human Relations, 4*(1), 3–38. doi:10.1177/001872675100400101.

Turner, G., & Myerson, J. (1998). *New Workspace New Culture: Office Design as a Catalyst for Change.* Aldershot: Gower Publishing Limited.

Veitch, J. A., Charles, K. E., Farley, K. M. J., & Newsham, G. R. (2007). A model of satisfaction with open-plan office conditions: Cope field findings. *Journal of Environmental Psychology, 27*(3), 177–189.

Vischer, J. C. (2005). *Space Meets Status: Designing Workplace Performance.* Oxford: Routledge.

Vos, P., & van der Voordt, T. (2001). Tomorrow's offices through today's eyes: Effects of innovation in the working environment. *Journal of Corporate Real Estate, 4*(1), 48–65.

Waterson, P. E. (2005). Sociotechnical design of work systems. In J. R. Wilson & N. Corlett (eds), *Evaluation of Human Work* (3rd ed., pp. 769–792). London: Taylor & Francis.

Wohlers, C., & Hertel, G. (2017). Choosing where to work at work: Towards a theoretical model of benefits and risks of activity-based flexible offices. *Ergonomics, 60*(4), 467–486. doi:10.1080/00140139.2016.1188220.

Zalesny, M. D., & Farace, R. V. (1987). Traditional versus open offices: A comparison of sociotechnical, social relations, and symbolic meaning perspectives. *Academy of Management Journal, 30*(2), 240–259. doi:10.2307/256272.

PART III

The physical environment of work and work design

8

CONNECTING WORKSPACE, WORK CHARACTERISTICS, AND OUTCOMES THROUGH WORK DESIGN

Themes, models, and directions

M.K. Ward and Sharon K. Parker

Organizations and research institutions are challenged to understand the interactive and dynamic effects of contemporary changes such as an older workforce (Andel, Finkel, & Pedersen, 2016), alternative workspaces (Hills & Levy, 2014), and new types of work (Parker, 2014). Attention to new workspaces (e.g. success of entrepreneurial co-working spaces) highlights the importance of the physical context to performance and organizational behaviours in general. The importance of context in organizational behaviour is widely recognized – and has been considered in relation to topics from entrepreneurship (Gloss, Pollack, & Ward, 2017), to online survey design (Ward & Meade, 2017), to work design (e.g. Oldham & Brass, 1979; Morgeson, Dierdorff, & Hmurovic, 2010; Parker, Van den Broeck, & Holman, 2017).

Physical workspace (i.e. workplace design; e.g. Sundstrom, Burt, & Kamp, 1980) is a substantial part of work and refers to specific elements of a workspace including location, layout, and sensation factors such as light, colours, sounds, smells, and dimensions of spaces. Work design is a broader concept, referring to the content, structure, and organization of the tasks, roles, and responsibilities of work (Parker, 2014). Work design is often assumed to be mostly about psychosocial elements of work (Humphrey, Nahrgang, & Morgeson, 2007), but the physical environment can also be considered part of work design (Morgeson & Humphrey, 2006). More generally, considering work design in isolation from physical factors such as workspace might be nonsensical, especially in some lines of work where there is a tight interconnection between these elements (e.g. ballet dancer).

Estimates of the amount of time people spend indoors are as high as 90% in some cases (Anthes, 2016), which means there is ample time for the workspace to influence workers and their work designs. Consequently, close attention has been paid to indoor spaces, particularly workspaces, in various disciplines (e.g. architecture, ergonomics) and research entities (e.g. the Well Living Lab). Perceptions of the physical workspace relates to job satisfaction (Carlopio, 1996) and performance (Sundstrom et al., 1980; Wineman, 1986), and relates indirectly to organizational commitment and turnover (Carlopio, 1996). Performance and satisfaction of workers partially depends on: physical enclosures, furniture, privacy (both acoustic and visual), and ergonomics (Brill, Margulis, & Konar, 1984). In addition to important organizational outcomes, decisions regarding workspace property and facilities can be notably visible, constraining, and expensive (Omara, 1999). In sum, workspaces have important implications for organizational behaviour, and paying more attention to the connection to work design may better explain links between workspace and important outcomes.

Building upon the argument that physical environments are part of work design, work design should be included when modeling the relationships between workspace and work outcomes. Elements of workspace can enable people to do their job in ways that utilize positive aspects of their work design to promote sustained performance. For example, workspace can foster social support and promote feelings of control/autonomy. In this way, workspace can be an important component of good work design. Unfortunately, however, workspace can also have negative effects on work design. For example, leaders of an organization may want to give employees more social contact and feedback in their workspace, and therefore move employees into a completely open layout and shared space. But this change may actually reduce feedback and intimate conversations because of lack of privacy. Moreover, the open space design may negatively impact employees' sense of control, and over time may create strain. Inconsistency between workspace and desired work design, therefore, can lead to negative work outcomes.

Although rigorous findings from extensive research have connected work design to important work outcomes (e.g. performance, wellbeing), the quantity and quality of research connecting workspace to work outcomes is lacking. The purpose of this chapter is to begin to better understand the connection between work design, workspace, and outcomes. We argue that while there are other ways that workspace and work design might work together (e.g. they could have interactive effects; or one could look at, for example, 'autonomy over the physical space'), our focus is on work design as a mediating mechanism that links workspace to outcomes. To put it another way, we focus on how work space can shape the psychological aspects of work.

In the remainder of the chapter, we present a synthesis across the literatures of physical workspace and work design, and highlight major themes. We then specify future research directions that build from proposed models.

Overview of workspaces: emergent themes from the literatures

To date, workspace has been an important subject of thought pieces, projects, observations, case studies, interviews, and experiments from architecture, design, human factors and ergonomics, and neuro-architecture. The amalgamation of all of these works is a detailed, complex, and nuanced perspective of workspaces. Numerous features of workspace can be grouped into three dimensions: layout, location, and use (de Croon, Sluiter, Kuijer, & Frings-Dresen, 2005). Coradi, Heinzen, and Boutellier (2015) refer to these dimensions as covering three types of elements: (1) functional, including furniture, coffee machines, or food equipment, and other infrastructure elements, (2) geographic, including locations of distinct areas within a building or floor of a building, and (3) architectural, including openness, accessibility, and proximity to people/objects. The structure, dimensions, objects, materials, light, colour, sound, smell, humidity, and temperature can all impact users of a space. Here we discuss a selection of the numerous elements of (work)space by underscoring three major themes.

Theme 1: Benefits of the 'natural' workspace

Findings across multiple publications and studies indicate that the natural environment is increasingly being recognized as an important influence on people in a variety of spaces, including workspaces. The cluster of workspace characteristics related to nature is termed biophilia. It is defined qualitatively and quantitatively with biophilic stimuli being: plants, light, vistas (actual or paintings of nature scenes, preferably non-winter), water fixtures, and temperature, all mimicking what would evolutionarily be considered natural and safe. Focusing on plants, for example, Ulrich (1984) found that patient recovery following surgery improved (fewer pain medications and shorter hospital stays) for patients with views of nature versus a brick wall. Using stronger research designs, Nieuwenhuis, Knight, Postmes, and Haslam (2014) found from three field experiments (two longitudinal designs) that, compared with lean offices, workspaces with plants that had nothing to do with the work itself (call centre, business consultancy) increased subjective perceptions of air quality, concentration, and workplace satisfaction, as well as objective measures of productivity (e.g. taking less time on vigilance tasks). Each of the three studies separately addressed issues in the design of the prior study. The lean and green workspaces of Study 1 were on the same floor and thus, the plants of the green workspaces were occasionally noticeable to participants in the lean condition. Study 2 had inadequacies in the objective measures of performance, with longer times on calls at a phone centre can indicate inefficiency or superior customer service. Finally, Study 3 addressed the internal validity issues using an experimental design, yet it used a cross-sectional design. Objective indicators (time spent, and errors) of performance were strong, and the types of tasks were relevant to future work, requiring information processing and vigilance. Nevertheless, taken together, the set of three studies provides good evidence that plants affect work performance, although the research leaves much to be learned regarding the duration and shape of that effect over time, as well as what that relationship looks like in terms of information processing and vigilance objective indicators in the real work tasks that employees do for their actual jobs.

Further research indicates desirable outcomes from workspace characteristics that are similar to safe, natural environments, achieved through having plants, sunlight, fresh air, natural vistas, and dark floors to lighter walls to light ceilings. Such outcomes include: improved perceived air quality (De Croon et al., 2005), increased cognitive activity, increased relaxation, suppressed autonomic nervous system activation and stress-related negative emotions (Ulrich, 1984), increased parasympathetic activity, increased electroencephalographic (EEG) activity (Choi et al., 2016), and improved concentration and increased positive emotions (Lee, 2010). In sum, there appear to be several potential benefits to employees when workspaces are more like the natural environment.

This restorative effect of nature can be seen through the lens of the job demands–resources model (Demerouti, Bakker, Nachreiner, & Schaufeli, 2001). This model theorizes that work entails demands, or aspects that require sustained effort, concentration, or energy; and at high levels, demands can create strain, burnout, and other health impairments (Parker, Morgeson, & Johns, 2017). Job resources are aspects of work that support workers in dealing with work demands and enable them to progress toward work goals. Job resources increase motivation and engagement (Parker, 2014). Since evidence from several studies indicates that biophilia can energize and restore depleted cognitive resources of workers, natural elements can be conceptualized as a job resource. When there are fixed, high demands (e.g. accountants during tax season), leveraging the workplace to energize workers through changing the workspace may improve performance.

Much of the empirical work in this field, however, is cross-sectional, non-experimental, or self-report. These elements of research design have severely constrained the ability to estimate any direct, causal relationships from natural elements in the workplace on employees. Additionally, there is an unanswered call to consider and study clusters of workspace variables together (Parker, 2014). In real office settings, people do not take in one aspect of the workspace at a time and behave based solely off of that one element. In other words, painting a mural in the office of a natural vista will not necessarily have the same effect in an office that is consistently musty, cold, and smelly compared with an office that also has good air quality, movement, and no pungent, displeasing odours. Experimental studies researching workspace effects on performance have generally manipulated one variable at a time to determine singular relationships. The internal validity of these studies does not outweigh the costs to external validity. Future research can address this issue by adapting the person-centred approach to analyse meaningful clusters of office characteristics, manipulating those clusters, and assessing how those clusters interact with person variables to result in different behaviours (e.g. performance) and emotions/perceptions (e.g. wellbeing).

The explanatory mechanisms underlying the relationships between biophilia and various objective and subjective work outcomes also remain somewhat unknown. As we discuss later, an organizational neuroscience approach may provide the micro-perspective to look at the neural and cognitive processes occurring in the brains of workers as they do their jobs in various office environments.

An organizational neuroscience perspective can use neuroimaging (e.g. EEG activity measurements) with task positive/default mode network showing effortful attention/non-directional, restorative attention when doing particular parts of the job in particular workspaces. For example, what would be the best biophilia setup based on how employees' brains are responding (not subjective assessments)? Overall, research is needed that goes beyond subjective, self-report, cross-sectional studies to assess the effects of natural elements (e.g. water fixture) in the office.

Theme 2: Mixed effects of open workspaces

A second major theme indicates that removing walls, or the open office concept, does not guarantee success. Open workspaces are intended to sustain high levels of productivity and collaboration at higher efficiency than traditional closed-office layouts (Hills & Levy, 2014). When workers are in close proximity, there can be increases in communication, collaboration, innovation, creativity, improved workers' perceptions of creativity, and increased creative performance (Dul & Ceylan, 2011; Oksanen & Ståhle, 2013). However, many studies show that transitions to open office designs have negative effects.

Although open workspaces can – in theory – increase collaboration and creativity, more interaction does not mean better interaction. Open spaces mean uncontrolled and, at times, unwanted interactions (Davis, Leach, & Clegg, 2011). Stimuli, such as having to hear conversations that are irrelevant or having to look at someone else's computer screen, are distracting (Oldham, Kulik, & Stepina, 1991). These distractions can lead to lower performance, satisfaction, and privacy (de Croon et al., 2005). Perceptions of work demands increase as a result of needing to deal with the additional task of managing interactions and irrelevant speech (Smith-Jackson & Klein, 2009). Open workspaces also remove aspects of physical space that might previously have been tools that workers utilize to control the timing, amount, and type of social interactions in socially acceptable ways (i.e. without being seen as rude). Limited empirical evidence suggests that open workplaces increase demands (increased cognitive load, worse interpersonal relations).

All together, the available evidence suggests that open workspaces threaten productivity and performance via potentially detrimental effects to employee health. Employees exhibit increased physiological and psychological stress in open, non-traditional workspace layouts (Roper & Juneja, 2008). Employees' satisfaction levels drop in open, non-traditional workspaces compared with traditional closed workspaces because of differences in privacy (both visual and sound), and amounts of space and noise (Kim & de Dear, 2013; Sundstrom, Town, Rice, Osborn, & Brill, 1994). Absenteeism due to sickness (Pejtersen, Feveile, Christensen, & Burr, 2011) and physical symptoms of ill health (Pejtersen, Allermann, Kristensen, & Poulsen, 2006) both increase in large, shared workspaces compared with enclosed offices.

Hot-desking, a specific open workspace setup in which no worker has an assigned desk (individuals choose their workspace each time they go in to work), also appears to have negative effects. Just like the wider research on open office spaces, there is more negative interactions and distrust, and fewer co-worker friendships, in hot-desking workspaces (Morrison & Macky, 2017). In addition, 'first-come, first-served' systems in hot-desking give preferential spaces to early risers and arrivers to work, which might penalize those with dependants (e.g. who need to drop kids off or check in on parents). Hot-desking also requires a new setup at the desk each day, and minimizes ownership over the space where, in more permanent setups, workers can express themselves through the space (e.g. display photos; Hirst, 2011). If electronic communication is sufficient, hot-desking can result in less identification with a team and more with the organization (Millward, Haslam, & Postmes, 2007). Just as in other forms of open layouts, it is generally unclear as to whether there are any positive effects of hot-desking on workers and organizations.

The job characteristics model (JCM) of Hackman and Oldham (1976) may be a useful framework through which to view the relationships between objective workspace features and resulting subjective perceptions among workers. The JCM posits five core job characteristics: task identity, autonomy, task variety, interdependence, and significance. Research has found autonomy to be particularly important for objective outcomes such as organizational performance, employee engagement, and employee wellbeing (Parker, 2014). This is consistent with results in the workspace literature that show negative outcomes when open offices reduce autonomy by reducing one's control over interruptions. On the other hand, open offices might have other work design benefits. For example, they might enable employees to literally see more of the work processes that are required to create and deliver a finished product/service, thereby increasing task identity (degree to which a job requires completion of a whole job from beginning to end). More interactions with internal customers, brought about by closer proximity, might also expose employees to feedback from customers regarding a product/service feature they developed. This means increased feedback and perceptions of significance, or the degree to which the work impacts others (Parker, 2014).

Having autonomy might also mitigate some of the negative effects of open offices. Control over the physical work context leads to positive outcomes such as increased satisfaction, diversity, and creativity (Kuratko, Hornsby, & Covin, 2014). Research shows that when employees have control over facets of their workspaces, they value open, non-traditional layouts (Hills & Levy, 2014; Kim & de Dear, 2013). Workers attribute close proximity of co-workers to increased collaboration, but proximity means increased distractions as well (Hills & Levy, 2014). If there is no option for employees to control when the additional stimuli and demands are seen or heard, autonomy can decrease (reduced resources). Thus, ensuring autonomy in open office layouts becomes particularly salient from a work design perspective. There is also the possibility that the drawbacks of open workspaces may be lessened given the changing nature of work, with increasing technologically facilitated communication (e.g. texts, tweets, direct messaging via Slack, Instagram, and Snapchat). These options may pair well with open workspaces to maintain privacy and reduce noise (Davis et al., 2011).

Theme 3: The influence of workspace varies across types of work and types of workers

A final, important point to make regarding workspace is that how workspace and work design interrelate varies. Work differs in terms of the workspaces in which the work can be done. With knowledge work, there can be substantial flexibility, particularly in terms of online, virtual, and technologically intense work such as coding or technical support positions. These jobs can be done wherever there is an internet connection and computer on which to work. Other types of work are more rigid in terms of workspaces in which the work itself can be performed. Examples include, but are not limited to: submariners, mechanics, geologists, marine biologists, and construction site managers. Thus work (and work design) can be highly constrained by workspace, or it can be performed in almost any workspace. Where jobs sit on this continuum is likely to shift in future work as technological changes occur and there is more automation across industries.

In addition to technology, work also evolves in response to shifts in economics, demographics, and other such factors. Workspaces, for example, must adapt to evolving work interactions of an age-diverse workforce (Van der Voordt, 2003). Work design has already started to focus on the ageing workforce in which the workforce globally is getting older, which can mean shifting needs and preferences (e.g. colour contrasts, temperature, lighting, noise levels, non-traditional layouts, distractions) in terms of workspace (McElroy & Morrow, 2010). Future research is needed in work design to investigate probable differences in employees' workspace preferences across the lifespan, which we discuss later in this chapter.

A socio-technical systems theory may be a theoretical framework to use in setting up needed research in work design/workspaces across the lifespan (Parker, 2014). A socio-technical systems approach is particularly useful given it is focused on optimizing the technical (i.e. tools and elements of workspace) and social facets of work (e.g. Davis et al., 2011). Thus, socio-technical systems theory suggests that workspaces must fit with the work itself such that work that requires sustained, critical, and analytical thinking would be poorly suited to workspaces set up for hot-desking. Given the constant need to reduce overhead and stay competitive, open workspaces and new types of flexible workspaces will likely remain.

Future work will see continued development in technical systems and tools used across industries outside of traditionally technical jobs. One example is the application of autonomous vehicles to disrupt the trucking industry. If human truck drivers are replaced by self-driving trucks, this would represent a dramatic shift in the technical systems in the trucking industry, and the resulting changes to that workforce mean drastically reduced size of social system requirements. Yet, for the few who remain, those social systems will remain as important as ever. The socio-technical perspective suggests a helpful way to monitor and adapt to changes in future work is to adapt the workspace, which includes the tools and technical systems of the job, while considering the effects of those changes on social systems. In essence, it is nonsensical to consider work design separately from workspace when evidence shows they are related. Research to date also indicates that there is ample work left to be done to understand relationships between workspace and work design.

Synthesis of literature and plausible models

Figure 8.1a–c presents three ways suggested by our review discussed previously in which work design might interrelate with workspace to affect important outcomes. First, aspects of the workspace can be seen as elements of the work design itself (Figure 8.1a). For example, the distraction and interruptions that occur as a result of some open space working can be considered as a type of job demand. From this perspective, aspects of the workspace have direct effects on outcomes such as performance and wellbeing, alongside other work design characteristics. In considering both work design and workspace, it might be more meaningful to investigate and describe clusters of variables together rather than individually. One possibility is that particular 'bundles' of workspace attributes and work design characteristics will be especially important for outcomes. For example, future research of the effect of increased biophilia in a workspace may relate differently from multiple work design variables. Those relationships may help develop work design profiles.

One theoretical framework that may help to connect workspace with work design is via psychological space in Lewin's field theory (1951). Lewin posited that an individual's behaviour in, and interpretation of, a space (e.g. workspace) follow from said individual's memories, and physical and social surroundings. Life-spaces consist of individuals' (i.e. workers') subjective interpretations of objective elements of situations (e.g. open door to the CEO's office) in the environment (e.g. office), and the importance of objective elements is based on subjective meanings (Kristensen, 2004; Lewin, 1951). Simply put, life-spaces include psychological, social, and physical elements of a space in order to predict and explain individual behaviours within that space. Those behaviours may be measures of work performance, organizational commitment, or other work outcomes. Future research is needed to develop profiles of workspace and work design, and to investigate relationships between the two.

Second, as shown in Figure 8.1b, psychosocial aspects of work design can mediate the effects of workspace on outcomes. Above, we gave several examples of this model, such as how open workspaces can increase social contact or reduce one's autonomy over their work environment. One could systematically map how each key workspace attribute can shape the major psychosocial work experiences, with the advantage that this approach links relatively less well-understood features of work (such as biofilia and open space working) to very well-understood features of work. From a practical perspective, since we know a great deal about the psychosocial aspects of work design, this means practitioners (e.g. architects, designers, managers) should actively consider how workspace features can shape these well-known aspects of work. It is possible that different choices can be made with respect to workspace features that will then flow through to more positive effects on psychosocial aspects of work. For example, we know that social contact is an important and positive aspect of work design, but we also know that excess noise creates distractions and demands, so workspaces could be deliberately designed to minimize demands (such as by preserving offices for those who prefer them) while maximizing social contact opportunities (such as by creating plenty of communal spaces to facilitate interaction).

A third model, Figure 8.1c, recognizes workspace and work design as two drivers of outcomes, but which can also interact. For example, above we cited research suggesting that the effect of open spaces on performance and wellbeing can be moderated by job autonomy, with autonomy buffering some of their negative effects. One could theorize other such interactions. For example, the positive effects of biophilia on employee wellbeing might be severely curtained if individuals have jobs with exceptionally high levels of job demands and/or low resources.

All of the models potentially have moderators, both the work itself and the workers themselves. For example, knowledge work – which typically allows employees to craft their own work environment – means that specific facets of a work context may have relatively weaker effects than a workspace in which there is little opportunity for customizing and adjusting one's own individual workspaces. On the other hand, biophilia aspects might be especially important for those individuals who work very long hours in an office. With respect to workers themselves, illustrative possible moderating processes include that: older workers who have more trouble hearing might be relatively more distracted by open space working; individuals with extroverted personalities might prefer open space working; and people with particular values (e.g. commitment to nature) might especially thrive in highly natural physical workspaces.

Future research directions

There are numerous routes for future research, and we highlight four that have high potential for impact in the field of work design and to inform and strengthen research in workspace. We focus on the first part of the model because of the ample research that has previously established links between work design and work outcomes. Of course, any future studies should include objective and subjective measures of work outcomes where possible. This will pay off in terms of increasing the practical implications of future studies.

Co-working spaces

A new type of workspace has recently emerged, which is the co-working space. In these spaces, individuals from many different startups and workplaces are provided with space as well as other possible resources (e.g. training opportunities). Such spaces are commonly used by entrepreneurs for their startups. Entrepreneurship is a key driver of economic growth and job creation (U.S. Bureau of Economic Analysis, 2015). Although entrepreneurs, particularly successful ones, often shape

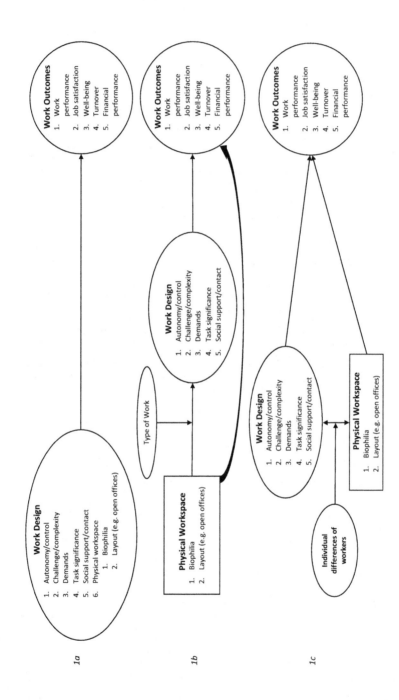

FIGURE 8.1 Integrative models of plausible relationships between workspace and work outcomes

future work, there is still much to learn about how work design (Baron, 2010) and workspace can be leveraged to improve the success of entrepreneurs.

Co-working spaces are shared workspaces that are nearly always multi-use spaces, often containing some combination of: private office spaces, meeting rooms to rent, tiny rooms for phone calls, silent work zones, shared restrooms, kitchen area, reception, mail, and recreational/social areas. Co-working spaces are similar to open offices in that co-working space often has open areas where people can share desk space and see others working. Unlike many of the studies regarding open offices, co-working spaces are voluntary workspaces such that entrepreneurs sign up to become members of their own accord. Future research should investigate whether entrepreneurs in co-working spaces experience the mixed effects reported from studies of open offices. Does the co-working space decrease control (via unexpected interruptions)? Or, in fact, because entrepreneurs have deliberately chosen these environments, perhaps benefits – such as for social contact – outweigh any downsides? Answering questions such as these has implications for entrepreneurs, informing them about how best to set up their workspace and work design. There are implications for organizations that provide co-working spaces. In order to compete and grow, they need to create workspaces that foster good work design for their members.

There are also implications for work design that should be considered alongside workspace choices. Co-working spaces are communities that are part of entrepreneurial ecosystems (Shepherd & Patzelt, 2017) – a multi-level context deemed important to supporting entrepreneurial performance. Little is known about ways in which work design fosters identity development, and co-working spaces may be an ideal setting for future research. The work design growth model posits that good work design (including social support, autonomy, complexity, feedback) can impact cognitive, motivational, and behavioural processes that can grow a collective identity in workers, and increase identity complexity (Parker, 2014). Entrepreneurial co-working spaces have numerous members from multiple organizations working in the same, co-working community. Future research is needed to investigate whether and how collective identities are developed in entrepreneurs who are members of co-working spaces. Answers to these and related questions may require investigations into clusters of characteristics of work design and workspaces.

Implicit work design of those involved in designing work and workspaces

The new work experience suggests it may be important to focus on designing work and workspaces with the full work experience in mind. In the experience economy, consumers buy experiences and those consumers have jobs where they, as employees, invest in their experience and expect particular work experiences from their jobs and careers. Thus, there may be preconceived notions of what is good versus bad experiences in work, and just as there are implicit leadership theories, people may have implicit work design theories.

Implicit notions of work design may influence the creation of workspace. Architects, interior designers, and technology experts that outfit future workspaces may not have the understanding of how their planned features of a workspace may affect work design. Not considering work design explicitly may shape their choices in building out workspaces. Alternatively, their implicit ideas about work design (e.g. that high social contact in work is good) may design an open space with few boundaries for sight and sound to maximize points where workers intermix throughout their work day. As described earlier in this chapter, high social contact in open offices does not necessarily create a desirable work experience. Future research can investigate ways in which preconceived notions of good work design in architects influences them to include workspace elements that create demands or resources for workers.

After the space is built, implicit notions of good and bad work design may be particularly relevant for entrepreneurs who pursue new ventures spurred by bad work design (bad work experience) from previous employers (Baron, 2010). Future research is needed to investigate relationships between the preconceived notions about work that are held by people. How do those preconceptions influence work designs they create for themselves? How does the workspace influence the development of preconceptions about work design? What are adequate ways to measure cognitive conceptualizations where self-report is not feasible nor appropriate?

Neural processes as explanatory mechanisms underlying relationships between workspace and work design

A third option for future research would involve taking an organizational neuroscience approach to investigate non-conscious, neural processes that may be explanatory mechanisms for relationships between workspace, work design, and work outcomes. Neural processes certainly are not sufficient to explain the work experience, but they are necessary. Therefore, the brain may be a potentially useful mediator wherein the cluster of workspace variables is perceived and interpretations relate to clusters of work design variables. Of the many neural processes that are implicated when working, future research should focus on neural processes with ample research and highest potential for relevance. Following this logic, we expect executive functioning, particularly attention, to be especially relevant to workspace and work design.

In looking to cognitive and neurological processes that offer explanatory mechanisms to connect physical workspace with work design, attention emerges as a necessary point of discussion. In a broad sense, attention is selective cognitive processing related to the constraint of limited cognitive resources (Shiffrin & Schneider, 1977). Processes of attention can be bottom–up (external stimuli engage and passively induce awareness through sensation and perception of neurological and cognitive processes) or top–down (internal goals, intentions, cognitions that are not necessarily related to the current physical workspace then influence increased awareness to particular stimuli and decreased conscious awareness of other stimuli). Overt attention means that the observer re-orients (via body, head, eye movement) towards the focus of attention. Covert attention refers to attention that can be focused on something using cognitive processes (Posner, Snyder & Davidson, 1980). No physical movement is necessary for covert attentional shifts, and covert attention can have multiple foci simultaneously.

Visual attention may be particularly useful to determine ways in which workspace influences work design. There is substantial research that measures visual attention via eye movements such as saccades, drifts, and microsaccades. Detailed explanations of each of these types of movements is beyond the scope of this chapter.

N-SEEV (Wickens, 1984) is a useful theory of attention from which to describe likely mechanisms that connect the external workspace with the experience of work through work design. N-SEEV stands for Noticing-Salience Effort Expectancy Value, and when taken together the theory includes different forms of attention. Salience refers to the ability of a visual stimuli to elicit attention by contrast or movement for example. Effort is the amount of work (cognitive, movement) needed to notice the stimuli. Both are bottom–up processes to influence visual attention, by attracting attention and dictating how easy it is to visually notice something. Workspace elements influence these bottom–up attentional processes. The expectancy and information value are top–down attention processes, and are the perceived probability of the occurrence of an important event, and value is the level of importance given to that event. These top–down processes likely are influenced by work design (e.g. previous feedback in relation to a co-worker makes one see that co-worker everywhere). Thus, visual attention viewed from the N-SEEV model framework may be particularly useful to delineate cognitive and neural processes underlying ways in which workspace impacts work outcomes through work design.

Future research is needed that employs methods such as eye-tracking and EEG to determine how people neurologically process particular clusters of workspace and work design variables. Such studies may help organizations and individuals design work from a cognitive perspective such that we can redesign work to fit our brains, rather than the common situation of making workers (and their brains) fit the job.

The ageing workforce

Work design and workspace research has already started focus on the ageing workforce; job-crafting and fitting work to workers can inform the workspace literature and workspace can assist work design scholars in developing both more comprehensive and positive approaches to supporting those who stay in the workforce later in the lifespan such that workspaces can be designed to align employee behaviour with the organization's mission and culture (Mencl & Lester, 2014). Such alignment can potentially increase employee job satisfaction, creativity, and productivity (Lee & Brand, 2005; Rothe, Lindholm, Hyvönen, & Nenonen, 2012).

Workspace literature can inform work design by informing work design of potentially important generational differences. For example, older workers (e.g. workers in the Baby Boomers and Generation X) have higher preference for control over temperature and furniture in their workspaces (Rothe et al., 2012) and are more dissatisfied with the noise, distraction, and lack of privacy in open office layouts, whereas Millennials prefer the open layouts and contemporary designs (McElroy & Morrow, 2010). This research aligns with results from Binnewies, Ohly, and Niessen (2008) that revealed generational shifts in terms of work design variables such as autonomy and support for creativity. Thus, physical elements of the workspace may in part explain Binnewies et al.'s (2008) finding, and point to multi-use workspaces given the mutually exclusive preferences of these two age groups of the workforce. We echo the call for more research in this area (Kim & de Dear, 2013; Rasila & Rothe, 2012), and urge further investigation to connect workspace as an antecedent to work design preferences of an aging workforce.

Practical implications

Several recommendations for workspaces flow from the above findings.

First, as a general rule, bring in biophilic design elements. Mimic nature in the components of the building using dark flooring, lighter walls (red/yellow correlates with socializing, blue with calming effects), and lightest for the ceilings to imitate the sky. Avoid monochrome spaces because the single hue is visually stressful, and can increase accidents among older adults who may not see changes in depth on stairs, for example. Where possible, create safe/power positions for employees so they have a clear vista, preferably with their backs to a wall with a view of doors to induce a sense of safety. Scenery of winter is not restorative compared with greener seasons that often have sunny weather.

The second recommendation is to minimize physical stressors. For example, ensure appropriate lighting, temperature, ventilation, and adequate space for work and storage (Spreckelmeyer 1993). Defined and clear traffic flow through corridors can reduce physical stressors.

Third, ensure privacy, interaction, and appropriate acoustics by using a configurable, multi-use, or bullpen in the open layout (Lee, 2010).

Fourth, for workers already operating in open workspaces, create and enforce the use of protocols (Hedge, 1982) that are designed to increase perceptions of privacy and control. Examples of protocols include respecting the privacy of others and minimizing telephone conversation noise (Brennan, Chugh, & Kline, 2002). Protocols can minimize social stressors and enable workspace to create good work design (e.g. by maintaining autonomy in an open environment).

Finally, give workers autonomy over their workspace. When considering a particular workspace, consider potential effects it may have on the control workers have over the way in which they prefer to work.

Conclusion

The goal of our synthesis across literatures was to inspire scholars and practitioners from a variety of training backgrounds (entrepreneurship, organizational behaviour, architecture, neurosciences, human factors, and ergonomics) to consider the potentially important intersection between workspace and work design. Both workspaces and work design will need to evolve alongside changes in the workforce and in work itself. A better understanding of how workspace and work design relate will help us ensure that future work will benefit workers as well as the economies they grow.

References

Andel, R., Finkel, D., & Pedersen, N. L. (2016). Effects of preretirement work complexity and postretirement leisure activity on cognitive aging. *Journals of Gerontology, Series B: Psychological Sciences and Social Sciences*, 71, 849–856. http://dx.doi.org/10.1093/geronb/gbv026.

Anthes, E. (2016). The office experiment: Can science build the perfect workspace? *Nature*, 537(7620), 294–296. https://doi.org/10.1038/537294a.

Baron, R. A. (2010). Job design and entrepreneurship: Why closer connections = mutual gains. *Journal of Organizational Behavior*, 31(2–3), 370–378.

Binnewies, C., Ohly, S., & Niessen, C. (2008). Age and creativity at work. *Journal of Managerial Psychology*, 23(4), 438–457.

Brennan A, Chugh JS, Kline T. (2002). Traditional versus open office design: A longitudinal field study. *Environment and Behavior*, 34(3), 279–299.

Brill, M., Margulis, S. ,& Konar, E. (1984). *Using Office Design to Increase Productivity*. Buffalo, NY: Workplace Design and Productivity.

Carlopio, J. R. (1996). Construct validity of a physical work environment satisfaction questionnaire. *Journal of Occupational Health Psychology*, 1(3), 330–344. https://doi.org/10.1037/1076-8998.1.3.330

Choi, J. Y., Park, S. A., Jung, S. J., Lee, J. Y., Son, K. C., An, Y. J., & Lee, S. W. (2016). Physiological and psychological responses of humans to the index of greenness of an interior space. *Complementary Therapies in Medicine*, 28, 37–43. https://doi.org/10.1016/j.ctim.2016.08.002.

Coradi, A., Heinzen, M., & Boutellier, R. (2015). A longitudinal study of workspace design for knowledge exploration and exploitation in the research and development process. *Creativity and Innovation Management*, 24(1), 55–71. Retrieved from http://search.ebscohost.com/login.aspx?direct=true&db=bth&AN=101024090&site=ehost-live

Davis, M. C., Leach, D. J., & Clegg, C. W. (2011). The physical environment of the office: Contemporary and emerging issues. *International Review of Industrial and Organizational Psychology*, 26(2011), 193–237. doi:10.1002/9781119992592.ch6.

de Croon, E. M., Sluiter, J. K., Kuijer, P. P. F. M., & Frings-Dresen, M. H. W. (2005). The effect of office concepts on worker health and performance: A systematic review of the literature. *Ergonomics*, 48(2), 119–134. https://doi.org/10.1080/0014013051233 1319409.

Demerouti, E., Bakker, A. B., Nachreiner, F., & Schaufeli, W. B. (2001). The job demands–resources model of burnout. *Journal of Applied Psychology*, 86(3), 499–512.

Dul, J., & Ceylan, C. (2011). Work environments for employee creativity. *Ergonomics*, 54(1), 12–20. https://doi.org/10.1080/00140139.2010.542833.

Gloss, A., Pollack, J. M., & Ward, M. K. (2017). A risky shift? An exploration of the measurement equivalence of entrepreneurial attitudes and entrepreneurial orientation across socioeconomic gradients. *Journal of Business Venturing Insights, 7*, 32–37.

Hackman, J. R., & Oldham, G. R. (1976). Motivation through the design of work: Test of a theory. *Organizational Behavior and Human Performance, 16*(2), 250–279. https://doi.org/10.1016/0030-5073(76)90016-7.

Hedge, A. (1982). The open-plan office: A systematic investigation of employee reactions to their work environment. *Environment and Behavior, 14*, 519–542.

Hills, R., & Levy, D. (2014). Workspace design and fit-out: What knowledge workers value. *Property Management Facilities, 32*(5), 415–432. https://doi.org/http://dx.doi.org/10.1108/PM-02-2014-0011.

Hirst, A. (2011). Settlers, vagrants and mutual indifference: Unintended consequences of hot-desking. *Journal of Organizational Change Management, 24*(6), 767–788. https://doi.org/10.1108/09534811111175742.

Humphrey, S. E., Nahrgang, J. D., & Morgeson, F. P. (2007). Integrating motivational, social, and contextual work design features: a meta-analytic summary and theoretical extension of the work design literature. *Journal of Applied Psychology, 92*(5), 1332–1356.

Kim, J., & de Dear, R. (2013). Workspace satisfaction: The privacy–communication trade-off in open-plan offices. *Journal of Environmental Psychology, 36*, 18–26. doi:10.1016/j.jenvp.2013.06.007.

Kristensen, T. (2004). The physical context of creativity. *Creativity and Innovation Management, 13*(2), 89–96. doi:10.1111/j.0963-1690.2004.00297.x.

Kuratko, D. F., Hornsby, J. S., & Covin, J. G. (2014). Diagnosing a firm's internal environment for corporate entrepreneurship. *Business Horizons, 57*(1), 37–47.

Lee, Y. S. (2010). Office layout affecting privacy, interaction, and acoustic quality in LEED-certified buildings. *Building and Environment, 45*(7), 1594–1600. https://doi.org/10.1016/j.buildenv.2010.01.007.

Lee, S. Y., & Brand, J. L. (2005). Effects of control over office workspace on perceptions of the work environment and work outcomes. *Journal of Environmental Psychology, 25*(2005), 323–333.

Lewin, K. (1951). *Field Theory in Social Science*. New York: Harper & Row.

McElroy, J. D., & Morrow, P. C. (2010). Employee reactions to office redesign: A naturally occurring quasi-field experiment in a multi-generational setting. *Human Relations, 63*(5), 609–636. doi:10.1177/0018726709342932.

Mencl, J., & Lester, S. W. (2014). More alike than different: What generations value and how the values affect employee workplace perceptions. *Journal of Leadership and Organizational Studies, 21*(3), 257–272. doi:10.1177/1548051814529825.

Millward, L. J., Haslam, S. A., & Postmes, T. (2007). Putting employees in their place: The impact of hot desking on organizational and team identification. *Organization Science, 18*(4), 547–559. https://doi.org/10.1287/orsc.1070.0265.

Morgeson, F. P., Dierdorff, E. C., & Hmurovic, J. L. (2010). Work design in situ: Understanding the role of occupational and organizational context. *Journal of Organizational Behavior, 31*(2–3), 351–360.

Morgeson, F. P., & Humphrey, S. E. (2006). The Work Design Questionnaire (WDQ): Developing and validating a comprehensive measure for assessing job design and the nature of work. *Journal of Applied Psychology, 91*(6), 1321.

Morrison, R. L., & Macky, K. A. (2017). The demands and resources arising from shared office spaces. *Applied Ergonomics, 60*, 103–115. https://doi.org/10.1016/j.apergo.2016.11.007.

Nieuwenhuis, M., Knight, C., Postmes, T., & Haslam, S. A. (2014). The relative benefits of green versus lean office space: Three field experiments. *Journal of Experimental Psychology: Applied*, *20*(3), 199–214. https://doi.org/10.1037/xap0000024.

Oksanen, K., & Ståhle, P. (2013). Physical environment as a source for innovation: Investigating the attributes of innovative space. *Journal of Knowledge Management*, *17*(6), 815–827. doi:10.1108/jkm-04-2013-0136.

Oldham, G. R., & Brass, D. J. (1979). Employee reactions to an open-plan office: A naturally occurring quasi-experiment. *Administrative Science Quarterly*, 267–284.

Oldham, G. R., Kulik, C. T., & Stepina, L. P. (1991). Physical environments and employee reactions: Effects of stimulus-screening skills and job complexity. *Academy of Management Journal*, *34*(4), 929–938.

Omara, M. A. (1999). *Strategy and Place*. New York: The Free Press

Parker, S. K. (2014). Beyond motivation: Job and work design for development, health, ambidexterity, and more. *Annual Review of Psychology*, *65*(1), 661–691. https://doi.org/10.1146/annurev-psych-010213-115208.

Parker, S. K., Morgeson, F. P., & Johns, G. (2017). One hundred years of work design research: Looking back and looking forward. *Journal of Applied Psychology*, *102*(3), 403.

Parker, S. K., Van den Broeck, A., & Holman, D. (2017). Work design influences: A synthesis of multilevel factors that affect the design of jobs. *Academy of Management Annals*, *11*(1), 267–308.

Pejtersen, J., Allermann, L., Kristensen, T. S., & Poulsen, O. M. (2006). Indoor climate, psychosocial work environment and symptoms in open-plan offices. *Indoor Air*, *16*(5), 392–401.

Pejtersen, J. H., Feveile, H., Christensen, K. B., & Burr, H. (2011). Sickness absence associated with shared and open-plan offices: A national cross sectional questionnaire survey. *Scandinavian Journal of Work, Environment and Health*, *37*(5), 376–382.

Posner, M. I., Snyder, C. R. R., & Davidson, B. J. (1980). Attention and the detection of signals. *Journal of Experimental Psychology: General*, *109*, 160–174.

Rasila, H., & Rothe, P. (2012). A problem is a problem is a benefit? Generation Y perceptions of open-plan offices. *Property Management*, *30*(4), 362–375. doi:10.1108/02637471211249506.

Roper, K. O., & Juneja, P. (2008). Distractions in the workplace revisited. *Journal of Facilities Management*, *6*(2), 91–109. doi:10.1108/14725960810872622.

Rothe, P., Lindholm, A., Hyvönen, A., & Nenonen, S. (2012). Work environment preferences: Does age make a difference? *Journal of Facilities Management*, *30*(1), 78–95. doi:10.1108/02632771211194284.

Shepherd, D. A., & Patzelt, H. (2017). *Trailblazing in Entrepreneurship: Creating New Paths for Understanding the Field*. New York: Springer.

Shiffrin R. M., & Schneider, W. (1977). Controlled and automatic information processing: II. Perceptual learning, automatic attending, and a general theory. *Psychological Review*, *84*, 127–190.

Smith-Jackson, T. L., & Klein, K. W. (2009). Open-plan offices: Task performance and mental workload. *Journal of Environmental Psychology*, *29*(2), 279–289.

Spreckelmeyer, K. F. (1993). Office relocation and environmental change: A case study. *Environment and Behavior*, *25*, 181–204.

Sundstrom, E., Burt, R. E., & Kamp, D. (1980). Privacy at work: Architectural correlates of job satisfaction and job performance. *Academy of Management Journal*, *23*(1), 101–117. https://doi.org/10.2307/255498.

Sundstrom, E., Town, J. P., Rice, R. W., Osborn, D. P., & Brill, M. (1994). Office noise and satisfaction, and performance. *Environment and Behavior*, *26*, 195–222.

Ulrich, R. (1984). View through a window may influence recovery from surgery. *Science*, *224*(4647), 420–421. https://doi.org/10.1126/science.6143402.

United States Bureau of Economic Analysis. (2015). *GDP-by-Industry* [Data files]. Retrieved from http://www.bea.gov/iTable/index_industry_gdpIndy.cfm

van der Voordt, D. J. M. (2003). *Costs and Benefits of Innovative Workplace Design*. Naarden: Centre for People and Buildings, Delft & Centrum Facility Management.

Wickens, D. D. (1984). Processing resources in attention. In R. Parasuraman, D. R. Davies, & J. Beatty (eds), *Varieties of Attention* (pp. 63–102). New York: Academic Press.

Wineman, J. D. (ed.) (1986). *Behavioral Issues in Office Design*. New York: Van Nostrand Reinhold.

Ward, M. K., & Meade, A. W. (2017). Applying social psychology to prevent careless responding during online surveys. *Applied Psychology: An International Review*, *67*(2), 231–263.

9

GREENING THE PHYSICAL ENVIRONMENT OF ORGANIZATIONAL BEHAVIOUR

William J. Bingley, Katharine H. Greenaway, and Kelly S. Fielding

Greening the physical environment of OB

Office greenery has become so ubiquitous that it is the subject of jokes in satirical comedy television programmes (Shields, 2016). A typical feature of these jokes is that greenery is an expensive waste of taxpayer money – a sentiment echoed in other forms of media. For example, the Australian government has been criticized for spending over AUD$1 million on office plants in two years (Shields, 2016). This echoes criticism of the previous government in Australia, which spent around AUD$2 million on office plants in three years. Similar accusations have been made in the United Kingdom, with spending on greenery seen as emblematic of a general tendency towards waste in the public sector (Morris, 2011). However, despite these criticisms, there is evidence that employees increasingly want natural elements in their workplaces. Earle (2003) found that 22% of employees considered the physical environment of a workplace to be a key factor when looking for a new role. Similarly, according to the Global Human Spaces Report (2015), 33% of employees say that office design would affect their decision to work at an organization. This figure is a global average, ranging from 27% in the United States to 67% in India. According to this report, indoor plants were the second most wanted physical element in an office space – identified as the key factor by 20% of employees surveyed. As a result of this employee demand, organizations in the private sector are increasingly willing to spend money on office greenery (Kimmorley, 2015; Loten & Monga, 2014).

OB outcomes of greening office spaces

Controversy over this issue raises the question: is office greenery a waste of money? Research suggests that greening the physical environment of organizations can improve a wide range of employee outcomes, leading to increased productivity and job satisfaction as well as more positive mood and attitudes towards the workplace, while also decreasing stress, physical discomfort, and even reducing recovery time from illness (e.g. Adachi, Rohde, & Kendle, 2000; Bringslimark, Hartig, & Patil, 2007; Dravigne, Waliczek, Lineberger, & Zajicek, 2008; Mitchell & Popham, 2008). However, some studies investigating the role of greenery in office environments have found inconsistent results, with beneficial effects appearing under some conditions but not others (Bringslimark, Hartig, & Patil, 2009). In this chapter, we review research on the organizational behaviour (OB) outcomes of physical greening. We go on to discuss several theories that have been used to explain these effects, and argue that the social identity approach may help to explain the inconsistent results found in these studies. In addition, we discuss how installing greenery may have the added benefit of increasing pro-environmental behaviour in organizations.

Greening promotes positive organizational outcomes

Productivity and attention

Several studies suggest that office greenery may improve employee productivity (Khan, Younis, Riaz, & Abbas, 2005; Knight & Haslam, 2010a; Nieuwenhuis, Knight, Postmes, & Haslam, 2014; Raanaas, Evensen, Rich, Sjøstrøm, & Patil, 2011). For example, Lohr, Pearson-Mims, and Goodwin (1996) found that participants working at a computer workstation with decorative plants had significantly faster reaction times on a computer-based productivity task compared with participants working at a workstation without plants. A correlational study of Norwegian office workers conducted by Bringslimark et al. (2007) found that after controlling for gender, age, and physical and psychosocial workplace factors such as office noise and job demands, having plants in view of a workstation was associated with increased self-reported productivity, although this was not a particularly strong association ($\beta = 0.12$).

However, the effects of office greenery on productivity and attention appear to be contingent on task type, control condition, and the gender of participants (Bringslimark et al., 2009; Thomsen, Sonderstrup-Andersen, & Muller, 2011; Doxey, Waliczek, & Zajicek, 2009). For example, a series of studies by Shibata and Suzuki (2001, 2002, 2004) found that participants showed improved performance on word association and attention tasks when plants were present compared with a variety of controls, such as a magazine rack, plants to the side of participants as opposed to in front, or no plants present. However, there was no effect of plants on sorting task performance. In addition, these results were moderated by gender – in the 2004 study the positive effect of plants on word association was found for women but not for men, while in the 2002 study the same effect was found for men but not women. Similarly, Liu, Mattson, and Kim (2004) found that exposure to lavender fragrance and cut flower arrangements had positive effects on cognitive performance compared with a no-plants control condition, but these differed by gender, sensory experience type, and outcome measure – men showed greater calculating accuracy when exposed to the cut flower arrangements, while women showed greater calculating speed when exposed to the lavender fragrance.

These results suggest that greening offices may improve employee performance under some conditions, although it is unclear exactly what those conditions are. In contrast, a study by Larsen, Adams, Deal, Kweon, and Tyler (1998) found that increasing the number of plants in a workstation actually worsened performance on a productivity task, with the no-plant condition being associated with the highest productivity. While it seems as though office plants have the capacity to improve employee productivity, it is difficult to draw definite conclusions based on the results of these studies because of the lack of consistency in outcome measures, the small effect sizes observed, and the lack of empirical studies conducted in an organizational setting, as opposed to a laboratory setting (Bringslimark et al., 2009).

Moving beyond productivity outcomes, other studies have found that plants can improve attentional capacity in both an academic environment (Khan et al., 2005) and in an office setting (Raanaas et al., 2011). This effect can also be produced more generally by exposure to the natural environment (Cimprich & Ronis, 2003; Hartig, Evans, Jamner, Davis, & Gärling, 2003; Hartig, Mang & Evans, 1991; Ottosson & Grahn, 2005; Tennessen & Cimprich, 1995), or even by viewing pictures of green spaces (Berto, 2005). For example, Berman, Jones, and Kaplan (2008) found that walking in nature or viewing pictures of nature improved attentional capacity across several tasks. However, while the evidence for the restorative effect of natural environments on attention is well established, few studies have demonstrated the effects of office greenery on employee attention and more research is therefore needed focusing on this specific environment.

Mood

One purported benefit of office greenery is that it makes employees feel happier. There is some empirical evidence to support this notion. Studies have shown that walking through nature or being exposed to natural scenes can improve positive affect, compared with walking through an urban environment or being exposed to urban scenes (Beute & de Kort, 2014; Bratman, Hamilton, Hahn, Daily, & Gross, 2015b). However, the effect of office greenery on mood is less clear. Some experimental studies have found that exposing participants to plants increased positive and decreased negative affect relative to a no-plant control condition, although these effects were moderated by gender and plant type such that a cut flower arrangement reduced negative affect among men but not women, while flowering geraniums increased positive affect among women but not men (Kim & Mattson, 2002; Liu et al., 2004). Similarly, Shibata and Suzuki (2004) found that plants increased positive mood compared with a no-plants control condition, but only for men. In addition, similar experiments by the same authors (Shibata & Suzuki, 2001, 2002) and others (Larsen et al., 1998) failed to find any effects of plants on mood compared with a no-plant control condition. Interestingly, Adachi et al. (2000) found that while a flower display decreased feelings of uncertainty relative to a no-plant control condition, it also increased annoyance. A foliage display without flowers, on the other hand, did not increase annoyance relative to control. The effects of the different conditions (flower, foliage, control) on mood differed depending on the gender of participants – overall men felt more positive in the foliage condition, while women felt more positive in the flower and control conditions. The results of these studies suggest that while greening offices may have a positive effect on mood, this is dependent on the type of plant, the setting, and the employee.

Job satisfaction

A survey of office workers in the United States found that employees who worked in offices with plants or views of exterior natural spaces reported higher job satisfaction compared with employees who worked in offices without plants or views (Dravigne et al., 2008). Other studies have found similar results (e.g. Lottrup, Stigsdotter, Meilby & Claudi, 2015). However, a study by Shoemaker, Randall, Relf, and Geller (1992) did not find any effect of introducing plants on employee job satisfaction compared with a control condition with no plants, although the authors noted that all employees in the study reported high job satisfaction before the manipulation, implying that a ceiling effect may be responsible for the lack of significant results. An experiment by Knight and Haslam (2010a) found that an 'enriched' workstation (one with potted plants and pictures) improved employee job satisfaction relative to a 'lean' space (one without any decoration). However, it is not clear whether this effect was due to introduction of the plants or the pictures, as these were both included in the enriched condition. More persuasively, Nieuwenhuis et al. (2014) found that participants in an office space reported higher satisfaction after the introduction of plants compared with participants in an office space without plants. However, they did not find this difference between conditions in another study, potentially because both office spaces were located on the same floor, which could have explained the results as participants in both conditions were exposed to plants to some degree. Based on the results of these studies, it seems that office greenery can potentially improve job satisfaction, but as with the other outcomes described above, the conditions of optimal effectiveness are not clear.

Self-control

There are several other purported benefits of natural environments related to self-control that could potentially apply to office plants. Exposure to natural spaces has been found to reduce future discounting compared with exposure to urban spaces – in other words, natural landscapes lead people to prefer long-term rewards over immediate rewards, whereas exposure to urban scenes may have the opposite effect

(Taylor, Kuo, & Sullivan, 2002; van der Wal, Schade, Krabbendam, & Van Vugt, 2013). Related to this, there is evidence that exposure to nature can be beneficial to other aspects of self-regulation. For example, Beute and de Kort (2014) found that viewing pictures of the natural environment improved self-control compared with viewing urban pictures or no pictures. However, this effect has yet to be tested with plants in a workplace setting.

Greening reduces negative organizational outcomes

Stress and discomfort

Another way that greening offices may improve organizational outcomes is by reducing stress and discomfort experienced by employees. Indoor plants have been associated with reduced anxiety, perceived stress, and fear across a variety of settings (Bratman, Daily, Levy, & Gross, 2015a; Chang & Chen, 2005; Dijkstra, Pieterse, & Pruyn, 2008; Han, 2009; Liu et al., 2004; Lottrup, Grahn, & Stigsdotter, 2013; Park & Mattson, 2008). Research by Lohr et al. (1996) found that plants reduced stress reactivity and improved stress recovery in a college computer lab, compared with a no-plant control condition. In addition to reducing psychological symptoms, office plants may also reduce physical discomfort (Park, Mattson, & Kim, 2004; Qin, Sun, Zhou, Leng, & Lian, 2014). For example, Fjeld, Veiersted, Sandvik, Riise, and Levy (1998) found that installing plants on the desks of office workers resulted in a 21% reduction in physical symptoms such as fatigue, dry throat, cough, and dry skin over a three-month period compared with a no-plant control condition. Fjeld (2000) found similar results in a junior high school setting.

Across these studies, as with the effects on productivity, the effects of plants on stress and discomfort are inconsistent, and sometimes differ depending on moderating variables such as gender. For example, Kim and Mattson (2002) found that plants reduced stress amongst women compared with a no-plant control condition, but had no effect on men. Coleman and Mattson (1995) did not find any effect of plants on stress, compared with a photo of a plant or a no-plant control condition. The inconsistent results found in these studies may be a function of the variety of outcomes related to stress and discomfort measured, which may be affected by greening to a greater or lesser extent; including rumination (Bratman et al., 2015b), self-reported anxiety (Park & Mattson, 2008; Chang & Chen, 2005), physical discomfort (Fjeld et al., 1998), and psychophysiological outcomes such as brain activity and skin temperature (Chang & Chen, 2005; Coleman & Mattson, 1995).

Physical illness

One interesting effect of exposure to nature is that it can improve physical health and recovery from illness (Mitchell & Popham, 2008; Ulrich, 1984). An example is research by Park and Mattson (2008, 2009), who found that hospitalized patients in rooms with plants and flowers had significantly shorter hospitalization times compared with patients in a control group, as well as reduced pain, anxiety, and fatigue. However, other studies have found less promising results – an indoor plant-based intervention conducted by Raanaas, Patil, and Hartig (2010) in a residential rehabilitation centre did not produce any extra improvements in patient recovery compared with a control condition, while Bringslimark et al. (2007) found that indoor plants were *positively* associated with self-reported sick leave in organizational settings, such that the greater the number of plants nearby, the more sick leave taken. While installing office greenery shows promise as a means of reducing employee absence due to illness, this effect has yet to be experimentally tested in an organizational setting.

Summary

In sum, the body of evidence showing the effect of office greenery specifically, and natural spaces more generally, suggests that physically greening workspaces can be beneficial. However, these effects appear to be contingent on a wide range of other factors, from gender, to task type, to the specific plant involved. Given this variability, it is important to consider the major theoretical frameworks that have been used to explain these effects. While the variety of effects attributed to office plants calls for a range of theoretical explanations, we argue that the social identity approach in particular provides a broad framework to help understand some of the gaps in knowledge concerning when these effects may appear.

Theoretical frameworks

Theories explaining the positive effects of office plants can be divided into two general categories: biophilia explanations and social explanations. Biophilia theories are those that explain the psychological and physiological effects of greening as being due to qualities inherent in plants themselves. The theories we include in this category are attention restoration theory (Kaplan, 1995), stress recovery theory (Ulrich et al., 1991), and improvement of air quality explanations (i.e. Orwell, Wood, Tarran, Torpy, & Burchett, 2004; Wood, Orwell, Tarran, Torpy, & Burchett, 2002). Social theories are those that attribute the positive effects of plants to the social meaning created by introducing plants into the workplace. The theories we include in this category are managerial attention (i.e. Haslam, 2004), territoriality (Brown, Lawrence, & Robinson, 2005), and social identity theories (Tajfel & Turner, 1979; Turner, Hogg, Oakes, Reicher, & Wetherell, 1987). These theories are not mutually exclusive, as the social theories do not attempt to explain the physiological effects of plants. However, they do overlap somewhat in their explanation of the psychological effects and employee productivity outcomes that are attributed to greening.

Biophilia explanations

The term 'biophilia' was coined by biologist Edward Wilson in 1984, and refers to the idea that humans have an affinity with the natural world (Wilson, 1984). While the following theories address different outcomes of greening, they all operate under the assumption that plants themselves have a special quality beyond other types of decoration that explains their effect on psychological and physiological outcomes.

Attention restoration theory

Attention restoration theory (ART) states that psychological effectiveness is dependent on recovery from fatigue caused by constant directed attention (Kaplan, 1995). According to ART, natural environments are inherently attention grabbing, but not in a way that activates or requires deliberate directed attention – instead, they attract our 'fascination', or involuntary attention. This allows for recovery from attention-related fatigue. There is a large body of research supporting ART in relation to the natural environment (e.g. Berman et al., 2008; Berto, 2005; Bratman et al., 2015a; Hartig et al., 2003; Tennessen & Cimprich, 1995). In addition, as our review of the literature demonstrates, there is some empirical evidence suggesting that plants can have a restorative effect on attention in an office setting (Lohr et al., 1996; Raanaas et al., 2011; Shibata & Suzuki, 2001, 2002, 2004). Overall, the evidence in favour of attention restoration as a mechanism for the positive effects of office plants on productivity tasks is persuasive. However, this explanation does not directly account for the effects of office plants on physical health.

Stress recovery theory

According to Ulrich (1983), natural environments evoke positive emotions, which lead to a reduction in the physiological arousal associated with exposure to stressors. This is a psycho-evolutionary theory known as stress recovery theory (SRT). While SRT overlaps with ART to some extent, it differs in that it focuses on the effect of natural environments on emotions rather than cognition, with stress as an outcome rather than attentional fatigue. These processes are compatible in that, although the two often go hand in hand, stress may occur without attentional fatigue, and attentional fatigue does not always cause stress (Berto, 2014). Exposure to natural environments has been found to reduce stress and help stress recovery (Ulrich et al., 1991; Hartig et al., 1991, 2003; Lottrup et al., 2013). However, when it comes to indoor greenery specifically, there are mixed results in relation to the proposed mechanism that reduces stress (i.e. emotion) and to the ultimate physiological outcomes of stress. In relation to these outcomes, while some studies have found a positive effect of indoor greenery on mood and stress, others have found an effect for men or women only, or no effect at all (Dijkstra et al., 2008;

Kim & Mattson, 2002; Larsen et al., 1998; Lohr & Pearson-Mims, 2000; Lohr et al., 1996; Shibata & Suzuki, 2001, 2002, 2004).

Air quality

Research supports the idea that indoor plants can improve physical health by removing air-borne contaminants (Orwell et al., 2004; Wood et al., 2002). In particular, indoor plants reliably remove volatile organic compounds such as benzene from the air, which can cause 'sick building syndrome', as well as other physical symptoms such as headache, sore eyes, and nausea (Carrer et al., 1999; Mølhave & Krzyzanowski, 2003; Wood et al., 2006;). Plants also reduce CO_2 levels (Khan et al., 2005), which are associated with reduced performance (Seppänen, Fisk, & Lei, 2006; Shaughnessy, Haverinen-Shaughnessy, Nevalainen, & Moschandreas, 2006).

Social explanations

While biophilia theories seek to explain the effect of office plants on psychophysiological organizational behaviour outcomes such as attention, stress, and physical health, social theories tend to focus on outcomes such as job satisfaction and organizational identification.

Managerial attention

One simple way that greening may promote employee satisfaction is by signalling to employees that management are paying attention to their needs. In other words, it may not be anything about office plants per se that increases employee satisfaction; rather, they may be one of many ways to enrich the working environment (Haslam, 2004; Vischer, 2005). Making employees feel as if they are listened to and valued is a key element of transformational leadership, which is positively associated with employee motivation and satisfaction (Bass, 1990; Judge & Piccolo, 2004). The results of the Global Human Spaces Report (2015) suggest that employees increasingly desire office plants in their workspaces, which makes them a potentially effective way to communicate managerial attention.

Territoriality

Territoriality refers to 'an individual's behavioural expression of his or her feelings of ownership toward a physical or social object' (Brown et al., 2005, p. 578). One way that employees can construct and communicate their ownership over their workspace is by a territorial behaviour called 'marking', in which gestures or symbols are used to delineate territorial boundaries. Research has shown that having clearly delineated social boundaries can reduce conflict in an organization (Becker & Mayo, 1971; Wollman, Kelly, & Bordens, 1994). Office plants may be an effective way for employees to mark their organizational territory, provided they are installed by the employees themselves (Knight & Haslam, 2010a; Wells, 2000). Personalization of one's space can enhance psychological wellbeing in a variety of ways, whether by allowing for the expression of emotion, increasing one's sense of control, or strengthening attachment to the environment (Edney & Buda, 1976; Hess, 1993; Scheiberg, 1990). In turn, this may improve wellbeing and satisfaction (Averill, 1973; Sundstrom, Herbert, & Brown, 1982).

Social identity

The social identity approach consists of two theories: social identity theory (SIT; Tajfel & Turner, 1979) and self-categorization theory (SCT; Turner et al., 1987). SIT argues that group membership is an important part of people's self-concept, determining their attitudes, emotions, and behaviour (Tajfel & Turner, 1979). SCT builds on SIT, arguing that the extent to which a particular social identity becomes self-defining depends on how salient (relevant, or available) that particular identity is (Turner et al., 1987). In other words, people's social identities regulate how they think, feel, and behave, and these identities become more or less important depending on the social context (Haslam, 2004). The social identity approach can help explain why there is inconsistent evidence for the organizational behaviour outcomes of physically greening office spaces (i.e. installing plants in offices). Namely, the extent to which office plants have psychological benefits beyond their impact on physical health may depend on the way that employees relate to green spaces, which is determined in part by their social identities.

The social identity approach may be useful in explaining variability in the attentional outcomes of greening. ART posits that compatibility between an environment and an individual's purposes and inclinations is an important factor in restoring attention-related fatigue (Kaplan, 1995). In other words, the way that an individual relates to the environment will determine whether they find it restorative or not. There is some research suggesting that people have different responses to the same environment depending on whether it is relevant to a salient social identity (Alnabulsi & Drury, 2014; Novelli, Drury, Reicher, & Stott, 2013; Pandey, Stevenson, Shankar, Hopkins, & Reicher, 2014; Schmitt, Davies, Hung, & Wright, 2010). For example, Morton, van der Bles, and Haslam (2017) found that when an urban identity was made salient, participants performed better on an attentional task after being exposed to urban images compared with natural images. This effect was reversed when a rural identity was made salient. Overall, performance was highest when there was compatibility between identity and image type.

Social identity can also affect the social outcomes of greening. Knight and Haslam (2010a) found that participants in an 'enriched' office space (with plants) showed increased organizational identification, physical comfort, and job satisfaction relative to a 'lean' office space (without plants). However, these effects were stronger for participants who were allowed to decorate the desk themselves, compared with those who had the decoration done for them by the experimenter.

A similar study by the same authors (2010b) found that managerial control of workspaces was associated with reduced psychological comfort, which in turn was associated with lower organizational identification and, through this, reduced job satisfaction and wellbeing. These results are similar to those showing that empowering residents of an aged care facility increased their identification with other staff and residents, in turn increasing their wellbeing (Knight, Haslam, & Haslam, 2010). The results of these studies suggest that allowing employees to decorate their own workspaces with plants might bolster positive psychological outcomes by fostering organizational identity.

A final way in which identity can affect the outcomes of greening is through its relationship with identity-oriented marking, which refers to the modification of an environment to reflect the identities of its occupants (Brown et al., 2005). Social identity affects what form identity-oriented marking will take, and in turn the process of engaging in identity-oriented marking can shape social identity (Elsbach, 2004; Gioia, Chultz, & Corley, 2000; Weick, 1995). A hypothetical example of the latter might be if an employee noticed that their fellow employees had decorated their workspaces with plants and so voluntarily followed suit – this might signal that the employee is a dedicated member of the group, potentially strengthening organizational identity. Importantly, decorating workplaces in a way that reflects identities has been shown to increase productivity relative to lean spaces that do not signal relevant identities (Greenaway, Thai, Haslam, & Murphy, 2016).

Given the wide range of outcomes attributed to office greenery, it seems likely that a number of the theories discussed have explanatory value, although to a greater or lesser extent depending on the context. For example, introducing office plants might clean the air, reducing physical symptoms such as dry skin and respiratory illness. At the same time, it might help employees to replenish their attentional resources and de-stress, particularly if they are thinking of themselves as members of a social group that has a positive relationship with the natural environment. Allowing employees to decorate their workspace with plants may provide them with a way to indicate ownership over the space and increase their organizational identification. If the office greening is initiated by management, it might signal to employees that management cares about their wellbeing. All of these effects could potentially improve employee mood and increase the productivity of the organization.

Our review of the literature suggests that, under some conditions, there is a positive relationship between office greenery and beneficial outcomes. However, it is difficult to draw firm conclusions because of inconsistent findings across the literature. We have advanced a social identity explanation to help explain some of the inconsistency in these findings: whether or not office greenery is associated with positive organizational outcomes may depend on identity signalling qualities. That is, if greenery aligns with organizational identity or signals the value of the identity, this may lead to positive outcomes. In addition, physically greening organizations may have another positive consequence – increasing employee pro-environmental behaviour.

Physical greening may increase pro-environmental behaviour

The idea that office greenery could motivate employee pro-environmental behaviour is underpinned by past research showing that exposure to nature is associated with increased pro-environmental behaviour (Nord, Luloff, & Bridger, 1998; Zelenski, Dopko, & Capaldi, 2015). The mechanism often cited as mediating this relationship is 'connection to nature'; that is, individuals' affective, cognitive, and experiential sense of connection to the natural world (Nisbet, Zelenski, & Murphy, 2009; Mayer & Franz, 2004). Exposure to the natural environment has been found to be positively associated with connection to nature (Hinds & Sparks, 2008, Nisbet et al., 2009). In turn, connection to nature has been found to be associated with increased pro-environmental behaviour (Dutcher, Finley, Luloff, & Johnson, 2007; Gosling & Williams, 2010; Sparks, Hinds, Curnock, & Pavey, 2014).

Supporting the mediated relationship between nature exposure and pro-environmental behaviour, research conducted by Kals, Schumacher, and Montada (1999) found that past and present exposure to the natural environment predicted emotional affinity with nature, which in turn predicted positive environmental behaviour. Similarly, studies have found that children's exposure to nature predicts their positive pro-environmental beliefs, intentions, and behaviour, mediated by emotional affinity towards nature (Collado, Corraliza, Staats, & Ruíz, 2015; Collado, Staats, & Corraliza, 2013). Based on past research, it is therefore possible to conclude that introducing office greenery may increase employees' sense of connection to nature, which in turn may motivate them to engage in pro-environmental behaviour. However, this idea has yet to be directly tested in an organizational setting, providing an avenue for future research.

Another way in which physical greening may motivate employee pro-environmental behaviour is by reinforcing a social norm that nature is important. There is a large body of research demonstrating that norms, in particular descriptive norms (what people actually do, rather than what they are supposed to do) are a powerful motivator of pro-environmental behaviour (Cialdini, Reno, & Kallgren, 1990; Dwyer, Maki, & Rothman, 2015; Nolan, Schultz, Cialdini, Goldstein, & Griskevicius, 2008; Fornara, Carrus, Passafaro, & Bonnes, 2011). For example, Goldstein, Cialdini, and Griskevicius (2008) found that appeals for hotel guests to reuse towels were more effective when they focused on what other guests generally do, rather than on the importance of environmental protection.

In an organizational context, Norton, Zacher, and Ashkanasy (2014) found that while an organization's official policies predicted employees' intentions to engage in the environmental duties and responsibilities included as part of their jobs, descriptive organizational norms (the actions of co-workers) predicted their willingness to do more for the environment than was expected as part of their jobs. In other words, while physically greening an organization in a top–down, management-driven way may communicate to employees that the environment is important and encourage employees to fulfil their job-related environmental responsibilities, the actions of co-workers may create a descriptive norm that may be more effective in getting employees to go 'above and beyond' what they are required to do in their jobs. Allowing employees to bring in their own office plants may therefore be an important extra step in encouraging pro-environmental behaviour because it signals to ingroup members that nature is important.

Conclusion

At the beginning of this chapter we noted that office greenery is often criticized as a frivolous waste of money. However, the evidence we have reviewed suggests that greening can have a variety of psychological and physiological benefits, including but not limited to decreased stress, reduced physical discomfort, and improved recovery time from illness. No wonder, then, that office plants are sought after and appreciated by employees. In addition, greening the workplace may increase employee productivity and job satisfaction. While there are a variety of theoretical frameworks that seek to explain the effects of office greenery, these are not mutually exclusive and may in fact be interactive. In particular, the social identity approach may be useful in reconciling some of the inconsistent results of the studies reviewed in this chapter.

There are a range of interesting and important questions to be addressed to fully understand the impact of office greenery on organization outcomes. These include whether office greenery might motivate employee green behaviour through encouraging greater connection to nature, whether less than optimal plant health could lead to negative employee outcomes, and whether the function of the plants (e.g. for privacy versus decoration) makes a difference to workplace outcomes, to name just a few. Future research should investigate these questions in order to build a more nuanced and flexible understanding of how to best utilize office greenery across a variety of contexts.

Although the research evidence is somewhat mixed in terms of some organizational outcomes, few studies show negative effects of office greening and most show positive effects – at least for some people. On balance, then, it makes sense for organizations to invest in greening office spaces, and to install greenery that might align with the identities of employees (e.g. tropical plants in tropical regions). Based on our review of the literature, it is clear that greening the physical space of organizations can be a worthwhile investment, especially if it is done in such a way that it aligns with the needs and social identities of employees.

References

Adachi, M., Rohde, C. L. E., & Kendle, A. D. (2000). Effects of floral and foliage displays on human emotions. *HortTechnology*, *10*(1), 59–63.

Alnabulsi, H., & Drury, J. (2014). Social identification moderates the effect of crowd density on safety at the Hajj. *Proceedings of the National Academy of Sciences*, *111*(25), 9091–9096. doi: 10.1073/pnas.1404953111.

Averill, J. R. (1973). Personal control over aversive stimuli and its relationship to stress. *Psychological Bulletin, 80*(4), 286–303. doi: http://dx.doi.org/10.1037/h0034845.

Bass, B. M. (1990). From transactional to transformational leadership: Learning to share the vision. *Organizational Dynamics, 18*(3), 19–31. doi: 10.1016/0090-2616(90)90061-S.

Becker, F. D., & Mayo, C. (1971). Delineating personal distance and territoriality. *Environment and Behavior, 3*(4), 375–381.

Berman, M. G., Jones, J., & Kaplan, S. (2008). The cognitive benefits of interacting with nature. *Psychological Science, 19*(12), 1207–1212. doi: 10.1111/j.1467-9280.2008.02225.x.

Berto, R. (2005). Exposure to restorative environments helps restore attentional capacity. *Journal of Environmental Psychology, 25*(3), 249–259. doi: doi.org/10.1016/j.jenvp.2005.07.001.

Berto, R. (2014). The role of nature in coping with psycho-physiological stress: A literature review on restorativeness. *Behavioral Sciences, 4*, 394–402. doi: 10.3390/bs4040394.

Beute, F., & de Kort, Y. A. W. (2014). Natural resistance: Exposure to nature and self-regulation, mood, and physiology after ego-depletion. *Journal of Environmental Psychology, 40*, 167–178. doi: 0.1016/j.jenvp.2014.06.004.

Bratman, G. N., Daily, G. C., Levy, B. J., & Gross, J. J. (2015a). The benefits of nature experience: Improved affect and cognition. *Landscape and Urban Planning, 138*, 41–50. doi: 10.1016/j.landurbplan.2015.02.005.

Bratman, G. N., Hamilton, J. P., Hahn, K. S., Daily, G. C., & Gross, J. J. (2015b). Nature experience reduces rumination and subgenual prefrontal cortex activation. *Proceedings of the National Academy of Sciences, 112*(28), 8567–8572. doi: 10.1073/pnas.1510459112.

Bringslimark, T., Hartig, T., & Patil, G. G. (2007). Psychological benefits of indoor plants in workplaces: Putting experimental results into context. *HortScience, 42*(3), 581–587.

Bringslimark, T., Hartig, T., & Patil, G. G. (2009). The psychological benefits of indoor plants: A critical review of the experimental literature. *Journal of Environmental Psychology, 29*, 422–433. doi: 10.1016/j.jenvp.2009.05.001.

Brown, G., Lawrence, T. B., & Robinson, S. L. (2005). Territoriality in organisations. *Academy of Management Review, 30*(3), 577–594.

Carrer, P., Alcini, D., Cavallo, D., Visigalli, F., Bollini, D., & Maroni, M. (1999). Home and workplace complaints and symptoms in office workers and correlation with indoor air pollution. *Indoor Air, 1*, 129–134.

Chang, C. Y., & Chen, P. K. (2005). Human response to window views and indoor plants in the workplace. *HortScience, 40*(5), 1354–1359.

Cialdini, R. B., Reno, R. R., & Kallgren, C. A. (1990). A focus theory of normative conduct: Recycling the concept of norms to reduce littering in public places. *Journal of Personality and Social Psychology, 58*(6), 1015. doi: 10.1037/0022-3514.58.6.1015.

Cimprich, B., & Ronis, D. L. (2003). An environmental intervention to restore attention in women with newly diagnosed breast cancer. *Cancer Nursing, 26*(4), 284–292.

Coleman, C. K., & Mattson, R. H. (1995). Influences of foliage plants on human stress during thermal biofeedback training. *HortTechnology, 5*, 137–140.

Collado, S., Corraliza, J. A., Staats, H., & Ruíz, M. (2015). Effect of frequency and mode of contact with nature on children's self-reported ecological behaviors. *Journal of Environmental Psychology, 41*, 65–73. doi: 10.1016/j.jenvp.2014.11.001.

Collado, S., Staats, H., & Corraliza, J. A. (2013). Experiencing nature in children's summer camps: Affective, cognitive and behavioural consequences. *Journal of Environmental Psychology, 33*, 37–44. doi: 10.1016/j.jenvp.2012.08.002.

Dijkstra, K., Pieterse, M. E., & Pruyn, A. (2008). Stress-reducing effects of indoor plants in the built healthcare environment: The mediating role of perceived attractiveness. *Preventive Medicine, 47*(3), 279–283. doi: 10.1016/j.ypmed.2008.01.013.

Doxey, J. S., Waliczek, T. M., & Zajicek, J. M. (2009). The impact of interior plants in university classrooms on student course performance and on student perceptions of the course and instructor. *HortScience, 44*(2), 384–391.

Dravigne, A., Waliczek, T. M., Lineberger, R. D., & Zajicek, J. M. (2008). The effect of live plants and window views of green spaces on employee perceptions of job satisfaction. *HortScience, 43*(1), 183–187.

Dutcher, D. D., Finley, J. C., Luloff, A. E., & Johnson, J. B. (2007). Connectivity with nature as a measure of environmental values. *Environment and Behavior, 39*(4), 474–493. doi: 10.1177/0013916506298794.

Dwyer, P. C., Maki, A., & Rothman, A. J. (2015). Promoting energy conservation behavior in public settings: The influence of social norms and personal responsibility. *Journal of Environmental Psychology, 41*, 30–34. doi: 10.1016/j.jenvp.2014.11.002.

Earle, H. A. (2003). Building a workplace of choice: Using the work environment to attract and retain top talent. *Journal of Facilities Management, 2*(3), 244–257. doi: 10.1108/14725960410808230.

Edney, J. J., & Buda, M. A. (1976). Distinguishing territoriality and privacy: Two studies. *Human Ecology, 4*(4), 283–296.

Elsbach, K. D. (2004). Interpreting workplace identities: The role of office decor. *Journal of Organizational Behavior, 25*, 99–128. doi: 10.1002/job.233.

Fjeld, T. (2000). The effect of interior planting on health and discomfort among workers and school children. *HortTechnology, 10*, 46–52.

Fjeld, T., Veiersted, B., Sandvik, L., Riise, G., & Levy, F. (1998). The effect of indoor foliage plants on health and discomfort symptoms among office workers. *Indoor and Built Environment, 7*, 204–209.

Fornara, F., Carrus, G., Passafaro, P., & Bonnes, M. (2011). Distinguishing the sources of normative influence on proenvironmental behaviors: The role of local norms in household waste recycling. *Group Processes and Intergroup Relations, 14*(5), 623–635. doi: 10.1177/1368430211408149.

Gioia, D. A., Schultz, M., & Corley, K. G. (2000). Organizational identity, image, and adaptive instability. *Academy of Management Review, 25*(1), 63–81. doi: 10.5465/AMR.2000.2791603.

Global Human Spaces Report. (2015). *The Global Impact of Biophilic Design in the Workplace.*

Goldstein, N. J., Cialdini, R. B., & Griskevicius, V. (2008). A room with a viewpoint: Using social norms to motivate environmental conservation in hotels. *Journal of consumer Research, 35*(3), 472–482. doi: 10.1086/586910.

Gosling, E., & Williams, K. J. (2010). Connectedness to nature, place attachment and conservation behaviour: Testing connectedness theory among farmers. *Journal of Environmental Psychology, 30*(3), 298–304. doi: 10.1016/j.jenvp.2010.01.005.

Greenaway, K. H., Thai, H. A., Haslam, S. A., & Murphy, S. C. (2016). Spaces that signal identity improve workplace productivity. *Journal of Personnel Psychology, 15*, 35–43. doi: 10.1027/1866-5888/a000148.

Han, K. (2009). Influence of limitedly visible leafy indoor plants on the psychology, behaviour, and health of students at a junior high school in Taiwan. *Environment and Behavior, 41*, 658–692. doi: 10.1177/0013916508314476.

Hartig, T., Evans, G. W., Jamner, L. D., Davis, D. S., & Gärling, T. (2003). Tracking restoration in natural and urban field settings. *Journal of Environmental Psychology, 23*(2), 109–123. doi: 10.1016/S0272-4944(02)00109-3.

Hartig, T., Mang, M., & Evans, G. W. (1991). Restorative effects of natural environment experiences. *Environment and Behavior, 23*(1), 3–26.

Haslam, S. A. (2004). *Psychology in Organizations: The Social Identity Approach*. London: SAGE.

Hess, J. A. (1993). Assimilating newcomers into an organization: A cultural perspective. *Journal of Applied Communication Research, 21*(2), 189–210.

Hinds, J., & Sparks, P. (2008). Engaging with the natural environment: The role of affective connection and identity. *Journal of Environmental Psychology, 28*(2), 109–120. doi: 10.1016/j.jenvp.2007.11.001.

Judge, T. A., & Piccolo, R. F. (2004). Transformational and transactional leadership: a meta-analytic test of their relative validity. *Journal of Applied Psychology, 89*(5), 755. doi: 10.1037/0021-9010.89.5.755.

Kals, E., Schumacher, D., & Montada, L. (1999). Emotional affinity toward nature as a motivational basis to protect nature. *Environment and Behavior, 31*(2), 178–202. doi: 10.1177/00139169921972056.

Kaplan, S. (1995). The restorative benefits of nature: Toward an integrative framework. *Journal of Environmental Psychology, 15*(3), 169–182.

Khan, A. R., Younis, A., Riaz, A., & Abbas, M. M. (2005). Effect of interior plantscaping on indoor academic environment. *Journal of Agriculture Research, 43*, 235–242.

Kim, E., & Mattson, R. H. (2002). Stress recovery effects of viewing red-flowering geraniums. *Journal of Therapeutic Horticulture, 13*, 4–12.

Kimmorley, S. (2015, March). Here's why putting plants in your office will improve productivity and the bottom line. *Business Insider Australia*. Retrieved from https://www.businessinsider.com.au

Knight, C., & Haslam, S. A. (2010a). The relative merits of lean, enriched, and empowered offices: An experimental examination of the impact of workspace management strategies on wellbeing and productivity. *Journal of Experimental Psychology: Applied, 16*(2), 158–172. doi: 10.1037/a0019292.

Knight, C., & Haslam, S. A. (2010b). your place or mine? Organizational identification and comfort as mediators of relationships between the managerial control of workspace and employees' satisfaction and well-being. *British Journal of Management, 21*(3), 717–735. doi: 10.1111/j.1467-8551.2009.00683.x.

Knight, C., Haslam, S. A., & Haslam, C. (2010). In home or at home? How collective decision making in a new care facility enhances social interaction and wellbeing amongst older adults. *Ageing and Society, 30*(8), 1393–1418. doi: 10.1017/S0144686X10000656.

Larsen, L., Adams, J., Deal, B., Kweon, B. S., & Tyler, E. (1998). Plants in the workplace: The effects of plant density on productivity, attitudes, and perceptions. *Environment and Behavior, 30*(3), 261–281.

Liu, M., Mattson, R. H., & Kim, E. (2004). Influences of lavender fragrance and cut flower arrangements on cognitive performance. *International Journal of Aromatherapy, 14*(4), 169–174. doi: 10.1016/j.ijat.2004.09.015.

Lohr, V. I., & Pearson-Mims, C. H. (2000). Physical discomfort may be reduced in the presence of interior plants. *HortTechnology, 10*(1), 53–58.

Lohr, V. I., Pearson-Mims, C H., & Goodwin, G. K. (1996). Interior plants may improve worker productivity and reduce stress in a windowless environment. *Journal of Environmental Horticulture, 14*, 97–100.

Loten, A., & Monga, V. (2014, September). Small firms poised to spend more on plants, equipment. *Wall Street Journal*. Retrieved from https://www.wsj.com

Lottrup, L., Grahn, P., & Stigsdotter, U. K. (2013). Workplace greenery and perceived level of stress: Benefits of access to a green outdoor environment at the workplace. *Landscape and Urban Planning, 110*, 5–11. doi: 10.1016/j.landurbplan.2012.09.002.

Lottrup, L., Stigsdotter, U. K., Meilby, H., & Claudi, A. G. (2015). The workplace window view: A determinant of office workers' work ability and job satisfaction. *Landscape Research, 40*(1), 57–75. doi: 10.1080/01426397.2013.829806.

Mayer, F. S., & Franz, C. M. (2004). The connectedness to nature scale: A measure of individuals' feeling in community with nature. *Journal of Environmental Psychology, 24*(4), 503–515. doi: 10.1016/j.jenvp.2004.10.001.

Mitchell, R., & Popham, F. (2008). Effect of exposure to natural environment on health inequalities: An observational population study. *The Lancet, 372*(9650), 1655–1660. doi: 10.1016/S0140-6736(08)61689-X.

Mølhave, L., & Krzyzanowski, M. (2003). The right to healthy indoor air: Status by 2002. *Indoor Air, 13*, 50–53. doi:10.1034/j.1600-0668.13.s.6.7.x.

Morris, N. (2011, April). Coalition ministers spend £40,000 on potted plants. *Independent.* Retrieved from https://www.independent.co.uk

Morton, T. A., van der Bles, A. M., & Haslam, S. A. (2017). Seeing our self-reflected in the world around us: The role of identity in making (natural) environments restorative. *Journal of Environmental Psychology, 49*, 65–77. doi: 10.1016/j.jenvp.2016.11.002.

Nieuwenhuis, M., Knight, C., Postmes, T., & Haslam, S. A. (2014). The relative benefits of green versus lean office space: Three field experiments. *Journal of Experimental Psychology: Applied, 20*(3), 199–214. doi: 10.1037/xap0000024.

Nisbet, E. K., Zelenski, J. M., & Murphy, S. A. (2009). The nature relatedness scale: Linking individuals' connection with nature to environmental concern and behavior. *Environment and Behavior, 41*(5), 715–740. doi: 10.1177/0013916508318748.

Nolan, J. M., Schultz, P. W., Cialdini, R. B., Goldstein, N. J., & Griskevicius, V. (2008). Normative social influence is underdetected. *Personality and social psychology bulletin, 34*(7), 913–923. doi: 10.1177/0146167208316691.

Nord, M., Luloff, A. E., & Bridger, J. C. (1998). The association of forest recreation with environmentalism. *Environment and Behavior, 30*(2), 235–246. doi: 10.1177/0013916598302006.

Norton, T. A., Zacher, H., & Ashkanasy, N. M. (2014). Organisational sustainability policies and employee green behaviour: The mediating role of work climate perceptions. *Journal of Environmental Psychology, 38*, 49–54. doi: 10.1016/j.jenvp.2013.12.008.

Novelli, D., Drury, J., Reicher, S., & Stott, C. (2013). Crowdedness mediates the effect of social identification on positive emotion in a crowd: A survey of two crowd events. *PloS One, 8*(11), e78983. doi: 10.1371/journal.pone.0078983.

Orwell, R. L., Wood, R. L., Tarran, J., Torpy, F., & Burchett, M. D. (2004). Removal of benzene by the indoor plant/substrate microcosm and implications for air quality. *Water, Air, and Soil Pollution, 157*(1–4), 193–207.

Ottosson, J., & Grahn, P. (2005). A comparison of leisure time spent in a garden with leisure time spent indoors: on measures of restoration in residents in geriatric care. *Landscape Research, 30*(1), 23–55. doi: 10.1080/0142639042000324758.

Pandey, K., Stevenson, C., Shankar, S., Hopkins, N. P., & Reicher, S. D. (2014). Cold comfort at the Magh Mela: Social identity processes and physical hardship. *British Journal of Social Psychology, 53*(4), 675–690. doi: 10.1111/bjso.12054.

Park, S. H., & Mattson, R. H. (2008). Effects of flowering and foliage plants in hospital rooms on patients recovering from abdominal surgery. *HortTechnology, 18*(4), 563–568.

Park, S. H., & Mattson, R. H. (2009). Therapeutic influences of plants in hospital rooms on surgical recovery. *HortScience, 44*(1), 102–105.

Park, S. H., Mattson, R. H., & Kim, E. (2004). Pain tolerance effects of ornamental plants in a simulated hospital patient room. *Acta Horticulturae, 639*, 241–247.

Qin, J., Sun, C., Zhou, X., Leng, H., & LIan, Z. (2014). The effect of indoor plants on human comfort. *Indoor and Built Environment, 23*(5), 709–723. doi: doi.org/10.1177/14 20326X13481372.

Raanaas, R. K., Evensen, K. H., Rich, D., Sjøstrøm, G., & Patil, G. (2011). Benefits of indoor plants on attention capacity in an office setting. *Journal of Environmental Psychology, 31*(1), 99–105.

Raanaas, R. K., Patil, G. G., & Hartig, T. (2010). Effects of an indoor foliage plant intervention on patient wellbeing during a residential rehabilitation program. *HortScience, 45*(3), 387–392.

Scheiberg, S. L. (1990). Emotions on display: The personal decoration of work space. *American Behavioral Scientist, 33*(3), 330–338.

Schmitt, M. T., Davies, K., Hung, M., & Wright, S. C. (2010). Identity moderates the effects of Christmas displays on mood, self-esteem, and inclusion. *Journal of Experimental Social Psychology, 46*(6), 1017–1022. doi: 10.1016/j.jesp.2010.05.026.

Seppänen, O., Fisk, W. J., & Lei, Q. H. (2006). Ventilation and performance in office work. *Indoor Air, 16*, 28–36. doi:10.1111/j.1600-0668.2005.00394.x.

Shaughnessy, R. J., Haverinen-Shaughnessy, U., Nevalainen, A., & Moschandreas, D. (2006). The effects of classroom air temperature and outdoor air supply rate on the performance of school work by children. *Indoor Air, 16*, 465–468. doi:10.1111/j.1600-0668.2006.00440.x.

Shibata, S., & Suzuki, N. (2001). Effects of indoor foliage plants on subjects' recovery from mental fatigue. *North American Journal of Psychology, 3*(3), 385–396.

Shibata, S., & Suzuki, N. (2002). Effects of the foliage plant on task performance and mood. *Journal of Environmental Psychology, 22*(3), 265–272. doi:10.1006/jevp.2.

Shibata, S., & Suzuki, N. (2004). Effects of an indoor plant on creative task performance and mood. *Scandinavian Journal of Psychology, 45*(5), 373–381.

Shields, B. (2016, January). Budget cuts don't dent the government's Utopia-esque penchant for office plants. *Sydney Morning Herald*. Retrieved from www.smh.com.au

Shoemaker, C. A., Randall, K., Relf, D., & Geller, E. S. (1992). Relationships between plants, behavior, and attitudes in an office environment. *HortTechnology, 2*, 205–206.

Sparks, P., Hinds, J., Curnock, S., & Pavey, L. (2014). Connectedness and its consequences: a study of relationships with the natural environment. *Journal of Applied Social Psychology, 44*(3), 166–174. doi: 10.1111/jasp.12206.

Sundstrom, E., Herbert, R. K., & Brown, D. W. (1982). Privacy and communication in an open-plan office: A case study. *Environment and Behavior, 14*(3), 379–392.

Tajfel, H., & Turner, J. C. (1979). An integrative theory of intergroup conflict. In W. G. Austin & S. Worchel (eds), *The Social Psychology of Intergroup Relations* (pp. 33–47). Monterey, CA: Brooks-Cole.

Taylor, A. F., Kuo, F. E., & Sullivan, W. C. (2002). Views of nature and self-discipline: Evidence from inner city children. *Journal of Environmental Psychology, 22*(1–2), 49–63. doi: 10.1006/jevp.2001.0241.

Tennessen, C. M., & Cimprich, B. (1995). Views to nature: Effects on attention. *Journal of Environmental Psychology, 15*(1), 77–85. doi: 10.1016/0272-4944(95)90016-0.

Thomsen, J. D., Sonderstrup-Andersen, H. K. H., & Muller, R. (2011). People–plant relationships in an office workplace: Perceived benefits for the workplace and employees. *HortScience, 46*(5), 744–752.

Turner, J. C., Hogg, M. A., Oakes, P. J., Reicher, S. D., & Wetherell, M. S. (1987). *Rediscovering the Social Group*. Oxford: Blackwell.

Ulrich, R. (1984). View through a window may influence recovery. *Science, 224*(4647), 224–225. doi: 10.1126/science.6143402.

Ulrich, R. S. (1983). Aesthetic and affective response to natural environments. In I. Altman, & J. F. Wohlwill (eds), *Human Behavior and the Natural Environment* (pp. 85–125). New York: Plenum.

Ulrich, R. S., Simons, R. F., Losito, B. D., Fiorito, E., Miles, M. A., & Zelson, M. (1991). Stress recovery during exposure to natural and urban environments. *Journal of Environmental Psychology, 11*(3), 201–230. doi: 10.1016/S0272-4944(05)80184-7.

Van der Wal, A. J., Schade, H. M., Krabbendam, L., & Van Vugt, M. (2013). Do natural landscapes reduce future discounting in humans? *Proceedings of the Royal Society of London B: Biological Sciences, 280*(1773), 20132295. doi: 10.1098/rspb.2013.2295.

Vischer, J. C. (2005). *Space Meets Status*. Abingdon: Routledge.

Weick, K. E. 1995. *Sensemaking in Organizations*. Thousand Oaks, CA: SAGE.

Wells, M. M. (2000). Office clutter or meaningful personal displays: The role of office personalization in employee and organizational wellbeing. *Journal of Environmental Psychology, 20*(3), 239–255. doi: 10.1006/jevp.1999.0166.

Wilson, E. O. (1984). *Biophilia*. Cambridge, MA: Harvard University Press.

Wollman, N., Kelly, B. M., & Bordens, K. S. (1994). Environmental and intrapersonal predictors of reactions to potential territorial intrusions in the workplace. *Environment and Behavior, 26*(2), 179–194.

Wood, R. A., Burchett, M. D., Alquezar, R., Orwell, R. L., Tarran, J., & Torpy, F. (2006). The potted-plant microcosm substantially reduces indoor air VOC pollution: I. Office field-study. *Water, Air, & Soil Pollution, 175*(1), 163–180. doi: 10.1007/s11270-006-9124-z.

Wood, R. A., Orwell, R. L., Tarran, J., Torpy, F., & Burchett, M. (2002). Potted-plant/growth media interactions and capacities for removal of volatiles from indoor air. *Journal of Horticultural Science and Biotechnology, 77*(1), 120–129. doi: 10.1080/14620316.2002.11511467.

Zelenski, J. M., Dopko, R. L., & Capaldi, C. A. (2015). Cooperation is in our nature: Nature exposure may promote cooperative and environmentally sustainable behavior. *Journal of Environmental Psychology, 42*, 24–31. doi: 10.1016/j.jenvp.2015.01.005.

Author note

Katharine H. Greenaway is supported by an Australian Research Council Discovery Early Career Researcher Award (DE160100761).
Corresponding author: William Bingley, School of Psychology, University of Queensland, Australia.

10

THE GENDERED AESTHETICS OF THE PHYSICAL ENVIRONMENT OF WORK

Varda Wasserman

Introduction

FIGURE 10.1 Manspreading

Do men use space differently than women? Many of us are familiar with the situation depicted in Figure 10.1. According to the *Oxford English Dictionary*, this phenomenon – nowadays termed 'manspreading' – refers to 'the practice whereby a man, especially one on public transportation, adopts a sitting position with his legs wide apart, in such a way as to encroach on an adjacent seat or seats'. Public awareness of this gendered spatial practice was raised in 2013, when many social media websites initiated a feminist campaign against manspreading and precipitated vigorous public debate in New York, Madrid, Toronto, and many other cities, some of which has brought about official bans on manspreading in city transport, especially on trains and buses. Does manspreading also occur in organizational spaces and in daily work situations? Do men and women differ in their spatial practices within the office space? Do men tend to take up more space than women, or do they differ merely in the ways that they territorialize their work environment? Are there gender differences in all cultures?

Expansive body postures (such as open legs, legs on the desk, spread hands, and more) were found to be linked to greater feelings of power and dominance. The symbolic meanings of those postures have attracted the attention of many psychologists and communication researchers (e.g. Henley, 1977), but were overlooked in the context of work environments. Since even in modern, Western societies, young girls and women are often encouraged (even if not explicitly) to take up less space than boys (Trethewey, 1999, Bird & Sokolofski, 2005), and given the fact that the literature on proximities and personal space shows that women's boundaries are not as respected as men's, causing their personal space to be invaded more easily (Jane, 2017; Puwar, 2004), it is unlikely that workspaces are an exception.

Examining work settings as sites where many forms of gendered spatial practice take place draws our attention to power relations and status differences as they are reflected in organizational spaces and bodily territoriality (Bartky, 1990, p. 74). Specifically, though women are nowadays much more integrated in organizations and their status has improved, focusing on spatial/aesthetic aspects allows us to expose the implicit, tacit ways in which women may be marginalized, and to expose how workplaces in all societies are still fairly gendered.

Critical research in organizational aesthetics has expanded this theoretical trajectory and placed special emphasis on the role of space in general – and open-space designs in particular – in the construction of social hierarchies and in processes of inclusion and exclusion of various identities, including gender (e.g. Dale & Burrell, 2008; Wasserman & Frenkel, 2011). While this scholarship reveals how design styles, colours, shapes, furniture, textures, and other spatial elements transmit messages regarding how employees are supposed to feel and behave in a specific surrounding, very little attention has been paid to gender and women's experiences within organizational spaces.

Based on the growing literature on organizational aesthetics (Dale & Burrell, 2008; Strati, 1996; Taylor & Spicer, 2007; Warren, 2008), this chapter aims to illuminate the various ways in which the physical work environment is segregated according to gender, how it is experienced by men and women, and how it is enacted by them. Specifically, the chapter suggests a typology of the literature on gender and organizational aesthetics by pointing to three main theoretical trajectories and then offering some theoretical arenas to be further developed in the future. In order to highlight the gendered biases of contemporary workplaces' layouts, I will focus mainly on open-space settings and cubicles by using illustrative examples both from literature and from my own experience in several organizational sites.

The aesthetics of separation: segregated workspaces

One way in which organizational aesthetics becomes a means to 'genderize' workplaces is through physical separation/segregation – that is, to separate women's and men's areas. However, most studies focusing on the various ways in which women are excluded in organizations do not relate to spatial segregation, under the assumption that it is no longer relevant today. Indeed, while in the past women were limited to at-home, unpaid jobs and were excluded from organizations and from the public sphere in general, we have witnessed in recent decades a process of desegregation in the labour market, and gender equality in organizations has been enhanced. However, by using a spatial lens and examining the historical development of spatial segregation within organizations, one sees that gender segregation still exists, though in different forms, mainly through job segregation.

Only a few decades ago, women were excluded from the central organizational space by various mechanisms of zoning and separation, including separate entrances, isolation, and physical partitions between men and women. Their entry into the labour market not only created gender-segregated spaces, but a unique aesthetics typical of women's areas has also been implemented – one that is based on stereotypical perceptions of gender and femininity. For example, at the beginning of the 20th century, when many women began working as service clerks and secretaries, their work environment was designed as spatially fixed (for instance, chairs and desks were fixed to the floor), tied to their machines and work positions, while men (mainly as managers) enjoyed workspaces that allow mobility and flow in space (Boyer, 2004).

Nowadays, with the gradual disappearance of formal gendered zoning in modern organizations, spatial segregation has become subtle and is manifested mainly through the occupational distinction between 'men's jobs' (often senior positions) and 'women's jobs' (mainly junior positions) (Deemer, Thoman, Chase & Smith, 2014; Nash, forthcoming; Twomey & Meadus, 2016).

The tendency of men and women to do different work, a phenomenon often labelled 'occupational segregation', remains one of the most persistent problems in gender equality even today (Gomberg-Muñoz, 2018). Secretaries, cashiers, teachers, and nurses are still the most common positions for women in the year 2017.[1] In many organizations this occupational segregation is not only reflected but also reproduced in many organizational layouts through spatial segregation based on space allotment according to rank and/or status. Managers and high-status jobholders are overwhelmingly male and thus often placed in enclosed, large, and private offices, whereas the supporting, low-status staff are predominantly female and are mostly located in open spaces that are small and lack privacy (Baran & Teegarden, 1987; Paliadelis, 2013; Sundstrom & Sundstrom, 1986; Wasserman, 2012). Since space allotments in contemporary organizations are often based on rank and status (Elsbach, 2003), which, in turn, often follow gender divisions, the unintended consequence is often that such allotments are not gender-neutral. In other words, although architects and managers do not deliberately design the organizational layout to reflect gender inequalities, the separation of 'closed-door jobs' from 'open-floor jobs' cloaks contemporary practices of gender exclusion and reinforces status differences (Spain, 1993; Wasserman, 2012).

Further, while the initial concept of open spaces aimed to enhance equality and communication, open spaces are often criticized for their noise and lack of privacy, which interferes with the concentration of workers, their ability to have interpersonal interactions with colleagues, and their wellbeing and general comfort (Elsbach & Pratt, 2007; Kaufmann-Buhler, 2016). The gap between the improved physical conditions of closed, private offices and the less desirable ones of open spaces arouse, in some cases, severe dissatisfaction and frustration on the part of employees who are located in those spaces. In organizations where a clearer gender division of labour is evident (for example, hospitals), many women (especially those of low status) are located in substandard spaces (Kaarlela-Tuomaala, Helenius, Keskinen & Hongisto, 2009).

One such example can be found in an extensive study I conducted on the Israeli Ministry of Foreign Affairs (see Wasserman, 2012; Wasserman & Frenkel, 2015). For its relocation to a new facility, the ministry's architects and management placed much emphasis on power and status symbols. Thus, as is common in many organizations, the dominant logic driving the allotment of space followed a hierarchical order. Specifically, senior employees (i.e. diplomats or managers) were located near the windows, in closed rooms, and on a high, spacious, and prestigious floor. Junior employees (administrative staff or junior diplomats) were located in the centre of the floor in open, simple, small, and visible cubicles. This allegedly 'neutral' logic has caused (even if not deliberately) a gender-segregated space that places many women (those who are not diplomats) in spaces that are inferior in terms of size, surveillance, aesthetics, and privacy. The separation carried symbolic and emotional implications, as it mirrored organizational hierarchies and power relations and was manifested in additional spatial practices. For instance, women in cubicles were subjugated to anyone passing by and felt themselves to be under constant surveillance, a situation that resulted in many women testifying that they felt anxious about their own aesthetics (their dress and bodily postures) during the day. Further, the lack of privacy, the inability to control the desired temperature of the air conditioning, the bolting of furniture to the floor, the high level of noise, disturbance, and visual ambience in the open-plan areas had increased their sense of distress (they even named their area a 'ghetto') and de facto had reinforced their exclusion. Even though these may be seen as problems that are not necessarily related to gender, in this case it was clear to all interviewees (men and women alike) that the number of women in the open cubicles is much larger. Further, since most of them are not part of the diplomatic staff – and thus are not expected to be promoted to senior positions – they are destined to remain in these spaces throughout their entire working life.

Although most of the literature on gender–spatial separations concentrates on occupational segregation, some studies show that gender segregation also exists between women and men who are employed in the same job or occupation. In the 1970s, researchers in the United States were already pointing to the tendency of men employed as sales clerks to be concentrated in high-end, relatively high-status stores, while women in the same occupation were concentrated mainly in discount or department stores (Talbert & Bose 1977). Although this sector, and the employment market in general, has changed significantly in recent decades, the preservation of status gaps between men and women employed in the same profession or role is expected to preserve the hierarchical division of the spaces between them. In a much more recent study, Johansson and Lundgren (2015) describe gender segregation in a Swedish supermarket that was divided into a pre-store (outside the store), where only women worked, and the inner space of the store, where both men and women work together (and where a job rotation practice was customary). The study showed that this spatial separation created a hierarchy among the workers, whose perception was that the pre-store is a peripheral and inferior space – in effect, a dead-end. Women who worked in this space perceived it as a space of high pressure and abrasive routines.

Aesthetics as a gendered experience

A second way in which organizational aesthetics may become gendered is associated with the different ways in which men and women experience their surroundings. Organizational buildings have long become tools for making work more efficient by turning them into homogenous, standardized, and transparent spaces, without taking into consideration differences in gender (or ethnicity, culture, and age). In many workplaces, the internal walls and partitions have been removed, with the intention of creating a work environment that will allow people to work flexibly according to projects and tasks. But this has also resulted in turning the workspace into a 'gaze-able', watchable sphere in which some are more subjected to surveillance than others. Studies show that these are not experienced as culture-neutral (see, for example, Ayoko and Härtel (2003) on the role of cultural norms in the experience of spatial layout and in interpersonal conflicts in workgroups) or gender-neutral. Generally speaking, women tend to assess their workspaces more critically than men (De Been & Beijer, 2014).

One of the few studies to explore the gendered experience of the physical work environment is that of Hirst and Schwabenland (2018), who examined the embodied experience of women in a UK authority office that moved to a new building with open cubicles. The authors showed that female employees associated the new office with a nudist beach-type feeling, whereby they were exposed to a male gaze.

As a result of being constantly watched, women were dressing more smartly in the new office, signalling their status through their attire. The researchers concluded that while some women felt discomfort about their visibility and others enjoyed it, there is no doubt that organizational spaces are gendered in many different ways.

Tyler and Cohen's (2010) study reached similar conclusions. In their research, the authors initiated a focus group exposing 30 women to an artist clip that was presented in an exhibition in a gallery in London, and which described a comic office situation. The focus group was designed to trigger emotional responses to organizational aesthetics and to generate gender-related associations with the women's own daily experience in their office space. Based on Butler's performativity and on Lefebvre's concept of lived space, Tyler and Cohen detail several sources of women's frustration in organizational spaces. First, they illustrate how women described feelings of constraint in standardized, transparent workspaces, typically open cubicles, amplifying claustrophobic feelings and the inability to develop a sense of belonging to what they perceived as a 'masculine environment'. They show that many organizations are designed with power symbols for transmitting to their clients and employees feelings of prestige and high status, but these are not interpreted as gender-neutral symbols. Second, women portrayed their experiences in terms of both invisibility and overexposure, reflecting their feelings in regard to their (lack of) right to space, privacy, and distinctiveness. Third, as suggested by Figure 10.1 at the beginning of this chapter, many women reported a sense of spatial invasion and 'spillage' of their male office partners, both symbolically and physically. Many of Tyler and Cohen's interviewees felt that their male colleagues take up much more space than they do, that their desks are much messier than their own, and that they feel they are expected to make their work environment welcoming and pleasing for their male colleagues.

The most prominent challenge facing many women is the increasing demand of organizations to stay in the office for long hours, to subordinate their personal/private concerns to those of the organization, and to blur the distinction between home and work, especially for highly skilled workers. Since women still bear the primary responsibility for household affairs, they are most often the victims of increased organizational control over workers' time and space (Collinson & Collinson, 1997). Thus, women (especially young mothers) prefer private spaces where they can talk to their children, their parents (for whom they are often the caregivers), and the babysitter, as well as address other daily routine arrangements for which they are responsible at home. But the open-cubicle layout makes this much more difficult, and the result is that they feel their privacy has been significantly invaded (Wasserman, 2012).

These experiences are likely to intensify for young women who are breastfeeding. When they are required to pump milk during working hours, they may feel particularly exposed to the gaze of others in their workspace, especially when it is an open or semi-open space. In such cases, women are forced to search for empty rooms, cars, toilets, and temporary hiding places – a circumstance that is likely to increase their sense that they lack the right to space, as well as their inability to develop a sense of belonging to the physical work environment and to the organization in general (Johnson & Salpini, 2017).

Nevertheless, even in more everyday cases, studies show that women and men tend to interpret and experience organizational aesthetics in different ways. One such explanation may stem from Berdahl and Anderson's (2005) study, in which the authors argue that women tend to favour egalitarian norms in work groups and therefore tend to divide space in a more equal manner, whereas men prefer hierarchical power relations and thus tend to occupy as much space as possible for themselves. Other studies found that women tend to gravitate toward homey and intimate designs with bright colours, whereas men tend to prefer dark colours, larger rooms, high-status symbols, and prestigious furniture pieces, particularly those incorporating leather and wood details (Pressly & Heesacker, 2001). Since most office layouts are set up in a more traditional and hierarchical style favouring men's preferences (especially in high-status jobs such as lawyers and accountants), women are likely to feel uncomfortable with this kind of organizational aesthetics.

Whether men and women differ in their preferences or whether it is a myth or a result of social construction (Massey, 1994), the common belief is that there is a difference between 'masculine design' and 'feminine design', each of which dictates how men and women are expected to feel in each of these designs. While tall buildings, linear and angular lines, and phallic symbols signify masculinity, rounder, softer lines are often seen as more feminine in character. These widespread views are further reinforced by architects, designers, and other professionals, who tend to express themselves in this manner when explaining their architectural choices to the general public. Since people are subjected to these common images – which are further reinforced and reconstructed by films, books, and other cultural means (Panayiotou, 2015) – it is reasonable to assume that experiences of aesthetics are not gender-neutral. In the following discussion, I will elaborate on how and why future research in organizational studies should delve deeper into the non-neutral styles of design and the emotions they trigger in various social groups.

Aesthetics as a gendered enactment of space

A third trajectory of studies referring to the gendered aesthetics of organizations has emerged in recent years following the shift in the field of organizational aesthetics from an emphasis placed on space as a container of organizational practices and identities toward a processual understanding of the production of organizational spaces – namely, 'spacing' rather than 'spaces' (Beyes, 2010; Beyes & Steyaert, 2012; Vásquez & Cooren, 2013; Wasserman & Frenkel, 2011). These studies argue that spatio-organizational analyses should focus on the *processes* at work in determining the ways in which employees, managers, clients, and other users of a specific organizational space enact space in a dynamic process of negotiation and continuous movement between complying and resisting it, how various actors within the organization take part in designing their own spaces, and how they perpetuate or change spatial boundaries and restrictions.

Various studies point to the ways in which employees mark their distinctiveness and try to embody their identity and feelings through crafting their own spaces within the organization. Many of these studies point to the ways in which employees, especially women, domesticate and personalize their offices as a strategy by which they feel more 'at home' in their work environment and achieve a sense of belonging to the workplace (Elsbach, 2003; Shortt, Betts, & Warren, 2013; Kanter, 1977; Warren, 2008; Wasserman, 2012). Wells's (2000) study showed that women not only tend to personalize their offices much more than men, but that their style of personalization is different. While the motives of women in personalizing their offices are to express their individuality and their emotions as well as to feel better, men who personalize their offices do so to show their status. Thus, women tend to display symbols of personal relationships (photographs with family, friends, pets, etc.) as well as items associated stereotypically with 'femininity' and with domestic-themed items (such as plants, trinkets, knick-knacks, or art), whereas men tend to exhibit sports-related items and markers of their achievements (such as diplomas and various certificates). Similar findings were described by Goodrich (1986), who observed that women tend to personalize their surroundings with aesthetic items (such as plants, posters, and personal items), whereas men tend to personalize their offices with items illustrative of their achievements. Dinc (2009) provides a possible explanation for this gender difference, arguing that women are characterized by attachment motives (creating a 'home-away-from-home' atmosphere in their offices), whereas men are characterized by ownership motives (showing off their status and making a place their own).

Domesticating space is a unique way of spatial enactment that is not only aimed at enhancing individual feelings of home, comfort, and belonging to the organization; it also serves as a means of constructing a sense of identity and identification with the organization (Shortt, Betts, & Warren, 2013). Since domestication and personal items displayed at work often trigger conversations and spontaneous interactions that connect different people, they should be perceived as both an individualistic and a collective act that establishes a communal identity in the organization. Therefore, they are of great importance in shaping the experiences and relationships of employees with others and with the organization in general.

The differences between 'female' and 'masculine' styles of space enactment are also reflected (and further reconstructed) in films, as documented by Panayiotou (2015), who demonstrates that offices of female senior executives are often represented as colourful, decorated, domestic environments. She argues that 'female' designs that typically blur the difference between offices and living rooms should be interpreted as an act of resistance whereby women take ownership of the office space and turn it into a place of their own, to which they feel a sense of belonging and where they feel at home. A similar argument has been raised by Warren (2005) in a study of non-territorial workspaces, also known as 'hot-desking' – that is, a spatial setting wherein desks are shared by many employees and no one has a permanent desk/workstation. These aesthetic arrangements, which are becoming increasingly popular, pose a potential emotional threat to employees who are unable to exhibit their own physical 'identity markers' (i.e. items that reflect the distinctive features of one's identity, such as being a mother or an athlete – see Elsbach, 2003). To cope with these anonymous workspaces, many women tend to engage in what Warren (2005) has named 'hot-nesting', that is, they resist management's hot-desking instructions by sticking to their desks and marking them with their own items to re-establish a sense of belonging and distinctiveness.

Another way in which female employees reject the formality and anonymity of the office space is by displaying 'office folklore' (cartoons, parodies, and sayings) in visible areas. In a case study focused on female researchers in an American university, Bell and Forbes (1994) argue that office folklore is used as a 'survival kit . . . as constant sources of laughter and entertainment, as escape valves and reality "checks," as reflections and fun-house mirrors of their organizational lives' (p. 186). The gendered enactment of artefacts, they argue, is aimed at subverting organizational control and the masculine discourse by displaying emotions usually perceived as illegitimate or inappropriate (e.g. rage, irrationality, pleasure, open criticism, and more).

The extent to which personalization is to be interpreted as a resistance tactic is questioned in Tyler and Cohen's (2010) article, in which they contend that personalization is not only intended to create a sense of comfort and control, but also to comply with gender expectations of being perceived as an excellent 'hostess'. Thus, women are expected to design an appealing, organized, comfortable, and inviting environment. By emphasizing how women take extra care when designing their work environment not to deviate from what they perceive as the unofficial instructions of the organization as to what is appropriate to their gender, Tyler and Cohen (2010) argue that organizational aesthetics is 'a materialization of the cultural norms according to which particular gender performances are enacted, and through which adherence to those norms is signified, successfully evoking recognition of viable gender subjectivity' (p. 193). While some women consciously choose not to put into their workspace objects that reveal their family lives and to keep this aspect of their lives secret, they do not deviate much from gender expectations. Many of them exhibit objects that emphasize their skills (such as diplomas) and portray them as professionals, but at the same time they display personal objects that reveal their identities and interests outside of work and portray them as 'well-rounded'.

A previous study that I conducted with a colleague (Wasserman & Frenkel, 2015) on the Israeli Ministry of Foreign Affairs corroborates these findings, differentiating between women of higher and lower status within the organization. By using the term 'spatial gender-class work', my colleague and I point to the ways in which women of differing class and status enact their spatial surroundings to reflect, perpetuate, and/or resist their organizational positioning. Inspired by the notion of 'doing gender' (West & Zimmerman, 1987) and more recent ideas of 'gender work' (Gherardi, 1994) and 'class work' (Gray & Kish-Gephart, 2013), we demonstrated how upper-class women, who share a class habitus with upper-class men in top organizational positions, designed their offices through a specific type of spatial gender-class work, which we named 'aesthetic work', in order to distinguish themselves from lower-class women and to position themselves as professionals who are entitled to top positions. Their offices were very similar to those of men of equivalent status – that is, a formal and restrained design, neutral and non-gender-specific colours and pictures, and symbols that stress their senior professional status. On the other hand, women from the administrative staff filled their cubicles with colourful pictures, accessories, toys and trinkets, mirrors, drawings done by their children, and family photos, resulting in a 'maternal aesthetics' that starkly challenges the planners' efforts to eradicate indicators of femininity and domesticity. This means that compliance with gender expectations and the way in which employees shape and enact their space is not only gendered, but also influenced and constructed by other social belongings.

Concluding remarks and reflections on future directions of study

In the final part of this chapter, I would like to point out some potential research directions that emerge from the typology I have suggested above and to elaborate on how each of three trajectories – gender segregation of space, gendered experience of space, and gendered enactment of space – could be further advanced. My suggestions will rely mainly on the growing organizational literature on the French philosopher Henri Lefebvre (Beyes & Steyaert, 2012; Dale & Burrell, 2008; Hancock & Spicer, 2011; Kingma, 2008; Taylor & Spicer, 2007; Wasserman & Frenkel, 2011, 2015; Zhang & Spicer, 2014; Zhang, Spicer, & Hancock, 2008), which has, in my view, the greatest potential to push forward the 'spatial turn' in organizational studies and to help us to develop a more nuanced and sophisticated analysis of organizational aesthetics and everyday spatial practices.

At the core of Lefebvre's theory of space stands his distinction between three spaces: *the conceived space* (also known as 'representations of space': the planners' discourse and conceptualization of space); *the perceived space* (also called 'spatial practices': the translation of the architectural discourse into material artefacts and users' bodily gestures); and *the lived space* (also referred to as 'the spaces of representation': the users' interpretations of space and the ways in which they experience and use it). Together these three spaces become a mechanism for reproducing power relations and constructing them as a taken-for-granted social order. Although Lefebvre has inspired a growing number of organizational researchers, especially those from the theoretical field of critical management, and although Lefebvre himself did refer directly to gender in his writings – arguing that spaces are shaped according to a masculine, phallic power – almost none of them has addressed gendered spaces (but see Hirst & Schwabenland, 2018; Nash, forthcoming). In what follows I would like to put forward some ideas on how to use Lefebvre's theory to enrich each of the three above-mentioned trajectories and to deepen our understanding of the gendered aspects of organizational aesthetics. While the following discussion is research-oriented, more practical implications for organizations to implement in their re-design processes may also emerge from the suggestions to follow.

The first trajectory discussed above refers to spatial segregation based on gender/occupational separation. While the most obvious suggestion to organizational managers might be to avoid any such spatial separations, in some cases women may *choose* it and even feel empowered in the company of women only, as advocated by some feminist movements (see Spain, 1993). Specifically, despite some of these efforts' success in increasing the visibility of women and feminist issues in a broader social struggle, organizational studies should define a set of criteria as to when such a separation perpetuates gender inequality and exclusion and in what circumstances it has the potential to reduce them. In order to expose the gendered assumptions of such a decision, we should inquire: who initiated the separation? What was its purpose? How was it rationalized by the planners and the management? How do women interpret this decision? By applying Lefebvre's conceived space in a feminist analysis, we can adopt a more political perspective, questioning the architectural and managerial discourses: their rationalizations and ideologies as to how space should be divided, who should get more space in the organization, and how offices should be designed and with which colours and materials. If, for instance, managerial/architectural discourse is phallocentric (i.e. space allotment is based on hierarchy and/or achievements, disregarding gender differences and division of labour), a unified conceptualization of space and male-centred planning processes will inevitably perpetuate women's invisibility and inequality. As suggested earlier in the chapter, managers should avoid spatial allocation based on rank and hierarchical position, since these decisions are never gender-neutral.

The second trajectory I indicated above suggests that organizational aesthetics is not experienced as gender-neutral. Despite some studies that have acknowledged that space is not homogeneously interpreted, most studies do not distinguish between different social groups, men and women, and users from different cultures (nor do the architects and managers involved in planning programmes). To integrate the limited literature on culture-based and gendered experiences of space (including perceptions regarding territoriality, privacy, artefacts, symbols, interpersonal distance, etc.), I suggest incorporating more insights from the growing interest in diversity as well as in intersectionality within organizations (Brah & Phoenix, 2013), which has yielded abundant empirical studies and documentations of the different experiences of women of colour, women of different national and ethnic backgrounds, sexual orientations, diverse religions and religiosity, and different class or professional backgrounds. By integrating insights from the literature on intersectionality into the literature on organizational aesthetics, we could avoid the homogenization of the essentialist category 'women' and develop a much more nuanced perspective on the ways in which space is lived and experienced by women of various social groups. I believe that qualitative/hermeneutic methodologies are more sensitive to the amplitude of emotional and cultural narratives and thus are more suitable for studies of this kind.

Managers can also use insights from this theoretical direction, especially in a globalized world in which diversity management has become a significant managerial tool. Assuming that the spatial experience is not only different for women and men, but also among women of different cultures, managers must examine and consider the different preferences of these women and provide diverse spatial options to workers from different cultures.

The third trajectory – spatial enactment – forgoes the notion of space as a container of organizational processes and urges us to deepen our understanding of how men and women use space to comply with or resist managerial agendas and surveillance. Inspecting spatial enactment through the lens of power and resistance theory provides a particularly fertile ground for understanding the role of gender (and other identities) in perpetuating or changing social order within organizations. In recent years there has emerged a growing body of literature on the ways in which people resist anonymous and/or regulated spaces imposed upon them (Dale & Burrell, 2008; Shortt, 2015; Spicer & Taylor, 2006) and how space can enhance political efforts (Courpasson, Dany, & Delbridge, 2017), but none of them refer to gender. Drawing on Lefebvre's triad, Spicer and Taylor (2006) present a variety of spatial resistance tactics that can be further explored, such as sabotaging the spatial surroundings or escaping to liminal places – for example, hidden corners, stairwells, or toilets – where employees can gain a sense of privacy and evade the gaze of their managers, customers, or colleagues. Broadening this framework will, in my opinion, enrich our analytical perspective on the ways in which organizational spaces become gendered (Jane, 2017). For instance, Lefebvre's ideas of embodiment and spatial practices can expose how artefacts are designed according to men's bodies. One anecdote that clarifies how the male body constitutes the standard on which the organization is based refers to a case that I encountered during my observations at the Ministry of Foreign Affairs, where I saw that women deliberately avoid shaking hands when sitting around the impressive table in the conference room. When I asked them about it, they answered that the width of the table was designed so that two people could shake hands across it, but the height of those people was 175cm. Since most women are shorter, they were forced to go around the table to shake hands. Thus, they avoided it as much as possible and advocated their refusal as a form of protest against this masculine architectural design. Recent studies have begun to acknowledge the theoretical potential of delving into these types of behaviours by examining the growing female protest against 'manspreading' and the ensuing changes in transportation policy in some cities (Jane, 2017). In organizations, too, a similar phenomenon might appear in the future, when female employees will resist the invasion of their space by their male colleagues and reclaim their right to shape their workspace according to their needs and preferences.

To sum up, aesthetics decisions within organizations form symbolic boundaries that become a key mechanism in the perpetuation of social inequality, direct and self-exclusion, and in the camouflage of power relations underlying the creation of spatial-social significance. Since architectural decisions are often embedded in a specific culture (or gender, for that matter), the inevitable result is a gendered space that reinforces the separate identities and distinct work experiences of men and women in an organization, making the glass ceiling very clear to women – not merely metaphorically, but in a very tangible manner.

Note

1 See for instance in the USA: www.dol.gov/wb/stats/most_common_occupations_for_
women.htm

Bibliography

Ayoko, O. B., & Härtel, C. E. J. (2003). The role of space as both a conflict trigger and a conflict control mechanism in culturally heterogeneous workgroups. *Applied Psychology, 52*(3), 383–412.

Baran, B., & Teegarden, S. (1987). Women's labor in the office of the future: A case study of the insurance industry. In L. Beneria & C. R. Stimpson (eds), *Households and the Economy* (pp. 201–224). New Brunswick, NJ: Rutgers University Press.

Bartky, S.L. (1990). *Femininity and Domination: Studies in the Phenomenology of Oppression.* New York: Routledge.

Bell, E., & Forbes, L. C. (1994). Office folklore in the academic paperwork empire: The interstitial space of gendered (con)texts. *Text and Performance Quarterly, 14*, 181–196.

Berdahl, J. L., & Anderson, C. (2005). Men, women, and leadership centralization in groups over time. *Group Dynamics: Theory, Research, and Practice, 9*(1), 45–57.

Beyes, T. (2010). Uncontained: The art and politics of reconfiguring urban space. *Culture and Organization, 16*(3), 229–245.

Beyes, T., & Steyaert, C. (2012). Spacing organization: Non-representational theory and performing organizational space. *Organization, 19*(1), 45–61.

Bird, S. R., & Sokolofski, L. K. (2005). Gendered socio-spatial practices in public eating and drinking establishments in the Midwest United States. *Gender, Place and Culture, 12*(2), 213–230.

Boyer, K. (2004). 'Miss Remington' goes to work: Gender, space, and technology at the dawn of the information age. *Professional Geographer, 56*(2), 201–212.

Brah, A., & Phoenix, A. (2013). 'Ain't I a woman?' Revisiting intersectionality. *Journal of International Women's Studies, 5*(3), 75–86.

Collinson, D. L., & Collinson, M. (1997). 'Delayering managers': Time-space surveillance and its gendered effects. *Organization, 4*(3), 375–407.

Courpasson, D., Dany, F., & Delbridge, R. (2017). Politics of place: The meaningfulness of resisting places. *Human Relations, 70*(2), 237–259.

Dale, K., & Burrell, G. (2008). *The Spaces of Organisation and the Organisation of Space: Power, Identity and Materiality at Work.* Basingstoke: Palgrave Macmillan.

De Been, I., & Beijer, M. (2014). The influence of office type on satisfaction and perceived productivity support. *Journal of Facilities Management, 12*(2), 142–157.

Deemer, E. D., Thoman, D. B., Chase, J. P., & Smith, J. L. (2014). Feeling the threat: Stereotype threat as a contextual barrier to women's science career choice intentions. *Journal of Career Development, 41*(2), 141–158.

Dinc, P. (2009). Gender (in)difference in private offices: A holistic approach for assessing satisfaction and personalization. *Journal of Environmental Psychology, 29*, 53–62.

Elsbach, K. D. (2003). Relating physical environment to self-categorizations: Identity threat and affirmation in a non-territorial office space. *Administrative Science Quarterly, 48*, 622–654.

Elsbach, K. D., & Pratt, M. G. (2007). The physical environment in organizations. *Academy of Management Annals, 1*(1), 181–224.

Gherardi, S. (1994). The gender we think, the gender we do in our everyday organizational lives. *Human Relations, 47*(6), 591–610.

Gomberg-Muñoz, R. (2018). On gender, labor, and inequality by Ruth Milkman. *Labor: Studies in Working-Class History, 15*(1), 115–116.

Goodrich, R. (1986). The perceived office: The office environment as experienced by its users. In J. D. Wineman (ed.), *Behavioral Issues in Office Design* (pp. 109–133). New York: Van Nostrand Reinhold.

Gray, B., & Kish-Gephart, J. J. (2013). Encountering social class differences at work: How 'class work' perpetuates inequality. *Academy of Management Review, 38*(4), 670–699.

Hancock, P., & Spicer, A. (2011). Academic architecture and the constitution of the new model worker. *Culture and Organization, 17*(2), 91–105.

Henley, N. (1977). *Body Politics: Power, Sex, and Non-verbal Communication.* Englewood Cliffs, NJ: Prentice-Hall.

Hirst, A., & Schwabenland, C. (2018). Doing gender in the 'new office'. *Gender, Work and Organization, 25*(2), 159–176.

Jane, E. A. (2017). 'Dude. . . stop the spread': Antagonism, agonism, and manspreading on social media. *International Journal of Cultural Studies, 20*(5), 459–475.

Johansson. K., & Lundgren, A. S. (2015). Gendering boundary work: Exploring excluded spaces in supermarket job rotation. *Gender, Place and Culture, 22*(2), 188–204.

Johnson, K. M., & Salpini, C. (2017). Working and nursing: Navigating job and breastfeeding demands at work. *Community, Work and Family, 20*(4), 479–496.

Kaarlela-Tuomaala, A., Helenius, R., Keskinen, E., & Hongisto, V. (2009). Effects of acoustic environment on work in private office rooms and open-plan offices: Longitudinal study during relocation. *Ergonomics, 52*(11), 1423–1444.

Kanter, R.M. (1977). *Men and Women of the Corporation.* New York: Basic Books.

Kaufmann-Buhler, J. (2016). Progressive partitions: The promises and problems of the American open plan office. *Design and Culture, 8*(2), 205–233.

Kingma, S. F. (2008). Dutch casino space or the spatial organization of entertainment. *Culture and Organization, 14*(1), 31–48.

Lefebvre, H. (1991). *The Production of Space.* Oxford: Blackwell.

Massey, D. (1994) *Space, Place and Gender.* Minneapolis, MN: University of Minnesota Press.

Nash, L. (forthcoming). Gendered places: Place, performativity and flânerie in the City of London. *Gender, Work and Organization.*

Paliadelis, P. (2013). Nurse managers don't get the corner office. *Journal of Nursing Management, 21*(2), 377–386.

Panayiotou, A. (2015). Spacing gender, gendering space: A radical 'strong plot' in film. *Management Learning, 46*(4), 427–443.

Pressly, P. K., & Heesacker, M. (2001). The physical environment and counseling: A review of theory and research. *Journal of Counseling and Development, 79*(2), 148–160.

Puwar, N. (2004). *Space Invaders: Race, Gender and Bodies out of Place.* Oxford and New York: Berg.

Shortt, H. (2015). Liminality, space and the importance of 'transitory dwelling places' at work. *Human Relations, 68*(4), 633–658.

Shortt, H., Betts, J., & Warren S. (2013). Visual workplace identities: Objects, emotion and resistance. In E. Bell, J. E. Schroeder, & S. Warren (eds), *The Routledge Companion to Visual Organization* (pp. 289–305). Abingdon: Routledge.

Spain, D. (1993). Gendered spaces and women's status. *Sociological Theory, 11*(2), 137–151.

Spicer, A., & Taylor, S. (2006). The struggle for organizational space. *Journal of Management Inquiry, 27*, 325–346.

Strati, A. (1996). Organizations viewed through the lens of aesthetics. *Organization, 3*(2), 209–218.

Sundstrom, E., & Sundstrom, M. G. (1986). *Work Places: The Psychology of the Physical Environment in Offices and Factories.* New York: Cambridge University Press.

Talbert, J., & Bose C. 1977. Wage-attainment processes: The retail clerk case. *American Journal of Sociology, 83*(2), 403–424.

Taylor, S., & Spicer, A. (2007). Time for space: A narrative review of research on organizational spaces. *International Journal of Management Reviews, 9*(4), 325–346.

Trethewey, A. (1999). Disciplined bodies: Women's embodied identities at work. *Organization Studies, 20*(3), 423–450.

Twomey, J. C., & Meadus, R. (2016). Men nurses in Atlantic Canada: Career choice, barriers, and satisfaction. *Journal of Men's Studies, 24*(1), 78–88.

Tyler, M., & Cohen, L. (2010). Spaces that matter: Gender performativity and organizational space. *Organization Studies, 31*(2), 175–198.

Vásquez, C., & Cooren, F. (2013). Spacing practices: The communicative configuration of organizing through space-times. *Communication Theory, 23*(1), 25–47.

Warren, S. (2005). Hot nesting? A visual exploration of personalized workspaces in a hot-desk office environment. In P. Case, S. Lilley, & T. Owens (eds), *The Speed of Organization* (pp. 119–146). Liber: Copenhagen Business School Press.

Warren, S. (2008). Empirical challenges in organizational aesthetics research: Towards a sensual methodology. *Organization Studies, 29*(4), 559–580.

Wasserman, V. (2012). Open spaces, closed boundaries: Transparent workspaces as clerical female ghettos. *International Journal of Work, Organization and Emotion, 5*(1), 6–25.

Wasserman, V., & Frenkel, M. (2011). Organizational aesthetics: Caught between identity regulation and culture jamming. *Organization Science, 22*(2), 503–521.

Wasserman, V., & Frenkel, M. (2015). Spatial work in between glass ceilings and glass walls: Gender-class intersectionality and organizational aesthetics. *Organization Studies, 36*(11), 1485–1505.

Wells, M. M. (2000). Office clutter or meaningful personal displays: The role of office personalization in employee and organizational wellbeing. *Journal of Environmental Psychology, 20*(3), 239–255.

West, C., & Zimmerman, D. H. (1987). Doing gender. *Gender and Society, 1*, 125–151.

Zhang, Z., & Spicer, A. (2014). 'Leader, you first': The everyday production of hierarchical space in a Chinese bureaucracy. *Human Relations, 67*(6), 739–762.

Zhang, Z., Spicer, A., & Hancock, P. (2008). Hyper-organizational space in the work of JG Ballard. *Organization, 15*(6), 889–910.

11

SOCIO-MATERIALITY AND THE PHYSICAL ENVIRONMENT OF ORGANIZATIONS[1]

Leonore van den Ende, Thijs Willems, and Alfons van Marrewijk

Introduction

The relation between the physical environment and organizational behaviour has received renewed academic attention in organization and management studies (Brennan, Chugh, & Kline, 2002; Kornberger & Clegg, 2004; Elsbach & Bechky, 2007; Dale & Burrell, 2008; e.g. McElroy & Morrow, 2010; Van Marrewijk & Yanow, 2010; Ashkanasy, Ayoko, & Jehn, 2014). The physical environment of an organization is understood as its spatial configuration such as offices and workplace design, including material artefacts like machines, technologies, desks, and office supplies. The physical environment is crucial for understanding organizational behaviour and how behaviour can be changed, transformed, or modified (Van Marrewijk & Van den Ende, forthcoming). For example, the physical features of offices have been identified as factors stimulating organizational change (Hancock, 2006; Cameron, 2003). According to Kornberger and Clegg (2004), changing office spaces can be a powerful intervention in changing work practices. Similarly, constructing a new corporate building, renovating existing buildings, and (re)designing interior spaces can be important means for organizational transformation (Van Marrewijk, 2009). The physical environment of an organization thus impacts the fabric of social relations and behaviour in that organization (Dale & Burrell, 2010).

At the same time, scholars argue that the physical environment cannot merely determine behaviour in a unidirectional or foreseeable way (Dale, 2005; Orlikowski & Scott, 2008). Kenis, Kruyen, and Baaijens (2010), for example, show how employees of a prison facility, in dealing with design imperfections, developed creative solutions which changed the character of tasks, procedures, and rules in the prison. In turn, these changes served to transform the ways in which the prison as a space, including its material artefacts and technologies, was used by employees and prisoners alike. In other words, the relationship between the physical environment and behaviour is complex and characterized by unintended consequences and trade-offs (e.g. Elsbach & Pratt, 2007; Dale & Burrell, 2008). Yet, many studies treat the physical environment and employee behaviour as distinct spheres of organizational life: 'material objects, stimuli, and arrangements distinguish the physical environment from other types of organizational environments such as the social environment' (Elsbach & Pratt, 2007, p. 182). The aim of this chapter is to rethink this assumption by demonstrating how the physical environment and behaviour are intrinsically interrelated: the physical environment shapes social behaviour, while this behaviour, in turn, shapes how the physical environment is used and perceived (Hernes, Bakken, & Olsen, 2006).

To help us understand the dynamic and recursive interrelation between social and material spheres of life, we introduce a 'socio-material' lens through which 'social processes and structures and material process and structures are seen as mutually enacting' (Dale, 2005, p. 641). This lens challenges Cartesian dualistic thinking, where the mind is seen as distinct from the material world – a perspective that has long dominated in organization studies (Dale & Burrell, 2008). Latour (1993) criticizes this perspective, as it imposes a binary division on the world where human experience would somehow stand apart from its material surroundings. He therefore deconstructs the artificial separation of human and non-human spheres and brings to light their intersections and hybrids. Based upon Latour and others (e.g. Barad, 2007; Pickering, 1995; Suchman, 1987), a growing number of organization scholars has recently attempted to move beyond the separation of human and material worlds, developing a theory of organizing where 'the social' and 'the material' are understood as entwined spheres of organizational life – also referred to as socio-materiality theory (Dale, 2005; Orlikowski, 2007; Orlikowski & Scott, 2008; Leonardi, 2012, 2013).

While philosophically enlightening, socio-materiality theory remains difficult to grasp and engage with empirically (Mutch, 2013; Faulkner & Runde, 2012; Leonardi, 2013). To address this critique, in this chapter we will utilize the theory as a lens – i.e. a socio-material lens – to analyse two empirical case studies (Van den Ende, Van Marrewijk, & Boersma, 2015; Willems & van Marrewijk, 2017) in the form of vignettes. The first vignette draws on a longitudinal ethnographic study of the national coordination centre of the Dutch railway system (the OCCR). The OCCR was designed as a new space where several organizations were co-located with the intention to improve inter-organizational collaboration during incidents on the railway. The vignette focuses on the territorial practices that emerged in the kitchen of the OCCR. Although the kitchen was designed to stimulate informal communication, employees used this physical environment and its material artefacts to contest and challenge collaboration. The second vignette draws from an ethnographic case study of the 'North-South line' metro construction project in Amsterdam. The project had the difficult task to restart the construction of the metro after serious technical mishaps, as water leaked through the dam wall of a new station causing several monumental buildings to sink into the ground at the historic Vijzelgracht avenue. This vignette illustrates how the project organization, and particularly the tunnel boring team, redefined their perception of and meaning attributed to the dangerous physical environment and risky technology of underground tunnelling by naming and baptizing the tunnel boring machines (TBMs) during a ritual. In both vignettes, we aim to illustrate and explain the dynamic, multidirectional relation between the physical environment and organizational behaviour through a socio-material lens.

The chapter is structured as follows. We first define the concepts of the material, materiality and socio-materiality, after which we introduce our socio-material lens as a means to study the physical environment and its interrelation with organizational behaviour. We then present our vignettes in which we illustrate our two case studies, followed by a discussion to integrate our analyses and provide the main contributions of applying a socio-material lens. Finally, the conclusion summarizes the value of a socio-material lens for researching the physical environment in organizational settings and provides theoretical and practical implications and suggestions for future research.

Material, materiality, and socio-materiality

Our lives, personally and professionally alike, are intrinsically bound up with our physical environment. Entering the office of any university, we are welcomed by posters presenting the latest research, piles of books and documents to be read or marked, in often cramped office spaces where roller-blinds keep out much of the direct sunlight. Sitting down, the office chair is adjusted to fit the height of the desk, after which the computer is switched on. Although these objects can be understood as materials by referring to their physicality – i.e. the fact that these objects are made of matter – they are also material in a sense going beyond their immediate physicality, being their materiality. The materiality of an object refers to how 'its physical and/or digital materials are arranged into particular forms that endure across differences in place and time' (Leonardi, 2012, p. 29). When talking about materiality, we refer to both tangible (i.e. chairs, books, computers) as well as intangible phenomena (i.e. computer software, emails, electricity) and how these have qualities that are inherent to their materiality. Thus, material and digital objects have certain 'affordances' (Gibson, 1986) that allow you to use it in a specific way. The materiality of a knife allows you to cut while its qualities are less readily available to use for drinking or painting. Thus, although closely related, the materiality of an object goes beyond its pure physicality.

Although the above may sound somewhat deterministic – i.e. that the materiality of an object could be equated with its use – scholars theorizing *socio-materiality*, on the contrary, aim to fuse the ontological distinction made between the social and the material world. In other words, socio-materiality represents the 'enactment of a particular set of activities that meld materiality with institutions, norms, discourses, and all other phenomena we typically define as "social"' (Leonardi, 2012, p. 42). The extent to which the social and material are ontologically distinct or fused is currently debated (e.g. Leonardi, 2013; Mutch, 2013). Winch (2017) distinguishes 'sociomateriality' and socio-materiality (with hyphen); 'sociomateriality' emphasizes the deep and recursive entangling of the social and the material, while 'socio-materiality' (with hyphen) offers possibilities that the material and social have evolved separately as well as being entangled. Therefore, Winch (2017, p. 2) states that 'sociomateriality views humans and technology as ontologically fused while socio-materiality views them as ontologically separated.'

The recent advances in conceptualizing the relationship and entanglement between the social and material has established an important shift in the locus of inquiry of what socio-materiality scholars study. Rather than studying materials or physical spaces as such, for socio-materiality scholars *practice* is the focal point of social and material entanglement (Orlikowski & Scott, 2008). Essentially, practices, as something that actors *do*, involve both social and material factors in (re)constructing meaning and reality. As such, a practice embodies and performs an entanglement between the social and material, i.e. the socio-material, just like the practice of programming in an office on a computer can create a program for others to use at other times and places. Although most studies have hitherto sufficed to show that the social and the material are thoroughly entangled in practice, and that all practices are therefore socio-material, scholars are just beginning to consider *how* this occurs.

Introducing a socio-material lens

To study how social and material facets are entangled in practice, we introduce a 'socio-material lens'. This means that rather than engaging in an in-depth discussion about socio-materiality theory, we wish to utilize the theory as a lens through which we can make sense of and analyse empirical phenomena in a new light, thereby providing novel insights. Specifically, by using a socio-material lens, three main insights will be provided in this chapter, which we will return to in our discussion.

First, a socio-material lens gives credit to the significance of materiality in its own right, as it problematizes the tendency of scholars to privilege the social over the material where objects are merely seen as signs mediated by humans or treated as peripheral (Orlikowski & Scott, 2008; Leonardi, Nardi, & Kallinikos, 2012). Rather, visible, tangible, and material spatial settings and artefacts play a leading role in constituting organizational realities and shaping behaviour. Brown et al. (2005), for instance, analyse the concept of territoriality as a matter of psychological ownership. Although their study does focus on the role of material objects in creating boundaries and territories (e.g. nameplates on doors; family pictures to claim a desk in open offices), they see the material world as mainly socially constructed, defining territoriality 'as an individual's behavioural expression of his or her feelings of ownership toward a physical or social object' (Brown, Lawrence, & Robinson, 2005, p. 578). Without denying the value of their conceptualization, we believe it downplays the active role of boundaries and territories in their own right, which may 'act' by enabling or constraining human behaviour, regardless of how or why they were initially constructed (Taylor & Spicer, 2007; Dale, 2005). Similarly, Elsbach (2003) showed how employees in open offices who did not 'own' a specific desk felt a threat to their identity and distinctiveness resulting from the unavailability of physical identity markers.

Second, and building on the previous point, a socio-material lens casts light on the agential role of the physical environment. Though agency – the ability for an actor to act – has been characterized as uniquely human in the past, especially when it comes to intentionality, the notion of material agency has recently gained recognition in the field of organization science (Putnam, 2013). Namely, it is argued that materials can exercise agency through the things they do that humans cannot control or predict (Putnam, 2013; Leonardi, 2012). Agency is thus not only human, but a capacity realized through the relational and shifting association of human and material actors. For example, Gregson (2011) offers a reading of ship disposal, focusing on the 'death dance' of obsolete battle ship 'Clementeau'. The author reminds us that the physical environment and artefacts too, are agential in that they challenge human agency and control. When a ship can no longer be used – i.e. its 'social death' – humans cannot simply make it disappear. Instead, an arduous socio-material process follows, taking many years, places, and actors before the ship's 'material death' can be realized. Thus, using a socio-material lens to study the physical environment in relation to human behaviour can show how material *and* human agencies shape organizations and processes of organizing.

Third, a socio-material lens can show not only that the social and material are entangled, but how their entanglement takes place over time and in practice (Leonardi, 2013; Winch, 2017). In other words, analysing organizational practices through a socio-material lens can elucidate how boundaries between the social and the material are not predefined or fixed but continuously enacted and (re)defined in practice (Orlikowski & Scott, 2008). Pickering (1995) describes this as a 'dance of agency', where human and non-human agencies temporally emerge in everyday practice, causing their interrelation to change continuously in unpredictable ways, contingent on time, place, and context. Similarly, Winch (2017) asks for a temporal approach to the entanglement of the social and the material and views the material as having different temporal dynamics than the social. For example, mobile technology develops at a much faster rate than our use of it. Leonardi (2013), too, advises to link social and material agencies over time and in practice, in order to engage socio-materiality theory empirically.

Below we illustrate the value of using a socio-material lens to make sense of physical environments in relation to organizational behaviour, by sharing two ethnographic vignettes of organizations in the infrastructure sector.

Vignette 1: The OCCR kitchen

For the largest part of the 20th century, the Dutch railway system was managed by one, state-owned company. However, between 1995 and 2003 and under

European legislation, this company was split up into different organizations to separate the management and the exploitation of the infrastructure. One of the rationales behind this split-up was the conviction that disentangling processes would increase the efficiency and quality of train services. However, soon after the split-up several system failures and large disruptions plagued the railways. The different companies were criticized by the Dutch government and public alike, urging them to improve collaboration and communication. To manage disruptions quicker and better, the OCCR was established as a control centre where most of the organizational actors involved in railway operations are co-located. The idea behind the OCCR is that collaboration improves once physical distance between different organizations is reduced.

The people responsible for the design of the OCCR realized that a powerful way to improve collaboration was to design for sufficient informal spaces, where the tense relation between the organizations could be soothed more easily: 'We needed common spaces for informal interaction between people' (interview, project manager). In designing the OCCR, where people work on a 24/7 basis, the kitchen became an important space, as it was thought that cooking and sharing food is more than just a basic human necessity but also a way through which people bond.

The other control centres of the railways were different from the OCCR: regional, rather than national, and consisting of just one organization, rather than different co-located organizations. In these control centres, food traditionally is an important aspect of work, and people may have breakfast, lunch, or dinner together. An OCCR coordinator reflects on his time at a regional control centre: ordering or cooking food was something you would do 'with the whole crew' and it 'really belonged to the work'. Collective meals, parties, spontaneous after-work drinks ('drinking with the boys') and even self-organized holidays with colleagues – stories about the past stood in stark contrast to how informal spaces in the OCCR were perceived. The kitchen, for example, turned out to be anything but a place to cook. Even if people tried to arrange an event, such as a barbeque, these usually failed because of low participation and enthusiasm.

The kitchen turned into a place where few informal interactions happened and even fewer would stay to actually enjoy their meal: 'The television, which is always on, broadcasts the opening ceremony of the Olympic Winter Games in Sochi; the couches, where nobody ever sits, are empty; the chairs, never occupied, are turned upside down on the tables. The fluorescent light shines bright, but a faint mood prevails' (observation during fieldwork). Rather than a meaningful place to informally meet, the kitchen became a 'non-place', 'a space which cannot be defined as relational, or historical, or concerned with identity' (Auge, 1995, p. 77). What is more, rather than uniting different organizations, we observed instances of what we interpreted as 'territoriality'. As a co-located space, designed to improve collaboration and overcome the differences of railway organizations, the kitchen became exemplary of a place where employees of the respective organizations defended and maintained the existing territorial boundaries.

Collectively, OCCR employees constructed the kitchen as a place to avoid or at least tread lightly. A myth circulated that right after the OCCR started its operation, the kitchen became a place where employees would sometimes go and vent their aggression to show their disapproval with the design of the building that 'demanded' collaboration, resulting in broken kitchen objects. Implicitly, this myth constructed the kitchen as a taboo, as a place to avoid at all costs: 'It has become a kind of no-man's-land. The social pressure of your own tribe is so high that you just shouldn't show your face in the kitchen' (interview, OCCR consultant).

The kitchen, as a 'non-place' devoid of any collectively shared meaning, became in fact a space of contestation where issues of identity and inter-organizational relations were fought out. Before the OCCR had even started its operations, employees had already labelled fridges in the kitchen: they had applied stickers to each fridge, indicating to what specific organization it belonged. This illustrates how the kitchen was not just a *physical* environment but a space where power relations were *socio-materially* enacted. The almost banal labels on the fridges were the result of the 'spatial legacies' (Vaujany & Vaast, 2014) of the railway system, materializing the already strained relationships between the organizations. An OCCR consultant reflects: 'All conversations about the OCCR were poisoned by discussions between the organizations about who would become the boss of the building. . ... If this is what managers communicate to their people, the result will be fridges with stickers.' Labelling fridges was a way through which employees were able to maintain their individual identities: 'We knew we needed several fridges because we had to facilitate a large group of people. But eventually this resulted in fridges that were earmarked per "blood type"' (interview, project manager). The socio-materiality of such practices in the kitchen was not simply determined by how the kitchen was designed. On the contrary, these practices came to constitute how the kitchen was used and perceived, and managers found it hard to counter this development: 'We can hardly force people to put their rolls in another fridge' (interview, project manager).

In conclusion, the kitchen was a place where already existing territorial boundaries were preserved, through name-tagging fridges, constructing the space as a taboo, and refusing to share food or eat together. The examples illustrate that these boundaries in the physical environment are not merely material (i.e. constituted in its design or layout of objects) and neither merely social (i.e. constructed in discourse or with a sense of psychological ownership). On the contrary, the boundaries and territories are socio-material and exist because they are enacted in practice. In other words, the relation between the physical environment of the kitchen and how the kitchen is used, is exemplified as one in which agency is distributed between social and material worlds; power relations and organization emerge through entangled socio-material practices. Moreover, in this vignette it is illustrated how the physical environment should be understood within its (historical) context. The practices of name-tagging or constructing the kitchen as taboo should be interpreted considering the split-up of the railway system. These practices were not 'invented anew' to create territories or distinctive identities, but they were aimed at *maintaining* already existing territorial boundaries. Collaboration is not just a result of changing the space in which this collaboration happens (e.g. by increasing physical proximity), but how collaboration as well as the use of this space emerges is co-constituted in socio-material practices.

Vignette 2: The machine baptism in the North-South line metro project

The construction of metros in Amsterdam has a difficult, traumatic history starting in the 1960s, when buildings and neighbourhoods were demolished to build the first metro, 'the East line'. This harsh approach to constructing metros sparked a series of social movements and riots from local residents, followed by the government's mobilization of military police to keep the riots at bay – historically referred to as 'the metro riots' and after which 'the metro' became taboo in Amsterdam. Three decades later in the late 1990s, 'the North-South line' metro project was initiated to the dismay of many residents. Especially when buildings started to sink into the ground at the historical street Vijzelgracht during preparatory work between 2004 and 2008 (and they had yet to drill the actual metro tunnel), it wasn't surprising that many locals, once again, resisted the construction of the metro and actively attempted to shut it down. Within this context, we focus on a ceremony marking the official kick-off of tunnel drilling during which the tunnel boring machines used to excavate the metro tunnel were baptized and given names according to the traditional ritual of tunnel workers.

The technologies to build metro lines had developed since the 20th century, particularly the innovative soft subsoil tunnel boring machine (TBM) that enabled the underground tunnel excavation without the demolition of aboveground buildings. 'We had a solution; we could do it underground' (interview, technical director). As the technology was new and risky, fears for the submergence of monumental buildings in Amsterdam, which are supported by a foundation of stilts, were justified. To prove that the project was possible, the project organization ran several tests for the TBM technique between 1997 and 2002 in different areas in the Netherlands. It was predicted they could bore underground with a small chance of submergence, and that they could inject the ground with a mixture of grout, stabilizing the earth to prevent (further) submergence. This, of course, did not convince everyone that tunnel drilling would not pose problems for Amsterdam's watery underground.

What followed next during the preparations were major complications resulting in the shut-down of the project. The incidents at historical street Vijzelgracht were by far the most serious, drawing heated criticism from the public and media. This is where the first submergence took place in 2004, and in June 2008 10 more buildings on this street sank into the ground due to a leakage of soil. The residents of the buildings had to be evacuated. Further evidence showed that the concrete of the dam walls was of low quality, resulting in weak spots and ultimately leakages. Consequently, the project was put on hold by the Amsterdam municipality. Only after fierce debates in the Amsterdam municipality and new studies on risks of the TBM technology, the project was granted permission to start again.

To drill the tunnel with the TBMs, the project organization hired two German tunnel construction companies. These constructors brought with them the traditional baptism and naming of the TBM before it is used (a very old ritual, pre-dating Christianity). 'They won't start boring without it,' the contractor explained. The dangers and risks associated with this machine's capacity (i.e. the workers' lives depend on the machine's reliability) traditionally gave rise to the need to bless and baptize it for safety, and to personify it with a female name, perhaps to render it less hazardous. When the project organization planned the first ceremony, during which the first two TBMs would be baptized as the official kick-off of the tunnel boring task in April 2010, they invited stakeholders such as state officials, politicians, contractors, investors, citizens, and the press, including journalists, photographers, and television crews from local and national news companies. Thus, the event was widely publicized and mediatized, even on a national scale.

The ritual started when a Catholic priest from Amsterdam dressed in traditional robes came to the front at the dark cold construction site, wearing a helmet. He started by presenting a small statue of Santa Barbara, a patron saint acknowledged by the Catholic Church as the protector of harm and later espoused by mine and tunnel workers for this purpose. Reciting holy texts from the Bible, he blessed water in a shiny goblet with which he then baptized the statue using a special staff. Then, the names of the TBMs would be revealed. As they counted down, a giant poster was released from the first machine, reading 'Noortje' in big bold letters, followed by the release of the second poster from the second machine reading 'Gravin'. The names were female in accordance to the tradition and chosen by schoolchildren from Amsterdam, who were also present at the site. The priest then baptized the machines, finishing in the renowned words 'in the name of the father, the son, and the holy spirit'. Afterward, the statue of Santa Barbara was carried by the 'bore master' and delicately placed in a glass cupboard hanging on the wall next to the machine – the shrine from which Santa Barbara would watch over the workers. Subsequently, the boring manager and the alderman smashed a bottle of champagne against the first machine and then the second, after which confetti was cast down from above in celebration of this moment. At that time, a group of engineers recited a traditional German mining song – Gluck Auf – after which a fascinated and clapping audience further indulged themselves with food and drinks, striking up conversations in reflection of the bizarre yet intriguing phenomenon they had just collectively experienced.

This case demonstrates the immense impact and risky nature of the physical environment: the soggy underground of Amsterdam, the historic monumental buildings built on a foundation of stilts, some of which sank into the ground during construction, the power of the machine with a capacity for disaster if technology would fail. It is not unexpected, then, that the physical environment has been an integral part of and shaped human behaviour: a Catholic priest baptizing the machine, the children of Amsterdam choosing a name for it, the alderman breaking a bottle of champagne against it, the tunnel boring master placing a statue of Santa Barbara next to it for protection, and the engineers reciting a traditional mining song in the underground construction site. This behaviour shows how human actors acknowledge the agency of the material because they do not have complete or direct control over it: 'we give our lives into the hands of this object' (interview, contractor).

Furthermore, the ritual shows what the machine and the underground mean for the people who work with it. The risks and dangers associated with the physical underground and the machine provoked particular human responses and appropriations, where humans make sense of and give meaning to the material as they deem appropriate within a certain context. This, in turn, can change the way the material is used and perceived, also by others. For example, after the ceremony all project members and the media would refer to the TBMs by their given names: 'What was extraordinary was that the whole name-giving was adopted by everyone who followed [the project]. The names were consistently used by the media' (communication advisor). Similarly, the behaviour performed during the ceremony put the underground in the spotlight and made it visible, especially for outsiders who could physically see the cold dark construction site 25 metres below the surface where workers were risking their lives every day. In sum, it can be argued that this ritual was a *practice of socio-material entanglement*, manifesting the inherent interrelation between social and material worlds.

Discussion

In this chapter, we explored the interrelation between the physical environment of two organizational settings and the behaviour of organizational actors through a socio-material lens in the form of two empirical vignettes. The first vignette focused on the kitchen of a newly built national control centre where major railway organizations were co-located to collaborate and manage complex and large disruptions in the Netherlands. Zooming in on the design and materiality of the kitchen, we showed the unintended consequences of the designed physical environment and how the space was appropriated in practice by employees. The second vignette illustrated a TBM baptism and name-giving ritual in Amsterdam, showing how organizational actors responded to the immense impact and unpredictability of the physical environment and manifesting how social and material worlds are entangled. Taken together, both vignettes demonstrate the recursive process of how the physical environment of spaces and artefacts are an integral part of and shape organizational behaviour, which, in turn, serves to (re)configure the perception, meaning, and use of the physical environment.

The application of a socio-material lens in this chapter makes three main contributions. First, the socio-material lens challenges the tendency for scholars to privilege the social over the material by granting equal credit to the role of the physical environment in its own right. By placing a spotlight on the physical environment, including its material artefacts and technologies, we come to acknowledge the significant and active role they play in organizational practices and processes. Indeed, in the OCCR case, the kitchen and its material artefacts like the refrigerators were not used as they were designed to be used, proving how the actual physical space is not secondary or peripheral to human intentions. In the metro line case, the dangerous underground and risky machine were given a privileged status, showing how the lives of the workers literally depended on the reliability of the machine and the stability of the underground space.

Second, and going a step beyond the previous point, a socio-material lens elucidates how the social and material are equally and simultaneously agential in the world's becoming. The physical environment is not passive or immutable but an active participant, thereby cutting agency loose from its human circuit (Barad, 2007). Likewise, in the two vignettes we see that employees struggled to control or predict the material as it 'acted' on its own accord. In the metro line project, organizational members attempted to control the physical environment by laser measurement technology, freezing methods, grout injections, and warning systems; yet technology still failed to fulfil its purpose, leakages still happened, and buildings still sank into the ground, beyond human control. In the OCCR, managers tried to consolidate inter-organizational collaboration through office designs, architectural maps, consultants, and the construction of informal spaces such as the kitchen. However, there was little real control, and employees could not predict how the material would 'act' when used (e.g. the fridges afforded the labelling, which was in turn appropriated by employees to preserve existing territories), which is a clear indication of material agency (Leonardi, 2013). In both vignettes, the materiality became a context in which human agents could not call all the shots (Pickering, 1993), confirming that the material is equally agential and co-constitutive of meaning and reality (Orlikowski & Scott, 2008; Putnam, 2013).

Third, a socio-material lens shows how socio-material entanglement transpires over time and in practice from a historical and contextual perspective. In both vignettes, we use the socio-material lens first to 'zoom out' to describe the context of each research case, such as the description of the organization, its history, its physical environment, and its members, after which we 'zoom in' on specific organizational activities and behaviour at certain places and times, in order to trace and analyse how the social vis-à-vis material is (re)configured in practice, and continuously shifting over time. Specifically, in the OCCR case we follow the initial spatial design of the kitchen and observe how the employees appropriated the space and materials in practice over time in empirically unique ways. Likewise, in the metro project case, we emphasize the difficult historical process of metro construction in Amsterdam that involved much social unrest and resistance, technical mishaps and failures, followed by a focus on the machine baptism and name-giving ritual which temporally served to redefine socio-material circumstances and realities.

In sum, a socio-material lens casts light on the inherent interrelation between social and material spheres of organizational life and their co-constitution of meaning and reality, thereby discrediting their ontological separation. Essentially, then, all organizational processes and practices can be perceived as socio-material configurations.

Conclusion

In this chapter, we aimed to introduce a socio-material lens to better understand the unpredictable, dynamic, and recurrent relationship between physical environments and organizational behaviour. We have shown that physical environments are *especially* places where the social and material worlds co-constitute how organizing happens and how organizations emerge. Specifically, through the analysis of our two cases through a socio-material lens, we have provided insight into how physical environments shape social settings, and how organizational members in that setting appropriate – i.e. make sense of, attribute meaning to, and use – the physical environment as they deem appropriate, often regardless of how the physical environment and the materials in that environment were intentionally designed. Thus, how the physical environment 'acts' and influences people, and how people simultaneously choose to (re)construct, manage, modify, adapt, or respond to the physical environment in return is an unpredictable process that unfolds in empirically unique ways. This process changes over time, thereby entangling the social and material spheres of life in dynamic and ever-changing ways. Hence, we advise scholars to observe and analyse, through a socio-material lens, the inherent interrelation between the physical environment and social behaviour within context, over time, and in practice.

The relation between the physical environment of organizations and the behaviour of employees will remain a fascinating theme for future research. Large amounts of funding are spent, such as in the case of the OCCR, on spatial interventions, while we do not exactly know how the material interacts with the social behaviour of employees, and how the material can have agency in organizational processes and practices. We hope that this chapter, with the use of a socio-material lens, can help future scholars to explore this interesting topic, both empirically and theoretically.

Note

1 Parts of this chapter have been published earlier in:Van der Ende, L.,Van Marrewijk,A. H., & Boersma, F. K. (2015). Machine baptisms and heroes of the underground: Performing socio-materiality in an Amsterdam metro project. *Journal of Organizational Ethnography,* 4(3), 260–280; and in Willems, T., & Van Marrewijk, A. H. (2017). Building collaboration? Co-location and 'dis-location' in a railway control post. *Revista de Administração de Empresas,* 57(6), 542–554.

References

Ashkanasy, N. M., Ayoko, O. B., & Jehn, K. A. (2014). Understanding the physical environment of work and employee behavior: An affective events perspective. *Journal of Organizational Behavior, 35,* 1169–1184.

Auge, M. (1995). *Non-Places: Introduction to an Anthropology of Supermodernity.* London: Verso.

Barad, K. (2007). *Meeting the Universe Halfway: Quantum Physics and the Entanglement of Matter and Meaning.* Durham, NC: Duke University Press.

Brennan, A., Chugh, J., & Kline, T. (2002). Traditional versus open office design. A longitudinal field study. *Environment and Behavior, 34,* 279–299.

Brown, G., Lawrence, T. B., & Robinson, S. L. (2005). Territoriality in organizations. *Academy of Management Review, 30,* 577–594.

Cameron, K. S. (2003). Organizational transformation through architecture and design: A project with Frank Gehry. *Journal of Management Inquiry, 12,* 88–92.

Dale, K. (2005). Building a social materiality: Spatial and embodied politics in organizational control. *Organization, 12,* 649–678.

Dale, K., & Burrell, G. (2008). *The Spaces of Organisation and the Organisation of Space: Power, Identity and Materiality at Work.* Basingstoke: Palgrave Macmillan.

Dale, K. & Burrell, G. (2010). 'All together, altogether better': The ideal of 'community' in the spatial reorganization of the workplace. In A. H. Van Marrewijk and D. Yanow (eds), *Organizational Spaces: Rematerializing the Workaday World* (pp. 19–41). Cheltenham: Edward Elgar.

Elsbach, K. D. (2003). Relating physical environment to self-categorizations: Identity threat and affirmation in a non-territorial office space. *Administrative Science Quarterly, 48,* 622–654.

Elsbach, K. D., & Bechky, B. A. (2007). It's more than a desk: Working smarter through leveraged office design. *California Management Review, 49,* 80–101.

Elsbach, K. D., & Pratt, M. G. (2007). The physical environment in organizations. *Academy of Management Annals, 1,* 181–224.

Faulkner, P., & Runde, J. (2012). On socio-materiality. In P. M. Leonardi, B. M. Nardi, & J. Kallinikos (eds), *Materiality and Organizing. Social Interaction in a Technological World* (pp. 49–66). Oxford: Oxford University Press.

Gibson, J. (1986). *The Ecological Approach to Visual Perception.* Hillsdale, NJ: Lawrence Arlbaum Associates.

Gregson, N. (2011). Performativity, corporeality and the politics of ship disposal. *Journal of Cultural Economy, 4,* 137–156.

Hancock, P. (2006). The spatial and temporal mediation of social change. *Journal of Organizational Change Management, 19,* 619–639.

Hernes, T. T., Bakken, P., & Olsen, O. (2006). Spaces as process: Developing a recursive perspective on organisational space. In S. Clegg & M. Kornberger (eds), *Space, Organizations and Management Theory* (pp. 33–63). Copenhagen: Liber and Copenhagen Business School Press.

Kenis, P., Kruyen, P. M., & Baaijens, J. (2010). Bendable bars in a Dutch prison: A creative place in a non-creative space. In A. H. Marrewijk & D. Yanow (eds), *Organisational Spaces: Rematerializing the Workaday World* (pp. 58–76). Northampton, MA: Edward Elgar.

Kornberger, M., & Clegg, S. (2004). Bringing space back in: Organizing the generative building. *Organization Studies, 25,* 1095–1114.

Latour, B. (1993). *We Have Never Been Modern.* London: Harvester Wheatsheaf.

Leonardi, P. M. (2012). Materiality, sociomateriality, and socio-technical systems: What do these terms mean? How are they different? Do we need them? In P. M. Leonardi, B. M. Nardi, & J. Kallinikos (eds), *Materiality and Organizing: Social Interaction in a Technological World* (pp. 25-48). Oxford: Oxford University Press.

Leonardi, P. M. (2013). Theoretical foundations for the study of socio-materiality. *Information and Organization, 23,* 59–76.

Leonardi, P. M., Nardi, B. M., & Kallinikos, J. (2012). *Materiality and Organizing: Social Interaction in a Technological World.* Oxford: Oxford University Press.

McElroy, J. C., & Morrow, P. C. (2010). Employee reactions to office redesign: A naturally occurring quasi-field experiment in a multi-generational setting. *Human Relation, 63,* 609–636.

Mutch, A. (2013). Socio-materiality: Taking the wrong turning? *Information and Organization, 23,* 28–40.

Orlikowski, W. J. (2007). Socio-material practices: Exploring technology at work. *Organization Studies, 28,* 1435–1448.

Orlikowski, W. J., & Scott, S. V. (2008). Socio-materiality: Challenging the separation of technology, work and organization. *Academy of Management Annals, 2,* 433–474.

Pickering, A. (1993). The mangle of practice: Agency and emergence in the sociology of science. *American Journal of Sociology, 99,* 559–589.

Pickering, A. (1995). *The Mangle of Practice: Time, Agency, and Science.* Chicago, IL: University of Chicago Press.

Putnam, L. L. (2013). Dialectics, contradictions, and the question of agency. In *Organization and Organizing: Materiality, Agency, and Discourse* (pp. 23–36). London: Routledge.

Suchman, L. (1987). *Plans and Situated Actions: The Problem of Human–Machine Communication* Cambridge: Cambridge University Press.

Taylor, S., & Spicer, A. (2007). Time for space: A narrative review of research on organizational spaces. *International Journal of Management Reviews, 9,* 325–346.

Van den Ende, L., Van Marrewijk, A. H., & Boersma, K. (2015). Machine baptisms and heroes of the underground: Performing socio-materiality in an Amsterdam metro project. *Journal of Organizational Ethnography, 4,* 260–280.

Van Marrewijk, A., & Van den Ende, L. (forthcoming). Changing academic work places: The introduction of open-plan offices in universities. *Journal of Organizational Change Management.*

Van Marrewijk, A. H. (2009). Corporate headquarters as physical embodiments of organisational change. *Journal of Organisational Change Management, 22,* 290–306.

Van Marrewijk, A. H., & Yanow, D. (2010). The spatial turn in organization studies. In A. H. Marrewijk & D. Yanow (eds), *Organizational Spaces: Rematerializing the Workaday World* (pp. 1–19). Northampton, MA: Edward Elgar.

Vaujany, F. X., & Vaast, E. (2014). If these walls could talk: The mutual construction of organizational space and legitimacy. *Organization Science, 25,* 713–731.

Willems, T., & Van Marrewijk, A. (2017). Building collaboration? Co-location and 'dislocation' in a railway control post. *Revista de Administração de Empresas, 57,* 542–554.

Winch, G. (2017). The morphogenesis of socio-material relations in organisations. 38th International Conference on Information Systems. Seoul.

12

A SOCIAL SEMIOTIC APPROACH TO THE PHYSICAL WORK ENVIRONMENT

Ken Tann and Oluremi B. Ayoko

Introduction

Since the Hawthorne Studies of 1927–1932 (see Haynes, 2007), the study of the physical environment of work has considerably multiplied (Altman, 1975; Sommer, 1974; Ayoko & Härtel, 2003; Ayoko, Ashkanasy, & Jehn, 2014; Brown, Lawrence & Robinson, 2005; Elsbach, 2003; Chigot, 2003; Elsbach & Pratt, 2007; Kim & De Dear, 2013; Rafaeli & Vilnai-Yavetz, 2004a, 2004b). While the initial Hawthorne studies showed that performance was driven more by human relations than illumination (Jones, 1990), recent studies have since shown that the physical environment of work is a context that may be significant to social interactions (Vischer, 2008) in the workplace. In this way, researchers in the social sciences (e.g. environmental psychology) have preoccupied themselves with studies that explore the link between the physical environment and employee performance (e.g. Baron, 1994; Boyce, Berman, Collins, Lewis, & Rea, 1989).

While environmental psychologists are exploring the connection between the physical environment and employee interactions (Chigot, 2003), research in organizational behaviour (OB) relating the physical environment of work to employees' attitudes and behaviours is still relatively scarce (Ayoko et al., 2014; Ashkanasy, Ayoko & Jehn, 2014; Brown et al., 2005; Elsbach, 2003). Those that exist in the OB area have consistently shown that the characteristics of the office environment can have a significant effect (positive or negative) on employees' behaviours, perceptions, and productivity (see Ayoko & Härtel, 2003; Chigot, 2003; Rafaeli & Vilnai-Yavetz, 2004a). These streams of research (from the environmental and OB scholars) generally regard the physical environment simply as a stimulant that impacts on employee interactions.

Faced with the mixed results in this body of literature, researchers (e.g. Ashkanasy et al., 2014; Elsbach, 2003, 2004; Elsbach & Pratt, 2007) call for more research into the role of the physical work environment and employees' behaviours. In the present chapter, we address their call by arguing that the physical environment is more than a material container that shapes any employee behaviour inside it: it plays a symbolic and discursive role (Wilhoit, 2016) in the construction of social meaning in the workplace (Baldry, 1997). For example, Joiner (1971) in his classic study demonstrates that spatial relationships between people may be employed to sustain and strengthen social relationships, while personal distance, orientation, and symbolic decorations can be used to mediate understandings of territoriality and identity. Despite the fact that the social and the material are intimately connected, the social and symbolic facet of the material is often overlooked in OB research. However, there has been substantial work on the relationship between them outside of OB (e.g. Lefebvre, 1991; Dale, 2005; Dale & Burrell, 2008; Orlikowski, 2009; Leonardi, 2011, 2012), and the present study seeks to extend this line of inquiry by providing a detailed analytical framework for examining the meanings that mediate the social and the material in situated interaction.

To do so, we examine the connection between physical workspaces and employee behaviours through the lens of social semiotics (Halliday, 1978; Hodge & Kress, 1988; van Leeuwen, 2005). From a social semiotic perspective, employees construct and negotiate their understanding of their context socially, and hence their environment is an inseparable part of their interaction. Building on Joiner's (1971) work that locates the communicative aspects of spatial organization alongside other forms of interaction (e.g. speech), we aim to demonstrate in this chapter how social semiotics provides a robust framework that allows us to conceptualize and model the relationship between features of the physical environment (e.g. noise and territoriality) and employee behaviours (verbal and non-verbal). Importantly, it provides a way to relate different levels of phenomena that have been discussed across the literature on the physical environment. The model does so by stratifying social meanings into the conceptual levels of context, content and expression, and proposing an alignment of social meaning across these levels. The model also provides a multifunctional account in which the physical environment simultaneously plays a part in relating employees with respect to their tasks, roles, and boundaries, without assuming that these different aspects are mutually exclusive.

Using the open-plan office space for illustration, we elaborate on these constructs in our model and how social meanings may be aligned functionally. We begin our discussion with the paradoxes of office space, and locate workplace interaction in the levels of context, content, and expression within the model. Then, we present different forms of meaning (representational, interactional, and organizational) and how the distinction may help to deepen our understanding of the relationship between the physical work environment and organizational behaviour as one that is mediated by social meanings.

The open-plan office

In this chapter, we focus on open-plan offices because differing configurations of open- plan offices are currently enjoying considerable popularity in contemporary organizations and the impact of the physical environment on workers' attitudes and behaviours (Ashkanasy et al., 2014). The idea of an open-plan office has its roots in the 'bullpen' office (sometimes referred to as the Taylorization of space, Baldry, 1997). The bullpen comprises a large open-plan area where desks were arranged in regimented rows facing the same way with no visual or acoustic privacy, and yet at the surrounding of such open-plan offices were cellular or traditional offices enclosed with walls, doors and usually occupied by an individual employee (Duffy, 1999; Bodin Danielsson & Bodin, 2009).

To date, many contemporary open-plan offices are modelled after the bullpen, and the management and supervisory staff sit in the cellular offices around the open-plan office, giving them visual supervision of their employees (see Aronoff & Kaplan, 1995). More specifically, contemporary open-plan offices are shared spaces that may provide accommodation for between 2 and 24 employees (see Bodin Danielsson & Bodin, 2009, for a review of types of open-plan offices). As such, open-plan offices provide an excellent example for a rich study on the relationship between the social and the material aspects of the work environment.

Paradoxes of the office space

Extant scattered research (e.g. Elsbach, 2004; Kim & De Dear, 2013) on the impact of open-plan offices on employee behaviours and performance suggest that some ambivalence surrounds the open-plan office. For example, while the open-plan office lends itself to low cost (Chigot, 2003), flexibility for reduced time in set-up and renovation times (Brennan, Chugh, & Kline, 2002), easier line-of-sight supervision (Baldry, 1997) and the adoption of team working and delayering of office hierarchies (Baldry, 1997), increased communication and interactions between employees (Brennan et al., 2002) as well as cohesion (Chigot, 2003), studies also show that employees in open-plan offices are increasingly concerned about the increased noise and poor privacy (Regoeczi, 2003) experienced in open-plan offices. The mixed results emanating from the research in open-plan offices suggest an underlying tension, paradox (Elsbach, 2003; Elsbach & Pratt, 2007) and the potential ambivalent relationship between employee behaviours and the physical environment of work. While OB studies have generally treated the physical work environment as a material container of work interactions, there has been a recent 'spatial turn' (van Marrewijk & Yanow, 2010) in organizational studies whereby scholars increasingly understand that the physical environment is not only material, but constitutes socially meaningful spaces for employees who embody them in interactions (Dale, 2005).

In this chapter, we propose that the mixed findings reported in OB research may partly be due to the treatment of space as a stable and predetermined container for employee interactions and behaviours, neglecting the social meanings that embodied space brings to those interactions, as well as how those social meanings shape understandings and use of the space. We further argue that prior research seems to have ignored the possibility that the physical environment is not just an objective space, but a lived and socially constructed place that is fluid, dynamic, and meaningful (Wilhoit, 2016). Space then is intricately bound with meaning (Tuan, 1976), and behaviour in the form of territoriality and identity. In this way, space and the built environment have both functional and symbolic properties that communicate identity and image (see Vischer, 2005).

The tension of territoriality and identity

We describe employee territoriality as 'an individual's behavioural expression of his or her feelings of ownership toward a physical or social object' (Brown et. al, 2005, p. 578). Altman and Chemers (1980) also refer to territorial behaviour as a mechanism that regulates the boundary between others and us and implies the personalization and the demarcation of a space. In this respect, Brown and colleagues (2005) distinguish between four territorial behaviours, namely: constructing, communicating, maintaining, and restoring territories. These behaviours allow employees to draw a territory around the objects for which an individual would claim ownership (Brown et al., 2005).

Central to territoriality is the notion of personalization (Wells, 2000). Personalization of space includes the decoration, modification, or deliberate design of a space by its user in order to reflect their personal values (Sommer, 1974; Brown et al., 2005). For example, an employee might personalize their workspace or objects by putting a name tag on the office door and potted plants to partition workspaces in open-plan offices and then communicating to others that the object or workspace belongs to an individual or a group of people. Scholars (e.g. Altman, 1975; Brown, 1987) argue that the key drivers of employees' territoriality include social and psychological intentions such as demarcating their workspaces to create a sense of place for themselves. In this regard, personalization is expected to regulate social interaction such that violation of a set boundary may elicit employee defensive reactions.

Although the full impact of the process of territoriality on organizations are yet to be fully understood (Kromah, 2017), available studies suggest that territoriality is connected with employees' creativity, performance, and wellbeing (Ashkanasy et al., 2014; Brown & Baer, 2015; Wells, 2000). The findings from a study conducted by Beggan (1992) show that people evaluate ideas and objects more favourably when they feel a sense of ownership for the target object and such feelings of psychological ownership are associated with positive attitudes about the target object.

While territoriality is beneficial for employees by giving them control over workspaces, providing an opportunity to personalize their space (Brown, 2009) and increased feeling of job satisfaction, and improved health (Wells, 2000), research also indicates that poorly managed territorial behaviours may trigger depression, stress, and emotional exhaustion (Brown, Crossley, & Robinson, 2014; Wells, 2000) and potential engagement in counterproductive behaviours (Nathan, 2002). Additionally, employees who engage in defence behaviours are perceived as less productive by their peers (Brown et al., 2014; Connelly & Ayoko, 2013).

Another potential tension is between organization and individual requirement regarding territoriality. Organizations may have a resisting policy on territoriality whereby personalization is perceived as office clutter while the individual worker may see personalization as establishing identity in the workplace. In this regard, the tension can be understood as one between competing interpretations, or meanings, of employee personalization.

An area where the socially constructed nature of space is evident is in the study of organizational and employees' identity and identification (Elsbach, 2003). Elsbach (2004) proposes that both individual organizational members' identities and the identity of the entire organization can be constituted by space (see van Marrewijk & Broos, 2012). Knox and Marston (2004) describe identity as the sense that people make of themselves through their subjective feelings, especially based on their everyday experiences and wider social relations. In this regard, there is growing evidence of the links between identity and spatial behaviour (Dixon & Durrheim, 2003; Hopkins & Dixon, 2006). Research in this area suggests that workers express and construct their identity by personalizing their workspaces (Brown et al., 2005; Elsbach, 2003, 2004; Pierce, Kostova, & Dirks, 2003). Additionally, through territoriality and other symbolic activities, behaviours, and/or gestures, workers share information about themselves, establish their desired boundary (Byron & Laurence, 2015), and build or reveal their professional and self-identity. Pierce and colleagues (2003) suggest that the sense of possession (which allows individuals to satisfy their basic needs for place, efficacy, and self-identity) is key to work-related attitudes (e.g. commitment and satisfaction), and behaviours such as performance and organizational citizenship.

Workspace is not only a conduit for expressing self-identity but also serves as a material vehicle for establishing an individual's organizational identity (Marquardt et al. 2002, p. 12). Research on the connection between space and identity is mixed. For example, employees with the highest identification with organizational space were found to have the most difficult time adapting to changes in organizational space (Rooney et al., 2010). Conversely, organizations that allow the expression of work identities are linked with increased performance (Knight & Haslam, 2010), while Brown and Baer (2015) found that people who negotiated in another person's office performed worse than if they were to negotiate in their own office or a neutral room. In another study, Greenaway, Thai, Haslam and Murphy (2016) investigated the impact of a space that contained identity cues relative to a lean space in which identity markers were absent. They expected that the in-group (where employees were similarly categorized) space would increase performance (e.g. communication and productivity) relative to lean space without identity cues. Especially, they expected the social meaning of the space to impact organizational performance positively when the space affirmed team identity, and indeterminately when the space threatened team identity. They found that participants in the in-group space showed greater individual and team productivity as well as increased identification than participants in the lean space. In sum, the above findings demonstrate that employees attach some symbolic meanings to organizational space and further highlight the importance the impact of physical space on psychological functioning in the workplace and beyond.

So far, the findings reported above show evidence of space having material, symbolic, and discursive functions. In line with Wilhoit's (2016) suggestion, we argue that the study of organizational space should integrate both its material and social aspects through communication theory. We therefore propose social semiotics as a useful framework to model this communicative relationship between the material and social aspects of organizational space.

Space and context

Organizational behaviour (OB) researchers (e.g. Ayoko et al., 2014; Elsbach, 2003; Elsbach & Pratt, 2007) tend to view organizational space as a backdrop to employee work, attitudes, and behaviours, and this backdrop is perceived as unchanging (Foucault, 1980). In this regard, space has generally been studied as a static and stable material object that can be manipulated by humans. It is seen as spatial affordances (Lefebvre, 1991) portraying how certain behaviours are facilitated or constrained as people interact within space (Leonardi, 2011). In this respect, space is often treated as a context of communication (Haslett, 2013; Sillince, 2007), a container as a backdrop for action and organizing, and/or a variable that can be changed and manipulated for increased productivity (Wilhoit, 2016).

Nevertheless, space is not only a medium for material functions but also a medium for social values (Lewin, 1951). In particular, space has the potential to control the strength and directness of communication while it conveys messages (e.g. values) about the individual and teams that are accommodated in it (Gärling, 1998). For example, areas where people converge, such as around photocopiers and water-coolers do not only function as means for printing and drinking water, but are places for informal interaction (Fayard & Weeks, 2007), conversation, and meaning. Similarly, the corridor and hallways are not just passages to get to offices, but spaces that assist certain encounters and prevent others.

Wilhoit (2016) argues that where work takes place matters, not just as a context or background for work, but as a constitutive element of work. The environment provides the setting that stimulates or prevents specific behaviours, such that a church, playground, movie theatre, or coffee shop are expected to trigger different spatial behaviours. Wilhoit (2016) further argues that while there is value in seeing organizational space as either primarily material or social, space as both material and social also should be integrated in the study of organizational space. While the material space provides organizations with a degree of stability and durability, socially constructed places contribute to the fluid and performative nature of organizations. She suggests that by integrating space and place's social and material facets through communication theory, communication becomes a means for better space theorizing as well as using space to better understand specific organizational communication phenomena. In this chapter, we agree that space is not just a container, but is also constituted by social interactions (Lefebvre, 1991).

In the next section, we draw on the work of Wilhoit (2016) and Joiner (1971) to provide a framework for studying the physical environment of work simultaneously as material (e.g. artefacts and partitions), content (e.g. designs, values, and belief systems), and context (e.g. work tasks, relationships, and boundaries). In doing so, we bring together the social and the material aspects as two ends of a continuum that constrain and shape employees' understandings of territoriality and identity, to provide a more holistic understanding of the relationship between the physical work environment and organizational behaviours.

Locating interaction in social context

Joiner (1971) provides a way for understanding how the social context relates to materiality in office spaces by focusing on the role of space in the construction of intersubjective meaning. Locating the communicative function of spatial features alongside verbal and non-verbal behaviours, he describes the way office spaces are designed across academic, commercial, and governmental organizations around particular 'social rituals' such as interviews, negotiations, administration, and group discussions, amongst others. While Joiner's (1971) study preceded the research in social semiotics, his insight is useful for informing a social semiotic model of spatial analysis.

These social rituals shape the way boundaries are established through the layout of furniture, seating arrangements and orientation, as well as the distances between them. While these spatial features facilitate the activities of the occupants, they simultaneously serve as impression management and establish the occupants' territory and identity. Finally, territoriality and identity are expressed through the use of physical markers such as doors and windows, furniture and displays. Conversely, the physical markers provide visitors with cues to the activities, boundaries, and identities that allow visitors to recognize the social ritual and their role in it.

Social semiotics (Halliday, 1978; Hodge & Kress, 1988; van Leeuwen, 2005) provides a systematic framework for modelling these relationships between social ritual, territoriality, identity, and physical markers that Joiner has observed. In this framework, meaning is understood to be contextual, and socially constructed through communication: communication is a social act, while forms of communication including artefacts and spatial relationships are resources for making meaning, alongside speech, documents, and others.

Hence instead of assuming a direct and causal relationship between the physical environment and individual behaviour, social semiotics situates boundaries and identity (and the conventions of how to respond to them) in the context of Joiner's (1971) 'social rituals', and specifies the way these social meanings are expressed in actual interaction. Martin (1992) describes the relationships between the three levels of analysis as connotative and denotative, represented by the arrows in Figure 12.1.

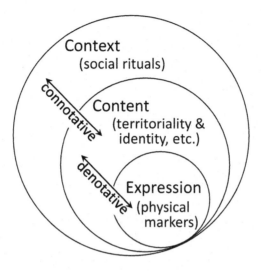

FIGURE 12.1 Context as a connotative semiotic

From a semiotic perspective, perceptible physical markers (among other behavioural cues) provide an 'expression' for territoriality and identity, while the 'content' of such social meanings connote the 'context' of interaction, thus allowing both occupants and visitors to infer the social ritual that they are collaboratively performing. Hence, the conventionalized use of physical markers is mediated by meanings in which participants are socialized, allowing them to arrive at a shared understanding of the context. Conversely, a shared understanding of context allows participants to disambiguate their roles and boundaries, and interpret the meanings behind the display of physical markers. This dialogic relationship between context and expression will be elaborated in the section below.

Towards a holistic model of the socio-material workplace

A similarly dialogic understanding of the social and material is increasingly adopted in organizational studies under the label of socio-materiality (Orlikowski & Scott, 2008; Orlikowski, 2009). Orlikowski (2009) argues strongly that it is no longer viable to consider social practices and the material aspects of the environment in isolation from each other. Instead, she proposes regarding them as co-constituting each other in what she calls 'entanglement in practice'. From this holistic perspective based on a relational ontology, social practices are necessarily shaped by the material qualities of embodied people located in actual environments, while aspects of the material are meaningful only by being part of a social practice.

This co-constitutive relationship can be systematically elaborated by the social semiotic model. In this model, meaning is theorized as social action (see Halliday, 2013), and the materiality of physical objects is socially meaningful insofar as they realize social practices. The physical environment can therefore be theorized as meaning-making resources alongside others, such as verbal language and gestures. In line with Joiner's (1971) observation, the design and manipulation of the physical environment are meaningful because they communicate information and cues to those who act socially in them, i.e. occupants and visitors.

Based on the theoretical foundation of systemic functional linguistics (e.g. Halliday & Matthiessen, 2004), the social semiotic framework provides a systematic way to examine the entanglement between the social and the material aspects of the workplace through a stratified model (Martin, 1992; Tann, 2017), as shown in Figure 12.2.

The model postulates a systematic relationship between social practices, situational variables, discourses, communicative resources such as spatial features, speech, and gestures, and the material affordances of each type of resource, as indicated by the arrows. A social semiotic approach aims to provide a description of these relationships and make them explicit, thus providing a systematic way to investigate context as both a 'cross-level effect' and a 'shaper of meaning' (Johns, 2006, p.388). The remainder of this chapter will outline some of these relationships.

Context: genre and register

Yates and Orlikowski (1992) describe the ritualistic nature of social interaction in terms of genre. They theorize organizational genres as a structuration process, through which the formalized characteristics of communication evolve over time in reciprocal interaction between institutionalized practices and individual actions. Genres are hence 'typified communicative action[s] invoked in response to recurrent situation[s]'

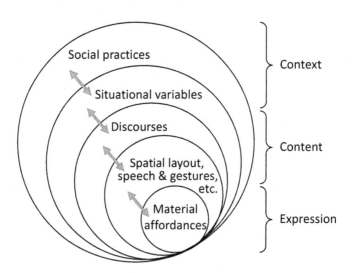

FIGURE 12.2 Stratification of social meaning

(p. 301), characterized by a mapping between their formal characteristics and social functions. While the literature did not make a direct connection, this concept can arguably be similarly applied to the socio-materiality of the work environment.

For instance, Joiner (1971) describes the stages of an interview, which involve greeting his interviewee, being invited to be seated, and discussing the contents of the interview, before performing a formal farewell. He provides a compelling account of how each of those stages occurs within a particular 'zone' in the office space. He argues that the zoning of the space through its layout and arrangement of furniture is highly formalized, and serves as conventionalized cues to the visitor on how to behave. In a similar vein to Yates and Orlikowski's account, the social ritual or genre of the interview involves the formalized displays of physical space as cues to facilitate its social functions. Importantly, he also demonstrates that the way space is used is culturally specific to the type of institution, and adapted by the individual for their specific situation.

The social semiotic framework combines both Joiner as well as Yates and Orlikowski's insight outlined above, by defining genres as 'staged, goal-oriented social processes' (Martin, 1999). A genre analysis therefore entails a description of both the functional aspect of the ritual's social purpose and how it is realized by its formal elements as schematic stages. For example, a committee meeting typically begins with the chairperson's opening remarks, followed by apologies and comments on minutes of the previous meeting, before addressing individual items on the agenda. When the items have been discussed, a date is set for follow-ups, before the chairperson closes the meeting. The stages of the meeting differ from that of the interview because they are designed to serve different social purposes. While it is not impossible for the sequence of meetings to deviate from what has been described here, we nonetheless recognize the canonical sequence of a meeting because it evolved specifically to achieve the goal of arriving at collective decision and action. The processes of the same individuals handling their own work tasks at their desks would again be very different.

Apart from genre, context in social semiotics can also be described in terms of register, which consists of the relationship between the people communicating, as well as the topic and the channel of their communication (Halliday & Hasan, 1989). Hence, while social rituals may constrain the layout of the office, Joiner (1971) is careful to point out that the layout is also dependent on the type of institution, the occupant's status, and familiarity with the visitor. An adequate account of context therefore has to consider both analytical levels, and establish how these situational variables relate to the genre of the workplace interaction. Specific workplace genres are constituted by particular actions, allocate particular roles, and involve particular channels of interaction. A committee meeting typically requires participants interacting verbally, a chairperson to regulate the discussion, and a secretary to render the spoken interaction into print. An interview requires at least an interviewer and an interviewee interacting either on email, over Skype, or face-to-face. The worker handling individual work tasks may be typing away quietly at the computer, and filling out electronic forms. These combinations of actions and roles are not fixed; they are allocated and constrained by the nature of the genre at hand: the same person may take on the role of a chairperson in a meeting, an interviewee in an interview, and a supervisor when responding to an email.

Important questions to be raised about the social context include what activities facilitate each stage of the genre, what responsibilities and roles are assigned to the participants, and how these aspects affect the difference in power, alignment, and distance between them.

Content: discourse and spatial layout

It was suggested earlier that context is both a 'cross-level effect' and a 'shaper of meaning'. As Joiner (1971) observes, the way space is zoned (i.e. genre) and situational variables (i.e. register) such as the degree of familiarity between the occupant and the visitor affect how they understand territorial boundaries and interaction distance. Where the office is used for business negotiation with strangers, there is usually a clear delineation between public and private space, and the visitor is seated at the furthest distance, and where the office is used for discussions in which power difference is downplayed, there is little boundary between private and public space. It is therefore necessary to establish how boundaries and identities enable different contextual configurations, and how different contexts constrain the interpretation of boundaries and identities.

However, the way space affects territoriality and identity is not a straightforward one, as they draw on different discourses (Halford & Leonard, 2005). When the same physical environment is used for different purposes, and hence genres, they can be part of different discourses, and carry a multitude of different and potentially conflicting meanings (Wapshott & Mallett, 2011). Discourses of boundaries and identities are communicated and maintained through language (Richardson & Jensen (2003), so it is important to consider spatial relations not in isolation, but alongside other communicative systems such as documents, speech, and gestures. The social semiotic framework models all of them as resources for communication and meaning-making, while acknowledging the different affordances that each one brings to the interaction, as elaborated in the following section. This provides a dynamic way to understand how different resources may come into play at different points in the interaction. For example, a worker may establish the boundaries of their territory with the use of physical barriers such as partitions. If that is not possible in an open-plan office, they may attempt to do so by marking the space with artefacts such as pictures and decorations. However, when those boundaries are disregarded by co-workers, shared understanding of territoriality between them breaks down, and the worker may have to resort to defending the space verbally with aggressive body language, hence triggering conflict. It is therefore important to examine how different discourses are communicated in different ways, and to evaluate the impact that these different resources have in turn on territoriality and identity. A dynamic modelling of how the different resources are used will also provide us with a broader understanding of their consequences.

Expression: material affordance

Joiner (1971) also attends to the materiality of the workplace, arguing that seating orientation physically constrains the occupant's visual contact with the surroundings, which affects their readiness to interact when approached by a visitor. This also helps to explain why not all aspects of the environment have an equally significant effect in a given instance. Moreover, he argues that the material quality of space means that locating a secretary on the main circulation route poses a physical barrier to the visitor. Other studies have also pointed out that physical objects such as decorations and photographs differ from speech because they continue to communicate information about the occupant to visitors even in the occupant's absence (Elsbach, 2004), while the material properties of partitions made from glass affect the nature of interaction between employees in an office (Chigot, 2003). In other words, the meetings, interviews, and other work tasks that we have discussed so far do not occur as abstract social phenomena. They are embodied practices carried out in physical environments with material properties that constrain the kind of interactions that are possible, and the material aspect of the environment confers an enduring quality to social organization (Leonardi, 2012).

Aside from constraining interactions in such practical ways, the material quality of objects also denote meanings that shape the interpretation of the social context indirectly. For example, the material used for carpeting and partitions, and the size of furniture symbolize the occupant's status and attitudes, thus serving as a front (Joiner, 1971). It is important to note, however, that not all aspects of an object's material qualities are necessarily meaningful at all times, because the affordances of materiality are always dependent on historically established social practices (van Dijk & Rietveld, 2017). Hence the affordance of a chair as a surface for sitting or an object for marvelling at depends on whether it plays a role in the genre of a meeting or an interview, or if it plays a role in the genre of an exhibition. In this way, the social and the material aspects of the work environment are always 'entangled in practice' (Orlikowski, 2009).

Multifunctionality of the work environment

The social semiotic framework also provides a multifunctional lens for investigating the relationship between the levels of meanings. Three simultaneous kinds of meanings have been identified across communication systems (Halliday, 2003; Kress & van Leeuwen, 2006; Ravelli & McMurtrie, 2016), known as representational, organizational and interactional meanings, shown in Figure 12.3.

Representational meanings in spatial features construct the experience of the world and how participants can act in it. For example, the presence of chairs around a desk would provide the room with a place to hold conversations, or the presence of a door would require a visitor to knock or open it to enter the room. Organizational meanings construct a sense of boundaries and relationships between spaces. Similarities in arrangement, design, and colour between the chairs around

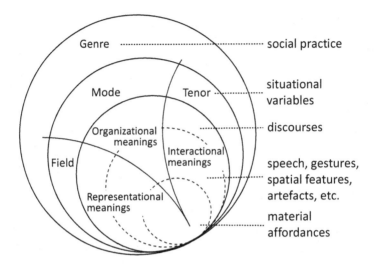

FIGURE 12.3 Metafunctional alignment

the desk mark the space around it as a distinct area for holding discussions, while the door marks the room as separate from the other parts of the office, even though the boundary marked by a door is more permeable than that of a wall. Interactional meanings construct a sense of how occupants and visitors relate to one another. Hence dissimilarity in size and arrangement between the chairs can mark a contrast in status or distance between people sitting in them, and having a door would mark a higher status of the occupant in a cell office compared with those without.

As the examples show, the three types of meaning correspond systematically to three different aspects of the context. Representational meanings correspond to the field, which comprises participants and their actions. Interactional meanings correspond to tenor, which is about social status and distance. Organizational meanings correspond to mode of communication, which is in this case the use of physical space, as distinct from speech and gestures. The specific combination of field, tenor, and mode in the example realize the genre of a meeting. In this way, we can distinguish between different functions of the use of the physical environment, while still accounting for their combination to enable social practices.

Discussion and further research

While recent OB research is paying increasing attention to the physical environment, this chapter argues that it has to move beyond the current treatment of space as a static container. The literature on territoriality and identity in the workplace within OB is fraught with paradoxes because the understanding of space is context-dependent, shaped by the complex interaction between the social and material aspects of organization. To understand how spaces are meaningful to employees (as the content of social meaning), it is necessary to take a more holistic approach by investigating both how they relate to (the context of) specific social practices, as well as their material affordance and expression.

The open-plan office is particularly challenging because without the traditional use of partitions, multiple practices and hence multiple social contexts overlap within the same physical space, and it is therefore unlikely that there is a single optimal design (Elsbach & Pratt, 2007). Collaborative tasks, for instance, may take place right beside individual tasks without a clear demarcation of activities and roles, social distance, and power relations. An implication for management therefore is to take the multifunctionality of the work environment into account. For instance, advocates of open-plan offices focus on the benefits of task coordination (representational meanings) and the removal of boundaries (organizational meanings), while critics are concerned with the impacts on relationship maintenance (interactional meanings).

However, not expressing these variables overtly through spatial boundaries does not necessarily mean that they no longer exist. Instead, by suppressing their expressions, employees may simply be forced to seek out and to renegotiate alternative forms of expression with their co-workers, with ramifications in terms of territoriality and identity as the meanings at stake between context and expression. When territorial boundaries and identities seem ambiguous, employees actively seek to re-establish them by displaying personal items, and adopting aggressive behaviours (Elsbach, 2003). The limits of this chapter preclude a discussion on de-personalized workspace arrangements that are variously called 'agile offices' or 'flexi-offices', where a clear-desk policy is often enforced to restrict territorial behaviour. However, the model suggests that when the communicative potential of the physical environment is limited, employees would seek out other behavioural or verbal means to organize themselves socially, which could be an important empirical enquiry.

We began this chapter by pointing out a number of tensions underlying the open-plan office. Territorial behaviours can vary, and the personalization of the workplace can be interpreted differently by the management and the employees; employees have a need for both territoriality and interaction, and expectations of appropriate behaviour have to be established and negotiated through the material environment; the use of identity markers at the workplace can impact on employee behaviour and interaction. While these varied aspects of the workplace are often dealt with separately in the OB literature, we argue in this chapter that a holistic model can provide a systematic way to understand the complex relationships between both the social and the material aspects of the physical work environment, as well as the levels of mediating meanings in between. Importantly, it provides a more dynamic picture of how changes to one aspect of the workplace can affect another. While the spatial turn in organizational studies literature provides insight to the interrelationship between the social and material aspects of the physical work environment, a social semiotic framework provides a holistic and detailed model for examining the meaningful understandings that underpin this relationship.

We suggest that the relationship between the social and material aspects can be investigated through using a combination of ethnographic observation, interviews, and sociometric badges. In contrast to previous studies that reduce the layout of the physical environment to a set of parameters, a social semiotic approach involves detailed notes of the layout of walls, doors, and furniture, as well as artefacts and decorations, complemented by extensive observations of how employees interact with each of these features as they go about their tasks. Following that, sociometric badges can be used to document how the features affect interactions between employees. Finally, interviews with the employees would reveal their understanding of the discourses and social context that inform those interactions. In this way, studies can provide a holistic and detailed understanding of how the physical layout of open-plan offices affect employees' understanding of their social context, and how they in turn act on their environment meaningfully as an ongoing dialogue.

References

Altman, I. (1975). *The Environment and Social Behavior*. Monterey, CA: Brooks/Cole.

Altman, I., & Chemers, M. (1980). *Culture and Environment*. Monterey, CA: Brooks/Cole.

Aronoff, S., & Kaplan, A. (1995). *Total Workplace Performance*. Ottawa: WDL Publications.

Ashkanasy, N. M., Ayoko, O. B., & Jehn, K. A. (2014). Understanding the physical environment of work and employee behavior: An affective events perspective. *Journal of Organizational Behavior*, *35*(8), 1169–1184.

Ayoko, O. B., Ashkanasy, N. M., & Jehn, K. A. (2014). Approaches to the study of employees' territoriality, conflict, emotions and wellbeing. In O. B. Ayoko, N. M. Ashkanasy, & K. A. Jehn (eds), *Handbook of Conflict Management Research* (pp. 363–381). Cheltenham: Edward Elgar.

Ayoko, O. B., & Härtel, C. E. J. (2003). The role of space as both a conflict trigger and a conflict control mechanism in culturally heterogeneous workgroups. *Applied Psychology: An International Review*, *52*, 383–412.

Baldry, C. (1997). The social construction of office space. *International Labour Review*, *136*(3), 365–378.

Baron, R. A. (1994). The physical environment of work settings: Effects on task performance, interpersonal relations, and job satisfaction. *Research in Organizational Behavior*, *16*, 1–46.

Beggan, J. K. (1992). On the social nature of nonsocial perception: The mere ownership effect. *Journal of Personality and Social Psychology*, *62*(2), 229–237.

Bodin Danielsson, C., & Bodin, L. (2009). Differences in satisfaction with office environment among employees in different office types. *Journal of Architectural and Planning Research*, *26*, 241–257.

Boyce, P. R., Berman, S. M., Collins, B. L., Lewis, A. L., & Rea, M. S. (1989). *Lighting and Human Performance: A Review*. Washington, DC: Lighting Equipment Division National Electrical Manufacturers Association and Lighting Research Institute.

Brennan, A., Chugh, J., & Kline, T. (2002). Traditional versus open office design: A longitudinal field study. *Environment and Behavior*, *34*(3), 279–299.

Brown, B. B. (1987). Territoriality. In D. Stokols & I. Altman (eds), *Handbook of Environmental Psychology* (Vol. 2, pp. 505–531). New York: Wiley.

Brown, G. (2009). Claiming a corner at work: Measuring employee territoriality in their workspaces. *Journal of Environmental Psychology, 29*(1), 44–52.

Brown, G., & Baer, M. (2015). Protecting the turf: The effect of territorial marking on others' creativity. *Journal of Applied Psychology, 100*(6), 1785–1797.

Brown, G., Crossley, C., & Robinson, S. L. (2014). Psychological ownership, territorial behavior and being perceived as a team contributor: The critical role of trust in the work environment. *Personnel Psychology, 67*, 463–485.

Brown, G., Lawrence, T. B., & Robinson, S. L. (2005). Territoriality in organizations. *Academy of Management Review, 30*(3), 577–594.

Byron, K., & Laurence, G. A. (2015). Diplomas, photos and tchotchkes as symbolic self-representations: Understanding employees' individual use of symbols. *Academy of Management Journal, 58*(1), 298–323.

Chigot, P. (2003). Controlled transparency in workplace design: Balancing visual and acoustic interaction in office environments. *Journal of Facilities Management, 2*(2), 121–130.

Connelly, A., & Ayoko, O. B. (2013). *Territorial Behaviours, Employee Perceptions and Conflict in Open-Plan Offices.* Paper presented at the 27th Australian and New Zealand Academy of Management Conference, Hobart, Australia.

Dale, K. (2005). Building a social materiality: Spatial and embodied politics in organizational control. *Organization, 12*, 649–678.

Dale, K., & Burrell, G. (2008). *The Spaces of Organization and the Organization of Space: Power, Identity and Materiality at Work.* Basingstoke and New York: Palgrave Macmillan.

Dixon, J., & Durrheim, K. (2003). Contact and the ecology of racial division: Some varieties of informal segregation. *British Journal of Social Psychology, 42*, 1–23.

Duffy, F. (1999). *The New Office* (2nd ed.). London: Conran Octopus.

Elsbach, K. D. (2003). Relating physical environment to self-categorizations: Identity threat and affirmation in a non-territorial office. *Space Administrative Science Quarterly, 48*, 622–654.

Elsbach, K. D. (2004). Interpreting workplace identities: The role of office décor. *Journal of Organizational Behavior, 25*, 99–128.

Elsbach, K. D., & Pratt, M. G. (2007). The physical environment in organizations. *Academy of Management Annals, 1*, 181–22.

Fayard, A. L., & Weeks, J. (2007). Photocopiers and water-coolers: The affordances of informal interaction. *Organization Studies, 28*(5), 605–634.

Foucault, M. 1980. *Power/Knowledge: Selected Interviews and Other Writings 1972–1977.* Edited by Colin Gordon. New York: Pantheon Books.

Gärling, T. (1998). Behavioural assumptions overlooked in travel choice modelling. *Travel Behaviour Research: Updating the State of Play*, 3–18.

Greenaway, K. H., Thai, H. A., Haslam, S. A., & Murphy, S. C. (2016). Spaces that signal identity improve workplace productivity. *Journal of Personnel Psychology, 15*(1), 35–43.

Halford, S., & Leonard, P. (2005). Place, space and time: Contextualizing workplace subjectivities. *Organization Studies, 27*, 657–676.

Halliday, M. A. K. (1978). *Language as Social Semiotic: The Social Interpretation of Language and Meaning.* Baltimore, MD: University Park Press.

Halliday, M. A. K. (2003). On the 'architecture' of human language. In *On Language and Linguistics* (Vol. 3 in the Collected Works of M.A.K. Halliday). London and New York: Equinox.

Halliday, M. A. K. (2013). Meaning as choice. In L. Fontaine, T. Bartlett, & G. O'Grady (eds), *Systemic Functional Linguistics: Exploring Choice.* Cambridge: Cambridge University Press.

Halliday, M. A. K., & Hasan, R. (1989). *Language, Context, and Text: Aspects of Language in a Social-Semiotic Perspective* (2nd ed.). Oxford: Oxford University Press.

Halliday, M. A. K., & Matthiessen, C. M. I. M. (2004). *An Introduction to Functional Grammar* (3rd ed.). London: Arnold.

Haslett, B. B. (2013). Structurational interaction. *Management Communication Quarterly, 27,* 615–622.

Haynes, B. P. (2007). The impact of the behavioural environment on office productivity. *Journal of Facilities Management, 5,* 158–171.

Hodge, R., & Kress, G. (1988). *Social Semiotics.* Cambridge: Polity.

Hopkins, N., & Dixon, J. 2006. Space, place, and identity: Issues for political psychology. *Political Psychology, 27*(2), 173–185.

Johns, G. (2006). The essential impact of context on organizational behavior. *Academy of Management Review, 31*(2), 386–408.

Joiner, D. (1971). Social ritual and architectural space. *Architectural Research and Teaching, 1*(3), 11–22.

Jones, S. R. (1990). Worker interdependence and output: The Hawthorne studies re- evaluated. *American Sociological Review, 55,* 176–190.

Kim, J., & de Dear, R. (2013). Workspace satisfaction: The privacy–communication trade-off in open-plan office. *Journal of Environmental Psychology, 36,* 18–29.

Knight, C., & Haslam, S. A. (2010). Your place or mine? Organizational identification and comfort as mediators of relationships between the managerial control of workspace and employees' satisfaction and well-being. *British Journal of Management, 21*(3), 717–735.

Knox, P. L., & Marston, S. A. (2004). *Places and Regions in Global Context: Human Geography* (3rd ed.). Upper Saddle River, NJ: Pearson Education.

Kress, G. & van Leeuwen, T. (2006). *Reading Images: The Grammar of Visual Design* (2nd ed.). London and New York: Routledge.

Kromah, M. D. (2017). *Workspace Territoriality: Role, Process and Consequences in the Context of Organizational Change.* An unpublished doctoral thesis of the University of Queensland, Brisbane, Australia.

Lefebvre, H. (1991). *The Production of Space.* Oxford: Blackwell Publishing.

Leonardi, P. M. (2011). When flexible routines meet flexible technologies: Affordance, constraint, and the imbrication of human and material agencies. *MIS Quarterly, 35,* 147–167.

Leonardi, P. M. (2012). Materiality, sociomateriality, and socio-technical systems: What do these terms mean? How are they different? Do we need them? In P. M. Leonardi, B. A. Nardi, & J. Kallinikos (eds), *Materiality and Organizing: Social Interaction in a Technological World* (pp. 25–48). Oxford: Oxford University Press.

Lewin, K. (1951). *Field Theory in Social Science.* New York: Harper.

Marquardt, C. J. G., Veitch, J. A., & Charles, K. E. (2002). *Environmental Satisfaction with Open-plan Office Furniture Design and Layout.* RR-106. Ottawa: Institute for Research in Construction, National Research Council of Canada.

Martin, J. R. (1992). *English Text: System and Structure.* Philadelphia, PA: John Benjamins Publishing.

Martin, J. R. (1999). Modelling context: A crooked path of progress in contextual linguistics. In M. Ghadessy (ed.), *Text and Context in Functional Linguistics* (pp. 25–61). Amsterdam: Benjamin.

Nathan, M. (2002). *Space SIG.* London: The Work Foundation.

Orlikowski, W. J. (2009). The sociomateriality of organisational life: Considering technology in management research. *Cambridge Journal of Economics, 34,* 125–141.

Orlikowski, W. J., & Scott, S. V. (2008). Sociomateriality: Challenging the separation of technology, work and organization. *Academy of Management Annals*, *2*(1), 433–474.

Pierce, J. L., Kostova, T., & Dirks, K. T. (2003). The state of psychological ownership: Integrating and extending a century of research. *Review of General Psychology*, *7*(1), 84–107.

Rafaeli, A., & Vilnai-Yavetz, I. (2004a). Instrumentality, aesthetics, and symbolism of physical artifacts as triggers of emotions. *Theoretical Issues in Ergonomics Science*, *5*, 91–112.

Rafaeli A., & Vilnai-Yavetz, I. (2004b). Emotion as a connection of physical artifacts and organizations. *Organization Science*, *15*, 671–686.

Ravelli, L. J,. & McMurtrie, R. J. (2016). *Multimodality in the Built Environment: Spatial Discourse Analysis*. London: Routledge.

Regoeczi, W. C. (2003). When context matters: A multilevel analysis of household and neighborhood crowding on aggression and withdrawal. *Journal of Environmental Psychology*, *23*, 457–470.

Richardson, T., & Jensen, O. B. (2003). Linking discourse and space: Towards a cultural sociology of space in analysing spatial policy discourses. *Urban Studies*, *40*(1), 7–22.

Rooney, D., Paulsen, N., Callan, V. J., Brabant, M., Gallois, C., & Jones, E. (2010). A new role for place identity in managing organizational change. *Management Communication Quarterly*, *24*, 44–73.

Sillince, J. A. A. (2007). Organizational context and the discursive construction of organizing. *Management Communication Quarterly*, *20*, 363–394.

Sommer, R. (1974). *Tight Spaces: Hard Architecture and How to Humanize It*. Englewood Cliffs, NJ: Prentice-Hall.

Tann, K. (2017). Context and meaning in the Sydney architecture of systemic functional linguistics. In T. Bartlett & G. O'Grady (eds), *The Routledge Handbook of Systemic Functional Linguistics*. London: Routledge.

Tuan, Y. F. (1976). Humanistic geography. *Annals of the Association of American Geographers*, *66*, 266–276.

Van Dijk, L., & Rietveld, E. (2017). Foregrounding sociomaterial practice in our understanding of affordances: The skilled intentionality framework. *Frontiers in Psychology*, *7*, 1969.

Van Leeuwen, T. (2005). *Introducing Social Semiotics*. New York: Psychology Press.

Van Marrewijk, A., & Broos, M. (2012). Retail stores as brands: Performances, theatre and space. *Consumption Markets and Culture*, *15*(4), 374–391.

Van Marrewijk, A., & Yanow, D. (2010). The spatial turn in organization studies. In A. Van Marrewijk & D. Yanow (eds), *Organizational Spaces: Rematerializing the Workaday World*. Northampton, MA: Edward Elgar.

Vischer, J. C. (2005). *Space Meets Status: Designing Workplace Performance*. Oxford: Routledge.

Vischer, J. C. (2008). Towards an environmental psychology of workspace: How people are affected by environments for work. *Architectural Science Review*, *51*(2), 97–108.

Wapshott, R., & Mallett, O. (2011). The spatial implications of homeworking: A Lefebvrian approach to the rewards and challenges of home-based work. *Organization*, *19*, 63–79.

Wells, M. (2000). Office clutter or meaningful personal displays: The role of office personalization in employee and organizational wellbeing. *Journal of Environmental Psychology*, *20*, 239–255.

Wilhoit, E. D. (2016). Organizational space and place beyond container or construction: Exploring workspace in the communicative constitution of organizations. *Annals of the International Communication Association*, *40*(1), 247–275.

Yates, J., & Orlikowski, W. J. (1992). Genres of organizational communication: A structurational approach to studying communication and media. *Academy of Management Review*, *17*(2), 299–332.

PART IV

Emotions, physical activity, and the physical environment of OB

13

WORKPLACE DESIGN, THE PHYSICAL ENVIRONMENT, AND HUMAN THRIVING AT WORK

Gretchen Spreitzer, Peter Bacevice, and Lyndon Garrett

Introduction

An important question that organizational scholars can and should be trying to answer is how organizations can enable their employees to thrive at work. Thriving, defined as the joint experience of vitality and learning, is associated with positive individual and organizational outcomes (Porath, Spreitzer, Gibson & Garnett, 2012), including performance and wellbeing. Most of the research on thriving at work has focused on how organizational culture, job character-istics, or the relational climate of the work unit affect human thriving. As with many organizational behaviour phenomena, the effects of the physical environ-ment are often overlooked or left in the background. This chapter examines how workspace design fosters or constrains human thriving at work. We pay specific attention to how new trends and practices in workspace design offer possibilities for organizations and workers themselves to generate resources that enhance the experience of thriving. We explore four types of affordances embedded in the physical environment: (1) affective affordances, (2) identity affordances, (3) social affordances, and (4) knowledge-sharing/creation affordances. These four types of affordances provide opportunities for workers to generate resources that enhance the experience of thriving. We conclude with implications for workplace design, with a particular emphasis on user control (throughout this chapter, we use the terms *users* and *end-users* to describe the people occupying the office spaces we discuss). The people working in any office environment can consist of company employees, contractors, customers, students, and any host of visitors. Architects and designers approach the planning and design of office space in a way that is human-centric, empathic, grounded in everyday practice, and focused on the needs and requirements of users. Similarly, people of any organizational affiliation may find themselves working from an array of places that are not traditional office buildings.

People work from coworking spaces, hotel lobbies, airports, coffee shops, home, and just about any place where power, wi-fi connectivity, and the social etiquette of users denotes a workplace.

Background

When we speak of the physical environment of work (Ashkanasy, Ayoko, & Jehn, 2014), we refer to the material features of the workspace that integrate with the work experience (Oldham & Rotchford, 1983; Elsbach & Pratt, 2007). The physical environment of work reflects the aesthetic (look and feel), symbolic (identity), and instrumental (creativity, collaboration) attributes of the workspace (Elsbach & Bechky, 2007). This chapter specifically focuses on how the material features that comprise the physical environment of work signal an organization's intent to promote values and encourage actions that influence the experience of thriving at work. At a large scale, examples of material features include the building architecture (such as the design of an office park campus that a work organization occupies). At a smaller scale, examples of material features can include office furnishings, desk chairs, computers, and other artefacts with which users engage as they work. These various material features create the functional, ambient, and social conditions that affect the user experience of work. For example, lighting, temperature, acoustics, air quality features, and layout are parts of building systems and architecture that affect our comfort and physiological responses in office settings (see Zhong & House, 2012 for a recent review). Moveable furniture, whiteboards, and conference room scheduling systems affect how we organize our work and our interactions with others when doing work. The intent of an organization to support user thriving is on display in the material features, which serve as conduits of culture, norms, and values, and shape everyday actions and routines in ways that enhance or hinder thriving at work.

What is thriving at work?

Thriving is defined as a psychological state that reflects the joint experience of vitality and learning at work (Spreitzer, Sutcliffe, Dutton, Sonenshein, & Grant, 2005). The vitality component of thriving refers to the positive feeling of being physically energetic (Nix, Ryan, Manly, & Deci, 1999). The learning component refers to the sense that one is acquiring and can apply knowledge and skills (Carver, 1998; Elliott & Dweck, 1988) and appears in the literature under labels such as the development of the self. Thriving is a continuum where people are more or less thriving at any point in time (Spreitzer et al., 2005; Carmeli & Spreitzer, 2009; Niessen, Sonnentag, & Sach, 2012). A construct validation study demonstrated significant within-person variation in thriving across contexts and time periods, indicating that thriving is a psychological state rather than an individual disposition (Porath et al., 2012). This suggests that attributes of the physical environment of work may influence a worker's everyday experience of thriving in a given spatial context.

And thriving matters for modern organizations because recent research suggests that human thriving at work contributes to human sustainability in terms of psychological (reduced burnout) and physical (health) wellbeing (Porath et al., 2012), change (Sonenshein, Grant, Dutton, Spreitzer, & Sutcliffe, 2013), career development (Porath et al., 2012), and job performance (Porath et al., 2012).

The physical environment and the experience of thriving

The physical environment of work is an assemblage of intent, function, and form that reveals assumptions about organizational life and offers interpretations of organizational reality through visual and aesthetic evidence (Meyer, Höllerer, Jancsary, & Van Leeuwen, 2013; Strati, 1996). Organizations define the intent of their work environments and how to deploy them strategically. Intent could represent priorities around efficiency, cost, location, or brand. Intent can also represent virtues such as community, tolerance, respect, transparency, or a range of other positive work practices. Together with architects and designers, organizational leaders collectively define the functionality of buildings, spaces, and other design features. Architects and designers ultimately interpret the stated intent and assenting functionality as enacted built form.

The physical environment affects the user experience (either positively or negatively) by means of material attributes that offer possibilities for (inter)action. Gibson (1979, p. 127) termed these possibilities affordances: 'The affordances of the environment are what it offers the animal, what it provides or furnishes, either for good or ill.' Originating from the field of ecological psychology, the concept of affordances captures the relationship between the physical environment and human experience. Specifically, affordances describe the action possibilities that the physical environment provides to users, as informed by the design, the social context, and individual perception (Fayard & Weeks, 2014; Maier, Fadel, & Battisto, 2009; Norman, 1988).

Affordances provide a suitable theoretical lens to study the relationship between the physical environment and thriving, as thriving is about vitality and opportunities for growth (Porath et al., 2012). Thriving is achieved in a process of 'continually developing and becoming, rather than achieving a fixed state wherein one is fully developed' (Ryff, 1989, p. 1071), as workers act in ways that expand themselves. For example, the placement of a fitness centre near the core of a work area in close proximity to key work areas may signal an organization's commitment to employee health and wellness, especially when organizational leaders are seen working out in the space during work hours. Similarly, the placement of a 'makerspace' in a prominent location may signal the organization's commitment to learning, especially when teams visibly hold working meetings in the space. As such, the physical environment enhances thriving when it affords possibilities for growth and vitality, and when it is embedded within a social environment imbued with virtuous intent. In this sense, an environment that promotes thriving contains elements that have been intentionally designed and constructed to afford growth and vitality. Further, thriving is a function of broadening the possibilities of (inter)action within the physical environment of work by letting users take more control over the features and functions of the workplace to suit their needs in the most effective way possible.

In the remaining sections, we will examine four types of affordances offered by the physical environment that promote thriving: affective affordances, identity affordances, social affordances, and knowledge-sharing affordances. These types of affordances are linked to existing research that touches the aesthetic, material, spatial, and environmental aspects of organizational life. In particular, we describe how these affordances open up possibilities for enhancing thriving in the doing of work (Spreitzer et al., 2005), namely positive affect, positive meaning, social connection, and knowledge.

Affective affordances

Affordances typically refer to action possibilities in the environment (e.g. such as a tree being 'climbable'), but the physical environment can also have affective affordances (Fuchs & Koch, 2014). Affective affordances are generally associated with the social environment, but they are also found in the physical environment. Emotions have two components, an affective component, which triggers a bodily resonance (being moved or touched), and a corresponding emotive component, which represents a readiness to action ('e-motion') (Fuchs & Koch, 2014). Positive emotions, an important driver of thriving, can result from the interaction between affective affordances in the physical environment and the user's bodily resonance, whether in the form of physical sensations, body postures, or expressive gestures. For example, Williams and Bargh (2008) found that holding a cup of hot coffee caused subjects to have a 'warmer' (more generous and caring) impression of another person than holding a cup of iced coffee. Bodily warmth directly affected the impression of warmth. Riskind (1984) found that subjects remembered more negative life events when sitting in a slumped position, and more positive events when sitting in an upright position. Evans and Johnson (2000) even found in an experimental setting that low-intensity noise typical of office settings reduced behavioural motivation. Relatedly, the physical work environment can influence our emotions by how it affords particular bodily responses. We describe several work-related office examples below.

As a result of a growing trend in supporting end-user health and wellness in the workplace, more users are choosing desks that can be adapted for sitting or standing. Studies have shown that when users are provided with sit-stand desks, they spend less time sitting (Alkhajah et al., 2012; Neuhaus et al., 2014) and experience less physical discomfort (Karakolis & Callaghan, 2014). A recent study (Alkhajah et al., 2012) compared users of sit-stand desks with a control group of users of traditional desks (which constrain their ability to stand) and found that the ability to control one's sitting or standing position resulted in choosing to spend less time sitting. The reduced sitting time was associated with higher levels of HDL ('good') cholesterol. In a similar controlled study, Thorp and colleagues (2014) found that users of sit-stand desks reported lower fatigue scores, further supporting the positively energizing affordance of this material office feature.

Another aspect of the physical environment at work, which can negatively impact worker affect, is the bad indoor air quality associated with 'sick building syndrome', or the presence of toxins in building materials, furnishings, and cleaning products that emanate in the air in an enclosed space (Frumkin, 2003). More generally, Gupta, Khare, and Goyal (2007) summarize 'sick building syndrome' as a condition that describes:

> situations in which building occupants experience acute health effects that appear to be linked with time spent in a building, but where no specific illness or cause can be identified. The complaints may be localized in a particular zone or may be widespread throughout the building.
>
> *(p. 2798)*

Given the high percentage of time that people spend indoors and at work with little control over certain systemic features of their physical environment, we suggest that the vitality aspect of thriving will be impacted by quality of built environment and its material components such as sick building syndrome.

Affective affordances also reside in aesthetic qualities such as beauty and sublimity, which can be found in architecture, visual arts, and even music in a workspace (Strati & de Montoux, 2002). Beauty is often associated with nature, and one strategy that architects and designers employ in office buildings is to bring naturalistic elements into interior office environments and to provide visibility and accessibility to the outdoors. Jackson (2003) provides a comprehensive review of the empirical link between visual and physical access to the outdoors and health-related outcomes. Research has indicated that exposure to nature and natural light help improve wellbeing (Kaplan & Kaplan, 2011). The natural light and views that come from having windows in the workspace can create the energy or feelings of vitality that are the essence of thriving. Other research has shown that exposure to green spaces enhances employee wellbeing and reduces stress (Louv, 2011; Seppala, 2017). Spending time in nature improves physical health (Williams, 2017), so having more plants as part of office design will likewise be beneficial for thriving. This can range from fresh flowers to green plants to entire walls covered with plants. It can even be captured in photographs or artwork of nature. Plants can also improve air quality, which can enable both the vitality and learning elements of thriving.

These examples illustrate how affective affordances in a physical environment can affect physical and emotional responses, generating positive emotion and energy that directly influence the experience of thriving.

Identity affordances

Another type of affordance in the physical environment, also increasingly recognized in the digital environment, is identity affordances (e.g. Majchrzak, Faraj,

Kane, & Azad, 2013; Poletti & Rak, 2014). The physical environment is replete with affordances that have relevance for user identity, which can enhance or diminish workers' identification with their work and organization. When identification increases, the work experience becomes more meaningful, which increases thriving (Spreitzer et al., 2005).

The physical environment plays a prominent role in affording the personal choice critical to the discovery and development of one's sense of self. The expressive characteristics of individual workspace and the choices people make to personalize (or not personalize) their individual workspace create opportunities to strengthen user identification with their workspace. The personal work setting (i.e. an enclosed office or open-plan workstation) offers a physical platform for self-representation of values and priorities while providing a mechanism that sparks dialogue and interaction among individuals in the workplace. Byron and Laurence's (2015) study of workspace personalization posits that personalization attributes communicate information about one's identity to others while simultaneously communicating identity to the self. The development and enhancement of a sense of self supported by the ability to personalize a workspace is crucial to the experience of growth, which is central to thriving.

Additionally, identity affordances extend beyond a particular office setting. As companies increasingly support worker mobility and flexibility, people have the option to structure their work routines around places and spaces that are suitable for them. In a study of coworking spaces that support freelance and remote workers with shared workspace and amenities, we found that the thriving of coworking space members was significantly higher than those working from traditional offices (Spreitzer, Bacevice, & Garrett, 2015). In a related qualitative study (Garrett, Spreitzer, & Bacevice, 2017), we found that in these settings where members self-organize and self-structure their work routines without the constraints of organizational group dynamics tied to being part of the same company, people could establish a more authentic sense of community and more comfortably be themselves at work, thereby eliciting increased thriving.

The physical environment also offers identity affordances at an organizational level. The physical environment can convey an organization's mission, values, and aspirations in spatial/aesthetic artefacts imbued with meaning (Khanna, van der Voordt, & Koppels, 2013; Klingmann, 2007; Mumby, 2016). Aesthetic choices that are incorporated into a workplace design such as its choice of furnishings (i.e. high end versus frugal), layout of team work areas (i.e. formal versus informal), or transparency of offices and meeting rooms (i.e. open and welcoming or closed and forbidding) can convey 'internal branding' (Brannan, Parsons, & Priola, 2015; Harquail, 2006; Land & Taylor, 2010; Mumby, 2016). Examples of workplace 'branded environments' (Hannigan, 2003; Klingmann, 2007) include the use of corporate logos within the architectural design, product imagery, or the incorporation of mission statements into wall graphics. A 'branded environment' serves as a sensegiving mechanism intended to reduce ambiguity in the interpretation of organizational purpose and values (Cappetta & Gioia, 2006; Maitlis & Lawrence,

2007; Vischer, 2011), which helps workers understand 'who am I, and how should I act?' in an organizational context (Alvesson, 2000). This branding can also serve to provide an increased sense of meaning in the work (Brannan et al., 2015). In short, the functionality and form of workplace design can reveal organizational intent around the expression of its values and commitment to them.

Social affordances

Social affordances represent the capacity of the physical environment to promote possibilities of social connection. An office is a social environment for supporting the cultivation of intra-organizational relationships (Vischer, 2011). In fact, the allocation of space for social interaction and collaboration as a proportion of over-all office square footage has increased in recent decades. Offices are increasingly designed to facilitate collaborative work. Even as a greater number of people work away from their primary office throughout the week (e.g. working from home part-time, meeting at client sites), the collaborative office archetype is intended to facilitate more meaningful social interactions and professional collaboration when people are in the office.

Social affordances in workplace design can counteract the isolation effects of increased virtual collaboration within daily workflow by increasing opportunities to experience high-quality connections (HQCs) and develop positive relationships (Stephens, Heaphy, & Dutton, 2012). HQCs have a profound impact on people's physical and emotional wellbeing, work engagement, and performance (e.g. Dutton & Ragins, 2007; Colbert, Bono, & Purvanova, 2016). By stimulating learning and growth, as well as health and vitality, HQCs are an important catalyst of thriving at work (Ragins & Verbos, 2007; Heaphy & Dutton, 2008; Suzuki et al., 2010).

Office design regularly incorporates multi-sensory design features (Clements-Croome, 2005) whose affordances are intended to stimulate social connectivity. Coffee bars and other food spaces generate sounds and scents that trigger affective responses that are associated with prosocial behaviours. Scents and sounds (i.e. coffee grinding and brewing) can be used to create an atmosphere of hospitality that creates an association with the space and encourages people to use it in a community-oriented way (Davies, Kooijman, & Ward, 2003). An organization's intent to build HQCs among employees may result in the placement of food and coffee spaces in central locations on a floor or in proximity to meeting areas or conference rooms so that they encourage employees to linger before and after meetings and engage in casual conversations. The scents and sounds produced in these spaces (i.e. the sound of coffee grinding or the smell of healthy food cooking) may be used to activate prosocial behaviours (Bradford & Desrochers, 2009; Herz, 2002) such as helpfulness (Baron, 1997) and vigilance (Warm, Dember, & Parasuraman, 1990).

While some affordances can trigger prosocial emotions and be useful in social settings where collaborative learning occurs, other affordances may be more useful in quiet settings where individual learning and focused work occurs. With noise being one of the biggest complaints of workers in open-plan office environments (Evans & Johnson, 2000), affordances in the transition zones between social areas and individual work areas can signal an etiquette of quiet in certain work areas and can lessen the strain of open-plan offices. The success of such affordances depends on prosocial behaviours such as reciprocity (i.e. 'we all need to share and respect this quiet space') and generosity (i.e. 'I will move my conversation outside because I know you need to focus').

Another way that the physical environment may afford social connection is by providing opportunities for playful and genuine moments of engagement (e.g. Mainemelis & Dionysiou, 2015; Mainemelis & Ronson, 2006). This includes examples such as putting a foosball table in the breakroom, posting funny comics on the office walls, or even keeping a kegerator in the kitchen. Additionally, many organizations have created dedicated social media platforms for social engagement (e.g. Huy & Shipilov, 2012). These platforms can be used for casual conversation, posting funny pictures, sharing music, or sharing pictures of families and pets. Also, as mentioned with identity affordances, workspace personalization helps provide information about one's work and non-work identities, which provides opportunities for individuals to connect around topics of personal interest. This type of social engagement serves to maintain energy and morale, foster personal relationships, and thereby enhance thriving.

The physical environment can also strengthen social connection by physically segregating or assimilating teams. Some organizations provide work groups with a 'kit-of-parts' (a menu of pre-determined furnishings or other workplace design features, along with a budget) from which they can assemble a team workspace that suits the needs of the individual team and expresses team identity, value, and function. In this manner, the workplace can divide 'the social world into "us" and, by implication although more or less clearly pronounced, "them" creates or sustains social distinctions and boundaries' (Alvesson & Willmott, 2002, p. 630). This sense of connection can enhance thriving by strengthening a member's sense of belonging and commitment to the group.

Knowledge-sharing affordances

Related to social affordances, the physical environment is increasingly being designed to promote and facilitate collaboration, coordination, and knowledge transfer. Practitioners often aim the rhetoric of 'increased workplace collaboration' (Chan, Beckman, & Lawrence, 2007; Congdon, Flynn, & Redman, 2014) at siloed organizational groups in an effort to break them down. Likewise, organizations often pursue workplace design projects with the same intent around increased collaborative behaviour. Viewed from a social capital lens, the strategy of employing workplace design as a means for increasing the quality and quantity of collaborative encounters strengthens workplace social capital and the wellness of people and teams.

Beyond providing spaces for collaboration as mentioned in the previous section, workplace technology is playing an increasingly important role in facilitating collaboration, namely virtual collaboration (i.e. Skype, Google Chats, Slack, Telepresence, etc.) and learning (smart whiteboards, cloud-based document sharing, etc.). For example, team communication platforms (TCPs) are a growing class of social collaboration technology that combines features of social networking platforms and instant messaging. The capabilities of these platforms provide affordances for efficient and generative team communication practices. The ubiquity of workplace technology and its potential to impact learning – a vital component of workplace thriving – suggests a link between the way people use technology and their ability to thrive at work.

Increased knowledge-sharing and social collaboration also has positive effects on social cohesion in teams and organizations. Studies have shown that collaboration and co-creation of knowledge, as compared with formalized knowledge-sharing, is a more effective way to share knowledge between cross-functional collaborations (Majchrzak, More, & Faraj, 2012). Additionally, communication visibility in collaboration promotes information symmetry, which is a key driver of social cohesion and productivity for cross-functional and virtual teams (Gardner & Mortensen, 2015). Ellison and colleagues (2015) emphasized the social benefits created by the affordances of collaboration technology for developing social capital and strengthening communication across traditional boundaries in organizational networks. Material artefacts are also useful in facilitating shared meaning and generating new knowledge in collaborative innovation processes (e.g. Stigliani & Ravasi, 2012; Islam, Endrissat, & Noppeney, 2016). Increasing collaboration, and making collaboration more effective, enhances user thriving by stimulating learning and growth, in addition to the vitality experienced from social connections.

Affordances and user control as means to enhance thriving at work

Each of the four types of affordances represents ways that the physical environment provides opportunities for users to generate resources in the doing of work that enhances thriving. An important element to consider for each affordance type to enhance thriving is the individual agency that users have in relation to the physical environment that they occupy. Giving workers agency, such as by giving them the choice to structure their work around achieving results rather than showing up to work at a set time and place, has been shown to improve health and wellbeing in the form of sleep quality, emotional exhaustion, personal mastery, psychological distress, and energy levels (Moen, Kelly, Tranby, & Huang, 2011). Similar benefits can be realized through control over the work environment (Lee & Brand, 2005; Hoskins, 2014).

The affordances embedded within the physical environment influence the way a user interprets an appropriate set of behaviours associated with them. For example, a conference room layout that includes a table and six chairs may suggest that a particular space is intended for group meetings of a certain size and purpose. Even subconsciously, one might liken a cubicle to a prison cell that invites little movement, whereas a space with a wide range of flexible seating options might encourage a much more relaxed attitude about work (von Thienen, Noweski, Rauth, Meinel, & Lang, 2012). In this context, user control is about providing ways to engage workplace users in the co-creation of their environment and providing them with multiple intuitive ways to adapt their environment to their needs. In this way, control of the work environment captures the autonomy and discretion that prior researchers have found to be important for fostering thriving at work (Spreitzer et al., 2005).

Sharing control over the design of office workspace and access to meeting places has been found to have numerous positive outcomes, including job attitudes and performance. For example, Knight and Haslam (2010) conducted an experiment where certain office workers were given more choice than others over the decoration and arrangement of artefacts in their workspace. They found that having a choice is associated with enhanced feelings of organizational identification, better physical and psychological comfort, better and more accurate task performance, and higher levels of organizational citizenship behaviours. In another example, Lee and Brand (2010) found that personal control over certain aspects of an office work environment (in particular choice over the organization of individual workstations, personalization of work areas, control over social contact, control of the ambient conditions of temperature and lighting, and control of work processes) mediated the negative aspects of distraction on perceived job performance. Today, more and more organizations are subjecting office workers to open office designs (Jones Lang LaSalle, 2017) that often are perceived as distracting to work in (Hedge, 1982; Kim & de Dear, 2013). Even in offices where collaboration is encouraged, providing people with choice as to where they collaborate matters because of the variability of social and cultural dimensions of interaction that can vary from group to group within the same space (Rashid, Kampschroer, Wineman, & Zimring, 2006).

Workers also benefit from having some control over the technology they use. The successful adoption of new technology requires a fit between the users' perceived usefulness of it and the task for which it is designed (Goodhue & Thompson, 1995). The social influence that occurs when other users buy into and choose to adopt new technologies is more effective than mandatory use compliance (Venkatesh & Davis, 2000). User choice can be expressed through the design and selection process for new workplace technologies to ensure a good fit for use and to help ensure that the tools help enable desired levels of learning and collaboration that are vital for thriving.

In taking a broader perspective on the evolving nature of work characterized by greater end-user choice around where and when work happens, and with greater environmental control over the experience of work, we are seeing how more choice enables thriving. However, there are two sides to the notion of user control. If the workplace places too many cognitive demands on the user and requires too many decisions on an ongoing basis (for example, the need to constantly move around to find a productive spot in which to work or to block out distractions), the environment and the unpredictable choices it requires to ensure functionality can be a source of stress (Vischer, 2007).

Implications for design strategy

Workplace design is a multi-stakeholder collaborative exercise that involves trade-offs that accommodate budgetary constraints and the competing requirements of individual and collective goals. People are more engaged when they have a say in and participate in workspace design (Alexander, Ishikawa & Silverstein, 1977). Participatory workplace design can take several forms. One form is the 'applied ergonomics' approach whereby users engage in hands-on fieldwork to document things they like and dislike about other environments (Broberg, Andersen, & Seim, 2011). Once a preliminary workplace concept has been developed, some organizations may choose to adopt it as a pilot to gauge user feedback or perform more rigorous and formal assessments before implementing it across a wider user base (Elsbach & Bechky, 2007; Kaczmarczyk & Murtough, 2002).

Workplace strategy (Becker & Steele, 1995; Laing, 2006; Schriefer, 2005) is the practice of managing the alignment among end-user needs, organizational and business goals, and design/real estate constraints. The aim of workplace strategy is to give each stakeholder a voice to weigh in on choices in the workplace design and change process so that users ultimately feel ownership in the outcome. Similarly, Vischer (2011) describes the relationship between people and space in an organization as the 'organization–accommodation relationship' whereby space and the strategic investment in it is seen as a means to supporting human capital. As opposed to viewing the physical environment as a cost to be minimized, the physical environment can be seen as a tool to support users in doing their work in ways that can contribute to organizational outcomes and user thriving.

Conclusion

In this chapter, we have explored how the physical environment of work enables user thriving. The four types of affordances by which workplace design and the physical environment of work may matter for thriving have unique but also intertwined effects. With each affordance, users should have some control to adapt the physical environment to meet their needs in order to promote growth and vitality. As workplace design involves user participation and accommodates end-user control, these affordances provide opportunities for organizations to enhance thriving in their workplaces.

References

Alexander, C., Ishikawa, S., & Silverstein, M. (1977). *A Pattern Language: Towns, Buildings, Construction.* New York: Oxford University Press.

Alkhajah, T. A., Reeves, M. M., Eakin, E. G., Winkler, E. A., Owen, N., & Healy, G. N. (2012). Sit–stand workstations: A pilot intervention to reduce office sitting time. *American Journal of Preventive Medicine, 43*, 298–303.

Alvesson, M. (2000). Social identity and the problem of loyalty in knowledge-intensive companies. *Journal of Management Studies, 37*, 1101–1123.

Alvesson, M., & Willmott, H. (2002). Identity regulation as organizational control: Producing the appropriate individual. *Journal of Management Studies, 39*, 619–644.

Ashkanasy, N. M., Ayoko, O. B., & Jehn, K. A. (2014). Understanding the physical environment of work and employee behavior: An affective events perspective. *Journal of Organizational Behavior, 35*, 1169–1184.

Baron, R. (1997). The sweet smell of. . . helping: The effects of pleasant ambient fragrance on prosocial behavior in shopping malls. *Personality and Social Psychology Bulletin, 23*(5), 498–503.

Becker, F. D., & Steele, F. (1995). *Workplace by Design: Mapping the High-Performance Workscape.* San Francisco, CA: Jossey-Bass.

Bradford, K., & Desrochers, D. (2009). The use of scents to influence consumers: The sense of using scents to make cents. *Journal of Business Ethics, 90*(S2), 141–153.

Brannan, M., Parsons, E., & Priola, V. (2015). Brands at work: The search for meaning in mundane work. *Organization Studies, 36*, 29–53.

Broberg, O., Andersen, V., & Seim, R. (2011). Participatory ergonomics in design processes: The role of boundary objects. *Applied Ergonomics, 42*, 464–472.

Byron, K., & Laurence, G. (2015). Diplomas, photos, and tchotchkes as symbolic self-representations: Understanding employees individual use of symbols. *Academy of Management Journal, 58*, 298–323.

Cappetta, R., & Gioia, D. (2006). Fine fashion: Using symbolic artifacts, sensemaking, and sensegiving to construct identity and image. In A. Rafaeli & M. Pratt (eds), *Artifacts and Organizations: Beyond Mere Symbolism* (pp. 199–219). Mahwah, NJ: Lawrence Erlbaum.

Carmeli, A., & Spreitzer, G. (2009). Trust, connectivity, and thriving: Implications for innovative behaviors at work. *Journal of Creative Behavior, 43*, 169–191.

Carver, C. (1998). Resilience and thriving: Issues, models, and linkages. *Journal of Social Issues, 54*, 245–266.

Chan, J., Beckman, S., & Lawrence, P. (2007). Workplace design: A new managerial imperative. *California Management Review, 49*, 6–22.

Clements-Croome, D. (2005). Consciousness, wellbeing and the sense. In D. Clements-Croome (ed.), *Creating the Productive Workplace* (2nd ed.) (pp. 14–24). New York: Taylor & Francis.

Colbert, A. E., Bono, J. E., & Purvanova, R. K. (2016). Flourishing via workplace relationships: Moving beyond instrumental support. *Academy of Management Journal, 59*, 1199–1223.

Congdon, C., Flynn, D., & Redman, M. (2014). Balancing we and me: The best collaborative spaces also support solitude. *Harvard Business Review, 92*, 51–57.

Davies, B. J., Kooijman, D., & Ward, P. (2003). The sweet smell of success: Olfaction in retailing. *Journal of Marketing Management, 19*(5–6), 611–627.

Dutton, J. E., & Ragins, B. R. (eds) (2007). *Exploring Positive Relationships at Work: Building a Theoretical and Research Foundation.* New York: Lawrence Erlbaum.

Elliott, E., & Dweck, C. (1988). Goals: An approach to motivation and achievement. *Journal of Personality and Social Psychology, 54*, 5–12.

Ellison, N. B., Gibbs, J. L., & Weber, M. S. (2015). The use of enterprise social network sites for knowledge sharing in distributed organizations: The role of organizational affordances. *American Behavioral Scientist, 59*, 103–123.

Elsbach, K. D., & Bechky, B. A. (2007). It's more than a desk: Working smarter through leveraged office design. *California Management Review, 49*, 80–101.

Elsbach, K. D., & Pratt, M. G. (2007). The physical environment in organizations. *Academy of Management Annals, 1*, 181–224.

Evans, G., & Johnson, D. (2000). Stress and open-office noise. *Journal of Applied Psychology, 85*, 779–783.

Fayard, A., & Weeks, J. (2014). Affordances for practice. *Information and Organization, 24*, 236–249.

Frumkin, H. (2003). Healthy places: Exploring the evidence. *American Journal of Public Health, 93*, 1451–1456.

Fuchs, T., & Koch, S. C. (2014). Embodied affectivity: On moving and being moved. *Frontiers in Psychology, 5*, 1–12.

Gardner, H. K., & Mortensen, M. (2015). Collaborating well in large global teams. *Harvard Business Review*, 1 July.

Garrett, L., Spreitzer, G., & Bacevice, P. (2017). Co-constructing a sense of community at work: The emergence of community in coworking spaces. *Organization Studies, 38*, 821–842.

Gibson, J. (1979). *The Ecological Approach to Visual Perception*. Boston: Houghton Mifflin.

Goodhue, D. L., & Thompson, R. L. (1995). Task–technology fit and individual performance. *MIS Quarterly*, 213–236.

Gupta, S., Khare, M., & Goyal, R. (2007). Sick building syndrome: A case study in a multistory centrally air-conditioned building in the Delhi City. *Building and Environment, 42*, 2797–2809.

Hannigan, J. (2003). Symposium on branding, the entertainment economy and urban place building: Introduction. *International Journal of Urban and Regional Research, 27*, 352–360.

Harquail, C. V. (2006). Employees as animate artifacts: Employee branding by 'wearing the brand'. In A. Rafaeli & M. Pratt (eds), *Artifacts and Organizations: Beyond Mere Symbolism* (pp. 161–180). Mahwah, NJ: Lawrence Erlbaum.

Heaphy, E. & Dutton, J. (2008). Positive social interactions and the human body at work: Linking organizations and physiology. *Academy of Management Review, 33*, 137–162.

Hedge, A. (1982). The open-plan office: A systematic investigation of employee reactions to their work environment. *Environment and Behavior, 14*, 519–542.

Herz, R. (2002). Influences of odors on mood and affective cognition. In C. Rouby, B. Schaal, D. Dubois, R. Gervais, & A. Holley (eds), *Olfaction, Taste, and Cognition* (pp. 160–177). New York: Cambridge University Press.

Hoskins, D. (2014). Employees perform better when they control their space. *Harvard Business Review*, 16 January.

Huy, Q., & Shipilov, A. (2012). The key to social media success within organizations. *MIT Sloan Management Review, 54*, 73.

Islam, G., Endrissat, N., & Noppeney, C. (2016). Beyond 'the eye' of the beholder: Scent innovation through analogical reconfiguration. *Organization Studies, 37*, 769–795.

Jackson, L. (2003). The relationship of urban design to human health and condition. *Landscape and Urban Planning, 64*, 191–200.

Jones Lang LaSalle, Inc. (2017). *Occupancy benchmarking: Occupancy planning annual report, 2017*.

Kaczmarczyk, S., & Murtough, J. (2002). Measuring the performance of innovative workplaces. *Journal of Facilities Management, 1*, 163–176.

Kaplan, R., & Kaplan, S. (2011). Wellbeing, reasonableness, and the natural environment. *Applied Psychology: Health and Wellbeing, 3*, 304–321.

Karakolis, T., & Callaghan, J. P. (2014). The impact of sit–stand office workstations on worker discomfort and productivity: A review. *Applied Ergonomics, 45*, 799–806.

Khanna, C., van der Voordt, T., & Koppels, P. (2013). Corporate real estate mirrors brand: A conceptual framework and practical applications. *Journal of Corporate Real Estate, 15,* 213–230.

Kim, J., & de Dear, R. (2013). Workspace satisfaction: The privacy–communication trade-off in open-plan offices. *Journal of Environmental Psychology, 36,* 18–26.

Klingmann, A. (2007). *Brandscapes: Architecture in the Experience Economy.* Cambridge, MA: MIT Press.

Knight, C., & Haslam, S. A. (2010). The relative merits of lean, enriched, and empowered offices: An experimental examination of the impact of workspace management strategies on well-being and productivity. *Journal of Experimental Psychology: Applied, 16*(2), 158–172.

Laing, A. (2006). North American office design at the start of the new millennium. In J. Worthington (ed.), *Reinventing the Workplace,* 2nd ed. (pp. 235–258). New York: Elsevier.

Land, C., & Taylor, S. (2010). Surf's up: Work, life, balance and brand in a new age capitalist organization. *Sociology, 44,* 395–413.

Lee, S. Y., & Brand, J. (2005). Effects of control over office workspace on perceptions of the work environment and work outcomes. *Journal of Environmental Psychology, 25,* 323–333.

Lee, S. Y., & Brand, J. (2010). Can personal control over the physical environment ease distractions in office workplaces? *Ergonomics, 53,* 324–335.

Louv, R., (2011). *Nature Principal.* New York: Algonquian Books.

Maier, J., Fadel, G., & Battisto, D. (2009). An affordance-based approach to architectural theory, design, and practice. *Design Studies, 30*(4), 393–414.

Mainemelis, C., & Dionysiou, D. D. (2015). Play, flow, and timelessness. In C. Shalley, M. Hitt, & J. Zhou (eds), *The Oxford Handbook of Creativity, Innovation, and Entrepreneurship* (pp. 121–140). New York: Oxford University Press.

Mainemelis, C., & Ronson, S. (2006). Ideas are born in fields of play: Towards a theory of play and creativity in organizational settings. *Research in Organizational Behavior, 27,* 81–131.

Maitlis, S., & Lawrence, T. B. (2007). Triggers and enablers of sensegiving in organizations. *Academy of Management Journal, 50,* 57–84.

Majchrzak, A., Faraj, S., Kane, G. C., & Azad, B. (2013). The contradictory influence of social media affordances on online communal knowledge sharing. *Journal of Computer-Mediated Communication, 19,* 38–55.

Majchrzak, A., More, P. H., & Faraj, S. (2012). Transcending knowledge differences in cross-functional teams. *Organization Science, 23,* 951–970.

Meyer, R., Höllerer, M., Jancsary, D., & Van Leeuwen, T. (2013). The visual dimension in organizing, organization, and organization research: Core ideas, current developments, and promising avenues. *Academy of Management Annals, 7*(1), 489–555.

Moen, P., Kelly, E., Tranby, E., & Huang, Q. (2011). Changing work, changing health: Can real work-time flexibility promote health behaviors and wellbeing? *Journal of Health and Social Behavior, 52,* 404–429.

Mumby, D. (2016). Organizing beyond organization: Branding, discourse, and communicative capitalism. *Organization, 23,* 884–907.

Neuhaus, M., Eakin, E. G., Straker, L., Owen, N., Dunstan, D. W., Reid, N., & Healy, G. N. (2014). Reducing occupational sedentary time: A systematic review and meta-analysis of evidence on activity-permissive workstations. *Obesity Reviews, 15*(10), 822–838.

Niessen, C., Sonnentag, S., & Sach, F. (2012). Thriving at work: A diary study. *Journal of Organizational Behavior, 33,* 468–487.

Nix, G., Ryan, R., Manly, J., & Deci, E. (1999). Revitalization through self-regulation: The effects of autonomous and controlled motivation on happiness and vitality. *Journal of Experimental Social Psychology*, 35, 266–284.

Norman, D. (1988). *The Design of Everyday Things*. New York: Basic Books.

Oldham, G., & Rotchford, N. (1983). Relationships between office characteristics and employee reactions: A study of the physical environment. *Administrative Science Quarterly*, *28*, 542–556.

Poletti, A., & Rak, J. (eds) (2014). *Identity Technologies: Constructing the Self Online*. Madison, WI: University of Wisconsin Press.

Porath, C., Spreitzer, G., Gibson, C., & Garnett, F. (2012). Thriving at work: Toward its measurement, construct validation, and theoretical refinement. *Journal of Organizational Behavior*, *33*, 250–275.

Ragins, B. R., & Verbos, A. K. (2007). Positive relationships in action: Relational mentoring and mentoring schemas in the workplace. In J. E. Dutton, & B. R. Ragins (eds), *Exploring Positive Relationships at Work: Building a Theoretical and Research Foundation* (pp. 91–116). New York: Lawrence Erlbaum.

Rashid, M., Kampschroer, K., Wineman, J., & Zimring, C. (2006). Spatial layout and face-to-face interaction in offices: A study of the mechanisms of spatial effects on face-to-face interaction. *Environment and Planning B: Planning and Design*, *33*, 825–844.

Riskind, J. H. (1984). They stoop to conquer: Guiding and self-regulatory functions of physical posture after success and failure. *Journal of Personality and Social Psychology*, *47*, 479–493.

Ryff, C. D. (1989). Happiness is everything, or is it? Explorations on the meaning of psychological wellbeing. *Journal of Personality and Social Psychology*, *57*, 1069.

Schriefer, A. (2005). Workplace strategy: What it is and why you should care. *Journal of Corporate Real Estate*, *7*, 222–233.

Seppala, E. (2017). Three surprising ways nature leads to success and joy. *Psychology Today blog*. Retrieved from www.psychologytoday.com/blog/feeling-it/201706/three-surprising-ways-nature-leads-success-and-joy

Sonenshein, S., Grant, A., Dutton, J., Spreitzer, G., & Sutcliffe, K. (2013). Growing at work: Employees' interpretations of progressive self-change in organizations. *Organization Science*, *24*, 552–570.

Spreitzer, G., Bacevice, P., & Garrett, L. (2015). Why people thrive in coworking spaces. *Harvard Business Review*, *93*, 28–30.

Spreitzer, G., Sutcliffe, K., Dutton, J., Sonenshein, S., & Grant, A. (2005). A socially embedded model of thriving at work. *Organization Science*, *16*, 537–549.

Stephens, J. P., Heaphy, E., & Dutton, J. (2012). High quality connections. In K. Cameron & G. Spreitzer (eds), *The Oxford Handbook of Positive Organizational Scholarship* (pp. 385–399). New York: Oxford University Press.

Stigliani, I., & Ravasi, D. (2012). Organizing thoughts and connecting brains: Material practices and the transition from individual to group-level prospective sensemaking. *Academy of Management Journal*, *55*, 1232–1259.

Strati, A. (1996). Organizations viewed through the lens of aesthetics. *Organization*, *3*(2), 209–218.

Strati, A., & de Montoux, P. (2002). Introduction: Organizing aesthetics. *Human Relations*, *55*(7), 755–766.

Suzuki, E., Takao, S., Subramanian, S., Komatsu, H., Doi, H., & Kawachi, I. (2010). Does low workplace social capital have detrimental effect on workers' health? *Social Science & Medicine*, *70*, 1367–1372.

Thorp, A., Kingwell, B., Owen, N., & Dunstan, D. (2014). Breaking up workplace sitting time with intermittent standing bouts improves fatigue and musculoskeletal discomfort in overweight/obese office workers. *Occupational and Environmental Medicine, 71*, 765–771.

Venkatesh, V., & Davis, F. (2000). A theoretical extension of the technology acceptance model: Four longitudinal field studies. *Management Science, 46*, 186–204.

Vischer, J. (2007). The effects of the physical environment on job performance: Towards a theoretical model of workplace stress. *Stress and Health, 23*, 175–184.

Vischer, J. (2011). Human capital and the organization–accommodation relationship. In A. Burton-Jones & J. Spender (eds), *The Oxford Handbook of Human Capital* (pp. 477–498). New York: Oxford University Press.

von Thienen, J., Noweski, C., Rauth, I., Meinel, C., & Lang, S. (2012). If you want to know who you are, tell me where you are: The importance of places. In H. Plattner, C. Meinel, & L. Leifer (eds), *Design Thinking Research: Studying Co-creation in Practice* (pp. 53–73). New York: Springer.

Warm, J., Dember, W., & Parasuraman, R. (1990). Effects of fragrances on vigilance, performance, and stress. *Perfumer and Flavorist, 15*, 16–17.

Williams, F. (2017). *The Nature Fix: Why Nature Makes us Happier, Healthier, and More Creative*. New York: W.W. Norton & Co.

Williams, L. E., & Bargh, J. A. (2008). Experiencing physical warmth promotes interpersonal warmth. *Science, 24*, 606–607.

Zhong, C., & House, J. (2012). Hawthorne revisited: Organizational implications of the physical work environment. *Research in Organizational Behavior, 32*, 3–22.

14

PERSON–ENVIRONMENT FIT

Optimizing the physical work environment

Rianne Appel-Meulenbroek, Pascale Le Blanc, and Yvonne de Kort

Introduction

Knowledge workers make up a significant proportion of advanced economies' workforces (Hvide & Kristiansen, 2012). In spite of automation, digitalization, and further implementation of technologies, the employee continues to be the most important asset for organizations. Besides their high costs, they have an important position as a knowledge producer (Drucker, 1999; Laing & Bacevice, 2013) and thus need to be supported well by their work environment. Although more and more people can work anywhere and anytime through technological advancements, a lot of the working time is still spent in the office. The physical office environment thus remains an important means to steer on organizational performance and employee productivity, and to win the war for new talent (Haynes, 2008; Riratanaphong, 2014).

Over the past three decades, management concepts have professionalized that plan, manage, and financially exploit a company's physical work environment: two related examples are corporate real estate management (CREM) (e.g. Brown, Lapides, & Rondeau, 1994) and facility management (FM) (e.g. Cotts, Roper, & Payant, 2009). These management departments are responsible for decisions on the design of the physical work environment, based on a consideration of costs and benefits (De Vries, De Jonge, & Van der Voordt, 2008). The cost transparency is usually relatively high (Haynes & Nunnington, 2010), but organizational benefits resulting from the design are more tacit and therefore less clear. Thus, in decision-making the criterion of cost minimization still dominates (Feige, Wallbaum, Windlinger, & Janser, 2013; Heywood & Kenley, 2008; Lindholm & Leväinen, 2006). However, recently the interest in benefits has risen among workplace managers, and also among academic researchers, because this is how the physical work environment might really add strategic value to the organization. It is expected that the multiplier effect of increased support of employees is crucial, as employee costs are roughly eight times higher than the costs of real estate (Pfnür, 2014).

One can take various perspectives on the role of physical context in worker productivity and health and, ultimately, in organizational success. Views may vary from the physical environment as a source of stress to an enabling asset, from a basic protective shell around activities and objects to the crystallization of corporate image and pride. The past three decades have seen a rise of research on possible effects of physical work environment characteristics on employee and/or organizational outcomes. An extensive literature review (Appel-Meulenbroek, Clippard, & Pfnür, 2018) has shown that thoughtful management of workplaces can impact employees in many ways. This review showed evidence for effects – positive and negative – of specific physical work environment characteristics on employee satisfaction, productivity, physical health, emotional state, attitude/engagement, comfort, concentration, privacy, and communication. The authors also mention that although empirical research focuses primarily on effects of psychosocial (distraction, privacy) and indoor climate characteristics, studies have also demonstrated effects of the office layout, characteristics of the individual space, aesthetics/architecture, accessibility, and services/facilities. Therefore, CREM and FM do not have an easy job in creating optimal conditions, especially when considering the diversity of employees in many contemporary organizations.

To complicate matters further, the majority of relevant research investigates isolated elements of environments and/or effects, often also from a monodisciplinary perspective, leaving matters of, for instance, complementarity, interrelationships between environmental design decisions and their relative importance untouched (Appel-Meulenbroek et al., 2018). Particularly findings from psychology remain scattered and poorly linked to the engineering and design disciplines that might make use of it (Veitch, Charles, Farley, & Newsham, 2007). Also, designers and workplace managers continue to ask for demonstrable proof of how the environment influences organizational outcomes (Veitch et al., 2007).

One theoretical umbrella perspective that at least tries to look at environments comprehensively and encompasses both sides (the good and the bad) of the coin of person–environment interaction is that of person–environment fit. According to person–environment fit (P–E fit) theory, person–environment interaction is optimal when the environment supports the most important needs of users, and does not demand more than their capabilities stretch. The theory states that suboptimal fit results in stress, defined as the subjective appraisal that supplies are insufficient to fulfil the person's needs (e.g. for privacy, for stimulation, for comfort), or that requirements outrun one's capacities (Edwards, Caplan, & Harrison, 1998). Or the environment could be too plain, minimalist or otherwise lacking stimuli, which may result in boredom. Importantly, stress arises not from the person or environment separately, but rather by their fit or congruence with one another.

Realizing that person–environment fit is important but that this optimization of workspace for knowledge workers is not necessarily straightforward, the current chapter is built up as follows: we first provide a brief explanation of P–E fit theory and then, in the main section of this chapter, discuss effects of the physical work environment on employee outcomes and the influence of choice and control. The chapter closes with general conclusions for workplace design and recommendations for more integrated research efforts towards this goal.

P–E fit theory

Central to P–E fit theory are three basic distinctions: the distinction between person and environment, the distinction between objective and subjective representations of the person and the environment, and the distinction between demands–abilities fit and needs–supplies fit (Edwards et al., 1998). Each of these distinctions will be elaborated below.

The distinction between the person and environment is a prerequisite for the conceptualization of P–E fit and provides the basis for examining reciprocal causation between the person and their environment. The objective person refers to attributes of the person as they actually exist, whereas the subjective person signifies the person's perception of their own attributes (i.e. person's self-identity or self-concept). Analogously, the objective environment includes physical and social situations and events as they exist independent of the person's perceptions, whereas the subjective environment refers to situations and events as encountered and perceived by the person. Though the objective person and environment are causally related to their subjective counterparts, these relationships are imperfect because of, for example, perceptual distortions, cognitive construction processes, limited human information processing capacities, and organizational structures that limit access to objective information (Harrison, 1978). By combining the two distinctions described above, four types of correspondence between person and environment constructs can be distinguished: (1) objective P–E fit, which refers to the fit between the objective person and the objective environment; (2) subjective P–E fit, or the fit between the subjective person and the subjective environment; (3) contact with reality, meaning the degree to which the subjective environment corresponds to the objective environment; and (4) accuracy of self-assessment (or accessibility of the self), representing the match between the objective person and the subjective person. Initially, P–E fit theory proposed that good mental health is signified by minimal discrepancies on objective P–E fit, subjective P–E fit, contact with reality, and accuracy of self-assessment (French, Rodgers, & Cobb, 1974; Harrison, 1978). However, subsequent refinements of the theory point out that objective P–E fit has little impact on mental health unless it is perceived by the person (e.g. House, 1974; Kahn, Wolfe, Quinn, Snoek, & Rosenthal, 1964; Lazarus & Folkman, 1984). Hence, currently P–E fit theory emphasizes subjective P–E fit as the critical pathway to mental health and other dimensions of wellbeing.

The final distinction of P–E fit theory differentiates two types of P–E fit. The first involves the fit between the demands of the environment and the abilities of the person. Demands include quantitative and qualitative job requirements, role expectations, and group and organizational norms, whereas abilities include aptitudes, skills, training, time, and energy the person may muster to meet demands. A second type of P–E fit entails the match between the needs of the person and the supplies in the environment that pertain to the person's needs. P–E fit theory characterizes needs in general terms, encompassing innate biological and psychological requirements, values acquired through learning and socialization, and motives to achieve desired ends (French & Kahn, 1962; Harrison, 1985). Supplies refer to extrinsic and intrinsic resources and rewards that may fulfil the person's needs, such as food, shelter, money, social involvement, and the opportunity to achieve (Harrison, 1978). The physical work environment is also part of these resources. For both needs–supplies fit and demands–abilities fit, P–E fit theory requires that person and environment constructs are commensurate, meaning they refer to the same content dimension. According to Cable and DeRue (2002), needs–supplies fit may be the most important type of fit from an employee perspective, because part of the basic motivation for people to enter the labour market and accept jobs is to gain access to the rewards that organizations offer as inducements (Simon, 1951). Cybernetic theories of stress (Cummings & Cooper, 1979) advance that the proximal cause of wellbeing is the perceived misfit between actual and desired states. In this way, 'needs–supplies misfit can be interpreted as stress when needs and supplies are both subjective and supplies fall short of needs' (Edwards & Shipp, 2007, p. 226). Therefore, in the remainder of this chapter we will focus mainly on the subjective fit between needs and supplies in the physical work environment that needs to be managed by those responsible for the physical work environment.

The three most basic human needs at work are the needs for competence, autonomy, and relatedness (Deci & Ryan, 2000). Employees are thus expected to be engaged and have high levels of wellbeing when they have these three psychological needs satisfied within their organization (Deci & Ryan, 1985). The need for relatedness is the desire of individuals to be connected to others and to experience feelings of security and belongingness (Van den Broeck, Vansteenkiste, Witte, Soenens, & Lens, 2010). Workplace managers might be able to affect the need for relatedness by, for example, designing the physical environment of the office in such a way that it facilitates interaction between employees (Meulensteen, 2017). The need for competence can be explained as the desire to feel effective in interacting with the environment, whereby the individual can adapt to complex and changing conditions (Deci & Ryan, 2000). Workplace managers might be able to play a role here by, for example, facilitating space that supports work processes. Van den Ouweland et al. (2014), for instance, demonstrated that noise nuisance, views of the outside, and personal control are key elements in office employees' perceived level of concentration and inspiration. The need for autonomy refers to people being able to self-organize and regulate their own behaviour while working toward inner integration and coherence among managerial demands (Deci & Ryan, 2000). As an example for workplace managers, Roelofsen (2002) showed that employees are more satisfied and less stressed if they are able to independently control the temperature and ventilation for their workspace.

Effects of physical work environment on employee outcomes

As Appel-Meulenbroek et al. (2018) report, abundant evidence for effects of specific physical work environment characteristics on employee satisfaction, productivity, physical and mental health has been found. Among others, significant effects are reported for humidity, temperature, air quality, volatile organic compounds, lighting, ergonomics of the workspace, privacy, level of enclosure, personal control, work-related interactions, spatial arrangement, interruptions, and noise (e.g. see Brill, Weidemann, & BOSTI Associates, 2001; Brennan, Chugh, & Kline, 2002; Van den Ouweland, et al. 2014; Van den Berg, 2017; Van der Voordt, Brunia, & Appel-Meulenbroek, 2016). Space does not allow a thorough review of individual environment characteristics here, but the current section will briefly summarize the literature on the most important outcomes.

First of all, it seems pivotal for companies to foster employee satisfaction, as the physical work environment can enhance individual productivity and overall organizational performance (e.g. De Been & Beijer, 2014; Lee & Brand, 2005; Veitch et al., 2007). Therefore, increasing employee satisfaction has become a major corporate real estate strategy in practice (Jensen, 2011). Satisfaction with the physical work environment has been defined as the extent to which the physical work environment meets employee needs (Van der Voordt, 2004), and is thus an essential outcome of subjective needs–supply fit.

In the scientific literature, especially the implementation of cell offices or open-plan offices has received much attention. As can be expected, such decisions on office layout and office use have far-reaching effects on work conditions, in particular on psychosocial (distraction, privacy) and indoor climate characteristics and, via these routes, on employees' environmental satisfaction (e.g. Kim & de Dear, 2013). Cell offices are generally found to show higher employee satisfaction while open-plan offices more often demonstrate inferior results (e.g. Bodin-Danielsson & Bodin, 2008; Kim & de Dear, 2013). Although it seems that in practice (specifically in some European countries) both cell offices and fully open offices are being transformed on a large scale into nomadic office concepts with a combination of open-plan workspaces and individual concentration spaces, a recent worldwide study of 17 countries has shown that most people still work in traditional office environments (Steelcase Inc, 2016). In their sample of over 12,000 employees, more than half worked in private offices (23% in individual private offices, 37% in shared private offices), and 33% in open-plan offices with an assigned space. Steelcase also showed that nearly a fourth of their sample worked in an entirely open office, despite the known pitfalls, such as distraction, lack of privacy, insufficient storage space, and a poor indoor climate (e.g. Brennan et al., 2002; Kamarulzaman, Saleh, Hashim, Hashim, & Abdul-Ghani, 2011; Kim & de Dear, 2013). On the other hand, an advantage of more open work environments is the increased frequency of unplanned face-to-face meetings during which knowledge is shared (Appel-Meulenbroek, 2014), although contrasting findings on the quality and quantity of interaction in open offices are also reported (e.g. Brill et al., 2001; Serrato & Wineman, 1997, 1999; Rashid, Kampschroer, Wineman, & Zimring, 2006).

Besides the overall workplace, the specific workspace used within the office also affects satisfaction (Kim & De Dear, 2013), just like indoor climate and accessibility. Physiological comfort is important and necessary, but not sufficient, to achieve psychological comfort, satisfaction, and wellbeing (Van den Ouweland, et al., 2014). From their overview of literature, Van der Voordt et al. (2016, p. 76) conclude that 'in particular the appropriate support of communication and concentration, well-designed desks and chairs, the comfort of the work place, indoor climate, and sound IT facilities are perceived as highly important by many employees, in general and in particular in flexible offices.' In this context, it is important to note that people's need for privacy and their need for socializing are relatively distinct motives (Haans, Kaiser & de Kort, 2007). Office environments are expected to accentuate the pros and diminish the cons of social contacts at work. Predictably, offices must be designed so that they can satisfy people's needs for social withdrawal (i.e. privacy in its narrow sense) and for social interaction without compromising either (Brill et al., 2001; see also Brennan et al., 2002).

Besides being related to employee satisfaction, increasing employee productivity is also a separate and important goal of organizations, and thus also for workplace managers (De Been & Beijer, 2014; Mawson & Johnson, 2014) when seeking P–E fit. Less productive employees can get less work done, have a lower contribution in meetings, create less value for organizations and are, in those respects, more expensive (Mawson & Johnson, 2014). But, more importantly, poor office buildings can result in occupants experiencing headaches, exhaustion, inability to concentrate and reduced work efficiency, symptoms also often caught under the term 'sick building syndrome' (Redlich, Sparer, & Cullen, 1997; Joshi, 2008). This will not only reduce their productivity, but also reduce the possibility to fulfil their need for competence. Productivity in a manufacturing sense is commonly defined as a ratio of input to output (Antikainen & Lönnqvist, 2006). However, for knowledge-intensive firms this definition is less applicable, since the input and output are far less tangible and more difficult to define (Haynes, 2007). Therefore, productivity of office workers is generally measured by asking effects of workplace characteristics on perceived productivity, thus again by assessing the subjective P–E fit. The difficulty of measuring productivity is one of the reasons why some knowledge-intensive organizations are currently not paying enough attention to fit supply to the needs and activities of knowledge workers in order for them to be productive (Feige et al., 2013; Chadburn, Smith, & Milan, 2017). They see measuring productivity as the 'holy grail' and an unreachable goal.

In addition to satisfaction and productivity, employees' physical and mental health is – or should be – of central importance in workplace management. It is important to realize that office concepts and conditions may directly or indirectly, via job demands and job resources, affect health, both in the short and longer term (De Croon, Sluiter, Kuijer, & Frings-Dresen, 2005). Occupational stress responses induced by, for instance, perceived inadequacy of space or privacy, or inability to concentrate and perform one's tasks, result in physiological and psychological short-term reactions, mental fatigue, the excretion of cortisol and increased levels of blood pressure. An accumulation of short-term reactions may, in the long term, result in more serious reactions and result in negative health outcomes, such as chronic fatigue, musculoskeletal disorders, deteriorated mental health, physical health, and executive functioning, and burnout (Maslach, Schaufeli, & Leiter, 2001; McEwen & Stellar, 1993; Sluiter, de Croon, Meijman, & Frings-Dresen, 2003). People with burnout report more daily cognitive blunders, increased fatigue, more headaches, and emotional exhaustion (e.g. Beer & Beer, 1992; Demerouti, Bakker, Nachreiner, & Schaufeli, 2001; Maslach & Jackson, 1981; van der Linden, Keijsers, Eling, & van Schaijk, 2005). As discussed above, working in open workplaces reduces privacy and job satisfaction, but the meta-analysis by De Croon et al. (2005) also suggested evidence for increased cognitive mental workload as well as worsening interpersonal relations. Moreover, they report that close distances between workstations intensify cognitive workload and reduce privacy. Interestingly, according to this same review, desk-sharing did appear to improve communication. Van den Ouweland et al. (2014) employed means–end chain interviews and follow-up questionnaires to relate a wealth of environmental attributes to health outcomes via employees' core values (i.e. needs). Clusters of attributes (related to effectiveness and functionality; meaningfulness; freedom and interaction; comfort and health; comprehensibility and manageability) were related explicitly to values (satisfaction, performing well, feeling at home, freedom, future, health), which in turn predicted measures of, among others, subjective health and burnout.

A bottom-line issue of organizations that seems to draw all the mentioned employee outcomes together into one concept might be employee engagement at work. Work engagement can be defined as 'a positive, fulfilling, affective-motivational state of work-related wellbeing that is characterized by vigour, dedication, and absorption' (Bakker, Schaufeli, Leiter, & Taris, 2008) and is also seen as the positive counterpart of burnout (Schaufeli, Salanova, Gonzalez-Roma, & Bakker, 2002). Employee engagement correlates positively with workplace satisfaction (Steelcase Inc., 2016) and productivity (Bakker & Demerouti, 2008), and engaged workers give their organization higher ratings for paying attention to their wellbeing and health (Steelcase Inc., 2016). So, work engagement appears to be related to many employee outcomes. 'When workers become disengaged, it costs companies money, slows projects, drains resources and undermines company goals, as well as the efforts of their engaged counterparts' (Steelcase Inc., 2016, p. 7). As Steelcase showed that more than a third of the workers in their world-wide sample are disengaged, exploring ways to minimize the risk for disengagement through better workplace design is certainly worthwhile.

As mentioned above, needs–supply fit refers to the congruence between personal needs on the one side and environmental supplies on the other (Kristof-Brown, Zimmerman, & Johnson, 2005). The wider the gap, the greater the likelihood of negative consequences on mental and physical wellbeing; conversely, the greater the fit, the greater the likelihood of positive consequences such as work engagement, meaningfulness, and job satisfaction (Edwards & Shipp, 2007; Tims, Derks, & Bakker, 2016; Travaglianti, Babic, & Hansez, 2016). Satisfaction of the three innate psychological needs of autonomy, competence, and relatedness (Deci & Ryan, 2000) can be considered a linking mechanism between perceived needs–supply fit and positive employee attitudes and behaviours.

Work-related positive emotions are described as relatively intense, short-lived affective experiences that are focused on specific objects or situations at work (Gray & Watson, 2001). Whereas positive emotions are immediate responses to the work environment, work engagement is relatively more enduring in nature (Schaufeli, Salanova, Gonzalez-Roma, & Bakker, 2002). Therefore, it is plausible to assume that short-term positive emotions precede work engagement (Schaufeli & van Rhenen, 2006). Broaden-and-build (B&B) theory posits that positive emotions not only make people feel good at a particular point in time, but these emotions may also predict future wellbeing (Fredrickson & Joiner, 2002). That is, positive emotions produce wellbeing. According to B&B theory, positive emotions broaden thought–action repertoires by inducing exploratory behaviours that create learning opportunities and goal achievement, and help to build enduring resources. Thus, by experiencing positive emotions, people enhance their resources, which, in turn, lead to a more enduring positive state of wellbeing, such as work engagement (Ouweneel, Le Blanc, & Schaufeli, 2012). Thus, work engagement can provide additional energy for workers in demanding situations (Bakker et al., 2008). When individuals are highly engaged, they have more energy and persistence to complete a task, while enhancing the successful implementation of needed strategies (Demerouti & Cropanzano, 2010).

Research has shown that engagement is related to bottom-line organizational outcomes such as job performance (Bakker & Bal, 2010; Halbesleben & Wheeler, 2008), client satisfaction (Salanova, Agut, & Peiró, 2005), and financial returns (Xanthopoulou, Bakker, Demerouti, & Schaufeli, 2009; for an overview, see Demerouti & Cropanzano, 2010). Moreover, Harter, Schmidt, and Hayes (2002) showed that levels of employee engagement were positively related to business-unit performance (i.e. customer satisfaction and loyalty, profitability, productivity, turnover, and safety) across almost 8,000 business units of 36 companies. The authors conclude that engagement is 'related to meaningful business outcomes at a magnitude that is important to many organizations' (p. 276). Last but not least, work engagement is also positively related to so-called extra-role or contextual performance (Demerouti & Cropanzano, 2010), i.e. behaviours of employees that are not part of their formal job requirements as they cannot be prescribed or required for a given job but help in the smooth functioning of the organization as a social system (for example, helping co-workers with a job-related problem; accepting orders without fuss; or protecting and conserving organizational resources; Bateman & Organ, 1983).

Choice and control

A relatively recent workplace trend is the implementation of non-territorial offices (with non-dedicated seats for all/most employees), which might alleviate individuals' strain of satisfying their subjective need–supply fit for several employee outcomes. Such offices have a variety of workspaces – both open and enclosed – to support the various activities conducted by the employees (Brunia, De Been, & Van der Voordt, 2016; Khamkanya & Sloan, 2009). Increased autonomy is an important advantage of this office concept (Ekstrand, Damman, Hansen, & Hatling, 2015; Vos & Van der Voordt, 2002), as employees can now decide themselves where to sit and what activities to perform where. This may help tailor environmental conditions to interpersonal differences. Joy and Haynes (2011), for instance, showed that in such non-territorial settings the selection of workspaces varied with age. Older employees used enclosed workspaces more frequently, perhaps indicating that their need for privacy is higher than for younger employees, or that the need for status expression differs between generations (some have reported that the oldest generation values hierarchy, while younger generations refute this (Earle, 2003)). Other studies have shown that for example age is related to environmental satisfaction (Bodin-Danielsson & Bodin, 2008; De Been & Beijer, 2014) and to workspace preferences regarding productivity support (Van den Berg, 2017). Gender is another factor impacting selection and experience of workspaces. Dinç (2009), for instance, found that female employees tend to value personalization, while status expression is perceived as more important by male employees.

Overall, employees in flexible offices seem to value the increased opportunities for communication (Gorgievski, Van der Voordt, Van Herpen, & Van Akkeren, 2010), the superior aesthetics (e.g. Van der Voordt, 2004), indoor climate (Appel-Meulenbroek, Kemperman, Van Susante, & Hoendervanger, 2015) and ergonomics (e.g. Vos & Van der Voordt, 2002). Steelcase Inc. (2016) found that as employees' ability to choose where to work increased, so too did their level of engagement. The diversity in available workspaces should increase workers' productivity as they can choose a workspace that fits their activities best, thus also supporting their need for competence. On the other hand, it could also lead to a decrease in productivity as employees will now spend more time on changing workspaces, organizing work and installing themselves (Van der Voordt, 2004). Also, research has shown that most employees do not change workspaces during the day in these flexible environments (Appel-Meulenbroek, Groenen, & Janssen, 2011), and that those who do not do so are less satisfied with their physical work environments than those who do (Hoendervanger, De Been, Van Yperen, Mobach, & Albers, 2016).

Although it certainly is no panacea, provision of meaningful personal control generally improves employee satisfaction and has the potential to support all three basic work-related needs in some way. Personal control certainly is a sound workplace strategy for tailoring to varying inter- and intrapersonal needs and preferences in an organization. Individuals may differ substantially, for instance in terms of noise sensitivity, need for privacy or need for socializing. Moreover, needs and available resources to meet environmental challenges differ with the type and complexity of tasks. Knowledge work typically includes different work-related activities, such as focused concentrated work, knowledge-sharing and social interactions (De Been, Van der Voordt, & Haynes, 2016). Whereas for individual concentrated work and formal interactions knowledge workers prefer enclosed environments with low noise levels, full control, and ergonomic furniture, for informal interactions noise-neutral, semi-enclosed environments are preferred (e.g. Van den Berg, 2017). Task complexity has also been related to, for example, privacy needs (e.g. Maher & Von Hippel, 2005). Person–environment fit theory emphasizes that a one-size-fits-all strategy can never be truly optimal. Control can be offered as decisional or design control, but also can be realized by offering various options to choose from (as in territorial/flex offices), or even in the form of information (e.g. on actual temperature, or on the rationale behind a certain light level).

Choice and control are also relevant in light of a second important trend in the office domain: that of so-called 'smart buildings'. Increasing attention for energy-efficient buildings combined with technological advances in sensors, processing power, lighting, and networks drive the development of building intelligence and automation in the work environment. But these too carry a risk that occupants lose their sense of control when decisions on environmental aspects such as temperature, electric lighting, and daylight are made by technology (Meerbeek, de Bakker, de Kort, van Loenen, & Bergman, 2016). Indoor climate and lighting are typical examples of environmental conditions that – through both psychological and biological pathways – have established effects on health and productivity, but which optimum differs substantially between individuals, due to varying preferences and varying metabolism and chronotype (e.g. De Kort & Veitch, 2014; Kingma & van Marken Lichtenbelt, 2015; Kingma, Frijns, Saris, Van Steenhoven, & Lichtenbelt, 2011; Smolders, 2013; Te Kulve, Schlangen, Schellen, Frijns, & van Marken Lichtenbelt, 2017). This explains why, for instance, female employees generally are more dissatisfied with climate comfort (Karjalainen, 2012). Offering users at least some form of (informational, selection or decisional) control increases user satisfaction and at the same time improves user conformance with system behaviour, as illustrated by reduced numbers of system actions that users corrected (Meerbeek et al., 2016).

Conclusions and recommendations

This chapter has provided an overview of the many roles that the physical work environment can play in achieving P–E fit at the office, specifically through improving employees' needs–supply fit. This overview underlines that CREM and FM have to take many potential characteristics of the physical work environment into account, when striving towards satisfying the three most basic human needs at work (competence, autonomy, and relatedness). Companies use a substantial amount of resources when recruiting new employees, so it should also be important for them to ensure that their environment will align with new hires' needs and abilities. If they do not, employee outcomes will be less optimal, affecting both employees' short-term emotions and long-term work engagement. In turn, this means that business performance will be less than it could be, including both objective measures such as financial returns and more subjective measures such as client satisfaction.

The present chapter has provided a very concise and undoubtedly incomplete review of workplace characteristics that have been shown to affect workers' well-being, satisfaction, and engagement. These included psychosocial (distraction, privacy) and indoor climate characteristics, office layout, design characteristics of the individual space, attractiveness of workspaces, accessibility, and services/facilities. Importantly, P–E fit theory explains that workplace management should not be geared towards maximization or minimization of threshold performance of such characteristics. Instead, optimization should be geared towards fit between employees' needs and abilities on the one hand and environmental supplies and demands on the other. Optimal fit thus depends on personal characteristics, as well as the task at hand, organizational culture, etc. This may also explain some of the mixed findings on, for instance, open office design. Without exception, however, studies do point at fulfilment of the three general basic needs – relatedness, competence, and autonomy – as key mechanisms connecting workplace characteristics to beneficial outcomes, and to control as a means towards optimal tuning towards such need fulfilment and P–E fit.

Despite the growing body of evidence on the potential of physical work environments to add value to organizations by optimally supporting office employees, it still does not receive sufficient attention in most organizations compared with the attention paid to the organizational work environment (human resource management). Also in academia, CREM and HRM-related academics do not often show joint research efforts towards integrating their theories and findings. Academic meta-analyses of what strategic human resource management can do for organizational outcomes disregard the physical work environment (e.g. Combs, Liu, Hall, & Ketchen, 2006), and CREM or FM studies are often limited to measuring effects of the physical (and sometimes behavioural) work environment without considering the organizational culture and management practices. Considering that both disciplines have the same overall aim of managing employees towards maximum job satisfaction, productivity and other objective and subjective employee outcomes, this is a missed opportunity and important research gap. We therefore call for more transdisciplinary future research on physical workplace effects on employees. Specific topics that would benefit from such an approach are achieving balance between concentration and privacy versus desired communication support, identifying the effect of workplace use and technologies on (mental) health, and effects of psychosocial conditions on mood/emotional state.

References

Antikainen, R., & Lönnqvist, A. (2006). *Knowledge Work Productivity Assessment*. Tampere, Finland: Institute of Industrial Management, Tampere University of Technology.

Appel-Meulenbroek, R. (2014). *How to Measure Added Value of CRE and Building Design: Knowledge Sharing in Research Buildings*. Dissertation, Eindhoven University of Technology, the Netherlands, available at: http://repository.tue.nl/762833.

Appel-Meulenbroek, R., Clippard, M., & Pfnür, A. (2018). The effectiveness of physical office environments for employee outcomes: An interdisciplinary perspective of research efforts. *Journal of Corporate Real Estate, 20*(1), 56–80.

Appel-Meulenbroek, R., Groenen, P., & Janssen, I. (2011). An end user's perspective on activity-based office concepts. *Journal of Corporate Real Estate, 13*(2), 122–135.

Appel-Meulenbroek, R., Kemperman, A., Van Susante, P., & Hoendervanger, J. (2015). Differences in employee satisfaction and productivity in new versus traditional work environments. *Proceedings of the 14th EuroFM Research Symposium*, June 1–3, Glasgow, Scotland, 2–10. Retrieved from https://www.eurofm.org/images/Papers/Section_4.2__Workplace_management.pdf

Bakker, A., & Demerouti, E. (2008). Towards a model of work engagement. *Career Development International, 13*(3), 209–223. doi.org/10.1108/13620430810870476.

Bakker, A. B., & Bal, P. M. (2010). Weekly work engagement and performance: A study among starting teachers. *Journal of Occupational and Organizational Psychology, 83*, 189–206.

Bakker, A. B., Schaufeli, W. B., Leiter, M. P., & Taris, T. W. (2008). Work engagement: An emerging concept in occupational health psychology. *Work and Stress, 22*, 187–200.

Bateman, T. S., & Organ, D. W. (1983). Job satisfaction and the good soldier: the relationship between affect and employee 'citizenship'. *Academy of Management Journal, 26*, 587–595.

Beer, J., & Beer, J. (1992). Burnout and stress, depression and self-esteem of teachers. *Psychological Reports, 71*, 1331–1336.

Bodin-Danielsson, C., & Bodin, L. (2008). Office type in relation to health, wellbeing and job satisfaction among employees. *Environment and Behavior, 40*(5), 636–668. doi: 10.1177/0013916507307459.

Brennan, A., Chugh, J. S., & Kline, T. (2002). Traditional versus open office design: A longitudinal field study. *Environment and Behavior, 34*(3), 279–299. doi: 10.1177/0013916502034003001.

Brill, M., Weidemann, S., & BOSTI Associates (2001). *Disproving Widespread Myths about Workplace Design*. Jasper, IN: Kimball International.

Brown, R. K., Lapides, P. D., & Rondeau, E. P. (1994). *Managing Corporate Real Estate: Forms and Procedures*. New York: John Wiley & Sons Inc.

Brunia, S., De Been, I., & Van der Voordt, T. (2016). Accommodating new ways of working: Lessons from best practices and worst cases. *Journal of Corporate Real Estate, 18*(1), 30–47. doi: 10.1108/JCRE-10-2015-0028.

Cable, D. M., & DeRue, D. S. (2002). The convergent and discriminant validity of subjective fit perceptions. *Journal of Applied Psychology, 87*, 875–884.

Chadburn, A., Smith, J., & Milan, J. (2017). Productivity drivers of knowledge workers in the central London office environment. *Journal of Corporate Real Estate, 19*(2), 66–79.

Combs, J., Liu, Y., Hall, A., & Ketchen, D. (2006). How much do high-performance work practices matter? A meta-analysis of their effects on organizational performance. *Personnel Psychology, 59*(3), 501–528. doi:10.1111/j.1744-6570.2006.00045.x.

Cotts, D. G., Roper, K. O., & Payant, R. P. (2009). *The Facility Management Handbook* (3rd ed.). New York: McGraw-Hill Professional.

Cummings, T. G., & Cooper, C. L. (1979). A cybernetic framework for studying occupational stress. *Human Relations*, *32*, 395.

De Been, I., & Beijer, M. (2014). The influence of office type on satisfaction and perceived productivity. *Journal of Facilities Management*, *12*(2), 142–157. doi: 10.1108/JFM-02-2013-0011.

De Been, I., Van der Voordt, T., & Haynes, B. (2016). Productivity. In P. A. Jensen & T. van der Voordt (eds), *Facilities Management and Corporate Real Estate Management as Value Drivers: How to Manage and Measure Added Value* (pp. 140–155). London: Routledge.

De Croon, E., Sluiter, J., Kuijer, P. P., & Frings-Dresen, M. (2005). The effect of office concepts on worker health and performance: a systematic review of the literature. *Ergonomics*, *48*(2), 119–134.

De Kort, Y. A. W., & Veitch, J. A. (2014). From blind spot into the spotlight. *Journal of Environmental Psychology*, *39*, 1–4.

De Vries, J. C., De Jonge, H., & Van der Voordt, T. J. M. (2008). Impact of real estate interventions on organisational performance. *Journal of Corporate Real Estate*, *10*(3), 208–223.

Deci, E. L., & Ryan, R. M. (1985). *Intrinsic Motivation and Self-Determination in Human Behavior*. New York: Plenum.

Deci, E. L., & Ryan, R. M. (2000). The what and why of goal pursuits: Human needs and the self-determination of behaviour. *Psychological Inquiry*, *1*, 227–268.

Demerouti, E., Bakker, B. A., Nachreiner, F., & Schaufeli, W. B. (2001). The job demands-resources model of burnout. *Journal of Applied Psychology*, *86*(3), 499–512.

Demerouti, E., & Cropanzano, R. (2010). From thought to action: Employee work engagement and job performance. In A. B. Bakker & M. P. Leiter (eds), *Work Engagement: A Handbook of Essential Theory and Research* (pp. 147–163). New York: Psychology Press.

Dinç, P. (2009). Gender (in)difference in private offices: A holistic approach for assessing satisfaction and personalization. *Journal of Environmental Psychology*, *29*, 53–62.

Drucker, P. F. (1999). Knowledge–worker productivity: The biggest challenge. *California Management Review*, *41*(2), 79–94.

Earle, H. A. (2003). Building a workplace of choice: Using the work environment to attract and retain top talent. *Journal of Facilities Management*, *2*(3), 244–257.

Edwards, J. R., Caplan, R. D., & Harrison, R. V. (1998). Person–environment fit theory: Conceptual foundations, empirical evidence, and directions for future research. In C. L. Cooper (ed.), *Theories of Organizational Stress* (pp. 28–67). Oxford: Oxford University Press.

Edwards, J. R., & Shipp, A. J. (2007). The relationship between person–environment fit and outcomes: An integrative theoretical framework. In C. Ostroff & T. A. Judge (eds), *Perspectives on Organizational Fit* (pp. 209–258). San Francisco, CA: Jossey-Bass.

Ekstrand, M., Damman, S., Hansen, G. K., & Hatling, M. (2015). Front and backstage in the workplace: An explorative case study on activity based working and employee perceptions of control over work-related demands. *Proceedings from EFMC 2015 Research Symposium*, June 1–3, Glasgow, Scotland.

Feige, A., Wallbaum, H., Windlinger, L., & Janser, M. (2013). Impact of sustainable office buildings on occupant's comfort and productivity. *Journal of Corporate Real Estate*, *15*(1), 7–34.

Fredrickson, B. L., & Joiner, T. (2002). Positive emotions trigger upward spirals to emotional wellbeing. *Psychological Science*, *13*, 172–175.

French, J. R. P., & Kahn, R. L. (1962). A programmatic approach to studying the industrial environment and mental health. *Journal of Social Issues*, *18*, 1–48

French, J. R. P., Rodgers, W. L., & Cobb, S. (1974). Adjustment as person–environment fit. In G. Coelho, D. Hamburg, & J. Adams (eds), *Coping and Adaptation* (pp. 316–333). New York: Basic Books.

Gorgievski, M. J., Van der Voordt, T. J., Van Herpen, S. G., & Van Akkeren, S. (2010). After the fire: New ways of working in an academic setting. *Facilities*, *28*(3/4), 206–224. doi: 10.1108/02632771011023159.

Gray, E., & Watson, D. (2001). Emotion, mood, temperament: Similarities, differences and a synthesis. In R. L. Payne & C. L. Cooper (eds), *Emotions at Work: Theory, Research and Applications for Management*. Chichester: John Wiley & Sons.

Haans, A., Kaiser, F. G., & de Kort, Y. A. W. (2007). Privacy needs in office environments: Development of two behavior-based scales. *European Psychologist*, *12*(2), 93–102.

Halbesleben, J. R. B., & Wheeler, A. R. (2008) The relative roles of engagement and embeddedness in predicting job performance and intention to leave. *Work and Stress*, *22*, 242–256.

Harrison, R. V. (1978). Person–environment fit and job stress. In C. L. Cooper & R. Payne (eds), *Stress at Work* (pp. 175–205). New York: Wiley.

Harrison, R. V. (1985). The person–environment fit model and the study of job stress. In T. A. Beehr & R .S. Bhagat (eds), *Human Stress and Cognition in Organizations* (pp. 23–55). New York: Wiley.

Harter, J. K., Schmidt, F. L., & Hayes, T. L. (2002). Business-unit-level relationship between employee satisfaction, employee engagement, and business outcomes: A meta-analysis. *Journal of Applied Psychology*, *87*, 268–279.

Haynes, B. P. (2007). An evaluation of office productivity measurement. *Journal of Corporate Real Estate*, *9*(3), 144–155.

Haynes, B. P. (2008). The impact of office layout on productivity. *Journal of Facilities Management*, *6*(3), 189–201.

Haynes, B. P., & Nunnington, N. (2010), *Corporate Real Estate Asset Management: Strategy and Implementation*. Amsterdam: Elsevier.

Heywood, C., & Kenley, R. (2008). The sustainable competitive advantage model for corporate real estate. *Journal of Corporate Real Estate*, *10*(2), 85–109.

Hoendervanger, J., De Been, I., Van Yperen, N., Mobach, M., & Albers, C. (2016). Flexibility in use: Switching behaviour and satisfaction in activity-based work environments. *Journal of Corporate Real Estate*, *18*(1), 48–62.

House, J. S. (1974). Occupational stress and coronary heart disease: A review and theoretical integration. *Journal of Health and Social Behavior*, *15*, 12–27.

Hvide, H., & Kristiansen, E. (2012). *Management of Knowledge Workers*. IZA discussion paper series no. 6609. Institute for the Study of Labor, Germany.

Jensen, P. (2011). Strategy and space: A longitudinal case study of broadcasting facilities. *International Journal of Strategic Property Management*, *15*(1), 35–47. doi: 10.3846/1648715X.2011.565868.

Joshi, S. M. (2008). The sick building syndrome. *Indian Journal of Occupational and Environmental Medicine*, *12*(2), 61–64.

Joy, A., & Haynes, B. P. (2011). Office design for the multi-generational knowledge workforce. *Journal of Corporate Real Estate*, *13*(4), 216–232.

Kahn, R. L., Wolfe, D. M., Quinn, R. P., Snoek, J. D., & Rosenthal, R. A. (1964). *Organizational Stress: Studies in Role Conflict and Ambiguity*. New York: Wiley.

Kamarulzaman, N., Saleh, A. A., Hashim, S. Z., Hashim, H., & Abdul-Ghani, A. A. (2011). An overview of the influence of physical office environments towards employees. *Procedia Engineering*, *20*, 262–268. doi: 10.1016/j.proeng.2011.11.164.

Karjalainen, S. (2012). Thermal comfort and gender: A literature review. *Indoor Air*, *22*, 96–109.

Khamkanya, T., & Sloan, B. (2009). Flexible working in Scottish local authority property: Moving on to the highest flexibility level. *International Journal of Strategic Property Management*, *13*(1), 37–52. doi: 10.3846/1648-715X.2009.13.37-52.

Kim, J., & De Dear, R. (2013). Workspace satisfaction: The privacy–communication trade-off in open-plan offices. *Journal of Environmental Psychology*, *36*, 18–26. doi: 10.1016/j.jenvp.2013.06.007.

Kingma, B., &. Van Marken Lichtenbelt, W. (2015). Energy consumption in buildings and female thermal demand. *Nature Climate Change*, *5*, 1054–1056.

Kingma, B. R., Frijns, A. J., Saris, W. H., Van Steenhoven, A. A., & Lichtenbelt, W. D. (2011). Increased systolic blood pressure after mild cold and rewarming: Relation to cold-induced thermogenesis and age. *Acta Physiologica*, *203*(4), 419–427.

Kristof-Brown, A. L., Zimmerman, R. D., & Johnson, E. D. (2005). Consequences of individuals' fit at work: A meta-analysis of person–job, person–organization, person–group, and person–supervisor fit. *Personnel Psychology*, *58*, 281–342.

Laing, A., & Bacevice, P. A. (2013). Using design to drive organizational performance and innovation in the corporate workplace: Implications for interprofessional environments. *Journal of Interprofessional Care*, *27*(Suppl 2), 37–45.

Lazarus, R. S., & Folkman, S. (1984). *Stress, Coping, and Adaptation*. New York: Springer.

Lindholm, A.-L., & Leväinen, K. I. (2006). A framework for identifying and measuring value added by corporate real estate. *Journal of Corporate Real Estate*, *8*(1), 38–46.

Lee, S. Y., & Brand, J. L. (2005). Effects of control over office workspace on perceptions of the work environment and work outcomes. *Journal of Environmental Psychology*, *25*(3), 323–333.

Maher, A., & Von Hippel, C. (2005). Individual differences in employee reactions to open-plan offices. *Journal of Environmental Psychology*, *25*, 219–229.

Maslach, C., & Jackson, S. E. (1981). The measurement of experienced burnout. *Journal of Organizational Behavior*, *2*, 99–113.

Maslach, C., Schaufeli, W., & Leiter, M. P. (2001). Job burnout. *Annual Review of Psychology*, *52*, 397–422.

Mawson, A., & Johnson, J. (2014), *The Six Factors of Knowledge Worker Productivity*. Advanced Workplace Associates, Center for Evidence-Based Management and Allsteel.

McEwen, B. S., & Stellar, E. (1993). Stress and the individual: Mechanisms leading to disease. *Archives of Internal Medicine*, *153*, 2093–2101.

Meerbeek, B. W., de Bakker, C., de Kort, Y. A. W., van Loenen, E. J., & Bergman, T. (2016). Automated blinds with light feedback to increase occupant satisfaction and energy saving. *Building and Environment*, *103*, 70–85.

Meulensteen, K. (2017). *Identifying the Underlying Process that Relates Aspects of the Physical Work Environment with Employee Work Performance*. Master's thesis, Eindhoven University of Technology, the Netherlands, available at: http://repository.tue.nl/864004.

Ouweneel, A. P. E., Le Blanc, P. M., & Schaufeli, W. B. (2012). Don't leave your heart at home: Gain cycles of positive emotions, resources, and engagement at work. *Career Development International*, *17*, 537–556.

Pfnür, A. (2014), *Economic Relevance of Corporate Real Estate in Germany, Berlin*. Retrieved from http://www.aurelis-real-estate.com/fileadmin/data/global/Download/Studien/Studie_CREM-EN.pdf.

Rashid, M., Kampschroer, K., Wineman, J., & Zimring, C. (2006). Spatial layout and face-to-face interaction in offices: A study of the mechanisms of spatial effects on face-to-face interaction. *Environment and Planning B: Planning and Design*, *33*(6), 825–844.

Redlich, C. A., Sparer, J., & Cullen, M. R. (1997). Sick-building syndrome. *The Lancet*, *349*(9057), 1013–1016.

Riratanaphong, C. (2014), *Performance Measurement of Workplace Change*. Dissertation, Delft University of Technology, Delft.

Roelofsen, P. (2002). The impact of office environments on employee performance: The design of the workplace as a strategy for productivity enhancement. *Journal of Facilities Management, 1*(3), 247–264.

Salanova, M., Agut, S., & Peiró, J. M. (2005) Linking organizational resources and work engagement to employee performance and customer loyalty: The mediation of service climate. *Journal of Applied Psychology, 90*, 1217–1227.

Schaufeli, W. B., Salanova, M., Gonzalez-Roma, V., & Bakker, A. B. (2002). The measurement of engagement and burnout: A two-sample confirmatory factor analytic approach. *Journal of Happiness Studies, 3*, 71–92.

Schaufeli, W. B., & Van Rhenen, W. (2006). Over de rol van positieve en negatieve emoties bij het welbevinden van managers: Een studie met de Job-related Affective Wellbeing Scale (JAWS) [About the role of positive and negative emotions in managers' wellbeing: A study using the Job-related Affective Wellbeing Scale (JAWS)]. *Gedrag en Organisatie, 19*, 323–344.

Serrato, M., & Wineman, J. D. (1997). Enhancing communication in lab-based organizations. In *Proceedings of the Space Syntax Symposium University College London*, London, volume *1*, pp. 15.1–15.8.

Serrato, M., & Wineman, J. D. (1999). Spatial and communication patterns in research and development. In *Proceedings of the Space Syntax Symposium University of Brasilia*, Brasilia, volume *1*, pp. 11.1–11.8.

Simon, H. A. (1951). A formal theory of the employment relationship. *Econometrica, 19*, 293–305.

Sluiter, J. K., de Croon, E. M., Meijman, T. F., & Frings-Dresen, M. H. W. (2003). Need for recovery from work related fatigue and its role in the development and prediction of subjective health complaints. *Occupational and Environmental Medicine, 60*, i62–i70.

Smolders, K. C. H. J. (2013). *Daytime Light Exposure: Effects and Preferences*. Dissertation, Eindhoven University of Technology, the Netherlands.

Steelcase Inc. (2016). *Engagement and the Global Workplace: Key Findings to Amplify the Performance of People, Teams and Organizations*. London: Steelcase Inc.

Te Kulve, M., Schlangen, L. J. M., Schellen, L., Frijns, A. J. H., & van Marken Lichtenbelt, W. D. (2017). The impact of morning light intensity and environmental temperature on body temperatures and alertness. *Physiology and Behavior, 175*, 72–81.

Tims, M., Derks, D., & Bakker, A. B. (2016). Job crafting and its relationship with person–job fit and meaningfulness: A three-wave study. *Journal of Vocational Behavior, 92*, 44–53.

Travaglianti, F., Babic, A., & Hansez, I. (2016). The role of work-related needs in the relationship between job-crafting, burnout, and engagement. *SA Journal of Industrial Psychology, 42*, a1308.

Van den Berg, J. (2017). *Preferred Workspace and Building Characteristics that Affect Knowledge Worker Productivity*. Master's thesis, Eindhoven University of Technology, the Netherlands, available at: http://repository.tue.nl/870615.

Van den Broeck, A., Vansteenkiste, M., Witte, H., Soenens, B., & Lens, W. (2010). Capturing autonomy, competence, and relatedness at work: Construction and initial validation of the Work-related Basic Need Satisfaction Scale. *Journal of Occupational and Organizational Psychology, 83*(4), 981–1002.

Van der Linden, D., Keijsers, G. P. J., Eling, P., & van Schaijk, R. (2005). Work stress and attentional difficulties: An initial study on burnout and cognitive failures. *Work and Stress, 19*, 23–36.

Van den Ouweland, E., Zeiler, W., de Kort, Y. A. W., Nierman, G., Boxem, G., & Maassen, W. H. (2014). A holistic approach to comfort in offices. In F. Nicol, S. Roaf,

L. Brotas, & E. Humphreys (eds), *8th Windsor Conference: Counting the Cost of Comfort in a Changing World, Proceedings* (pp. 324–334). Windsor: NCEUB.

Van der Voordt, T. J. (2004). Productivity and employee satisfaction in flexible workplaces. *Journal of Corporate Real Estate, 6*(2), 133–148. doi: 10.1108/14630010410812306.

Van der Voordt, T., Brunia, S., & Appel-Meulenbroek, R. (2016). Satisfaction. In P. A. Jensen & T. van der Voordt (eds), *Facilities Management and Corporate Real Estate Management as Value Drivers: How to Manage and Measure Added Value* (pp. 67–82). London: Routledge.

Veitch, J. A., Charles, K. E., Farley, K. M., & Newsham, G. R. (2007). A model of satisfaction with open-plan office conditions: COPE field findings. *Journal of Environmental Psychology, 27*(3), 177–189. doi: 10.1016/j.jenvp.2007.04.002.

Vos, P., & Van der Voordt, T. (2002). Tomorrow's offices through today's eyes: Effects of innovation in the working environment. *Journal of Corporate Real Estate, 4*(1), 48–65. doi: 10.1108/14630010210811778.

Xanthopoulou, D., Bakker, A. B., Demerouti, E., & Schaufeli, W. B. (2009). Work engagement and financial returns: A diary study on the role of job and personal resources. *Journal of Occupational and Organizational Psychology, 82*, 183–200.

15

THE PHYSICAL WORK ENVIRONMENT AND ITS RELATIONSHIP TO STRESS

Elizabeth J. Sander, Arran Caza, and Peter J. Jordan

Introduction

The prevalence of workplace stress continues to rise, with studies showing that in the US alone, work-related stress costs US$500 billion in lost productivity annually (Mental Health America, 2017). Similarly, more than 49% of Australian employees are estimated to be suffering from stress at work, costing employers over AUD$10 billion per year (APS, 2014; Medibank, 2008). The cost of stress is not just financial. Stress at work increases absenteeism and turnover, decreases job satisfaction, and reduces productivity (Harter, Schmidt, & Hayes, 2002). Additionally, the consequences of work stress are of significant public interest because of their association with ill health (Stansfield & Candy, 2006). Clearly, stress is a phenomenon we need to understand more about.

Although there are many potential stressors for employees, from dealing with ongoing change (Spector, 1986) to daily expectations for performance (Alarcon, 2011), one area that has recently attracted the attention of researchers and organizations is the physical work environment. Evidence suggests the physical work environment plays a powerful role in influencing stress, with alterations to design, materials, and layout resulting in better or worse outcomes for employees (Kim, Candido, Thomas, & de Dear, 2016; Nijp, Beckers, van der Voorde, Geurts, & Kompier, 2016). For example, high levels of noise emanating from the physical environment result in fatigue, tension headaches, and irritation (Ryherd, Persson, & Ljungkvist, 2008). Indeed, poor acoustics are a significant stressor, having been shown to elevate heart rates to levels associated with a heart attack (Ising & Kruppa, 2004; Tiesler & Oberdörster, 2008). As these examples illustrate, one's environment can play an important role in stress-related outcomes.

In this chapter, we review research findings examining the relationship between the physical work environment and stress. We begin with an overview of stress, including ways it is commonly defined and measured in the workplace. Next, we review the research on aspects of the physical work environment that influence stress, summarizing the literature and discussing the implications. Next, we propose evidence-based recommendations for using the physical environment to reduce employee stress. Finally, we conclude with suggestions for future research directions within the field.

Stress

Early conceptualizations of stress refer to it as a response by the body to a demand for change (Selye, 1955). More recently Folkman (2013) notes that stress is a relationship between the individual and the environment, where personally significant events are seen as overwhelming one's personal resources to cope with that situation. Stressors within the workplace result in strain which has subsequent effects on health and wellbeing (Ganster & Rosen, 2013). Stressors in the workplace refer to environmental events and work characteristics (for example in the Physical Work Environment, ergonomics) that result in either direct physical effects, or psychological reactions (Ganster & Rosen, 2013). Strains refer to the psychological, behavioural, and physiological reactions to environmental demands, threats, and challenges (i.e. stressors) and can result in a range of physical and psychological responses including anxiety, poor sleep, and increased blood pressure (Ganster & Rosen, 2013; Griffin & Clarke, 2011).

As noted, stressors may produce strain in one of two ways: physiological or psychological. Directly, some environmental factors such as noise, temperature, and ergonomics can lead to physical problems with associated physiological strain (Ganster & Rosen, 2013). For example, noise in the workplace has been associated with changes in heart rate variability and blood pressure (Kristiansen et al., 2009). Stressors may also have an indirect effect, and many studies of work-related stress also focus on how environmental conditions or events lead to cognitive and affective reactions that influence subsequent strain (Griffin & Clarke, 2011), rather than causing a direct physical consequence.

Workplace stressors lead to strains that include psychological responses such as fear, tension, and anxiety, as well as physiological responses such as increased cortisol and adrenaline or psychosomatic responses such as sleep disturbance, headaches, and fatigue (Ganster & Rosen, 2013). These responses can lead to changes in the immune, cardiovascular, and metabolic systems such as increases in blood pressure, body mass index, waist to hip ratio, and cholesterol. These sorts of health changes indicate strain, being associated with greater rates of cardiovascular disease, diabetes, depression, mental health disorders, and all-cause mortality (Ganster & Rosen, 2013).

Because of these complex and diverse reactions to stress, the measurement of stress is undertaken in a number of different ways. These ways include physiological reactions such as changes in cardiovascular activity (e.g. heart rate variability (HRV) and blood pressure), arousal indicators such as sweating, alterations to the immune system (e.g. epinephrine and norepinephrine), and the hypothalamic-pituitary adrenocorticol axis (e.g. cortisol), and changes in metabolic system indicators (e.g. body mass index, waist to hip ratio, and cholesterol) (Ganster & Rosen, 2013; McCoy & Evans, 2005).

Measurement of psychological effects from stress are generally less objective, including self-report assessments of affect, fatigue, tension, workload, and anxiety or depression (McCoy & Evans, 2005). Further, some researchers suggest that task performance can be used as a measure of psychological stress; that is, if performance drops, we can infer the effect of stress (McCoy & Evans, 2005). In sum, stressors can result in both psychological and physiological responses, resulting in strains that have both short-term and long-term health consequences (Ganster & Rosen, 2013). Since there are a range of factors within the physical work environment that can produce different mental and physical reactions amongst employees, designers and managers need to be aware of the factors that lead to stress and strains.

The physical work environment

The physical work environment in organizations includes the nature and arrangement of all the material objects and stimuli that people encounter in their organizational life (Davis, Leach, & Clegg, 2011; Elsbach & Pratt, 2007). While the physical work environment can powerfully influence employee stress, these effects are frequently not taken into consideration when undertaking workplace design. Workplace design decisions are more likely to be made with a focus on reducing escalating real estate costs (Nijp et al., 2016) or enhancing performance and collaboration (Kim et al., 2016). Indeed, the nature and design of work environments have altered dramatically, including practices such as open-plan offices, hot-desking, and shared office spaces. This has resulted in decreasing levels of visual and auditory privacy, reduced space per employee, and increased levels of noise and distraction (Davis et al., 2011; Kim et al., 2016).

Changes such as these are likely to have implications for stress on employees. A range of dimensions of the physical work environment, including a lack of access to views, increased noise, higher temperature, poor office layout, and a lack of nature-like surroundings, have been linked to increasing stress. Research has shown that environmental stress can reduce work performance by 2.4–5.8%, reducing motivation, and increasing tiredness and distractibility (Lamb & Kwok, 2016). Below, we summarize the ways in which different dimensions of the physical work environment may act as stressors resulting in physiological and psychological responses of strain.

Environmental sources of strain

Light and view

Physiological stress

Lighting levels, access to views and proximity to windows have been demonstrated to have direct physical effects on employees (Rashid & Zimring, 2008). For instance, natural light in offices decreases headaches and seasonal affective disorder (Franta & Anstead, 1994), decreases accidents and improves sleep quality (Luo, 1998), and decreases eyestrain (Rashid & Zimring, 2008).

Psychological stress

Psychologically, well-lit offices have been shown to increase positive mood (Heerwagen, Johnson, Brothers, Little, & Rosenfeld, 1998). Lighting effects, such as warm white light, positively influence social relations and reduce interpersonal conflicts (Baron, Rea, & Daniels, 1992). Likewise, perceptions of high-quality office lighting led to employees reporting more pleasant moods and having improved wellbeing at the end of the work day (Veitch & Newsham, 2000). A study by Leder, Newsham, Veitch, Mancini, and Charles (2016) found that employee-reported satisfaction with lighting was influenced by window access and levels of glare within the workspace, supporting previous findings about the importance of access to daylight and outside views (Frontczak et al., 2012; Yildirim, Akalin-Baskaya, & Celebi, 2007).

Summary

Visual cues appear to be a key stressor which contribute to the stress experienced by employees at work. The effects of light on workers have been of interest to researchers since the time of the original Hawthorne experiments (Izawa, French, & Hedge, 2011). Based on the evidence we have highlighted, lighting levels and access to natural light have an influence on employees' stress at work.

Noise

Physiological stress

Noise is amongst the most often cited complaints from employees regarding the physical work environment (Kim et al., 2016). Research has linked workplace noise exposure to physiological consequences of elevated cortisol levels (Kristiansen et al., 2009), changes in HRV and blood pressure (Chang, Jain, Wang, & Chan, 2003; Kristiansen et al., 2009). Noise has also been linked to increased sickness in employees (Kristiansen, 2010). Frequent self-reported exposure to disturbing noise at work is associated with increased risk of long-term sickness absence among office workers (Chou, Lu, & Huang, 2016; Clausen, Kristiansen, Hansen, Pejtersen, & Burr, 2013).

Psychological stress

Distraction and inability to concentrate is the most often noted complaint in relation to modern workplaces (see Elsbach & Pratt, 2007; Kim & de Dear, 2013). Noise has been demonstrated to cause annoyance (Rashid & Zimring, 2008) and decrease task performance (e.g. Cohen, 1980; Glass, Reim, & Singer, 1971). Distractions in open-plan offices lower cognitive performance (Yadav, Kim, Cabrera, & de Dear, 2017), as well as increasing levels of annoyance and mental workload (Zaglauer, Drotleff, & Liebl, 2017). All these factors have been identified as stressors in previous research.

Summary

In essence, auditory factors are also important as a stressor in the physical environment at work. While excessive noise has been a clear safety issue in industrial settings over an extended period (Nelson, Nelson, Concha-Barrientos, & Fingerhut, 2005), the above evidence suggests that noise is also an issue contributing to stress in modern office environments.

Temperature

Physiological stress

Sick building syndrome, which has been described as occupants experiencing acute health- or comfort-related effects linked to the amount of time spent in a building, has been consistently correlated with room temperatures above 22°C (e.g. Reinikainen & Jaakkola, 2001). Research also reveals that workers' performance on fine motor tasks and tasks requiring sensitive movement drops when temperatures are too cold (McCoy & Evans, 2005).

Psychological stress

In terms of psychological effects, research notes temperature as a significant stressor in office buildings that are either too hot or too cold (Rashid & Zimring, 2008). Research has shown that higher temperatures increased perceptions of crowding (Griffit & Veitch, 1971), which has been shown to contribute to aggression (Stokols, 1972). Cool offices can improve the performance on some cognitive tasks and reduce fatigue; however, extreme cold within the workplace will reduce performance on complex tasks (McCoy & Evans, 2005).

Summary

Drawing on another of the five senses (touch), the evidence suggest that temperature can be a significant stressor. Given the requirements for modern office buildings to be air-conditioned, difficulties in achieving and maintaining ideal temperatures throughout the workplace mean that resultant temperature extremes can contribute to a range of strains for employees.

Furniture and the arrangement of space

Physiological stress

A key development in recent office furnishings is the implementation of workstation modifications based on research highlighting problems with excessive sitting (Chia, Chen, & Suppiah, 2015). Indeed, workers spend up to 80,000 hours seated during their working life, leading to numerous health issues, including diabetes, cardiovascular disease, and obesity (MacEwen, MacDonald, & Burr, 2015; Neuhaus, Healy, Dunstan, Owen, & Eakin, 2014).

An experiment by Chia and colleagues (2015) randomly assigned groups of office workers to two different conditions: an office chair and a seat-cycle. After four weeks, the groups switched conditions. The results showed significant improvements for resting systolic blood pressure, resting heart rate, and sleep quality (Chia et al., 2015) for the seat-cycle group. However, using a stand-up desk all day may produce different health issues. Prolonged standing has been associated with musculo-skeletal pain and venous insufficiency (McCulloch, 2002).

Researchers have demonstrated a relationship between open-plan office design and health complaints including headaches and respiratory infections (Hedge, 1982; Klitzman & Stellman, 1989). Increased density within the workplace has also been shown to lead to greater risk of infection (Bodin Danielsson, 2010). Male and female occupants may experience the work environment differently, with researchers noting differences in satisfaction with the ambient environment, stress levels, and sick leave (Bodin Danielsson, Chungkham, Wulff, & Westerlund, 2014; Kim & de Dear, 2013).

Psychological stress

The layout of equipment and the degree to which enclosures and barriers (such as walls, desk dividers, and meeting rooms) are present in the workplace can influence levels of density and psychological comfort (Elsbach & Pratt, 2007). Open-plan offices, for example, generally have few enclosures or barriers, leading to issues with privacy, noise, and distraction (Kim & de Dear, 2013). Further, the level of density and crowding within the workplace can exacerbate issues relating to distraction, concentration, and productivity. Increasing the numbers of enclosures and barriers has been shown to increase satisfaction (e.g. Brennan, Chugh, & Kline,

2002), performance on simple tasks (e.g. Oldham, Cummings, & Zhou, 1995), task feedback, and trust in management (Zalesny & Farace, 1987). This would appear to support research on shared desk environments, where Morrison and Macky (2017) found that the perception of supervisor support decreased in environments where employees did not have allocated desks. Some research has suggested that increased stress levels in open-plan offices may be related to disturbance and a lack of personal control (Bodin Danielsson, 2010),

Further, while a greater number of enclosures and barriers assists with visual privacy, it may not assist with auditory privacy (Maher & von Hippel, 2005). Cain (2013) suggests that solitude is an essential ingredient in innovation, an important outcome sought in many organizations today.

Summary

Clearly our sensory experience of spaces is important. There are direct physiological effects based on ergonomics; however, the arrangement of space and our ability to arrange space to fit the necessary working conditions can also be seen as a stressor.

Natural factors

Physiological stress

Research has shown that exposure to nature resulted in decreased heart rate and decreased systolic and diastolic blood pressure (Park et al., 2007). In addition, studies have also found that the presence of plants and nature-like surroundings reduced cortisol for participants (Park et al., 2007), and supported improved autonomic control (measured using heart rate variability). The overall results of these studies suggest that there is a systemic relaxation effect experienced by individuals who have contact with plants and other natural features. These results have also been found when nature is simulated in indoor environments, with potential confounding factors such as weather, climate, sounds, and smells removed (Gladwell et al., 2012; Laumann, Garling, & Stormark, 2003).

Workplace air quality can have significant effects on workers' stress. In experimental conditions where researchers enhanced air quality, employees were found to have fewer headaches, respiratory complaints and slept better at night (Allen et al., 2016). Allen et al. (2016) argue that changing the quality of air in the physical work environment (at a cost of about $40 per person) had a $6,500 per year increase in employee productivity. Air quality is affected by levels of carbon dioxide (CO_2), as well as air-borne pollutants (Orwell, Wood, Tarran, Torpy, & Burchett, 2004). Other researchers confirm that high levels of CO_2 have resulted in reduced performance and productivity (Seppänen, Fisk, & Lei, 2006). Other studies have also demonstrated a reduction in sick building syndrome symptoms when air quality is increased (Seppänen, Fisk, & Mendell, 1999).

Psychological stress

In a field experiment introducing plants to three different workplaces, Nieuwenhuis, Knight, Postmes, and Haslam (2014) found that subjective perceptions of air quality, concentration, and workplace satisfaction improved for employees, as well as objective assessments of productivity. In addition, exposure to nature has been shown to have the capacity to improve attention (Berman, Jonides, & Kaplan, 2008). An explanation of plants' beneficial effects centres on the evolutionary explanation that a green, planted environment reflects the natural world and thereby supports human physiology (Orians & Heerwagen, 1992).

Summary

The proliferation in recent years of vertical gardens and green walls on both the exterior and interior of commercial office buildings attests to the recognition of the importance of the effects of natural environments for individuals in urban settings (Nieuwenhuis et al., 2014). The inclusion of nature within the workplace can reduce the effects of a range of environmental stressors.

Interventions to reduce stress in the physical work environment

Having outlined the ways in which the physical work environment creates stress, in this section we propose ways in which the environment can be modified to reduce employee stress. There is no question that physical work environments can have powerful effects on individual behaviour (Knight & Baer, 2014), and while the direct physiological effects are relatively straightforward (e.g. provide adequate lighting to reduce eye strain), the mechanisms through which psychological effects emerge are not clearly established. Oseland (2009) emphasizes the importance of considering how spaces support the psychological needs of employees, and previous research has established the importance of psychological reactions to the physical work environment. Further, the effect of stressors within the physical work environment is additive, and as such while the individual effect of one stressor such as noise or lighting may be low, the cumulative effect of stressors on employees may be significant (Lamb & Kwok, 2016). These considerations are important for both researchers and practitioners in examining the effects of physical work environments on stress.

Light and view

The use of high-quality lighting in the workplace will improve both mood and wellbeing (Veitch, Newsham, Boyce, & Jones, 2008), as well as enhancing social relations and reducing interpersonal conflicts (Baron et al., 1992). Providing all employees with access to natural daylight and outside views across the workspace may also reduce physiological strains, including headaches, eyestrain, and seasonal affective disorder. The provision of adjustable lighting such as task lighting to provide employees with personal control is also recommended (Danielsson & Bodin, 2008). In order to balance the access to views, the provision of barriers such as internal walls needs to be carefully considered in the design of the workplace.

Noise

Jahncke, Hygge, Halin, Green, and Dimberg (2011) found that open-plan office noise evoked cognitive and affective responses that led to reduced motivation and performance. Being able to control noise appears to moderate some of the negative effects experienced by employees (Danielsson & Bodin, 2008; Glass et al., 1971), likely due to the effects of the influence of personal control. Noise in the workplace can be managed through barriers such as walls, dividers and acoustic furnishings, wall treatments and fabrics, while hard surfaces such as concrete and timber floors can increase noise. As such, and particularly with the continued rise of open-plan workplaces (Kim et al., 2016), acoustic design is an essential factor to ensure that the effects of noise are minimized where possible. Giving employees access to a range of different spaces within the workplace to select to conduct their work will increase the perception of personal control, allowing employees to control the amount of noise exposure experienced during their work. The types of workspaces that facilitate this control are discussed later in this section.

Temperature

As modern air-conditioning systems develop, the ability for employees to control and adjust temperature within different areas of the work environment is increasingly available. The installation of such systems should be a key consideration for employers in refurbishing or fitting out new work environments.

Furniture and space

Cain (2013) has recently been involved in a project to create retreat spaces for introverts within the workplace. Refuge spaces allow employees to access a place where they can retreat from distraction to restore their mental and physical state. These types of spaces, as well as different furniture configurations with specific considerations for visual and acoustic privacy, are becoming increasingly important for employees to undertake focused work and reduce psychological stress.

In addition, modified workstations including stand-up desks, treadmill desks, and seat-cycling chairs are an increasingly prevalent feature in offices in an attempt to address the physical consequences of sitting for long periods. Careful consideration should be given to decisions around density, desk-ownership and where people work in relation to others who are important in their work team in the layout of the workplace having regard to the type of work being conducted and the needs of individual teams and employees.

Natural factors

Proponents of introducing greenery to the workplace argue that natural environments restore people's capacity for directed attention, whereas built environments tend to deplete this capacity (Kaplan, 1995). Natural environments exert less demand on directed attention and encourage more effortless brain functions, thereby allowing the capacity for attention to be restored. Thus, after an interaction with natural environments, one is able to perform better on tasks that rely on directed-attention abilities (e.g. data analysis, problem-solving tasks). According to this view, plants in the workplace should enhance employees' directed-attention capacity and therefore enhance their concentration and productivity levels. Despite these findings, Coon et al. (2011) argue further research is needed into the physiological mechanisms that arise with exposure to nature.

The benefits of working in physical work environments that are characterized by the inclusion of indoor plants, and/or views of greenery, are supported by evidence of the benefits of nature on employee attitudes and outcomes. Some researchers suggest humans have an innate need to be connected with nature, termed biophilia (Wilson, 1984). However, as housing density, commute times, and office hours increase, employees are spending less and less time in natural environments, placing greater emphasis on the inclusion of nature-like surroundings in the workplace.

Incorporating nature into the workplace can take many different forms, including living green walls, indoor trees, and planter boxes. Even where there aren't windows onto nature, and it isn't possible to bring in plants, some of the same effects can be achieved. Simulated views of nature, using high definition televisions, have also been shown to create positive effects, reducing physiological stress by lowering heart rates and blood pressure (Brown, Barton, & Gladwell, 2013).

More generally, research findings suggest that environment designers should take account of the cognitive, affective, and behavioural reactions of employees to achieve the outcomes desired by organizations of their employees (Sander, Caza, & Jordan, 2019). For example, physical work environments that are poorly designed in terms of layout and acoustics will likely contribute to levels of noise and distraction that make it difficult for employees to focus and concentrate, resulting in cognitive and affective outcomes that increase strains.

Likewise, environments that utilize unattractive materials, furnishings, and design will contribute to strain by increasing negative moods and perceptions of a lack of beauty (Wilson, 1984). The beauty of the workplace and its effects on employees may be a critical factor in reducing stress. With respect to the experience of a sense of beauty, scholars have shown that aspects of the physical work environment such as use of beautifying natural materials, colours, views, and lighting can influence mood and creativity (e.g. Ceylan, Dul, & Aytac, 2008; Larsen, Adams, Deal, Kweon, & Tyler, 1998). Indeed, it has been suggested that the aesthetic experience of beauty is a universal human response (Wilson, 1984).

Lastly, the physical work environment has been suggested to represent the body language of the organization (Doorley & Witthoft, 2011). If the design of the environment lacks functional and attractive spaces and items that convey a sense of welcome and meaning in terms of the organization's purpose, employees are unlikely to feel a sense of connection to the organization. Studies have shown that by not allocating permanent desks, employees report a decrease in the perception of supervisory support, indifference to co-workers, and reduced commitment to the organization (Morrison & Macky, 2017). When employees do not feel supported by the organization and are indifferent to their co-workers, they are likely to experience psychological strain.

While there are a broad range of physical and psychological stressors within the work environment, the ways in which employees react to those stressors may vary significantly based on individual differences and needs. Further, the importance of the ways in which aspects of the physical work environment influence psychological reactions is highlighted by Oseland (2009), who emphasizes the importance of considering aspects such as the variety, layout, purpose, and furnishing of spaces to ensure the psychological needs of employees are supported.

Indeed, previous research has shown that there is significant between-person variance in how individuals respond to the physical work environment (Sander et al., 2019), with individual perceptions of the working environment influencing responses to stress (Sohail & Rehman, 2015). For example, noise-sensitive individuals are more distracted by noise than insensitive individuals, with noise-sensitive subjects not only evaluating environmental noise as more annoying, but they also experience higher levels of strain than noise-insensitive individuals (Sandrock, Schütte, & Griefahn, 2009).

While this may seem unsurprising, the wide-scale adoption of open-plan and shared-desk work environments (Kim & de Dear, 2013; Kim et al., 2016) suggests that the importance of between-person variation is often not considered by those that design office space. That is, to suggest that all employees will respond in the same way to changes in the physical work environment ignores the basic foundation of psychology in relation to between-person differences.

This generally has not been considered by organizations in the design of their physical work environments and the subsequent effects this has on both physiological and psychological stress. As such, organizations should consider creating workplaces with a range of different spaces within the physical work environment that cater to different individual needs and the requirements of different types of work. For example, instead of one large open-plan work area, several smaller work areas could be provided along with café areas and meeting points for noisier collaborative work, as well as visually and acoustically private workspaces for employees to select based on their personal requirements.

As noted earlier, a sense of personal control may moderate the psychosocial stress, with increasing perceptions of personal control being shown to moderate stressors within the work environment (Danielsson & Bodin, 2008). As such, giving employees the ability to adjust factors within the workplace, including glare, light levels, furniture, temperature, and levels of privacy, may reduce the effects of environmental stressors.

Future directions

In this chapter we have summarized current knowledge about the ways in which the physical work environment influences stress. We have outlined the implications of these influences, and suggested ways in which the physical work environment might be modified to reduce employee stress. As employees spend increasing amounts of time at work, and levels of stress continue to rise, the environments where work is conducted are increasingly under focus.

Given that individuals respond to stress in a number of different ways, a diverse range of measures is required to record these responses. Researchers need to be aware that a single measure of stress may not give a complete picture of the ways in which stress is affecting an individual. Similarly, studying discrete aspects of the physical work environment, such as plants or noise, is likely to give an incomplete understanding of the complex ways in which reactions to the physical work environment influence stress.

Although many studies have examined effects of specific environmental features, they have frequently done so in atheoretical or theoretically incommensurate ways (Davis et al., 2011). So considering the work environment from an efficiency perspective (looking at workflows), will be different from a work environment designed for cost savings (focussing on the amount of space individuals need to work), will be different from a workplace designed to encourage innovation, will be different from a workplace designed to reduce stress. To this end, we encourage researchers in the field to incorporate a reliable and widely applicable means of assessing employees' reactions to their physical work environment. By focusing on the important role of individual reactions to the physical work environment and doing so using a consistent theoretical framework, future researchers may accumulate a body of knowledge of the ways in which reactions to the physical work environment influence stress.

Psychological reactions can provide the link between concrete features of the environment and employee behaviour, they can explain how features such as equipment, colour scheme, and office layout influence behaviour and reactions to that environment. In relation to focus, we know that employees need to focus on their tasks. Research has also shown that workplace environments vary in their ability to support focus, based in part on how much distraction is introduced into the space and how much support the space provides for individuals to adjust the level of distraction they experience (Lee & Brand, 2005). Using this knowledge, a well-designed workspace should reduce stress. For example, noisy workplaces disrupt cognitive processing, leading to significant deteriorations in concentration (Banbury & Berry, 2005) and resulting psychological stress. As such, investigating how levels of privacy, cognitive distraction, and environmental control in the physical work environment influence focus and psychological stress is an important next step. This research could lend itself to an experimental design where the environment is manipulated to assess its impact on an employee's ability to focus.

Scholars have noted that a sense of territory and control within the physical work environment is associated with a sense of belonging (Brown, Lawrence, & Robinson, 2005). Given that many employees now have much smaller spaces and less control over them (Davis et al., 2011), the effect of modern trends in efficient office design are worth investigating in terms of how they support or detract from a sense of connectedness or belonging. Density, spatial layout, furniture placement, and design may all contribute to a sense of connectedness or of isolation, thus increasing cognitive and affective stress responses. This type of research may lend itself to being conducted as action research examining reactions in actual workplaces.

Conclusion

This chapter reveals the numerous ways in which elements of the physical work environment can result in stress for employees. The outcomes of this stress can have significant negative effects on employee health and wellbeing as well as reducing task performance, job satisfaction, and productivity. We have suggested ways in which the physical work environment might be modified to reduce stressors for employees. With work-related stress costing employers billions of dollars per year, coupled with the continued rise of higher-density open-plan workplaces, understanding the effects of the physical work environment on stress is more important than ever.

References

Alarcon, G. M. (2011). A meta-analysis of burnout with job demands, resources, and attitudes. *Journal of Vocational Behavior, 79*(2), 549–562.

Allen, J. G., MacNaughton, P., Satish, U., Santanam, S., Vallarino, J., & Spengler, J. D. (2016). Associations of cognitive function scores with carbon dioxide, ventilation, and volatile organic compound exposures in office workers: A controlled exposure study of green and conventional office environments. *Environmental Health Perspectives, 124*(6), 805–812.

APS. (2014). Retrieved from www.psychology.org.au/Assets/Files/2014-APS-NPW-Survey-WEB-reduced.pdf

Banbury, S. P., & Berry, D. C. (2005). Office noise and employee concentration: Identifying causes of disruption and potential improvements. *Ergonomics, 48*(1), 25–37.

Baron, R. A., Rea, M. S., & Daniels, S. G. (1992). Effects of indoor lighting (illuminance and spectral distribution) on the performance of cognitive tasks and interpersonal behaviors: The potential mediating role of positive affect. *Motivation and Emotion, 16*(1), 1–33.

Berman, M. G., Jonides, J., & Kaplan, S. (2008). The cognitive benefits of interacting with nature. *Psychological Science, 19*(12), 1207–1212.

Bodin Danielsson, C. (2010). *The Office: An Explorative Study: Architectural Design's Impact on Health, Job Satisfaction and Wellbeing* (Doctoral dissertation, KTH).

Bodin Danielsson, C., Chungkham, H. S., Wulff, C., & Westerlund, H. (2014). Office design's impact on sick leave rates. *Ergonomics, 57*(2), 139–147.

Brennan, A., Chugh, J. S., & Kline, T. (2002). Traditional versus open office design: A longitudinal field study. *Environment and Behavior, 34*(3), 279–299.

Brown, D. K., Barton, J. L., & Gladwell, V. F. (2013). Viewing nature scenes positively affects recovery of autonomic function following acute-mental stress. *Environmental Science & Technology, 47*(11), 5562–5569.

Brown, G., Lawrence, T. B., & Robinson, S. L. (2005). Territoriality in organizations. *Academy of Management Review, 30,* 577–594.

Cain, S. (2013). *Quiet: The Power of Introverts in a World That Can't Stop Talking.* New York: Broadway Books.

Ceylan, C., Dul, J., & Aytac, S. (2008). Can the office environment stimulate a manager's creativity? *Human Factors and Ergonomics in Manufacturing and Service Industries, 18,* 589–602.

Chang, T. Y., Jain, R. M., Wang, C. S., & Chan, C. C. (2003). Effects of occupational noise exposure on blood pressure. *Journal of Occupational and Environmental Medicine, 45*(12), 1289–1296.

Chia, M., Chen, B., & Suppiah, H. (2015). Office sitting made less sedentary: A future-forward approach to reducing physical inactivity at work. *Montenegrin Journal of Sports Science and Medicine, 4*(2), 5–10.

Chou, C., Lu, C., & Huang, R. (2016). Effects of different ambient environments on human responses and work performance. *Journal of Ambient Intelligence and Humanized Computing, 7*(6), 865–874.

Clausen, T., Kristiansen, J., Hansen, J. V., Pejtersen, J. H., & Burr, H. (2013). Exposure to disturbing noise and risk of long-term sickness absence among office workers: A prospective analysis of register-based outcomes. *International Archives of Occupational and Environmental Health, 86*(7), 729–734.

Cohen, S. (1980). After effects of stress on human performance and social behavior: A review of research and theory. *Psychological Bulletin, 88,* 82–108.

Coon, J., Boddy, K., Stein, K., Whear, R., Barton, J., & Depledge, M. H. (2011). Does participating in physical activity in outdoor natural environments have a greater effect on physical and mental wellbeing than physical activity indoors? A systematic review. *Environmental Science and Technology, 45*(5), 1761–1772.

Danielsson, C. B., & Bodin, L. (2008). Office type in relation to health, wellbeing, and job satisfaction among employees. *Environment and Behavior, 40*(5), 636–668.

Davis, M. C., Leach, D. J., & Clegg, C. W. (2011). The physical environment of the office: Contemporary and emerging issues. In G. P. Hodgkinson & J. K. Ford (eds), *International Review of Industrial and Organizational Psychology* (pp. 193–235). Chichester: Wiley.

Doorley, S., & Witthoft, S. (2011). *Make Space: How to Set the Stage for Creative Collaboration.* Milton, Australia: John Wiley & Sons.

Elsbach, K. D., & Pratt, M. G. (2007). The physical environment in organizations. *Academy of Management Annals, 1,* 181–224.

Folkman, S. (2013) Stress: Appraisal and coping. In M. D. Gellman & J. R. Turner (eds), *Encyclopedia of Behavioral Medicine.* New York: Springer.

Franta, G., & Anstead, K. (1994). Daylighting offers great opportunities. *Window and Door Specifier-Design Lab, Spring,* 40–43.

Frontczak, M., Schiavon, S., Goins, J., Arens, E., Zhang, H., & Wargocki, P. (2012). Quantitative relationships between occupant satisfaction and satisfaction aspects of indoor environmental quality and building design. *Indoor Air, 22*(2), 119–131.

Ganster, D. C., & Rosen, C. C. (2013). Work stress and employee health: A multidisciplinary review. *Journal of Management, 39*(5), 1085–1122.

Gladwell, V. F., Brown, D. K., Barton, J. L., Tarvainen, M.P., Kuoppa, P., Pretty, J., Suddaby, J. M., & Sandercock, G. R. H. (2012). The effects of views of nature on autonomic control. *European Journal of Applied Physiology,* 1–8.

Glass, D. C., Reim, B., & Singer, J. E. (1971). Behavioral consequences of adaptation to controllable and uncontrollable noise. *Journal of Experimental Social Psychology, 7*(2), 244–257.

Griffin, M. A., & Clarke, S. (2011). Stress and wellbeing at work. In S. Zedeck (ed.), *APA Handbook of Industrial and Organizational Psychology: Vol. 3. Maintaining, Expanding, and Contracting the Organization* (pp. 359–397). Washington, DC: American Psychological Association.

Griffit, W., & Veitch, R. (1971). Hot and crowded: Influence of population density and temperature on interpersonal affective behavior. *Journal of Personality and Social Psychology, 17*(1), 92–98.

Harter, J. K., Schmidt, F. L., & Hayes, T. L. (2002). Business-unit-level relationship between employee satisfaction, employee engagement, and business outcomes: A meta-analysis. *Journal of Applied Psychology, 87*(2), 268–287.

Hedge, A. (1982). The open-plan office: A systematic investigation of employee reactions to their work environment. *Environment and Behavior, 14,* 519–542.

Heerwagen, J., Johnson, J. A., Brothers, P., Little, R., & Rosenfeld, A. (1998). *Energy Effectiveness and the Ecology of Work: Links to Productivity and Wellbeing* (No. CONF-980815). Richland, WA (USA): Pacific Northwest National Lab.

Ising, H., & Kruppa, B. (2004). Health effects caused by noise: Evidence in the literature from the past 25 years. *Noise and Health, 6*(22), 5–13.

Izawa, M. R., French, M. D., & Hedge, A. (2011). Shining new light on the Hawthorne illumination experiments. *Human Factors, 53*(5), 528–547.

Jahncke, H., Hygge, S., Halin, N., Green, A. M., & Dimberg, K. (2011). Open-plan office noise: Cognitive performance and restoration. *Journal of Environmental Psychology, 31*(4), 373–382.

Kaplan, S. (1995). The restorative benefits of nature: Toward an integrative framework. *Journal of Environmental Psychology, 15*(3), 169–182.

Kim, J., Candido, C., Thomas, L., & de Dear, R. (2016). Desk ownership in the workplace: The effect of non-territorial working on employee workplace satisfaction, perceived productivity and health. *Building and Environment, 103,* 203–214.

Kim, J., & de Dear, R. (2013). Workspace satisfaction: The privacy–communication trade-off in open-plan offices. *Journal of Environmental Psychology, 36,* 18–26.

Klitzman, S., & Stellman, J. M. (1989). The impact of the physical environment on the psychological wellbeing of office workers. *Social Science & Medicine, 29*(6), 733–742.

Knight, A. P., & Baer, M. (2014). Get up, stand up: the effects of a non-sedentary workspace on information elaboration and group performance. *Social Psychological and Personality Science, 5*(8), 910–917.

Kristiansen, J. (2010). Is noise exposure in non-industrial work environments associated with increased sickness absence? *Noise and Vibration Worldwide, 41*(5), 9–16.

Kristiansen, J., Mathiesen, L., Nielsen, P. K., Hansen, Å. M., Shibuya, H., Petersen, H. M., . . . & Søgaard, K. (2009). Stress reactions to cognitively demanding tasks and open-plan office noise. *International Archives of Occupational and Environmental Health, 82*(5), 631–641.

Lamb, S., & Kwok, K. C. (2016). A longitudinal investigation of work environment stressors on the performance and wellbeing of office workers. *Applied Ergonomics, 52,* 104–111.

Larsen, L., Adams, J., Deal, B., Kweon, B. S., & Tyler, E. (1998). Plants in the workplace the effects of plant density on productivity, attitudes, and perceptions. *Environment and Behavior, 30,* 261–281.

Laumann, K., Garling, T., & Stormark, K. (2003).Selective attention and heart rate responses to natural and urban environments *Journal of Environmental Psychology, 23,* 125–134.

Leder, S., Newsham, G. R., Veitch, J. A., Mancini, S., & Charles, K. E. (2016). Effects of office environment on employee satisfaction: A new analysis. *Building Research & Information*, *44*(1), 34–50.

Lee, S. Y., & Brand, J. L. (2005). Effects of control over office workspace on perceptions of the work environment and work outcomes. *Journal of Environmental Psychology*, *25*, 323–333.

Luo, C. (ed.). (1998). *To Capture the Sun and Sky: Lighting Futures*. New York: Rensselaer Polytechnic Institute Lighting Research Center.

MacEwen, B. T., MacDonald, D. J., & Burr, J. F. (2015). A systematic review of standing and treadmill desks in the workplace. *Preventive Medicine*, *70*, 50–58.

Maher, A., & von Hippel, C. (2005). Individual differences in employee reactions to open-plan offices. *Journal of Environmental Psychology*, *25*(2), 219–229.

McCoy, J. M., & Evans, G. W. (2005). Physical work environment. In J. Barling, E. K. Kelloway, & M. R. Frone (eds), *Handbook of Work Stress* (pp. 219–245). Thousand Oaks, CA: Sage.

McCulloch, J. (2002). Health risks associated with prolonged standing. *Work*, *19*(2), 201–205.

Medibank. (2008). Retrieved from www.medibank.com.au/content/dam/medibank/About-Us/pdfs/The-Cost-of-Workplace-Stress.pdf

Mental Health America. (2017). *Mind the Workplace*. Retrieved from www.mentalhealthamerica.net/sites/default/files/Mind%20the%20Workplace%20-%20MHA%20Workplace%20Health%20Survey%202017%20FINAL.pdf [Accessed 24 September 2017].

Morrison, R. L., & Macky, K. A. (2017). The demands and resources arising from shared office spaces. *Applied Ergonomics*, *60*, 103–115.

Nelson, D. I., Nelson, R. Y., Concha-Barrientos, M., & Fingerhut, M. (2005). The global burden of occupational noise-induced hearing loss. *American Journal of Industrial Medicine*, *48*(6), 446–458.

Neuhaus, M., Healy, G. N., Dunstan, D. W., Owen, N., & Eakin, E. G. (2014). Workplace sitting and height-adjustable workstations: a randomized controlled trial. *American Journal of Preventive Medicine*, *46*(1), 30–40.

Nieuwenhuis, M., Knight, C., Postmes, T., & Haslam, S. A. (2014). The relative benefits of green versus lean office space: Three field experiments. *Journal of Experimental Psychology Applied*, *20*(3), 199–214.

Nijp, H. H., Beckers, D. G., van de Voorde, K., Geurts, S. A., & Kompier, M. A. (2016). Effects of new ways of working on work hours and work location, health and job-related outcomes. *Chronobiology International*, *33*(6), 604–618.

Oldham, G. R., Cummings, A., & Zhou, J. (1995). The spatial configuration of organizations: A review of the literature and some new research directions. *Research in Personnel and Human Resource Management*, *13*, 1–37.

Orians, G. H., & Heerwagen, J. H. (1992). Evolved response to landscapes. In J. Barrow (ed.), *The Adapted Mind* (pp. 555–580). New York: Oxford University Press.

Orwell, R. L., Wood, R. L., Tarran, J., Torpy, F., & Burchett, M. D. (2004). Removal of benzene by the indoor plant/substrate microcosm and implications for air quality. *Water, Air, and Soil Pollution*, *157*(1–4), 193–207.

Oseland, N. (2009). The impact of psychological needs on office design. *Journal of Corporate Real Estate*, *11*(4), 244–254.

Park, B., Tsunetsugu, Y., Kasetani, T., Hirano, H., Kagawa, T., Sato, M., & Miyazaki, Y. (2007). Physiological effects of Shinrin-yoku (taking in the atmosphere of the forest): Using salivary cortisol and cerebral activity as indicators. *Journal of Physiological. Anthropology*, *26*(2), 123–128.

Rashid, M., & Zimring, C. (2008). A review of the empirical literature on the relationships between indoor environment and stress in health care and office settings: Problems and prospects of sharing evidence. *Environment and Behavior, 40*(2), 151–190.

Reinikainen, L. M., & Jaakkola, J. J. (2001). Effects of temperature and humidification in the office environment. *Archives of Environmental Health: An International Journal, 56*(4), 365–368.

Ryherd, E. E., Persson, K. W., & Ljungkvist, L. (2008). Characterizing noise and perceived work environment in a neurological intensive care unit. *Journal of the Acoustical Society of America, 123*(2), 747–756.

Sander, E. L. J., Caza, A., & Jordan, P. J. (2019). Psychological perceptions matter: Developing the reactions to the physical work environment scale. *Building and Environment, 148*, 338–347.

Sandrock, S., Schütte, M., & Griefahn, B. (2009). Impairing effects of noise in high and low noise sensitive persons working on different mental tasks. *International Archives of Occupational and Environmental Health, 82*(6), 779–785.

Selye, H. (1955). Stress and disease. *The Laryngoscope, 65*(7), 500–514.

Seppänen, O., Fisk, W. J., & Lei, Q. H. (2006). Ventilation and performance in office work. *Indoor Air, 16*(1), 28–36.

Seppänen, O. A., Fisk, W. J., & Mendell, M. J. (1999). Association of ventilation rates and CO_2 concentrations with health and other responses in commercial and institutional buildings. *Indoor Air, 9*(4), 226–252.

Sohail, M., & Rehman, C. A. (2015). Stress and health at the workplace: A review of the literature. *Journal of Business Studies Quarterly, 6*(3), 94.

Spector, P. E. (1986). Perceived control by employees: A meta-analysis of studies concerning autonomy and participation at work. *Human Relations, 39*(11), 1005–1016.

Stansfield, S., & Candy, B. (2006) Psychosocial work environment and mental health: A meta-analytic review. *Scandinavian Journal of Work, Environment and Health, 32*(6), 433–462.

Stokols, D. (1972). A social-psychological model of human crowding phenomena. *Journal of the American Institute of Planners, 38*(2), 72–83.

Tiesler, G., & Oberdörster, M. (2008). Noise – a stressor? Acoustic ergonomics of schools. *Building Acoustics, 15*(3), 249–261.

Veitch, J. A., & Newsham, G. R. (2000). Exercised control, lighting choices, and energy use: An office simulation experiment. *Journal of Environmental Psychology, 20*, 219–237.

Veitch, J. A., Newsham, G. R., Boyce, P. R., & Jones, C. C. (2008). Lighting appraisal, well-being and performance in open-plan offices: A linked mechanisms approach. *Lighting Research and Technology, 40*(2), 133–151.

Wilson, E. O. (1984). *Biophilia*. Cambridge, MA: Harvard University Press.

Yadav, M., Kim, J., Cabrera, D., & De Dear, R. (2017). Auditory distraction in open-plan office environments: The effect of multi-talker acoustics. *Applied Acoustics, 126*, 68–80.

Yildirim, K., Akalin-Baskaya, A., & Celebi, M. (2007). The effects of window proximity, partition height, and gender on perceptions of open-plan offices. *Journal of Environmental Psychology, 27*(2), 154–165.

Zaglauer, M., Drotleff, H., & Liebl, A. (2017). Background babble in open-plan offices: A natural masker of disruptive speech? *Applied Acoustics, 118*, 1–7.

Zalesny, M. D., & Farace, R. V. (1987). Traditional versus open offices: A comparison of sociotechnical, social relations, and symbolic meaning perspectives. *Academy of Management Journal, 30*(2), 240–259.

PART V

The physical environment of OB and the practitioner

16

A QUALITATIVE STUDY OF EMPLOYEES' EMOTIONS AND IDENTITIES DURING CHANGE

The role of place attachment

Momo D. Kromah, Oluremi B. Ayoko, Neal M. Ashkanasy, and Gemma L. Irving

For over two decades, organizational change researchers and practitioners (e.g. see Higgs & Rowland, 2007; Miller, Johnson, & Grau, 1994) have focused much of their attention on understanding the factors that underpin successful organizational change. Nevertheless, and as Probst and Raisch (2005) point out, most change initiatives fail to meet expectations, resulting in resistance (Oreg, Vakola, & Armenakis, 2011) or low commitment to change initiatives (Herscovitch & Meyer, 2002). We argue that this failure of change initiatives may be partly attributed to a lack of attention to the physical context of work (Johns, 2006) and its connections with employees' responses and attitudes to change (Herold, Fedor, & Caldwell, 2007). In particular, we propose that the psychological phenomenon of *place attachment* may help to explain employees' negative responses to change initiatives (see Lewicka, 2011 for a recent review). In this chapter, we report a study in this genre (i.e. organizational change) and outline practical implications for managing physical workspace change.

Physical workspaces, change, and place attachment

While contemporary organizations are adopting innovative workspaces to promote employee productivity, teamwork, and collaboration (Ricciotti et al., 2014; Zoller & Boutellier, 2013), there is evidence that such innovative workspaces may be problematic. In particular, organizational change initiatives, which often involve the redesign of physical workspace to improve employee communication or to reduce facilities costs (Hedge, 1982), seem often to promote unintended negative consequences such as reduced productivity, satisfaction, and cooperation (Brennan, Chugh, & Kline, 2002). This conundrum, we argue, may arise because managers fail to consider employees' feelings of attachment to their workspaces during the change process.

Moreover, while researchers are documenting the benefits that accrue to organizations through adoption of high-tech open-plan workspaces, research empirically examining workspace preferences and especially employees' place attachment during organizational change (for exceptions, see Goel, Johnson, Junglas, & Ives, 2011; Milligan, 2003) is limited.

To address this issue, we conducted a study to understand the role place attachment plays in influencing employees' attitudes and behaviours in the context of organizational change. We define place attachment as a positive affective relationship between an individual and a specific place that includes an individual's desire to stay close to that place, as well as their memories, knowledge, and meanings about that place (Scannell & Gifford, 2010).

Place attachment scholars (e.g. Low & Altman, 1992; Scannell & Gifford, 2010) portray the construct as a multidimensional concept involving person, process (e.g. affect, cognition), and place. As such, place attachment is distinct from related concepts such as territorial behaviour (behavioural expression of feelings of ownership toward physical or social objects, Brown, Lawrence, & Robinson, 2005). Whereas territorial behaviours involve marking and defending the territory, place attachment behaviours include maintaining affective closeness to place, place restoration, and pilgrimages to revisit the space (Scannell & Gifford, 2010).

Hidalgo and Hernández (2001) argue in particular that individuals often feel an emotional connection to a physical place and the people in that place. For example, in a review of 40 years of research on place attachment, Lewicka (2011) concluded that 'despite mobility and globalization processes, place continues to be an object of strong attachments' (p. 207). Given this evidence, we propose that employees' place attachment to their workspaces influences their responses (attitudes and behaviours) to workspace change. This proposition leads us to our guiding research question: *what is the relationship between organizational change involving changes to the physical environment and employees' place attachment, attitudes, and behaviours?*

Method

Traditionally, place attachment researchers (e.g. Brown & Perkins, 1992; Brown, Perkins, & Brown, 2003) have used observational and correlational designs, usually based on survey administration. While these approaches may help us understand place attachment from a large number of participants, and findings are assumed to be generalizable to workplace settings, survey research methods are prone to common method (Podsakoff, Mackenzie & Podsakoff, 2012) and retrospectivity (Ashkanasy, Zerbe, & Härtel, 2002) biases. To overcome these challenges, we relied upon face-to-face interviews to collect our data.

The rationale for this choice of research method is twofold. First, qualitative methods such as interviews are useful to gain deep and rich insights into organizations and activities for the purposes of generating theories (Christianson, Farkas, Sutcliffe, & Weick, 2009). Second, scholars (e.g. Brown et al., 2005; Scannell & Gifford, 2010) have noted that place attachment behaviours can sometimes be mistaken for other related phenomena such as territoriality and place dependence. In this case, to understand the role of place attachment and especially its intensity and occurrence during organizational change, a qualitative approach seems to be the appropriate method (Denzin & Lincoln, 2005). Moreover, qualitative research allows researchers to collect rich and in-depth information and to probe participants for further information (Warrick, 2005) that may not be apparent at first.

Research context

We conducted our study in nine Australian public and private organizations. As indicated in Table 16.1, employees from these nine organizations experienced various forms of organizational change. These included office relocation, organizational restructure, leadership change, technological change, and amalgamation of local government councils.

For example, in 2008, an Australian state government implemented changes to amalgamate local councils across the state. Through these amalgamations, the government sought to establish larger local government administrative units by combining two or more local councils. This amalgamation resulted in job losses for middle managers, reorganization of departments and work units, and extensive relocation of employees to the new (amalgamated) council office complex.

Additionally, the amalgamations created regional differences among employees working for the new councils. Indeed, most workers seemed not to view themselves as members of the newly established amalgamated councils, but continued to identify with their original (now defunct) council. This reluctance of employees to accept the reality that they were now working in the amalgamated council seemed to present managers with a further challenge on top of other more mundane issues. These issues include: a need to manage diverse cultures; the need to relocate employees from private offices to large open-plan offices (sometimes across different regions); the need to establish new reporting structures and work procedures; and the need to lay off redundant workers (who then often became angry ex-employees).

This change also came at a time when the state government itself was undergoing substantial political change, including a large-scale economy drive. These changes affected middle managers in both state and local government offices, who experienced increased job uncertainty, exacerbated by the need to relocate and/or to work in different teams.

Participants

We collected our data from 19 participants working in 9 different private and governmental organizations across 6 sectors: (1) a state government department, (2) a local council, (3) a public university, (4) a commercial law firm, (5) two healthcare organizations, and (6) three higher education institutes. Participants, whose ages ranged from 25 to 55, came from five continents (i.e. Australia, Africa,

TABLE 16.1 Social demographics of participants

No.	Interviewee	Age Group	Gender	Occupation	Tenure	Ethnicity	Industry	Organizational change types
1	Em01	30s	Male	Professional	2 years	American	Education	Office relocation
2	Em03	50s	Male	Professional	3 years	American	Healthcare	Leadership change
3	Em05	40s	Female	Clerical/Administrative	9 years	Asian	Education	Office relocation
4	Em06	30s	Female	Manager	3 years	Australian	Education	Office relocation
5	Em07	40s	Male	Professional	3 years	Asian	Healthcare	Office relocation
6	Em08	40s	Female	Manager	1 year	Asian	Healthcare	Organizational restructure
7	Em09	50s	Male	Manager	4 years	African	Government	Amalgamation of Councils
8	Em13	50s	Female	Clerical/Administrative	12 years	Australian	Government	Office relocation
9	Em15	30s	Female	Professional	3 years	Australian	Government	Office relocation
10	Em16	40s	Female	Professional	18 years	Australian	Government	Organizational restructure
11	Em17	50s	Male	Manager	10 years	Australian	Government	Office relocation
12	Em24	20s	Male	Professional	2 years	Asian	Legal services	Office relocation
13	Em25	40s	Female	Professional	14 years	Asian	Education	Leadership change
14	Em26	30s	Male	Professional	4 years	African	Government	Technological change
15	Em27	30s	Male	Professional	4 years	Australian	Government	Organizational restructure
16	Em28	40s	Male	Professional	10 years	African	Government	Leadership change
17	Em29	20s	Female	Professional	4 years	European	Education	Organizational restructure
18	Em30	30s	Female	Professional	8 years	African	Government	Organizational restructure
19	Em31	50s	Male	Professional	14 years	Australian	Education	Technological change

America, Europe and Asia). Forty-seven per cent were female and 47% worked in government organizations. Sixty-eight per cent were professionals (e.g. human resource consultants, researchers), 11% were clerical/administrative staff, and 21% were managers.

Participants' organizational tenure ranged from 1–18 years. We specifically selected employees who had experienced a recent or ongoing organizational change (Herscovitch & Meyer, 2002). This was because we were interested in understanding the processes through which place attachment affects individuals' attitudes and behaviours in the organizational change context. Table 16.1 displays the socio-demographic information of participants in this study.

Procedure

We contacted managers and human resource (HR) managers in each organization to act as our 'gatekeepers' (i.e. granting permission for the study in their organizations). We then scheduled meetings with our contact persons in each organization to ask for permission to conduct brief presentations and to distribute information sheets about the study. Notably, the role of managers in the study was limited to gatekeeping (i.e. no manager was involved in the sampling of participants). After we received access to the participating organizations, managers withdrew from being middle-person between the researchers and participants. Once all these precautions were in place, we then contacted the participants directly to explain the research purpose and to invite them to participate.

Participants interested in participating contacted us for either more information about the study's purpose, objectives, and methodology, or to book an interview appointment. The first author then scheduled a meeting with each participant and conducted the interviews, either in the employee's office (n=11) or a nearby meeting room (n=8). The interviews took between 30 and 60 minutes to complete.

The interviewer began with general questions about participants' experiences with their workspaces (e.g. what is it like to work in your physical workspace?). As the interview progressed, the interviewer asked participants to clarify or expand on their responses (e.g. 'How do you feel about interacting with others in your workspace?' 'How did you respond to the change process?' 'Can you give me examples of how you personalize your physical workspace?').

To conclude the interview, the interviewer asked participants questions about the impact of organizational changes on employees and their workspaces (e.g. 'Can you describe for me your ability in dealing with change in your physical workspace?' 'Can you describe for me how you control your physical workspace during the change process?' 'How did the change affect you and your workspace?'). At the end of each interview, the interviewer thanked the participant for their time. We recorded all the interviews and then subsequently transcribed them for quality, review, and verification.

Although the interviews were the main source of data collection, we also continued to collect data after the formal interviews. For example, in three large organizations, the first author participated in 'see for yourself' tours. He used these opportunities to observe office décor, symbols, and decorations (cf. Elsbach & Pratt, 2007) as well as to observe interactions between employees and co-workers. Although the tours were relatively brief, they nonetheless provided him with the opportunity to witness how employees were expressing themselves in relation to workspaces (Brown & Robinson, 2011). For example, in two organizations, the first author observed that all floors in the buildings of these organizations were secured and that visitors were only permitted access via monitored restricted-entry elevators. In these instances, the first author had to call each individual using a list of phone numbers with different colours (e.g. red, green, blue, etc.). The colours represented different teams (e.g. IT, human resources, finance, etc.) on the floor. This form of marking behaviour (Brown, 2009) was thus apparent to the researchers even before their interviews with participants.

After each visit, the first author recorded field notes as well as noting down the reactions and thoughts of the interviewees. These field notes provided contextual depth (Reay, Golden-Biddle, & Germann, 2006) in understanding employees' attachment to specific workspaces or place of work.

Analysis

We analysed the data in three stages (see Table 16.2). First, the first author browsed transcripts and briefly read paragraphs, sentences, and statements for each participant. Next, he generated initial codes from participants' statements, deriving meaning from these codes and ensuring codes were reliable by

TABLE 16.2 Data analysis levels and processes

Levels of analysis	Processes involved in each level of analysis

Level I:
   Content
   Analysis
	The primary focus at this first level was to get a general overview of how each participant felt and behaved in their workspace by browsing pages of transcripts, briefly reading responses to each question, statements, paragraphs, and taking note of length and number of pages of the content.

Familiarity with data	Transcribing data, reading and re-reading each transcript to note down initial ideas and grasp interviewee's perspective and understanding of the phenomenon.

Level II:
   Concept
   Analysis
	The focus of analysis at this level was on making sense of participants' statements of how they felt and behaved and deriving meaning out of statements and ensuring interpretations of meaning were reliable

Generating initial codes (In vivo codes)	Coding systematically by reading line by line, words, sentences, phrases, and paragraphs across the entire data set and collating data relevant to each code (e.g. feelings words such as happy, positive, and behaviours such as displayed trophies of hockey team, put jacket on chairs, created name tags, bring teddy bear to work).

Ensuring reliability of codes	*After coding three interview transcripts, the first author submitted coded transcripts to members of the research team and the research team had a 90-minute meeting to discuss coding procedures, initial codes identified, and ongoing data analysis.*
Level III: Thematic Analysis	*The focus of analysis at this last level was on translating Level II concepts into higher-order themes and cross-checking and validating those themes against specific statements of participants (Level I) as well as contacting a few participants to get initial reactions of themes.*
	Collating codes into potential themes and gathering all data relevant to each potential theme.
Identification of themes	*Checking themes in relation to coded extracts (Level I – in vivo) and*
Reviewing themes	*the entire data set (Level II). Member check with three research participants. Ongoing analysis to refine the specifics of each theme,*
Refining themes	*and the overall storyline of the analysis, generating concise names for each theme (i.e. Theme I – Workspace Identity, Theme II – Emotional Connection to Workspace, and Theme III – Maintain Closeness or Separation from Workspace).*

cross-checking with members of the research team. Finally, the research team discussed the initial codes to identify general themes from specific concepts. The research team also reviewed the themes with participants and organizational behaviour experts and refined themes continuously by checking them against participants' transcripts and feedback from experts. These procedures are similar to the methods commonly employed by other qualitative scholars (e.g. see Strauss & Corbin, 1998; Sandberg, 2000; Alvesson, 2003; Christainson et al., 2009; Griffiths & Gilly, 2012).

Lincoln and Guba (2000) suggest four factors are important in establishing integrity and trustworthiness of data: credibility, dependability, transferability, and confirmability (see Table 16.3). We consider that we addressed all four criteria in this research. For example, the criterion of transferability was achieved by collecting data from participants at different levels (i.e. employees, managers and co-workers) and occupational groups (e.g. IT administrators, HR consultants, researchers) from both public and private organizations (see Table 16.3 for strategies).

Results

Our analysis of participants' interviews revealed three significant themes. These themes concerned employees' place attachment, attitudes, and behaviours in the context of organizational change (and especially change in the physical environment). Specifically, the themes were: (1) employees' sense of identification with workspace; (2) emotional connections to workspace; and (3) how employees maintain closeness or separation from workspaces. We next discuss each of these themes in more detail.

TABLE 16.3 Strategies to ensure trustworthiness and integrity in present research

Criteria	Strategies
Credibility	Research was conducted in accordance with the university's code of research ethics and supervised by an ethics committee at the university. Approval was sought from the ethics committee at every stage of the data collection period to ensure adherence to guidelines of confidentiality, anonymity, storage of data, and voluntary participation.
	Acknowledgement of researcher bias and errors so that readers can take them into consideration when reading the findings of the research.
Transferability	Data were collected from participants at different levels (i.e. employees, managers, and co-workers), occupational groups (i.e. IT administrators, HR consultants, researchers, etc.), and both public and private organizations
Dependability	Data were collected using multiple research methods (i.e. interviews, non-participant observations, field notes) and informal discussions with academic and senior qualitative researchers from Australia, the USA, and UK. Although the interviews were the primary source of data for this study, observations, field notes, and informal discussions with experts enrich the researchers' understanding of the interview data and research contexts.
Confirmability	Researchers returned to some of the participants to ask them about the study's themes and whether these themes reflect participants' perceptions and experiences. Incorporate any changes offered by the participants into the final themes and findings of the study.

Workspace identity

Interviewees reported their experiences about their sense of identity, perceptions of attachment, close connection to organizations, and difficulty of managing separate identities in organizational change context. They noted in particular that their workspace forms part of their sense of identity. In effect, they saw their workspace as an extension of who they were as a person. It seems that these employees used their workspaces to express their views of themselves (i.e. who they are). The impression they conveyed is that they personally incorporated meaningful and valuable physical objects in workspaces into their overall sense of who they were. In this regard, seven interviewees (37%) reported explicitly that they identified with their workspace, as the following quote illustrates:

> My workspace is an extension of me and reflects who I am. I have pictures of my family, some quotes that I like, flowers, and African crafts.
>
> *(Em30, Female, Professional)*

One aspect of the identity theme that came out in the interviews was that employees appeared to establish close connections to their organization through their personal workspaces. In this regard, they told us that organizational change affected their sense of belonging to the organization and attachment to workspaces. In particular, interviewees described the effects of organizational change on their sense of belonging and attachment to workspaces.

Two (11%) mentioned specifically that the implementation of organizational change (e.g. mergers or departmental amalgamation) affected their sense of belongingness. As a corollary of this, when the small organization that these employees initially identified with became part of the larger organization, a sense of identification seemed to become lost. These participants noted that they became sceptical that the larger organization's values might not be consistent with the previous organization. This was evident in this excerpt from a government worker who was coping with organizational restructure:

> I guess for me, it is a change in our identity as a small organization becoming part of a bigger one that doesn't necessarily have the same organizational values as us.
>
> *(Em16, Female, 30s)*

In addition, organizational change also appeared to affect these employees' perceptions of attachment to their workspaces. Some (37%) found it difficult to connect closely to their workspaces during significant organizational change (e.g. mergers, leadership change, and organizational restructure). Employees told us how they identify less with workspaces following significant organizational changes (e.g. leadership change in the organization). For example:

> I identify less with it. Definitely! I don't care for it as much. Yeah; so although I think it's mine, I don't value it. I don't value it as much. I am not as dedicated to my work.
>
> *(Em03, Male, 50s)*

Finally, three participants (16%) told us about the difficulty of managing separate identities that resulted from amalgamation. For these workers, managing separate identities required them to work in two places (i.e. with two different workspaces). Participants mentioned in particular that they had to use two passwords or to work in multiple teams during the transitional period of the merger. One worker whose organization was undergoing a merger of two departments explained her challenge to manage separate identities and how it affects her sense of place attachment, as follows:

> We are still struggling at the moment in terms of how to define each centre. We are thinking of putting posters or pictures, maybe to say like this is YYYY and this is centre for XXXX. To divide things, you know, to make it more, you know to have an identity that makes it distinct. But for the meantime, it's been quite difficult.
>
> *(Em08, Female, 40s)*

Emotional connections to the workspace

Organizational change (e.g. office relocation, mergers) also affects individuals' attitude and feeling about their workspaces, including feelings of happiness, uncertainty, worry, and loss of attachment to workspaces. Participants reported both positive and negative emotions. Positive emotion employees mentioned that they experienced as a result of organizational change included happiness (e.g. 'I am quite happy with my physical workspace') and feelings of security, comfort, and relief. In contrast, negative emotion employees expressed included worry, uncertainty, frustration, upset, annoyance, dread, fear, and unhappiness (e.g. 'I feel that I have no control and unsure if I can continue to use my current workspace or will be moved to another floor').

Some participants (21%) indicated that they were worried and uncertain when they learned that the implementation of change would affect the location and form of their workspace. This feeling of uncertainty appeared to have affected these individuals' beliefs and confidence in coping with change in their workspaces. Employees told us that the organizational change severed the emotional connection they had with their workspaces. As a result, these participants noted that they began to feel unsure about themselves (e.g. 'I wasn't sure I could do what was required because of the change'). One executive assistant, whose organization had experienced a major office relocation, described how she responded to her loss of attachment to workspace (when the change was announced), as follows:

> Before we moved from building XXXX to here, we were a bit worried; I was a bit worried because this is very open-planned. We have to tour over here before we moved in once and it's just like you mingled with the others so you think you will get disturbed a lot.
>
> *(Em05, Female, Office relocation)*

Another employee, whose organization experienced changes in its leadership team, reported similarly that she felt less valued in her organization when she found she had no workspace to call her own:

> I'm fairly flexible as a casual academic, but it annoys me nonetheless not to have our own little space where we can even sit down to relax in between our teaching gaps. We felt less valued by the workplace, and realized we are not at all important as casual academics.
>
> *(Em25, Female, Leadership change)*

Not all employees appeared to consider disruptions and loss of attachment to their workspaces to be negative, however. Some employees (32%) described their attitudes about their workspace during organizational change as positive; that they were in fact happy with their new workspace. These individuals' relationship with their workspaces seemed to be enhanced through the organizational change. These participants experienced stronger ties to their workspaces and expressed a range of emotions including happiness, pride, feelings of comfort, security, and self-worth – as the following quote illustrates:

> I was given an assigned desk and a room (that can be locked). I felt like I possess an asset which gave me the feeling of security, maybe even an important/self-worth.
>
> *(Em29, Employee, Education)*

Other employees we interviewed (21%) reported that changes to their workspace had no noticeable effect on them. An executive assistant in her fifties noted that changes in workspaces do not make her happy if managers did not treat her or co-workers with respect:

> It doesn't matter how many posters you put up or green plants you buy, we lost green plants years ago, except for staff room and, yes, it is, I don't believe what colour you paint the walls, it's going to make people happier towards each other. You need to work on the people.
>
> *(Em13, Employee, Office relocation)*

Maintaining closeness or separation from a workspace

The final theme of this study concerns the closeness or separation employees have with their workspaces. For some of the employees we interviewed, being close to workspaces seemed to be very important to them. These participants noted that, when they maintain close relationship to workspaces, this reminds them of their home and being close to family – as one manager indicates:

> I suppose in some way I treat it like the way I treat my home. I take pride in it. I think I am quite welcoming with people coming in. We have a lot of outsiders coming in, so even though it's a space I work in and part of it is essentially mine, I try to make it a welcoming place that other people come into. I have personal effects like some photographs you know. I have some things to add my own personality specifically to my workspace.
>
> *(Em06, Female, Manager)*

In contrast, three participants (16%) told us that their workspaces were separate from who they were as individuals. For example, one administrative assistant working for a large public organization described her experience of keeping workspace and home activities separate:

> I don't personalize my desk space as I keep moving from project to project so all personal objects have been removed, not that I ever had very many to begin with. I like to keep personal and work separate.
>
> *(Em13, Female, Clerical/Administrative assistant)*

Another manager commented on separating home and workspace:

> I treat my office as my office and is not my house. I go there in the morn-
> ing, when I finish work, I don't, I never take my computer around and if I
> leave my office at 7 in the evening, I turn off my work phone until the next
> morning at 7. I make a very clear distinction between private time and office.
> So, I clearly separate my work.
>
> *(Em09, Male, Manager)*

Discussion

Our aim for this study was to understand the role of place attachment in influencing employees' attitudes and behaviours in the context of organizational change
involving changes to office location and/or configuration. The question we sought
to address was, 'What is the relationship between organizational change involving
changes to the physical environment and employees' place attachment, attitudes,
and behaviours?' Based on the results of our interviews and observations, we found
three broad themes. These were: (1) workspace identity, (2) emotional connections to workspace, and (3) maintaining closeness or separation from a workspace.

Workplace identity

The first theme we found related to employees' sense of identity to workspace in
the context of organizational change. Employees described their sense of identity
in two ways. First, they perceived their workspace as an extension of who they are
as a person. One government worker indicated, for example, that her workspace
was an 'extension of me and reflects who I am'.

The employees in other organizations related similar experiences of identifying with workspace. Place attachment theory suggests that an individual's sense
of place fulfils fundamental human needs (e.g. belonging, privacy, sense of place,
self-efficacy). This sense of place may consists of an individual's sense of identity,
attachment, and dependence to important and sacred places (Tuan, 1974; Relph,
1976; Jorgensen & Stedman, 2001).

In addition, psychological ownership theory (see Pierce, Kostova, & Dirks,
2003) suggests that individuals become psychologically tied to objects and feel possessive towards these objects. This feeling of possessiveness creates a special bond
between individuals and objects – such that employees see their possessions (including their workspace) as part of their extended self (Belk, 1988). Moreover, when
an individual's psychological ownership increases for an object, their sense of self
and object, though distinct, will increasingly overlap. Consequently, such employees may not distinguish between self and their possessions (Dirks, Cummings, &
Pierce, 1996; Pierce, Kostova, & Dirks, 2001). Indeed, for some employees we
interviewed, workspace appeared also to represent an important form of their ethnic identity (e.g. African, Australian Aboriginal, Asian, etc.). We speculate that

these individuals may connect to a place in the sense that it comes to represent who they are (Scannell & Gifford, 2010).

Research by Elsbach (2003) suggests further that employees may affirm their identities at work through physical artefacts and salient behaviours such as seating preferences, engaging in sports, aggressive body language, and public eating habits. In particular, individuals may affirm distinctiveness through displays of physical artefacts such as photos, mementos, equipment, and furniture (Wells & Thelen, 2002; Brown, 2009). Thus, organizational change (e.g. office relocation, mergers and acquisitions) as well as trends towards more non-territorial work arrangements (e.g. hoteling, hot-desking) are likely to create identity threats for many employees (Elsbach, 2003; Brown et al., 2005). This is because such individuals' affirmation of their identities (e.g. parent, researcher, manager) may depend on their ability to personalize their workspace in order to accentuate the central dimensions of their identities and sense of distinctiveness in the workplace (Elsbach, 2003).

Many of the employees we interviewed also told us that they felt connected and attached to workspaces. Nonetheless, in times of organizational change, some employees (16%) in our study told us that they struggled to maintain their sense of identity. For instance, one manager narrated her struggle to manage separate identities. During a merger of two hospital research centres, this manager was able to maintain her status as a manager in her existing organization. After the merger, however, she found herself working on projects across the facilities of the two hospitals. Thus, while she continued to associate with both hospitals (because she was working on projects in both), her role as manager was not constant across both hospitals. She mentioned that this struggle of managing separate identities was a challenge for her and co-workers in her organization because it affected their use of workspaces, including creating passwords on workstations, working in multiple teams, and personalizing workspaces with personal items (e.g. posters, flowers, awards).

Place identity research by Rooney et al. (2010) tells us that an individual's identification with the physical environments influences perceptions of organizational change. That is, employees at various levels of organizational hierarchy (e.g. managers, supervisors, employees) tend to evaluate change differently. In this regard, lower-level employees are more likely to report feelings of alienation and dislocation (Speller, Lyons, & Twigger-Ross, 2002), while middle and senior managers do not see change as a threat to their sense of identity. This is because, as Rooney et al. (2010) noted, middle and senior managers do not draw their professional identity from a particular location but from many sources (e.g. family, communities of practice, professional groups). Yet Ashforth and Mael (1989) suggest that individuals who compartmentalize their multiple identities may also connect with double standards such as apparent hypocrisy and selective forgetting. In this respect, multiple identities, especially given organizational change and lack of privacy in the open-plan office, may well have a negative influence on employees' wellbeing.

Additionally, the finding of sense of identity in relation to employees' workspaces is consistent with previous research on loss of self-identity during organizational change, natural disasters, displacements, wars, or relocations (Fried, 1963; Fullilove, 1996). In particular, some individuals in the present study found it difficult to manage their sense of identity because of organizational change (e.g. merger). Their struggle to manage their separate identities also appeared to influence their use of workspaces – including personalizing their workspaces.

Emotional connections

The second main theme to emerge from our study concerned employees' emotional connection to their workspaces. In general, our interviewees felt connected to workspaces and were positive about organizational changes (i.e. office relocation, restructure, mergers). This often resulted in positive outcomes (e.g. new workspace, improved working conditions, new project teams). Place attachment research by Scannell and Gifford (2010) tells us that connections to place can be affective, cognitive, and/or behavioural. Individuals' attachment to places can sometimes lead them to incorporate these places into their self-definitions. That is, self-definition occurs 'when individuals draw similarities between self and place and incorporate cognitions about the physical environment (memories, thoughts, values, preferences, categorizations) into their self-definitions' (p. 3).

In our study, employees who had a positive view of the organizational change (e.g. office relocation) also displayed positive attitudes and feelings about their workspace (e.g. happy or excited about workspace). One employee mentioned in particular that she felt a sense of self-worth after she was assigned a desk following an organizational restructure. In contrast, a female employee who experienced leadership change in her organization reported that she felt less valued by the workplace and did not feel important because she was a casual employee with no permanent workspace. This finding suggests a relationship between the themes of the study.

In particular, employees allocated workspaces either before or after the organizational change seem to associate strong emotions (e.g. feeling of security, sense of self-worth, happiness) to these workspaces. Conversely, employees who work in unallocated workspaces appeared to feel less valued, frustrated, and annoyed because there was no permanent space for them. In this regard, Elsbach (2003) suggests that managers underappreciate the value of office space for affirming their employees' egos, status, and distinctiveness. In the present study, we found that many employees appeared to have worked for ten or more years with their organizations as casual workers with no permanent workspaces.

Although many employees expressed positive feelings about workspaces, we also found four (21%) who reported that they were worried and uncertain about the organizational changes they were experiencing, especially when they learned that the implementation of change would affect their workspace. This feeling of uncertainty tended to affect these individuals' beliefs and confidence in coping with changes in workspaces. In this regard, our findings are consistent with the work of Ashford (1988), who found that perceived uncertainty and fears about the impact of transitions (i.e. divestiture) tend to relate to employees' experiences of stress. In contrast, affective feelings towards one's workspace tend to relate significantly to identity-oriented marking territorial behaviours and psychological ownership (Brown et al., 2005).

In other words, it seems that individuals who hold positive feelings (e.g. excitement, enthusiasm, pride) towards their (old or new) workspace also tend to feel strong feelings of ownership of the workspace. Consequently, these individuals seek to personalize the workspace. In times of organizational change, however, this sense of workspace identity is normally threatened (Elsbach, 2003) because of greater disruption, dislocation, and alienation (Rooney et al., 2010).

These findings appear to echo research by Oreg and Sverdlik (2011), who showed that two factors (i.e. individuals' personal orientation towards change and orientation towards change agents) appear to affect individuals' ambivalence towards imposed organizational change. That is, the relationship between employees' dispositional resistance to change (i.e. negative attitudes towards change) and ambivalence towards change is positive when employees have positive orientation towards change agents (e.g. high trust in management). The reverse outcome is also true when employees have negative orientation towards change agents. Our findings extend these concepts to the specific context of employees' emotional reactions to workspace change

Maintaining closeness or separation from a workspace

The final theme we found in the present study was participants' desire to maintain closeness or separation from workspaces. In general, we identified that some employees maintain close connection to workspaces because these places remind them of home and family. On the other hand, others report keeping home and workspace separate. These findings corroborate similar findings from recent studies on place attachment and collaborative workspaces.

In one such study, Irving, Kromah, Ayoko, and Ashkanasy (2015) examined employees' place attachment and interactions in a purpose-built 'collaborative precinct'. The researchers collected observational data over 6 weeks, including 40 semi-structured interviews with employees who had moved from 17 smaller sites into the precinct. Whereas the employer intended that the move would foster inter-organizational collaboration, results indicate that, after two years, the precinct appears to have done little to improve collaboration, and that, 'on the whole, people stay to themselves and their own area, do their work and then go home'. Additionally, many employees still expressed strong feelings of attachment to their old sites, and used metaphors that likened the move to 'a death in the family. It was a tragedy, because I really liked working out where we were.' While managers made few attempts to generate a sense of community at the precinct or to help employees identify with the precinct, employees continued to maintain connections with their old colleagues, rather than to form new connections. Altogether, these results suggest that place attachment influences employees' experience of workspace change and their reluctance to form new collaborative relationships in the precinct.

In sum, the results of the present study provide preliminary findings to understand the role of place attachment in influencing employees' attitudes and behaviours about workspaces in the context of organizational change.

Implications

Although place attachment has been studied in other disciplines such as environmental psychology and sociology (Lewicka, 2011), the concept has rarely been applied in organizational behaviour (Ayoko, Ashkanasy, & Jehn, 2009). We thus extend work on place attachment within the organizational behaviour literature and show that employees' place attachment can lead to unintended consequences (Scannell & Gifford, 2010) in the context of organizational and workspace change. Managers and workspace designers need to consider employee place attachment when implementing organizational change initiatives or changes to workspaces. Based on our findings, it seems safe to conclude that employees are unlikely to adopt new behaviour associated with a workspace change (e.g. collaboration, working with new people) if they still feel attached to their old workspace and the identities and relationships associated with that space. The main implication of our findings is that, to minimize the negative effect of place attachment during change, managers need to assist employees to deal with the trauma of ending connections to the old space (Brown & Perkins, 1992), while helping them to bond with the new workspaces even before they move.

Conclusion

Our findings in the current study suggest that organizational change has a significant influence on employees' sense of place attachment, attitudes, and behaviours. Specifically, our results demonstrate the importance of seriously considering employees' sense of identity, feelings, and sense of attachment to workspaces and place of work. Based on our findings, we conclude that place attachment is an important factor that seems to influence employees' attitudes and behaviours in organizational change settings.

References

Alvesson, M. (2003). Beyond neopositivists, romantics and localists: A reflexive approach to interviews in organizational research. *Academy of Management Review, 28*, 13–33.

Ashford, S. J. (1988). Individual strategies for coping with stress during organizational transitions. *Journal of Applied Behavioral Science, 24*, 19–36.

Ashforth, B. E., & Mael, F. (1989). Social identity theory and the organization. *Academy of Management Review, 14*, 20–39.

Ashkanasy, N. M., Zerbe, W. J., & Härtel, C. E. J. (eds). (2002). *Managing Emotions in a Changing Workplace*. Armonk, NY: M. E. Sharpe.

Ayoko, O. B., Ashkanasy, N. M., & Jehn, K. A. (2009). *Workplace Territorial Behaviors: A Conceptual Model of the Impact of Employees' Territorial Behaviors on Conflict and Outcomes in Diverse Teams*. Paper presented at the 22nd Annual Conference of IACM, Kyoto, Japan.

Belk, R. W. (1988). Possessions and the extended self. *Journal of Consumer Research*, *15*, 139–168.

Brennan, A., Chugh, J. S., & Kline, T. (2002). Traditional versus open office design: A longitudinal field study. *Environment and Behavior*, *34*, 279–299.

Brown, B. B., & Perkins, D. D. (1992). Disruptions in place attachment. In I. Altman & S. M. Low (eds), *Place Attachment* (pp. 279–304). New York: Plenum Press.

Brown, B., Perkins, D. D., & Brown, G. (2003). Place attachment in a revitalizing neighborhood: Individual and block levels of analysis. *Journal of Environmental Psychology*, *23*, 259–271.

Brown, G. (2009). Claiming a corner at work: Measuring employee territoriality in their workspaces. *Journal of Environmental Psychology*, *29*, 44–52.

Brown, G., Lawrence, T. B., & Robinson, S. L. (2005). Territoriality in organizations. *Academy of Management Review*, *30*, 577–594.

Brown, G., & Robinson, S. L. (2011). Reactions to territorial infringement. *Organization Science*, *22*, 210–224.

Christianson, M. K., Farkas, M. T., Sutcliffe, K. M., & Weick, K. E. (2009). Learning through rare events: Significant interruptions at the Baltimore & Ohio Railroad Museum. *Organization Science*, *20*, 846–860.

Denzin, N. K., & Lincoln, Y. S. (eds). (2005). *The Discipline and Practice of Qualitative Research* (2nd ed.). Thousands Oaks, CA: Sage.

Dirks, K. T., Cummings, L. L., & Pierce, J. L. (1996). Psychological ownership in organizations: Conditions under which individuals promote and resist change. In R. W. W. W. A. Pasmore (ed.), *Research in Organizational Change and Development* (Vol. *9*, pp. 1–23). Greenwich, CT: JAI Press.

Elsbach, K. D. (2003). Relating physical environment to self-categorizations: Identity threat and affirmation in a non-territorial office space. *Administrative Science Quarterly*, *48*, 622–654.

Elsbach, K. D., & Pratt, M. G. (2007). The physical environment in organizations. *Academy of Management Annals*, *1*(1), 181–224.

Fried, M. (1963). Grieving for a lost home. In L. J. Duhl (ed.), *The Urban Condition: People and Policy in the Metropolis* (pp. 124–152). New York: Simon & Schuster.

Fullilove, M. T. (1996). Psychiatric implications of displacement: Contributions from the psychology of place. *American Journal of Psychiatry*, *153*, 1516–1523.

Goel, L., Johnson, N. A., Junglas, I., & Ives, B. (2011). From space to place: Precincting users intentions to return to virtual worlds. *MIS Quarterly*, *35*, 749–771.

Griffiths, M. A., & Gilly, M. C. (2012). Dibs! Customer territorial behaviors. *Journal of Service Research*, *15*, 131–149.

Hedge, A. (1982). The open-plan office: A systematic investigation of employee reactions to their work environment. *Environment and Behavior*, *14*, 519–542.

Herold, D. M., Fedor, D. B., & Caldwell, S. D. (2007). Beyond change management: A multilevel investigation of contextual and personal influences on employees' commitment to change. *Journal of Applied Psychology*, *92*, 942–951.

Herscovitch, L., & Meyer, J. P. (2002). Commitment to organizational change: Extension of a three-component model. *Journal of Applied Psychology*, *87*, 474–487.

Hidalgo, M. C., & Hernández, B. (2001). Place attachment: Conceptual and empirical questions. *Journal of Environmental Psychology*, *21*, 273–281.

Higgs, M., & Rowland, D. (2007). All changes great and small: Exploring approaches to change and its leadership. *Journal of Change Management, 5*, 121–151.

Irving, G. L., Kromah, M. D., Ayoko, O. B., & Ashkanasy, N. M. (2015). *Organizational Change and Unintended Consequences: The Role of Place Attachment.* Paper presented at the Society for Industrial and Organizational Psychology, Philadelphia, USA.

Johns, G. (2006). The essential impact of context on organizational behavior. *Academy of Management Review, 31*, 386–408.

Jorgensen, B. S., & Stedman, R. C. (2001). Sense of place as an attitude: Lakeshore owners' attitudes toward their properties. *Journal of Environmental Psychology, 21*, 233–248.

Lewicka, M. (2011). Place attachment: How far have we come in the last 40 years? *Journal of Environmental Psychology, 31*, 207–230.

Lincoln, Y. S., & Guba, E. G. (eds). (2000). *Paradigmatic Controversies, Contradictions, and Emerging Confluences* (2nd ed.). Thousand Oaks, CA: Sage.

Low, S. M., & Altman, I. (1992). Place attachment: A conceptual inquiry. In I. Altman, & S. M. Low (eds), *Place Attachment* (pp. 1–12). New York: Plenum Press.

Miller, V. D., Johnson, J. R., & Grau, J. (1994). Antecedents to willingness to participate in a planned organizational change. *Journal of Applied Communication Research, 22*, 59–80.

Milligan, M. J. (2003). Loss of site: Organizational site moves as organizational deaths. *International Journal of Sociology and Social Policy, 23*, 115–152.

Oreg, S., & Sverdlik, N. (2011). Ambivalence toward imposed change: The conflict between dispositional resistance to change and the orientation toward the change agent. *Journal of Applied Psychology, 96*, 337–349.

Oreg, S., Vakola, M., & Armenakis, A. (2011). Change recipients' reactions to organizational change: A 60-year review of quantitative studies. *Journal of Applied Behavioral Science, 47*, 461–524.

Pierce, J. L., Kostova, T., & Dirks, K. T. (2001). Toward a theory of psychological ownership in organizations. *Academy of Management Review, 26*, 298–310.

Pierce, J. L., Kostova, T., & Dirks, K. T. (2003). The state of psychological ownership: Integrating and extending a century of research. *Review of General Psychology, 7*, 84–107.

Podsakoff, P. M., MacKenzie, S. B., & Podsakoff, N. P. (2012). Sources of method bias in social science research and recommendations on how to control it. *Annual Review of Psychology, 63*(1), 539–569.

Probst, G., & Raisch, S. (2005). Organizational crisis: The logic of failure. *Academy of Management Review, 19*, 90–105.

Reay, T., Golden-Biddle, K., & Germann, K. (2006). Legitimizing a new role: Small wins and microprocesses of change. *Academy of Management Journal, 49*, 977–998.

Relph, E. (1976). *Place and Placelessness.* London: Pion Limited.

Ricciotti, H. A., Armstrong, W., Yaari, G., Campion, S., Pollard, M., & Golen, T. H. (2014). Lessons from Google and Apple: Creating an open workplace in an academic medical department to foster innovation and collaboration. *Academic Medicine, 89*, 15.

Rooney, D., Paulsen, N., Callan, V. J., Brabant, M., Gallois, C., & Jones., E. (2010). A new role for place identity in managing organizational change. *Management Communication Quarterly, 24*, 44–73.

Sandberg, J. (2000). Understanding human competence at work: An interpretative approach. *Academy of Management Journal, 43*, 9–25.

Scannell, L., & Gifford, R. (2010). Defining place attachment: A tripartite organizing framework. *Journal of Environmental Psychology, 21*, 1–10.

Speller, G. M., Lyons, E., & Twigger-Ross, C. L. (2002). A community in transition: The relationship between spatial change and identity process. *Social Psychological Review, 4*, 39–58.

Strauss, A., & Corbin, J. (1998). *Basics of Qualitative Research: Grounded Theory Procedures and Techniques.* London: Sage.

Tuan, Y. (1974). *Topophilia: A Study of Environmental Perception, Attitudes, and Values.* Englewood Cliffs, NJ: Prentice Hall.

Warrick, D. D. (ed.). (2005). *Launch: Assessment and Action Planning* (2nd ed.). San Francisco, CA: John Wiley & Sons, Inc.

Wells, M. M., & Thelen, L. (2002). What does your workspace say about you? The influence of personality, status, and workspace on personalization. *Environment and Behavior, 34*, 300–321.

Zoller, F. A., & Boutellier, R. (2013). Design principles for innovative workspaces to increase efficiency in pharmaceutical R&D: Lessons learned from the Novartis campus. *Drug Discovery Today, 18*, 318–322.

17

CONCLUSIONS AND RECOMMENDATIONS FOR MANAGING THE PHYSICAL ENVIRONMENT OF WORK

Oluremi B. Ayoko and Neal M. Ashkanasy

Over the past few decades, researchers have begun to pay more attention to the context of organizational behaviour (e.g. see Cappelli & Sherer, 1991; Johns, 2006; Maaninen-Olsson & Müllern, 2009). In essence, this interest stems from a realization that the work context has the potential capacity to interact with personal, group, and organizational properties to influence outcomes for the individual, team, and organization. This focus was first taken up in disciplines such as environmental psychology and behaviour (e.g. Brown, Lawrence, & Robinson, 2005; Wineman, 1982), facilities management (Roelofsen, 2002), and education (Bohr, 2000). In the field of organizational behaviour (OB), however, the physical environment of work (PEW: buildings, furnishings, equipment, lighting, air quality, and the arrangements of these objects) has largely been ignored (Ayoko, Ashkanasy & Jehn, 2014; Ashkanasy, Ayoko & Jehn, 2014; Brown et al., 2005). The chapters in the present volume are intended to redress this omission. In this concluding chapter, we summarize some of the main conclusions and draw out some recommendations for managing the PEW, with particular references to open-plan offices (OPOs).

Throughout the book, authors note that OPOs represent a double-edged sword that can facilitate communication, collaboration, and support design thinking practices as well as creativity (Elsbach & Stigliani, Chapter 2) while impacting strategic management tools such as branding (Bodin Danielsson, Chapter 3). The PEW also affects employee psychological ownership and territorial behaviours with positive and negative consequences (Pierce & Brown, Chapter 4). Yet, the PEW, especially in the context of OPOs, is full of distractions and diminished privacy (Kim & de Dear, 2013). In Chapter 5, Kim and de Dear reiterate that the benefits of OPO (e.g. enhanced interaction between employees) are outweighed by penalties of noise and decreased privacy. Altogether, and as Ashkanasy et al. (2014) point out, findings from studies on PEW remain contradictory. As such, this constitutes a puzzle that both researchers and practitioners seek to resolve.

Irrespective of the apparent tension on the effects of the PEW (especially the OPO) on organizational behaviours and outcomes, organizations are currently adopting OPOs to accommodate their employees because it is cost-effective (Elsbach & Pratt, 2009). For example, in Australia employees of the largest communications company, Telstra, have just moved into an activity-based workplace (ABW, see Hoendervanger, de Been, van Yperen, Mobach, & Albers, 2016) in one of their locations, purportedly providing the organization some significant cost savings.[1] Nevertheless, the trend in contemporary organizations' adoption of the OPO as the primary accommodation for their employees has become a challenge for organizational leadership and managers. In this concluding chapter, we discuss the major challenges a manager might face in managing the physical environment of work and especially the open-plan office.

Issues in the PEW

Managing noise

One of the primary challenges that face employees working in an open-plan office is noise. Several researchers (e.g. Banbury & Berry, 2005; Bodin Danielsson & Bodin, 2009) have reported background noise as the most frequent complaint from open-plan office workers. Banbury and Berry (2005) especially demonstrate that 90% of their sample reported that their concentration was impaired in the open-plan office. This form of noise comes from ringing telephones and employee conversations resulting in employees' annoyance and frustration (Sundstrom, Town, Rice, Osborn, & Brill, 1994). This finding is nonetheless unsurprising in view of the fact that the concept of the OPO intrinsically invites some level of acoustical compromise. In effect, office designers seek to trade off the conflicting requirements of good speech and good speech privacy within the PEW (Banbury & Berry, 2005; Bodin Danielsson, 2008; Bodin Danielsson & Bodin, 2009). In this regard, it seems that managers expect good communication to be tempered with a risk of interruption and distraction from background noise.

Evans and Johnson (2000) argue that exposure to uncontrollable noise is associated with a fall in task motivation, resulting in a loss of personal control over their workspace (Brand & Smith, 2005; Bodin Danielsson & Bodin, 2009). Kim and de Dear (2013) demonstrate further that noise is linked with overstimulation resulting in workers' negative reactions towards their PEW. This negativity then affects individual performance on tasks, especially those requiring cognitive processing (Smith-Jackson & Klein, 2009).

Clearly, managers of employees in OPO settings must attend to noise. One of the ways in which noise may be managed is to address it at the office design and construction stages. Architects, for example, could use sound masking to lessen speech intelligibility in workstations and cover room surfaces and partitions with sound-absorptive materials to decrease speech sound levels (cf. Venetjoki, Kaarlela-Tuomaala, Keskinen, & Hongisto, 2006). Hongisto and Haapakangas (2008) point out that sound-masking systems, which add neutral background noise to mask disturbing noises or speech, need to be designed carefully so the level and spectrum of the noises they create may be adaptable to the acoustical conditions of a specific office area while spreading evenly throughout office space. This should in turn assist in effectively masking office noise but not be disturbing itself. Similarly, the use of higher dividing panels to separate workspace, or working in enclosed offices, can also serve as an effective improvement measure (Zhang, Kang, & Jiao, 2012).

Also from the stage of design and construction, it is important to think through how the PEW might also serve to shield office workers from undesirable stimuli. To do this, managers need to provide tall, enclosed, or frosted glass sound-insulating partitions between open workplaces, as well as textile floor coverings, acoustic ceiling tiles, and printer cabinets. In addition, high-tenure employees who do complex jobs have specific needs for privacy and these need to be considered when designing offices (de Croon, Sluiter, Kuijer, & Frings-Dresen, 2005).

Besides controlling ambient sound to create ideal acoustic conditions, disturbing noises (e.g. speech, printer noise) also need to be controlled. The sources of disturbing noises can be isolated and, with a good office layout, sound travelling between workstations can be blocked. For example, partitions that are high enough block noise travelling and even affect distribution of light and perceptions of air flow in office areas. Moreover, larger workstations decrease sound travelling to other workstations. The orientation of workstation openings and their arrangement as groups of workstations can also affect noise travelling around the office. In adjoining workstations, office occupants should be seated in positions that they face away from each other while working, thus, the speech is directed away from neighbouring workstations. Additionally, to isolate the sources of disturbing noises, some strategies are to place shared, noise-generating sources – such as meeting rooms and printers – away from office occupants who do demanding jobs or to position shared sources along a main path, and place workstations along less noisy paths (Charles et al., 2004).

Managing privacy and distractions in the PEW

Another frequent complaint from employees who work in OPOs is the lack of privacy. Privacy is described as an idea of control over the social contact and access to information (Justa & Golan, 1977), seclusion, withdrawal, and avoidance of interaction (Rashid & Zimring, 2008), while layout includes the number and groupings of workstations, which influence communications and privacy at work. Privacy also involves a sense of being on display (O'Neill, 1994). It may also be described as a psychological state and a feature of the physical environment (Sundstrom, Burt, & Kamp, 1980).

In this case, the large open office seems to be the major culprit. In a recent study, for example, Seddigh et al. (2015) found that normal working conditions in comparison with quiet conditions have a less negative effect on performance, especially on cognitively demanding tasks in smaller open-plan offices compared with larger settings. In particular, the benefit of larger open-plan offices in comparison with smaller when it comes to lower cost in both construction and maintenance might not be as advantageous when adding employees' performance loss to the calculation (see also Bodin Danielsson, 2008). Therefore, companies and organizations would likely gain more from creating smaller OPO environments when choosing among open-plan office types.

Underlying the concept of privacy is the notion that employees try to maintain an optimal level of social contact, and dissatisfaction arises from being in a situation that is far away from what an individual considers as optimal (Sundstrom et al., 1980), leading in turn to a feeling of overcrowding. Nevertheless, privacy may function to protect personal autonomy when providing an emotional outlet (e.g. withdrawal), while allowing for self-evaluation, opportunity to synthesize information, and decision-making (Pastalan, 1970). Rashid and Zimring (2008) also argue that an OPO layout of a workplace may reduce an individual's sense of privacy (a psychological need) and, therefore, their task performance and wellbeing may suffer.

On the one hand, psychological privacy refers to a sense of control over access to self or group members, and includes control over transmission of information about oneself to others and control over inputs from others (Altman, 1975; Margulis, 1977). On the other hand, the notion of architectural privacy refers to the visual and acoustic isolation supplied by an environment (such that a work area is completely enclosed by soundproof walls with lockable doors) and therefore inherently embodies a high degree of architectural privacy. In this case, a large room with many people where individuals occupy an undivided space would give minimal privacy. In this regard, Sundstrom and his colleagues (1980) argue that architectural privacy contributes to psychological privacy because employees in separate individual rooms with a door can control their accessibility to others more easily than those in open-plan offices. In three separate studies, Sundstrom and his team found that architectural privacy consistently links with psychological privacy.

Findings from more recent research in this area are not very different from those of Sundstrom et al. (1980). For example, Lee, Lee, Jeon, Zhang, and Kang (2016) found that noise sensitivity affects speech privacy, and that the longer the exposure to noise, the less satisfaction employees report. Sundstrom, Herbert, and Brown (1982) also found that speech privacy is associated with satisfaction with environment and job satisfaction. Employees also show a greater degree of satisfaction as the amount of privacy increases in offices, and a loss of privacy is associated with decreased opportunities for feedback, friendship formation, and a decrease in satisfaction (see Brennan, Chugh, & Kline, 2002; Wineman, 1986).

Altman (1975) argues, moreover, that although privacy regulation is a culturally universal capability, people from culture to culture use specific strategies and behaviours to control interaction. Therefore, regulation of privacy may be culturally distinct regarding the particular psychological and behavioural strategies used to regulate it. For example, in Western cultures, office employees systematically use doors to regulate access by others. Thus, when they wish to be alone, on the one hand, they choose to close their door and thereby use the physical environment to isolate themselves from others. When they prefer to be accessible, on the other hand, they partially open the door. Therefore, depending on their privacy preferences the 'closed' or 'open' part of the physical environmental circle predominates. Altman (1975) argues that some cultures do not use such a strategy; in fact, their 'environmental circle' often has the open part occupying the largest area.

In terms of managing privacy in the PEW, Rashid and Zimring (2008) argue that organizational factors such as leadership play a critical role. In this respect, unit culture may need to be built around the issue of privacy such that norms, values, beliefs, and expectations of the people in the same work unit should be shared. Hedge (1982) points out further that the connection of physical enclosure with privacy may be dependent on the type of job. In this regard, Block and Stokes (1989) found that employees working on more complex tasks are more satisfied with working in private offices than those working on simple tasks. This suggests that managers need to manage the notion of privacy especially in the PEW. We therefore argue that one way to reduce the challenge of privacy at the PEW may be to group employees working on similar tasks together. This should not only facilitate informal communication but it would also mean that those working on complex tasks should attain a greater level of privacy. In an open-plan office, more side rooms could be provided where employees working on complex work may also work in private when they need to. Cangelosi and Lemoine (1988) argue further that issues of privacy need to be managed in the PEW, especially in OPOs, including considerations of flexible furniture.

Office norms and rules of behaviour

To minimize noise and distractions, managers may need to encourage their employees in OPO settings to set up and to agree upon standard norms and rules for behaviours that respect other co-workers in an OPO setting. Banbury and Berry (2005) suggest that a policy can inspire employees to be mindful of how loud they speak, the need to use headphones (to listen to music and radio), as well as the need to be cognisant of the noise they make. In this respect, managers need to establish etiquettes for working such an environment from the onset of the movement to the install of OPOs (Fox, 1998). The policy should require employees to respond to private phone calls and short conversations in breakout rooms or a designated room for taking private calls. Other practical norms in OPOs should include using low speech levels whenever possible and not leaving their mobile phones ringing on work desks. Additionally, organizational policies in this area should confirm that all conference calls are conducted in conference rooms with closed doors and speaker phone usage at workers' desks should be discouraged (Smith-Jackson & Klein, 2009).

Moreover, telephone calls can be diverted to a central answering service if they are left unanswered after three to five rings, while headphones can be provided for employees to use when they need to concentrate on the task before them.

To complement this, the configurations should allow some private rooms where employee can withdraw and complete tasks needing privacy or high concentration (Jensen, Potts, & Jensen, 2005). Employers may also supply acoustic covers (Smith-Jackson & Klein, 2009). In sum, corporate decision-makers should take into account the task characteristics and need for interaction of employees before establishing open-plan office settings (Herbig, Schneider, & Nowak, 2016).

Managing interpersonal processes in the PEW

In Chapter 12, Tann and Ayoko note that workspaces are not just a medium of material functions, but also a medium of social values (Lewin, 1951). Similarly, according to Gärling (1998), space controls the strength and directness of communication and it sends a social message about the group or society that occupies it (i.e. its style of living and its values).

Research by Ayoko and Härtel (2003) also indicates that privacy invasion can trigger conflict (see also Bodin Danielsson, Bodin, Wulff, & Theorell, 2015). Specifically, Ayoko and Härtel found that employees have different interpretations about the use and invasion of space, rooted in differences in culture and different work orientations. These interpretations lead to employee turnover, absenteeism, poor time management, and stress (in one case, even a car accident). Thus, team leaders need to know how to manage conflict that may arise in the open-plan office, especially that related to privacy, territoriality noise, and space infringement (see also Ayoko et al., 2014).

Managing the PEW for effective work in the OPO

Hedge (1982) suggests that the main source of interference at work comes from co-workers rather than office machinery and other distractions. In this regard, it seems that employees need to be taught how to interact effectively in the OPO for increased productivity. Hedge recommends 'educating the users of open-plan offices on how to behave in, work in, and generally use it to maximum benefit' (p. 539). Given that a major reason for employees' dissatisfaction is lack of privacy and increased noise, extra breakout rooms for confidential conversations, meetings, and phone calls should be provided (Brennan et al., 2002). Especially, organizations need to design training programmes through which employees can acquire skills to boost their focused attention and filter irrelevant stimuli. Moreover, because attention can be regarded as a flexible information processing strategy or skill, self-report measures can be used to establish a standard based on which training activities can be developed (Smith-Jackson & Klein, 2009).

Need for employee behavioural change in the context of OPOs

According to Haynes (2007), behavioural changes may lead to a change in the perception of the physical environmental conditions. Indeed, Mulville, Callaghan, and Isaac (2016) show that employees' workplace behaviour is crucial for employee productivity, health, and wellbeing. Mulville and his associates demonstrate that workers who take frequent breaks are less likely to experience headaches or be dissatisfied with thermal comfort and noise. Therefore, it is important for managers of employees in OPOs to check the workplace ambient conditions constantly, especially to enact behavioural change (e.g. taking frequent breaks). Coupled with this, organizations need to ensure that all equipment is functioning correctly and that there is enough workspace.

Managing social withdrawal

The chapters in Part II of this volume deal with issues of employee territoriality and placement identity. Arising from this work, we can conclude that protected areas need to be provided for employees to 'refresh' themselves from the social disturbances of their work setting. In this regard, Evans, Rhee, Forbes, Allen, and Lepore (2000) found that social withdrawal constitutes an oft-used coping approach for minimizing short-term stress related to chronically populous residential conditions. As we previously discussed, space usage may be a conflict trigger. This is because employees lack the ability to personalize space, to close interaction distances, to retreat from interactions, or to obtain privacy. Employees may also be sensitive towards receiving instructions from persons other than supervisors (McFarlin & Sweeney, 1992). In open-space environments, it may therefore be useful to have areas that are available for 'cooling off' after conflict encounters.

Managing territoriality and place attachment

In spite of the surge in the building of high-tech workspaces, empirical research that seeks to find out what kind of workplaces employees actually prefer and how they establish emotional bonds is limited (Lewicka, 2011). Yet, we know that employees develop a place attachment with their workspaces (Lewicka, 2011; Rollero & De Piccoli, 2010). We define place attachment as a positive affective relationship between an individual and a specific place – that includes an individual's desire to stay close to that place, and their memories, knowledge, and meaning about that place (Scannell & Gifford, 2010). In effect, this concerns the emotional connection that individuals feel about a physical place and the people in that place (Hidalgo & Hernández, 2001). In a review of 40 years' work in the area of place attachment, Lewicka (2011) concluded that 'despite mobility and globalization processes, place continues to be an object of strong attachments' (p. 207).

In this regard, Fried (2000) reports that people with high levels of place attachment suffer emotionally and physiologically when forced to move or when places change. In this case, they are likely to have difficulty adapting to new places. In a study of a collaborative science building intended to foster inter-organizational collaborations between scientists, Irving (2016) found that the scientists showed little collaboration after two years. Altogether, these results portray place attachment as an important but unintended consequence of change in the PEW that may impact employees' wellbeing and productivity.

One of the practical ways to manage both place attachment and territoriality may be to structure the pace of changes to the PEW. Also, while employees may not be able to individually personalize their own new PEW, managers need to find ways for them to bring some elements of their old workplace into the new PEW. For example, facilities managers, designers, and planners may be able to capture some critical events or relics of the old physical workplace that remind employees of their sense of belonging to the organization in the new physical work environment. This should assist in managing the employees' emotional needs during and after moving to a new PEW. Organizations might also incorporate into their system pathways (e.g. sharing stories of success and failures and critical events) for employees to grieve and mourn their old place as they move on to their new workplace. It may also be useful to the organization to provide counsellors to assist employees with the sense of loss (Droseltis & Vignoles, 2010) that usually accompanies the movement from a favourably remembered old physical work environment to the new.

Managing the PEW via improved work design

As far back as 1979, Oldham and Brass reported that changes in job characteristics (e.g. task significance) that accompany the change in facilities explain much of the decline in employees' satisfaction and motivation. They demonstrated that the OPO is expected to affect task identity negatively and, from a social technical perspective, supervisors' and co-workers' feedback are expected to decrease when moving to an open-plan office because OPOs provide less privacy where evaluative feedback may be given.

Similarly, several authors (Block & Stokes, 1989; Brookes & Kaplan, 1972; Hackman & Oldham, 1975; Hedge, 1982; Sundstrom et al., 1980) have shown that task complexities influence how employees perform in and react to workspaces of various designs. In this regard, Sundstrom and his colleagues suggest that individuals performing highly complex jobs appear to be more likely to be distracted by the OPO, resulting in poor performance and negative attitudes. While the connection between open-plan office and task complexity is not straightforward (Maher & Von Hippel, 2005), nonetheless, the bulk of the evidence suggests that differing tasks require different levels of attention and thus different levels of concentration for their completion (Oldham & Fried, 1987).

Thus, employees with complex jobs are most influenced by open-plan offices in terms of satisfaction, workplace attitudes, withdrawal behaviours, and performance (Block & Stokes, 1989; Brookes & Kaplan, 1972; Stone, 2001; Sundstrom et al., 1980). For such employees working on complex tasks, Maher and Von Hippel (2005) suggest that they need to develop an inhibitory ability. Maher and Von Hippel's findings show that, in the context of lowly perceived privacy and highly complex tasks, individuals with a poor inhibitory ability also reported low job satisfaction.

Not only do these findings confirm that stimulus-screening ability is an important factor for determining an individual's ability to cope with the distractions inherent to the open-plan environment, but the ability to inhibit distractions aids performance when working in complex jobs. In this instance, training in the ability to inhibit distractions may be an important aspect to consider in overall training for employees moving into an OPO.

More specifically, Kaarlela-Tuomaala, Helenius, Keskinen, and Hongisto (2009) suggest the following steps in order to meet the job demands and individual needs in designing office space: (1) individual job requirements and individual needs for speech privacy should be considered such that private office rooms may be allocated to employees who perform mainly independent and cognitively demanding work and need private conversations; (2) small interactive teams should be placed in shared office rooms rather than large, open-plan offices; (3) open-plan offices can be used for non-demanding and dynamic work or travelling workers; (4) substitute workstation types in the same office environment may give flexibility that allows workers to choose the workstation type based on the type of work task, which ameliorates the feeling of control over the work environment at a given moment.

In the present volume, Ward and Parker in Chapter 8 propose work design as a mediator in the links between PEW and employee outcomes. They suggest further that the influence of workspace varies across types of work and workers. This means managers need to take a holistic approach to manage the PEW. In this respect, managers need to think carefully about the characteristic features of the job performed in the OPO and the employees' workload. Given that employees are likely to be better informed (than their managers) about work processes, job functions, and personal needs, we advocate that employees should be at the centre of the office design from the conception to the occupation stage. Therefore, to manage the PEW effectively, managers may also need to conduct focus groups, administer surveys, and interview employees to find out how they can best improve employees' satisfaction and wellbeing.

Managing individuality, identity, and cultural differences

Awareness of employee individuality

In Chapter 6 of this volume, Luong, Peters, von Hippel, and Dat draw on person–organization fit literature (see Kristof-Brown, Zimmerman, & Johnson, 2005) to discuss the link between employees' individuality and the physical work environment. In particular, Luong and her co-authors introduce the workplace self-space identity mode, which holds that the physical workspaces can activate mental representations that relate to a person's own identity (as well as the identities of other individuals and groups who belong to the organization). The authors propose that, when employees activate their self-space identities simultaneously, they are likely to be accompanied by an evaluation of their compatibility. In this respect, employees' perceptions of self-space identity compatibility should generally boost workers' sense of belonging and work motivation, while perceptions of incompatibility should erode them. This line of argument further suggests that effective PEW management must not ignore the need for managers to engage employees' individuality and identity.

In particular, self-identity (Watson, 2008) and collective identity (van Knippenberg, 2000) are crucial to work productivity and employee wellbeing. This becomes particularly important with issues related to the PEW. This is because we are aware that employees decorate their personal workspaces with objects (e.g. photos, diploma certificates, favourite sport teams, and personalities) to convey their interests and what matters to them (e.g. Graham, Gosling, & Travis, 2015) and other employees read identities from these objects (see Gosling, Ko, Mannarelli, & Morris, 2002; Perez-Lopez, Aragonés, & Amérigo, 2017). Research findings suggest that opportunities for employees to personalize their workspaces are connected with self-efficacy and increased perceived control of the events around them as well as feelings of personal accomplishment (Kromah, 2017). Yet, managers appears to overlook employees' need to express their identity and fit for the organization.

Based on this evidence, we suggest that managers willing to manage the PEW effectively need to pay more significant attention to employees' individuality. For example, a better understanding of the individual could be useful in designing office settings. In this instance, standard personality tests might be used to categorize respondents based on personality type. In the same way, questionnaires can include questions regarding how the individual employee works in groups to obtain a better knowledge of group dynamics and group behaviour (Haynes, 2007).

Awareness of cultural differences

Extant literature (Beaulieu, 2004; Sorokowska et al., 2017) suggests further that culture has a significant impact on employees' work orientation and use of the physical environment of work. For example, Remland (2000) indicates that people touch significantly more in Southern Europe than in Northern Europe, while North America and Europe are probably moderate- to high-contact cultures. Also, Northeast Asian cultures are extremely non-contact (McDaniel & Andersen, 1998; Remland, Jones, & Brinkman, 1991). These findings are consistent with other research suggesting that China and Japan are distinctly non-tactile cultures (see Samovar & Porter, 1976), and suggest that employees' cultural backgrounds have the capacity to influence their use of space, not only at home but also at work.

Relatedly, there is evidence that culture shapes people's interpretation of behaviours and their style of interaction with others in the workplace (Pelled, Eisenhardt, & Xin, 1999). In particular, scholars identify differing cultural orientations in engaging tasks and interpersonal norms as important conflict triggers. In this respect, Ayoko and Härtel (2003) argue that triggers of conflict are not limited to differences in cultural norms alone but also to employees' views of their physical and psychological workspaces. In their field study, Ayoko and Härtel found that different viewpoints regarding the use of space is a moderator between cultural diversity and type, frequency, and duration of conflict events in teams. Additionally, organizations have their own unique culture (e.g. openness, trust, performance, collaboration). Thus, we suggest that in managing the PEW effectively, managers should be cognisant of the fact that the PEW designs in the context of OPSs may enhance cross-cultural conflict. This is so because the OPO design makes more apparent the differences in employees' work orientations. Similarly, managers needing to manage employees' PEW will also need to build a culture of trust and openness and collaboration.

Sorokowska and her colleagues (2017) also report that temperature impacts people's social and intimate distance. In fact, in countries with warmer climates, people are more inclined to maintain more intimate distances towards strangers but more distant towards their intimate partners. They explain their result from the view that while increased temperatures might directly lead to smaller social distances, the prevalence of parasites in hotter climates might also indirectly explain distance preferences in close relationships, especially considering the increased risk of certain infections. In sum, managers need to be aware of the impact of the climatic conditions on employees' behaviours at work. Again, thermal comfort and correct lighting at work may be critical in managing employees' behaviours in the PEW that may be driven by climatic differences in different cultural settings.

Managing and improving employee wellbeing in the PEW

Researchers have also examined organizational workspaces as a lived experience (e.g. see Taylor & Spicer, 2007). In this regard, space is understood as our experience and understanding of distance and the meaning we give to walls. This suggests that the different experiences give rise to the radically different spaces. For example, Manchha (2017) found that employees experience and understand anxiety in the OPO in multiple ways, which include helplessness or vulnerability. These findings suggest that managers need to provide interventions for coping with anxiety presented in the open-plan office. Training in anxiety management (e.g. socialization, buddies at work) should also be provided for employees who suffer from anxiety in the OPO.

Overall, the evidence tells us that a lack of capacity to 'get away' in the OPO may be detrimental to employees' wellbeing. Managers therefore need to provide more breakout rooms to enable employees to escape from the OPO. Such rooms can also be used for meditation and prayers to help employees regain focus and refresh from the distractions in the OPO. Some organizations (e.g. Google) are already providing space for meditation to promote self-regulation, resilience, and avoid burnout. In another example, Zappo is also promoting employee spirituality in the workplace (see Dhiman & Marques, 2011). In a more recent study, Low and Ayoko (2018) found that such spiritual breaks could be critical for employees to maintain high performance.

Managing the OPO as change management

Scholars are beginning to turn their attention to the study of the connection between space and organizational change (see Taylor & Spicer, 2007, for a review). In this respect, researchers have now begun to examine space not only as a changing and multiple social production (Dale & Burrell, 2007) but also as an experience (see Beyes & Steyaert, 2011). This shift from traditional offices to open-plan offices (e.g. ABW, agile workspaces, etc.) is informed by the cost-effectiveness and flexibility of the OPO and increased informal interactions and communication (Papierska, 2018).

While such benefits appeal to managers, they nonetheless seem to ignore the fact that the changes to the physical environment of work are not only material but also social (van Marrewijk & van den Ende, 2018; Wilhoit et al., 2016) and psychological (Droseltis & Vignoles, 2010).

Indeed, Kromah (2017) argues that organizational change leaders seem to have ignored the influence of overall organizational change on changes in workers' workspaces and their intended and unintended consequences. In this respect, while there is a potential for OPOs to increase communication, they can also cause more restructuring and surveillances because of the need to cast an eye on employees' behaviours to improve productivity (Leonardi & Barley, 2011). Similarly, both organizational and spatial change can affect the identity of employees. This is because the employees are no longer able to control their territory (see Pierce & Brown, Chapter 4 of this volume). There is also evidence that buildings designed to symbolize openness through their materiality paradoxically decrease openness (Pepper, 2008). This suggests that in order to manage the PEW effectively, managers need skills in managing not only organizational change but the related changes to employees' behaviours within the PEW.

While there is a large body of research on the phenomenon of organizational change, there still appears to be little knowledge of approaches that may lead to successful change management in organizations (Burke, 2017; Hitt, Harrison, & Ireland, 2001; Todnem By, 2005). Nonetheless, as Nadler, Thies, and Nadler (2001) point out, effective change management hinges on eight key strategies: (1) active engagement of the CEO and executive team, (2) employee engagement at all levels, (3) consideration to human and cultural factors in change, (4) a proactive approach to the integration following change, (5) a solid framework to guide the implementation of the change, (6) managing the pace of the shift in organizational culture, (7) managing uncertainty, and (8) open communication and transparency. We suggest that these requirements (to manage general organizational change effectively) will also be pertinent for the effective management of changes in employees' PEW.

Effective change management also necessitates a change manager (Kotter & Schlesinger, 1989), who may also possess some facility management background to assist with the movement of employees to the new PEW. The role of the change manager is to reduce uncertainty and to support staff during this process and until all employees are settled in the new place. The role of the change manager also includes seeking constant feedback from the employees during the implementation phase with the focus on acting on the feedback to improve employees' satisfaction (Nadler & Tushman, 1990).

Altogether, involving employees in environmental change through participatory design practices and proper change management is also a way to enhance employees' feelings of control over the environment (e.g. see Chapter 7 in this volume; Davis, Leach, & Clegg, 2011). At the same time, following guidelines of effective change management should facilitate increased employee satisfaction and wellbeing after workspace change.

Conclusion

As far back as the 1980s, scholars have argued that the field of industrial and organizational psychology has paid little attention to the physical surroundings of people at work (Sundstrom et al., 1980). Specifically, Sundstrom and his colleagues contend that 'research on the role of the physical setting in interpersonal behaviour in organizations have been especially uncommon' (p. 101). In spite of the long-term acknowledgements of a lack of attention to the phenomenon of the physical context or setting and how this might shape employees' behaviours, there still seems to be reluctance to explore the nexus between the physical context of work and employee behaviours, wellbeing, and productivity (Ayoko et al., 2014; Ashkanasy, et al., 2014).

In the present volume, we set out to fill this vacuum and to explore in detail the connection between the PEW and OB. The book comprises 17 chapters arranged in 5 parts. The chapters in Part I set the scene, provide an overview of the nature of the PEW, and list some of the contradictory findings from the research in the PEW – especially how creative spaces may influence innovation. The chapters in Part II deal with the theoretical background to the physical environment to OB. In Part III, the authors take up a discussion of the relationship between the PEW and work design. In Part IV, the authors highlight the significance of emotions, physical activity, and the physical environment of work. Finally, Part V includes a look at the physical environment of OB and the practitioner. In particular, in this concluding chapter, we focus on the management of employees' physical environment of work and how to deal with its attendant challenges from a practical perspective.

While this volume has examined how the physical environment might shape employees' behaviours at work, there is much still to do. For example, the way the physical setting of work promotes physical activities that may impact wellbeing is still understudied in OB research. Pertinent questions in this regard might be: what level of access do employees have in terms of recreational facilities? What is the link between accessible recreational facilities and employee behaviours (conflict, bullying), productivity, and wellbeing? Is having good access to recreational facilities a necessary but sufficient condition to achieving productivity (e.g. see Giles-Corti & Donovan, 2002)?

Similarly, we are aware that, traditionally, employees have been rewarded with the allocation of more attractive spaces, including window and corner offices (Greenberg, 1988; Paliadelis, 2013). This pattern reproduces and preserves hierarchy and reinforces bureaucratic culture and organizational status (Kaufmann-Buhler, 2016). In this way, Paliadelis notes, organizational power appears embedded in role and environment, where the PEW still portrays powerful symbols of organizational culture and identity. More research is needed to explore how the PEW sustains power and hierarchy (e.g. through surveillance) and its impact in terms of OB. We hope the chapters presented in this volume represent a beginning of scholars' endeavours to enlarge and deepen our understanding of the important and critical issue of the physical environment of work in OB.

Note

1 See https://smarterbusiness.telstra.com.au/trends/industry-trends/hot-desking-how-successful-businesses-make-it-about-people-not- (Accessed 26 April 2019).

References

Altman, I. (1975). *The Environment and Social Behavior: Privacy, Personal Space, Territory, Crowding.* New York: Books/Cole.

Ashkanasy, N. M., Ayoko, O. B., & Jehn, K. A. (2014). Understanding the physical environment of work and employee behavior: An affective events perspective. *Journal of Organizational Behavior, 35,* 1169–1184.

Ayoko, O. B., Ashkanasy, N. M., & Jehn, K. A. (2014). Approaches to the study of employees' territoriality, conflict, emotions and wellbeing. In O. B. Ayoko, N. M. Ashkanasy, & K. A. Jehn (eds), *Handbook of Conflict Management Research* (pp. 363–381). Cheltenham: Edward Elgar.

Ayoko, O. B., & Härtel, C. E. J. (2003). The role of space as both a conflict trigger and a conflict control mechanism in culturally heterogeneous workgroups. *Applied Psychology: An International Review, 52,* 383–412.

Banbury, S. P., & Berry, D. C. (2005). Office noise and employee concentration: Identifying causes of disruption and potential improvements. *Ergonomics, 48,* 25–37.

Beaulieu, C. (2004). Intercultural study of personal space: A case study. *Journal of Applied Social Psychology, 34,* 794–805.

Beyes, T., & Steyaert, C. (2011). The ontological politics of artistic interventions: Implications for performing action research. *Action Research, 9* 100–115.

Block, L. K., & Stokes, G. S. (1989). Performance and satisfaction in private versus nonprivate work settings. *Environment and Behavior, 21,* 277–297.

Bodin Danielsson, C. (2008). Office experiences. In H. Schifferstein (ed.), *Product Experience* (pp. 605–628). New York: Elsevier.

Bodin Danielsson, C., & Bodin, L. (2009). Difference in satisfaction with office environment among employees in different office types. *Journal of Architectural and Planning Research, 26,* 241–257.

Bodin Danielsson, C., Bodin, L., Wulff, C., & Theorell, T. (2015). The relation between office type and workplace conflict: A gender and noise perspective. *Journal of Environmental Psychology, 42,* 161–171.

Bohr, P. C. (2000). Efficacy of office ergonomics education. *Journal of Occupational Rehabilitation, 10*, 243–255.

Brand, J. L., & Smith, T. J. (2005, September). Effects of reducing enclosure on perceptions of occupancy quality, job satisfaction, and job performance in open-plan offices. In *Proceedings of the Human Factors and Ergonomics Society Annual Meeting* (Vol. 49, No. 8, pp. 818–820). Los Angeles, CA: Sage Publications.

Brennan, A., Chugh, J. S., & Kline, T. (2002). Traditional versus open office design: A longitudinal field study. *Environment and Behavior, 34*, 279–299.

Brookes, M. J., & Kaplan, A. (1972). The office environment: Space planning and affective behavior. *Human Factors, 14*, 373–391.

Brown, G., Lawrence, T., & Robinson, S. L. (2005). Territoriality in organizations. *Academy of Management Review, 30*, 577–594.

Burke, W. W. (2017). *Organization Change: Theory and Practice*. Thousand Oaks, CA: Sage.

Cangelosi, V. E., & Lemoine, L. F. (1988). Effects of open versus closed physical environment on employee perception and attitude. *Social Behavior and Personality: An International Journal, 16*, 71–77.

Cappelli, P., & Sherer, P. D. (1991). The missing role of context in OB: The need for a meso-level approach. *Research in Organizational Behavior, 13*, 55–110.

Charles, K. E., Danforth, A., Veitch, J. A., Zwierzchowski, C., Johnson, B., & Pero, K. (2004). *Workstation Design for Organizational Productivity: Practical Advice Based on Scientific Research Findings for the Design and Management of Open-Plan Offices*. (Research Report, NRCC 47343). Ottawa, ON: National Research Council Canada, Institute for Research in Construction. Available at: http://doi.org/10.4224/20377787.

Dale, K., & Burrell, G. (2007). *The Spaces of Organisation and the Organisation of Space: Power, Identity and Materiality at Work*. London: Macmillan International Higher Education.

Davis, M. C., Leach, D. J., & Clegg, C. W. (2011). The physical environment of the office: Contemporary and emerging issues. In G. P. Hodgkinson & J. K. Ford (eds), *International Review of Industrial and Organizational Psychology* (Vol. 26, pp. 193–235). Chichester: Wiley.

de Croon, E., Sluiter, J., Kuijer, P. P., & Frings-Dresen, M. (2005). The effect of office concepts on worker health and performance: A systematic review of the literature. *Ergonomics, 48*, 119–134.

Dhiman, S., & Marques, J. (2011). The role and need of offering workshops and courses on workplace spirituality. *Journal of Management Development, 30*, 816–835.

Droseltis, O., & Vignoles, V. L. (2010). Towards an integrative model of place identification: Dimensionality and predictors of intrapersonal-level place preferences. *Journal of Environmental Psychology, 30*, 23–34.

Elsbach, K. D., & Pratt, M. G. (2009). Physical environment in organizations. *Academy of Management Annals, 1*, 181–223.

Evans, G. W., & Johnson, D. (2000). Stress and open-office noise. *Journal of Applied Psychology, 85*, 779–783.

Evans, G. W., Rhee, E., Forbes, C., Allen, K. M., & Lepore, S. J. (2000). The meaning and efficacy of social withdrawal as a strategy for coping with chronic residential crowding. *Journal of Environmental Psychology, 20*, 335–342.

Fox, G. (1998). *Office Etiquette and Protocol*. New York: Learning Express.

Fried, M. (2000). Continuities and discontinuities of place. *Journal of Environmental Psychology, 20*, 193–205.

Gärling, T. (1998). Introduction: Conceptualizations of human environments. *Journal of Environmental Psychology, 18*, 69–73.

Giles-Corti, B., & Donovan, R. J. (2002). The relative influence of individual, social and physical environment determinants of physical activity. *Social Science and Medicine, 54,* 1793–1812.

Gosling, S. D., Ko, S. J., Mannarelli, T., & Morris, M. E. (2002). A room with a cue: Personality judgments based on offices and bedrooms. *Journal of Personality and Social Psychology, 82*(3), 379–398.

Graham, L. T., Gosling, S. D., & Travis, C. K. (2015). The psychology of home environments: A call for research on residential space. *Perspectives on Psychological Science, 10,* 346–356.

Greenberg, J. (1988). Equity and workplace status: A field experiment. *Journal of Applied Psychology, 73,* 606–613.

Hackman, J. R., & Oldham, G. R. (1975). Development of the job diagnostic survey. *Journal of Applied Psychology, 60,* 159–170.

Haynes, B. P. (2007). The impact of the behavioural environment on office productivity. *Journal of Facilities Management, 5,* 158–171.

Hedge, A. (1982). The open-plan office: A systematic investigation of employee reactions to their work environment. *Environment and Behavior, 14,* 519–542.

Herbig, B., Schneider, A., & Nowak, D. (2016). Does office space occupation matter? The role of the number of persons per enclosed office space, psychosocial work characteristics, and environmental satisfaction in the physical and mental health of employees. *Indoor Air, 26,* 755–767.

Hidalgo, M. C., & Hernández, B. (2001). Place attachment: Conceptual and empirical questions. *Journal of Environmental Psychology, 21,* 273–281.

Hitt, M. A., Harrison, J. S., & Ireland, R. D. (2001). *Mergers and Acquisitions: A Guide to Creating Value for Stakeholders.* New York: Oxford University Press.

Hoendervanger, J. G., de Been, I., van Yperen, N. W., Mobach, M. P., & Albers, C. J. (2016). Flexibility in use: Switching behaviour and satisfaction in activity-based work environments. *Journal of Corporate Real Estate, 18,* 48–62.

Hongisto, V., & Haapakangas, A. (2008, June). Effect of sound masking on workers in an open office. *Proceedings of Acoustics, 8*(29), 537–542.

Irving, G. (2016). *Collaboration in Open-Plan Offices.* Unpublished PhD dissertation, the University of Queensland, Brisbane, Australia.

Jensen, C., Potts, C., & Jensen, C. (2005). Privacy practices of Internet users: Self-reports versus observed behavior. *International Journal of Human–Computer Studies, 63,* 203–227.

Johns, G. (2006). The essential impact of context on organizational behavior. *Academy of Management Review, 31*(2), 386–408.

Justa, F. C., & Golan, M. B. (1977). Office design: Is privacy still a problem? *Journal of Architectural Research, 6,* 5–12.

Kaarlela-Tuomaala, A., Helenius, R., Keskinen, E., & Hongisto, V. (2009). Effects of acoustic environment on work in private office rooms and open-plan offices: Longitudinal study during relocation. *Ergonomics, 52,* 1423–1444.

Kaufmann-Buhler, J. (2016). Progressive partitions: The promises and problems of the American open plan office. *Design and Culture, 8,* 205–233.

Kim, J., & de Dear, R. (2013). Workspace satisfaction: The privacy–communication trade-off in open-plan offices. *Journal of Environmental Psychology, 36,* 18–26.

Kotter, J. P., & Schlesinger, L. A. (1989). Choosing strategies for change. In C. Bowman & D. C. Asch (eds), *Readings in Strategic Management* (pp. 294–306). London: Palgrave.

Kristof-Brown, A. L., Zimmerman, R. D., & Johnson, E. C. (2005). Consequences of individuals' fit at work: A meta-analysis of person–job, person–organization, person–group, and person–supervisor fit. *Personnel Psychology, 58,* 281–342.

Kromah, M. (2017). *Workspace Territoriality: Role, Process and Consequences in the Context of Organisational Change*. PhD dissertation, University of Queensland, Brisbane, Australia.

Lee, P. J., Lee, B. K., Jeon, J. Y., Zhang, M., & Kang, J. (2016). Impact of noise on self-rated job satisfaction and health in open-plan offices: A structural equation modelling approach. *Ergonomics*, *59*, 222–234.

Leonardi, P. M., & Barley, W. C. (2011). Materiality as organizational communication: Technology, intention, and delegation in the production of meaning. In T. Kuhn (ed.), *Matters of Communication: Political, Cultural, and Technological Challenges to Communication Theorizing* (pp. 101–122). New York: Hampton Press.

Lewicka, M. (2011). Place attachment: How far have we come in the last 40 years? *Journal of Environmental Psychology*, *31*, 207–230.

Lewin, K. (1951). *Field Theory in Social Science: Selected Theoretical Papers* (edited by Dorwin Cartwright.). Oxford: Harpers.

Low, J. J., & Ayoko, O. B. (2018). The emergence of spiritual leader and leadership in religion-based organizations. *Journal of Business Ethics*. Published online ahead of print. https://doi.org/10.1007/s10551-018-3954-7.

Maaninen-Olsson, E., & Müllern, T. (2009). A contextual understanding of projects: The importance of space and time. *Scandinavian Journal of Management*, *25*(3), 327–339.

Maher, A., & von Hippel, C. (2005). Individual differences in employee reactions to open-plan offices. *Journal of Environmental Psychology*, *25*, 219–229.

Manchha, A. (2017). *Bring Your Understanding of Anxiety with You: Employees' Experiences of Anxiety in Open-Plan Offices*. Honours thesis, University of Queensland, Brisbane, Australia.

Margulis, S. T. (1977). Conceptions of privacy: Current status and next steps. *Journal of Social Issues*, *33*, 5–21.

McDaniel, E., & Andersen, P. A. (1998). International patterns of interpersonal tactile communication: A field study. *Journal of Nonverbal Behavior*, *22*, 59–75.

McFarlin, D. B., & Sweeney, P. D. (1992). Distributive and procedural justice as predictors of satisfaction with personal and organizational outcomes. *Academy of Management Journal*, *35*, 626–637.

Mulville, M., Callaghan, N., & Isaac, D. (2016). The impact of the ambient environment and building configuration on occupant productivity in open-plan commercial offices. *Journal of Corporate Real Estate*, *18*, 180–193.

Nadler, D. A., Thies, P. K., & Nadler, M. B. (2001). Culture change in the strategic enterprise: Lessons from the field. In C. L. Cooper, S. Carwright, & P. C. Earley (eds), *The International Handbook of Organizational Culture and Climate* (pp. 309–324). Chichester: John Wiley & Sons.

Nadler, D. A., & Tushman, M. L. (1990). Beyond the charismatic leader: Leadership and organizational change. *California Management Review*, *32*(2), 77–97.

Oldham, G. R., & Brass, D. J. (1979). Employee reactions to an open-plan office: A naturally occurring quasi-experiment. *Administrative Science Quarterly*, *24*, 267–284.

Oldham, G. R., & Fried, Y. (1987). Employee reactions to workspace characteristics. *Journal of Applied Psychology*, *72*, 75–80.

O'Neill, M. J. (1994). Work space adjustability, storage, and enclosure as predictors of employee reactions and performance. *Environment and Behavior*, *26*, 504–526.

Paliadelis, P. (2013). Nurse managers don't get the corner office. *Journal of Nursing Management*, *21*, 377–386.

Papierska, A. (2018). *Office Design and Employee Stress: An Office Design that Reduces Employees' Stress and Increases Employee Productivity*. Doctoral dissertation, University of Lisbon, Lisbon, Portugal.

Pastalan, L. A. (1970). Privacy as a behavioral concept. *Social Science, 45*, 93–97.

Pelled, L. H., Eisenhardt, K. M., & Xin, K. R. (1999). Exploring the black box: An analysis of work group diversity, conflict and performance. *Administrative Science Quarterly, 44*, 1–28.

Pepper, G. L. (2008). The physical organization as equivocal message. *Journal of Applied Communication Research, 36*, 318–338.

Perez-Lopez, R., Aragonés, J. I., & Amérigo, M. (2017). Primary spaces and their cues as facilitators of personal and social inferences. *Journal of Environmental Psychology, 53*, 157–167.

Rashid, M., & Zimring, C. (2008). A review of the empirical literature on the relationships between indoor environment and stress in health care and office settings: Problems and prospects of sharing evidence. *Environment and Behavior, 40*, 151–190.

Remland, M. S. (2000). *Nonverbal Communication in Everyday Life*. Boston, MA: Houghton Mifflin.

Remland, M. S., Jones, T. S., & Brinkman, H. (1991). Proxemic and haptic behavior in three European countries. *Journal of Nonverbal Behavior, 15*, 215–232.

Roelofsen, P. (2002). The impact of office environments on employee performance: The design of the workplace as a strategy for productivity enhancement. *Journal of Facilities Management, 1*, 247–264.

Rollero, C., & De Piccoli, N. (2010). Place attachment, identification and environment perception: An empirical study. *Journal of Environmental Psychology, 30*, 198–205.

Samovar, L. A., & Porter, R. E. (1976). *Intercultural Communication: A Reader*. Belmont, CA: Wadsworth.

Scannell, L., & Gifford, R. (2010). Defining place attachment: A tripartite organizing framework. *Journal of Environmental Psychology, 30*, 1–10.

Seddigh, A., Stenfors, C., Berntsson, E., Bååth, R., Sikström, S., & Westerlund, H. (2015). The association between office design and performance on demanding cognitive tasks. *Journal of Environmental Psychology, 42*, 172–181.

Smith-Jackson, T. L., & Klein, K. W. (2009). Open-plan offices: Task performance and mental workload. *Journal of Environmental Psychology, 29*, 279–289.

Sorokowska, A., Sorokowski, P., Hilpert, P., Cantarero, K., Frackowiak, T., Ahmadi, K., . . . & Blumen, S. (2017). Preferred interpersonal distances: A global comparison. *Journal of Cross-Cultural Psychology, 48*, 577–592.

Stone, N. J. (2001). Designing effective study environments. *Journal of Environmental Psychology, 21*(2), 179–190.

Sundstrom, E., Burt, R. E., & Kamp, D. (1980). Privacy at work: Architectural correlates of job satisfaction and job performance. *Academy of Management Journal, 23*, 101–117.

Sundstrom, E., Herbert, R. K., & Brown, D. W. (1982). Privacy and communication in an open-plan office: A case study. *Environment and Behavior, 14*, 379–392.

Sundstrom, E., Town, J. P., Rice, R. W., Osborn, D. P., & Brill, M. (1994). Office noise, satisfaction, and performance. *Environment and Behavior, 26*, 195–222.

Taylor, S., & Spicer, A. (2007). Time for space: A narrative review of research on organizational spaces. *International Journal of Management Reviews, 9*, 325–346.

Todnem By, R. (2005). Organisational change management: A critical review. *Journal of Change Management, 5*, 369–380.

van Knippenberg, D. (2000). Work motivation and performance: A social identity perspective. *Applied Psychology, 49*, 357–371.

van Marrewijk, A., & van den Ende, L. (2018). Changing academic work places: The introduction of open-plan offices in universities. *Journal of Organizational Change Management, 31*, 1119–1137.

Venetjoki, N., Kaarlela-Tuomaala, A., Keskinen, E., & Hongisto, V. (2006). The effect of speech and speech intelligibility on task performance. *Ergonomics, 49*, 1068–1091.

Watson, T. J. (2008). Managing identity: Identity work, personal predicaments and structural circumstances. *Organization, 15*, 121–143.

Wilhoit, E. D., Gettings, P., Malik, P., Hearit, L. B., Buzzanell, P. M., & Ludwig, B. (2016). STEM faculty response to proposed workspace changes. *Journal of Organizational Change Management, 29*(5), 804–815.

Wineman, J. D. (1982). Office design and evaluation: An overview. *Environment and Behavior, 14*, 271–298.

Wineman, J. D. (1986). *Behavioral Issues in Office Design*. New York: Van Nostrand Reinhold Company.

Zhang, M., Kang, J., & Jiao, F. (2012). A social survey on the noise impact in open-plan working environments in China. *Science of the Total Environment, 438*, 517–526.

INDEX